QUENTIN TARANTINO

QUENTIN TARANTINO

Poetics and Politics of Cinematic Metafiction

David Roche

UNIVERSITY PRESS OF MISSISSIPPI / JACKSON

www.upress.state.ms.us

Designed by Peter D. Halverson

The University Press of Mississippi is a member of the Association of University Presses.

Copyright © 2018 by University Press of Mississippi
All rights reserved

First printing 2018
∞

Library of Congress Cataloging-in-Publication Data

Names: Roche, David, 1976– author.
Title: Quentin Tarantino : poetics and politics of cinematic metafiction / David Roche.
Description: Jackson : University Press of Mississippi, [2018] | Includes bibliographical references and index. |
Identifiers: LCCN 2018010430 (print) | LCCN 2018015498 (ebook) | ISBN 9781496819178 (epub single) | ISBN 9781496819185 (epub institutional) | ISBN 9781496819192 (pdf single) | ISBN 9781496819208 (pdf institutional) | ISBN 9781496819161 (hardcover : alk. paper) | ISBN 9781496821157 (pbk. : alk. paper)
Subjects: LCSH: Tarantino, Quentin—Criticism and interpretation. | Film criticism.
Classification: LCC PN1998.3.T358 (ebook) | LCC PN1998.3.T358 R63 2018 (print) | DDC 791.4302/33092—dc23
LC record available at https://lccn.loc.gov/2018010430

British Library Cataloging-in-Publication Data available

CONTENTS

Acknowledgments   vii
Introduction   3

CHAPTER ONE
"What Shall the History Books Read?"
History and Film History   15

CHAPTER TWO
"Black Man, White Hell"
Identity Politics Vol. 1: Race and Ethnicity   32

CHAPTER THREE
"That's the Excuse You Guys Use Whenever You Want to Exclude Me from Something"
Identity Politics Vol. 2: Gender (and Sexuality)   75

CHAPTER FOUR
"Revenge Is Never a Straight Line"
A Neoformalist Approach Vol. 1: Narrative Structures and Paradigms   127

CHAPTER FIVE
"Everything's the Same Except for One Change"
A Neoformalist Approach Vol. 2: Narration and Style   160

CHAPTER SIX
"Lookin' Back on the Track, Gonna Do It My Way"
The Use of Preexisting Music   224

CHAPTER SEVEN
"Come On, Let's Get into Character"
Acting and Theatricality   244

CHAPTER EIGHT
"He's Just Not Used to Seein' a Man Ripped Apart by Dogs Is All"
Violence and Spectacle   270

Conclusion   288
Notes   293
Filmography and Bibliography   319
Index   332

ACKNOWLEDGMENTS

There weren't really any academic books when I started working on the films of Quentin Tarantino in 2005. I approached the material with anticipation and some anxiety. Like many members of my generation, I had found *Pulp Fiction* cool and stylish, but I was now worried that it wouldn't hold up under close scrutiny. In analyzing the movie, I discovered a complex, layered work, one in which a mere detail, such as the funny, now iconic line "*Le Big Mac*," opened the door onto a metafictional discourse on stereotypes of Frenchness in Hollywood cinema. I realized that the intertextual references weren't just hip and amusing; they intensely participated in the production of meaning, one that only the viewers could piece together. This impression was confirmed when working on other films. Studying *Death Proof* three years later, I realized that Tarantino's work was both informed by the history of modes of production and exhibition, as well as by film scholarship. So when *Inglourious Basterds* came out in 2009, I only saw it as a turning point insomuch as Tarantino's metafictional engagement with film history was even more explicit. In twelve years of studying his films, my respect and admiration for Tarantino's films has only grown. I want to start by thanking Tarantino and his many collaborators for their work, as well as fan sites and vids for their insights. And I hope this book will convince readers not necessarily that they should like his films (that's a question of taste), but that the films are sophisticated works that elicit serious engagement.

Warm thanks to Vijay Shah and Lisa McMurtray for their support, to the reviewers (Reynold Humphries and Oliver C. Speck) for their helpful comments, to copyeditor Peter Tonguette for seeing yet another manuscript through to the end. I'd like to thank my friends, students, and colleagues at Université Toulouse Jean Jaurès, Université de Bourgogne, and SERCIA. It is truly an honor to know so many passionate and intelligent people. Many thanks are due to the friends and colleagues who took the time to read various chapters: Jim Buhler, Christophe Gelly, Marianne Kac-Vergne, Xavier Lemoine—I'm grateful to you all for the insightful feedback you provided. Thanks are due to Elizabeth Cullingford, Alan Friedman, and Wendy Harding who gave me the wonderful opportunity of teaching the spring semester of 2017 at the University of Texas at Austin, where I finished the book. And to Mercedes Lynn de Uriarte just for being there. Discussions with my wonderful students in E379R Metafiction in English-language Cinema found their way into the introduction and analyses of *Inglourious Basterds*. The librarians in Dijon and Toulouse, at PLC in Austin, and at the Doe Library at the University of California, Berkeley were incredibly helpful. So were the many friends (Jean-François Baillon, Zachary Baqué, Marie Boyer, Florence Courriol, Christophe Damour, Celestino Deleyto, Sarah Hatchuel, Donna Kornhaber, Emeline Jouve, Cristelle Maury, Mark Niemeyer, Nathalie Rivère de Carles, Vincent Souladié, Benjamin Thomas, Shannon Wells-Lassagne) who helped me with translations or get my hands on various references and sources.

As always, love to my mother, brother, and sister, and to all my friends who have been following Tarantino since *Reservoir Dogs*.

And to Virginie and Lisa. Hey, little person, you must have had quite an intra-uterine experience when we went to the movies to see *Django Unchained* a couple of days before you were born! And to Tim, who'll be watching movies with us soon enough.

QUENTIN TARANTINO

INTRODUCTION

Is it even necessary to introduce Tarantino? Probably not. The biographies (Bernard 1995; Dawson 1995; Charyn 2006) and interview books (Peary 2013) all tell the same story: that of a young man, born in 1963 and raised by a strong, single mother named Connie, who went from working in a Los Angeles rental store called Video Archives to winning the Palme d'or for *Pulp Fiction* at the Cannes Film Festival in 1994, to being arguably the most famous American filmmaker of his generation, with just eight feature films—*Reservoir Dogs* (1992), *Pulp Fiction*, *Jackie Brown* (1997), *Kill Bill* (2003–2004), *Death Proof* (2007), *Inglourious Basterds* (2009), *Django Unchained* (2012), and *The Hateful Eight* (2015)—and several screenplays and stories—*True Romance* (Tony Scott, 1993), *Natural Born Killers* (Oliver Stone, 1994), *From Dusk Till Dawn* (Robert Rodriguez, 1996)—to his name, as well as a short film in the anthology movie *Four Rooms* (Allison Anders, Alexandre Rockwell, Robert Rodriguez, Quentin Tarantino, 1995) and episodes of *E.R.* (S1E24, NBC, 1995) and *CSI* (S5E24-E25, CBS, 2005). In a time when many American directors and screenwriters have been to film school, the Tarantino success story has largely contributed to his legend. The achievements of a self-taught director might call into question the usefulness of film schools. After all, Tarantino learned how to make films from watching movies, as he himself has said.[1] But he also learned from reading books. Lots of books.[2] And not just those of Elmore Leonard, whose dialogues he cited early on as a major influence, or James M. Cain, Raymond Chandler, and Dashiell Hammett.[3]

Tarantino has never been interested in just making films: he has been interested in participating in, and reflecting on, film history and, more largely, cultural history, as a means of making a name for himself and becoming one of the biggest star directors since Alfred Hitchcock. But more importantly for this book, it is the very heart of his vision of the creative act. This vision is inherently cinephilic, but in a broad and not a solipsistic sense, as I intend to demonstrate. It stems from having watched films from all over the world and from all eras: action movies, art movies, classics, exploitation films, independent films, silent films, propaganda movies,[4] mainly produced in the US, Europe, and East Asia. It has led him to read books on cinema: technical books on acting, cinematography and stuntmen, books about the history of German cinema, criticism by Pauline Kael, academic studies such as Carol Clover's *Men, Women, and Chainsaws* (1992).[5] And while some artists admit to losing interest in anything but the works they consumed during their formative years, Tarantino remains essentially a student of cinema, one who continues to read up and watch movies for each project. His is an ongoing process and reflection, evidenced by the fact that he regularly changes his mind about his favorite films. Compare the lists published by *Sight & Sound* in 2002, *The Independent* in 2005, and *Empire Magazine* in 2008, where only five of the ten—*The Good, the Bad and the Ugly* (Sergio Leone, 1966), *Rio Bravo* (Howard Hawks, 1959), *His Girl Friday* (Hawks, 1940), *Taxi Driver* (Martin Scorsese, 1976), and *Carrie* (Brian De Palma, 1976)—are the same.[6]

Tarantino is interested in each part of the filmmaking process: writing, rehearsal, production design, stunt choreography, cinematography, editing, etc. If he has deliberately sought to construct himself as an auteur and a brand, he is fully aware of the collaborative effort that goes into the filmmaking process. He has cultivated long-term relationships with actors (Samuel L. Jackson, Michael Madsen, Tim Roth, Uma Thurman), cinematographers (Robert Richardson since *Kill Bill*), and editors (the late Sally Menke up to and including *Inglourious Basterds*). Cast and crew have testified to the fact that Tarantino is curious about each aspect and values each collaborator for the part s/he plays. A student of mine, who doubled for Zoë Bell on the set of *Death Proof*, told me that Tarantino made a point of addressing every member of the cast and crew by her or his first name. The promotion of the unseen workers of cinema was made especially manifest in that film, both in terms of plot—Stuntman Mike acts as the return of the cinematic repressed—and casting, since Bell, a stuntwoman on *Kill Bill*, plays herself. Tarantino's love for cinema is not just a love of fiction films; it is a love for the day-to-day reality of cinema, its history and its process.

Tarantino is very much aware that he is not working alone and that he is not working in an artistic vacuum: his films are resolutely inscribed within film genres and film history. His interests go beyond cinema to include comics, music, and television,[7] but they also go beyond mainstream culture. The image of the "cool" defender of pop culture that stuck to him for quite a while, and that he largely cultivated—after all, Dawson's biography is subtitled *The Cinema of Cool*—masked the fact that Tarantino also has a taste for classic literature. He compared *Pulp Fiction* to "opera" and *Jackie Brown* to a "chamber piece,"[8] and Django and Schultz's journey into Candieland to the journey in Joseph Conrad's *Heart of Darkness*.[9] Discussing *The Hateful Eight* in an interview, Tarantino disclosed that he frequents theaters and knows his drama and opera, citing Eugene O'Neil and Giacomo Puccini.[10] Robert von Dassanowsky has illuminated how deliberate the integration of Beethoven and Wagner in *Django Unchained* is.[11] Reading through the book of interviews edited by Gerald Peary reveals that this "intellectual" side of Tarantino is something he has mainly displayed only since the mid-2000s, roughly at the time when he was working on *Inglourious Basterds*. The director even admits that, though he hated high school, he would have loved to go to college.[12] Tarantino is not just a proponent of low culture; he is a defender of culture *tout court*. One of the aims of this book is to emphasize the extent to which his feature films reflect on cultural history, and that it is this engagement that makes them so relevant.

Tarantino has often said that if he hadn't become a filmmaker, he would have been a film critic, and the fact that he has been conducting research suggests that he may one day decide to pursue that venue as well.[13] It is in this respect that his debt to Jean-Luc Godard, an influence Tarantino often cited early on,[14] is the most obvious; writing for *Film Comment* in 1994, Gavin Smith, probably one of the most perceptive among Tarantino's early interviewers, was one of the first to realize that Tarantino's movies are "movies commenting on themselves, movies, and movie history."[15] Godard and Tarantino differ in many respects, of course. One is seen as the epitome of cinematic modernism, the other as the epitome of cinematic postmodernism. Godard ultimately rejoined the avant-garde, while Tarantino remains firmly attached to mainstream cinema and is now considering directing a *Star Trek* movie. The French director's politics are resolutely Marxist and feminist, while the American director is mainly concerned with identity politics. These differences prove that both are very much in tune with the political debates of their times and cultures, and it is in this respect that they participate as cultural critics in the circulation of ideas via their films. Making movies about cinema that are about real-world concerns—that is, films that engage with culture politically and morally through a critical engagement with the medium and its history, which is what this book aims to prove is exactly what Tarantino's feature films do—is something I believe the American director learned from Godard's early movies. Tarantino, like Godard according to Richard Neupert, sees "films history as a series of modes of discourse rather than merely mise-en-scène options," with "each cinematic device [...] a signifier with multiple cultural effects."[16]

Audiences, critics, and scholars recognized from the start Tarantino's intertexual approach to filmmaking—the homage to East Asian martial arts and the spaghetti Western in *Kill Bill*, to blaxploitation in *Jackie Brown*; the references to the dance scene from *8½* (Federico Fellini, 1963), the rape scene from *Deliverance* (John Boorman, 1972) and the character of the "crime cleaner" from *Nikita* (Luc Besson, 1990) in *Pulp Fiction*; and some even accused *Reservoir Dogs* of being a mere rip-off of *City on Fire* (Ringo Lam, 1987). The director himself was all too happy to help out with the allusion spotting, going so far as to brag that he "steal[s] from everything."[17] As films that are indebted to specific "hypotexts"—*City on Fire* for *Reservoir Dogs*, *Django* (Sergio Corbucci, 1966) for *Django Unchained*—and/or that play on genre conventions, and thus participate in "architexuality," "the relation of inclusion that unites each text to the various types of discourses to which he is affiliated,"[18] Tarantino's films offer textbook illustrations of the typology of intertexuality Gérard Genette developed in *Palimpsests* (1982), with instances of citation—*The Losers* (Jack Starrett, 1970) in *Pulp Fiction* [82:40–83:44]; allusion—the above-mentioned scenes in *Pulp Fiction*; and plagiarism—the Ezekiel 25:17 speech from the opening of *Karate Kiba* (Ryuichi Takamori and Simon Nuchtern, 1976) in *Pulp Fiction*, the shot of the fighters' silhouettes from *Samurai Fiction* (Hiroyuki Nakano, 1998) in *Kill Bill Vol. 1*[19] [87:08]. Many critics saw this allusionism as symptomatic of the postmodernist delight in surface and in decontexualized and ultimately depoliticized signs. In his 2007 study of *Reservoir Dogs*, Mark T. Conard, for example, described the hypotexts of Tarantino's films as narrow—i.e., limited to action movies and comics—and stated that "these scenes and references lack any kind of critical element, so anyone who cares about such things will be disappointed that Tarantino's movies at best leave social inequalities and injustices in place and untouched."[20] Laurent Jullier similarly saw *Pulp Fiction* as abandoning "all pretense of ideological modelling."[21] Although the references do invite viewers to enjoy the sense of recognition or play at seeking them out, viewer activity ends there only if s/he so chooses. The chapters that follow will prove that the intertexuality in the films of Tarantino is the basis not just of artistic creation, but of the creation of meaning, and that our participation as meaning-makers is solicited in this process;[22] they also demonstrate that intertexuality is just one of the many strategies the films resort to in order to produce metafictional discourses. With the exception of Eve Bertelsen's 1999 article on *Pulp Fiction*, in which she discusses the film as exemplifying "metafiction's wilfully compromised 'complicitous critique,'"[23] it was only after the release of *Inglourious Basterds* that critics and scholars started to discuss the metafictional dimension of Tarantino's films, notably in the useful collected volumes on *Inglourious Basterds* and *Django Unchained*, edited by, respectively, Robert von Dassanowsky (2012) and Oliver C. Speck (2014). This book argues that the films were metafictional from the start.

Linda Hutcheon (1980) defines metafiction as works that "transform formal properties of fiction into its subject matter."[24] For Patricia Waugh (1984),

> [m]etafiction is a term given to fictional writing which self-consciously and systematically draws attention to its status as an artefact in order to pose questions about the relationship between fiction and reality. In providing a critique of their own methods of construction, such writings not only examine the fundamental structures of narrative fiction, they also explore the possible fictionality of the world outside the literary fictional text.[25]

Waugh's definition is a bit broader than Hutcheon's, since metafiction, for her, deals not just with fiction, but with its "relationship" to reality within and without fiction, and it does so "critically" and not just playfully as a formal exercise. Hutcheon's later work (1989) on "historiographic metafiction" proves that works like E. L. Doctorow's 1975 novel *Ragtime* can foreground how historiography and literature are both grounded in a history of discourse. Both Hutcheon and Waugh focus primarily on contemporary authors (John Barth, Donald Barthelme, Italo Calvino, Robert Coover, John Fowles, Gabriel García Márquez, Thomas Pynchon), who have often been labeled postmodernists or whose œuvre exemplifies the shift from modernism to postmodernism (Jorge Luis Borges, Vladimir Nabokov). This should come as no surprise given that metafiction has often been seen as a recurrent approach in postmodernist fiction, if not the dominant one, by critics and scholars such as Brian McHale[26] and Hutcheon herself,[27] who went from devoting a book to metafiction to writing two books about postmodernism.

The term "metafiction" is usually reserved for literary fiction, though Hutcheon cites Godard and admits that "the visual arts and music both have also shown signs of self-reflectiveness."[28] Film scholars have long refrained from using the term, instead privileging analyses of reflexivity (Robert Stam includes Brice Kawin, Noël Burch, Martin Walsh, Don Frederickson, Alfred Appel Jr., among his predecessors);[29] Christian Metz has even gone so far as to argue that, when "enunciation marks itself in the cinematic utterance," it does so "by means of reflexive constructions."[30] In his seminal *Reflexivity in Film and Literature* (1982), a book remarkable for its scope and clarity, Stam, in his prefatory discussion, acknowledges the connection between reflexivity and metafiction, citing Hutcheon's and Waugh's definitions,[31] but he does not distinguish between the two. To be fair, Stam is interested in looking at the broader phenomenon of reflexivity and tracing a tradition of anti-illusionist fiction that carries on from literature (Cervantes, Henry Fielding) and drama (Shakespeare, Alfred Jarry, Bertolt Brecht) into cinema. He identifies many reflexive devices either common to the three media (interruptions and narrative discontinuity, intertexuality, the thematization of creating or consuming a work of art, *mise en abyme*,[32] etc.) or specific to cinema (frame-within-the-frame composition, flat images, sharp primary colors, unmotivated camera movements, static images, violations of classical narration, the "counterpuntal" use of sound,[33] etc.).

It is only more recently that critics, scholars, and viewers have appended the prefix "meta-" to "film" or "cinema."[34] In his study of Hollywood films about Hollywood, Marc Cerisuello (2000) offers a very restrictive definition of the term "metafilm" by identifying it as a genre with specific conventions:

> a movie that deals explicitly with cinema by representing those responsible for the production (actors, directors, producers, techniques, publicity and public relations agents, studio personnel, etc.) through a strict storyline, regardless of the film genre the movie can eventually be associated with, and that proposes at a given moment in time a better understanding, whether achieved through a documentary style or through realist fiction, of the cinema world which it views in a critical light.[35]

From Cerisuello's perspective, *Inglourious Basterds* would be Tarantino's only metafilm, since it is the only one that portrays producers (Joseph Goebbels), actors (Bridget von Hammersmark, Frederick Zoller), critics (Archie Hicox), and exhibitionists (Marcel and Shosanna). Von Dassanowsky does not define "metacinema" in the introduction to the collected volume on *Inglourious Basterds*, but he does seem to have a broader understanding of the term than Cerisuello; he associates it with distancing and reflexive devices, evoking the French New Wave, Brecht, and Stanley Kubrick as models, and with the subversion of classical conventions and the postmodern deconstruction of master plots.[36] Fátima Chinita (2014) helpfully distinguishes between Cerisuello's metafilms and metacinema, which "reveals a taste for spectacle rather than just entertainment, a penchant for variety instead of narrative formulas, and a propensity for the eulogy of art and artists, connoting film with other artistic endeavors";[37] among such "metacinematic allegories," she includes films Cerisuello excludes, such as *Rear Window* (Alfred Hitchcock, 1954), *8 ½* (Federico Fellini, 1963), and *Blow-up* (Michelangelo Antonioni, 1966).³⁸

I agree with Chinita's distinction, but, like others, whether scholars (Jay McRoy 2008,³⁹ Robert Sinnerbrink 2011⁴⁰) or reviewers (Jonathan McCalmont 2016⁴¹), I prefer the term "cinematic metafiction" to "metacinema" because (1) prose does not have a monopoly on fiction; (2) using the same word makes it possible to emphasize what metafiction has in common in both media (and in others as well); and (3) the adjective "cinematic" is enough to assert media specificity. Of course, clarifying the relationship between metafiction and reflexivity is far more crucial than my terminological preference. Stam eventually provides such insight, even though he seems practically determined to avoid doing so, in his discussion of self-conscious adaptations like *Lolita* (Stanley Kubrick, 1962) and *Tom Jones* (Tony Richardson, 1963): "While they incorporate certain reflexive devices, they do not metalinguistically dissect their own practice or include critical discourse within the text itself."⁴² Stam's comment recalls Waugh's definition: in order to be identified as "meta-," so to speak, reflexive devices must produce some sort of "critical discourse" about the work and the medium itself. This is confirmed by Stam's brilliant analyses of certain films—*Contempt* (Jean-Luc Godard, 1963) and *Tout va bien* (Godard and Jean-Pierre Gorin, 1972)—and specific scenes—the Balzac plagiarism scene in *The 400 Blows*⁴³ (François Truffaut, 1959)—which prove that they are not just reflexively drawing attention to the artifice; they are proposing a meta-discourse on themselves as works of fiction, and are thus metafictional.

I adapt Hutcheon's and Waugh's definitions by defining as metafictional any work of fiction—or any scene—that, regardless of the medium, engages with its status as a work of fiction by producing a meta-discourse that can be explicit, implicit or, more often, an alliance of both. Metafiction implies a high degree of reflexivity; it is essentially reflexive, but reflexivity does not necessarily make a work metafictional. Classical Hollywood films such as those of Fritz Lang—for example, *The Woman in the Window* (1944), *House by the River* (1950)—abound in reflexive devices that foreground the artificiality of storytelling and genre conventions and reflect the spectator's look⁴⁴ without necessarily developing a meta-discourse—no doubt, because Lang wasn't in a position to do so. A documentary can be reflexive (Orson Welles's 1973 *F for Fake* is, perhaps, the most famous example), and reflexive devices can be merely playful "winks," as Stam notes;⁴⁵ elsewhere, I demonstrated that the references to previous films produced a metafictional discourse on horror in *Halloween* (Rob Zombie, 2007) but were merely playful in *Dawn of the*

Dead (Zack Snyder, 2004).⁴⁶ The high degree of reflexivity is by no means synonymous with the degree of explicitness. Indeed, expanding on Jean Ricardou (1975), Hutcheon explains that metafiction can be overt ("thematized or even allegorized within the 'fiction'") or covert ("structuralized, internalized, actualized").⁴⁷ Of course, the overtness of the device also depends on the reader or viewer's capacity to recognize the reference and activate it; in the case of intertexts, for instance, citations, such as the many discussions on slasher conventions in *Scream* (Wes Craven, 1996), would tend to be overt, while allusions can be overt or covert depending on how easy it is to identify them. Hutcheon also distinguishes between metafictional strategies that are diegetic or linguistic. Diegetic devices would tend to be the same regardless of the medium: overt diegetic devices include allegory, parody, and *mise en abyme*,⁴⁸ while covert diegetic devices include underlying structures that can be modeled, for instance, on the detective plot, fantasy, and games.⁴⁹ Linguistic devices would be medium-specific, but Hutcheon's notion of "building blocks,"⁵⁰ i.e., the formal foundations of the work, could easily be adapted to film; in film, they would comprise the specifically cinematic reflexive devices noted by Stam and listed above.

It is equally important to specify what we understand by metafiction being about "itself"—what lies behind the reflexive pronoun? The work of fiction can be about its own creation (its narrative, the strategies it deploys), about its inscription in an artist's body of work, but it can also be about the genre(s) it participates in (its architexuality), about cultural history or the industry, about the ontology of the medium, or about the essence and/or function of art in general. In practice, it is unlikely that the metafictional discourse(s) can ever be entirely limited to the film or œuvre. Nor is it likely to be absolutely singular and coherent. By exploring the creative and imaginative process, metafiction can be just as much about the writer, director, or actor's work, as about the work of a spectator whose activity participates in breathing life into the fiction; Hutcheon even argues that the acknowledgment of the reader's role in literary creation is characteristic of modern metafiction.⁵¹

Because metafiction is about itself, it has often been charged with both elitism and narcissism—the latter because metafiction seems to be about itself and nothing else, and the former because the works of most of the writers studied by Hutcheon and Waugh are considered difficult reads; their books not only solicit the reader's active participation,⁵² but posit a reader who has the requisite knowledge (notably of other literary works) to do so. Similar charges have been made by critics of Tarantino's films. Sharon Willis, for instance, deplores that "the central referent of *Inglourious Basterds* seems to be the auteur's own œuvre, from *Reservoir Dogs* to the *Kill Bill* franchise."⁵³

Tarantino is, however, not really criticized for being elitist, since many of the intertexual references are associated with pop culture, but some viewers do feel that their abundance blocks their access to, and enjoyment of, his films. Although the analyses in the body of this book will confirm that these references are key to interpreting Tarantino's films, the many informal conversations I have had with non-cinephile viewers have convinced me that not identifying these references does not prevent them from enjoying the films. Reactions such as frustration or annoyance can only be felt by those who know there are references but cannot identify them (or not all of them at least), or by those who consider that there are far too many and that the work is far too dependent on their presence (Tarantino's detractors often accuse him of plagiarism).[54] I can understand these viewers' annoyance, and I do not wish to convince them that they are wrong to feel that way because it is, in my opinion, a question of taste and sensibility. What I do intend to demonstrate, convincingly I hope, is that these references and other reflexive devices, in addition to being playful, actually invite the viewer to explore the meaning of the relationships thereby established, and that they do not make Tarantino's films solipsistic but, on the contrary, enable them to engage not just with cinema but with real-world concerns.

In other words, my defense of Tarantino's feature films is equally a defense of metafiction, and it pursues the arguments made by Hutcheon and Waugh about literary fiction. Hutcheon deliberately tackles head-on the charge of narcissism by coining the term "narcissistic narrative" instead of metafiction and attempting to rehabilitate the myth of Narcissus in her introduction;[55] she argues that by focusing on the imagination and the act of creation (both writing and reading), metafiction is very much about a "vital" human concern: "imaginative creation."[56] Waugh goes even further by suggesting that metafiction critically engages with the relationship between fiction and reality, how one can reflect (on) the other, and how both are seen, in our postmodern, poststructural era, as ongoing human constructs. Thus, engaging with its status as a work of fiction implies engaging with the relationship between fiction and reality. In so doing, metafiction provides the framework to analyze this relationship; the metafictional work, says Hutcheon, "embodies within itself its own critical frame of reference as part of its theme and often its form."[57] This entails that metafiction begs to be analyzed on its own terms, as metafiction; one can regret that they are metafictional to the core, that, like genre films, they are "made in imitation not of life but of other films,"[58] but viewing them as anything else is a misinterpretation, maybe even an "excercise in futility," to quote Mia Wallace in *Pulp Fiction* [44:36]. It also implies that metafictions would tend to be paradigmatic examples of what Umbert

Eco calls "closed" works. Yet one should bear in mind that, after defining the latter as "monosemic," Eco finally concludes that "nothing is more open than a closed work."[59] This is equally true of the films of Quentin Tarantino: as tightly knit works that lay bare their connections to the wider network of film history and cultural history, they provide us with—nay, they impose on us—the framework to analyze them, and yet, by connecting the framework to this larger network, they also invite us—and this is obviously an invitation we can choose to decline—to move far beyond and explore their limits and contradictions, as well as their real-world implications.

By arguing that Tarantino's work asks to be considered as cinematic metafictions, this book aims to provide an in-depth study of each feature film up to and including *The Hateful Eight*. It pursues venues opened by the major books on Tarantino: the collected volumes on *Inglourious Basterds* edited by von Dassanowsky and *Django Unchained* edited by Speck, Adilifu Nama's (2014) insightful investigation of the racial politics of Tarantino's films, and Philippe Ortoli's (2012) magnificent full-length study of Tarantino as director, producer, and self-fashioned authorial figure. It also seeks to open a few doors of its own, in the process hopefully encouraging further research. Each chapter focuses on a side of Tarantino's films that has been discussed or at least noted by fans and critics: the turn to historical material from *Inglourious Basterds* on; their engagement with identity politics, especially race and gender; their experimenting with narrative structure; their stylishness and use of trademark devices; their characteristic use of preexisting music; their theatricality and emphasis on role-playing; and their ambiguous treatment of violence. These features have not received the same degree of attention in academic studies. By and large, most publications have focused on gender, history, intertextuality, race, and violence, adopting a predominantly cultural studies perspective. The chapters dealing with these aspects dialogue with previous writings, those dealing with the other four aspects less so. This accounts for the overall structure of the book. I begin by attempting to shed new light on issues that have been widely discussed (chapters 1, 2, and 3), before moving on to less charted territory (chapters 4, 5, 6, and 7) and ending on the potentially unresolvable debates concerning cinematic violence (chapter 8). As in my previous work on horror cinema, my approach combines cultural studies and neoformalism and pays particular attention to the dialectics between form and content, aesthetics and representation.

Chapter 1 starts by considering Tarantino's turn to historical material from *Inglourious Basterds* on. Like many historical films, *Inglourious Basterds*, *Django Unchained*, and *The Hateful Eight* have been criticized for misrepresenting historical facts and experiences or, worse, disrespecting them, but I argue that this turn, in effect, makes explicit the mode by which metafiction investigates the relationship between fiction and reality. Engaging with film history through allegory does not preclude an engagement with history; on the contrary, it constitutes the means by which the films inscribe themselves within cultural history.

Chapters 2 (on race and ethnicity) and 3 (on gender and sexuality) deal with identity politics in all eight feature films. In order to foreground the intersectionality of identity politics and to compensate for what is ultimately an arbitrary separation, as films like *Jackie Brown* and *The Hateful Eight* prove, the chapters have been organized according to the same structure: the relation between film genre and identity politics, power relations within the diegeses, the use of gendered, racialized, racist, and misogynistic rhetoric, and the treatment of the body. This foregrounds certain parallels and links between the construction of ethnicity, gender, race, and sexuality, showing that Tarantino's films tackle these aspects of identity politics in the same fashion; they take the gendered and racialized conventions of the genres the films are tapping into as a starting point for an exploration of gendered and racialized discourses and practices in culture. I argue that it is through their high degree of self-consciousness of representation, characteristic of metafiction, that these films inscribe themselves in contemporary debates on identity as social construct. Like Nama, I demonstrate that Tarantino's fantasies "resonate with established and emerging discourses"[60] concerning real-world tensions, and that the focus on such tensions is evidence that our society is rife with them and that we have yet to move on to a post-racial, post-feminist world.

Chapters 4 and 5, devoted to narrative structure and style, also function in tandem. Both are grounded in a neoformalist approach largely indebted to the work of David Bordwell and Kristin Thompson, and more generally to French film studies. They seek to describe Tarantino's storytelling strategies in relation to classical and art-cinema paradigms, and thus to determine his position in the history of forms. Special attention is paid to how specific reflexive devices produce a meta-discourse on the aesthetics and politics of Tarantino's films, cinema, and culture in general. I demonstrate that Tarantino's style is not just "stylish": form is meant to be interpreted and complexifies the ethical and political issues the stories address. In fact, the poetics and politics of these films come together in the very contemporary notion that everything, notably art and identity, is a re-representation.

The same can be said of the use of preexisting music, the main focus of chapter 6. If the songs featured on the original motion picture soundtracks have unquestionably played an important role in constructing the Tarantino brand as an emblem of cool retro, their functions in the films have always been varied and complex: reinforcing and establishing structural and thematic relationships (notably regarding character relations), endowing specific scenes with a certain tone or emotional ambience, and also highly contributing, on a metafictional level, to the political subtexts by way of intertexuality.

Chapter 7 explores some of the key anti-illusionist strategies deployed in the films—namely, those that endow the films with theatricality through staging and performance. More than just an arsenal of reflexive devices, cinematic theatricality serves to frame the discourse on the aesthetics, ethics, and politics of role-playing. The *theatrum mundi* metaphor underlying the films takes them well beyond the restrictions of Hollywood cinema; it both contributes to an underlying fantasy and game structure typical of metafiction in general, and asserts the relevance of fiction to reflect on the world, or rather on representations of the world.

Chapter 8 analyzes both the treatment of violence and the metafictional discourses that the body of films develop on the topic. Despite the director's claims in interviews early in his career, the movies reveal an awareness of how sensitive and complex it is; violence is a core feature of the films not so much by token of its presence, but because it is the point at which the aesthetics, ethics, and politics of the films converge—this explains why discussions of violence inevitably crop up in each chapter, as they do in most writings on Tarantino. The conclusion then attempts to determine the films' place in American and world cinema and circumscribe the terms of their own brand of cinematic metafiction, before returning to the suspicion surrounding metafiction in general and its possible implications.

CHAPTER ONE

"WHAT SHALL THE HISTORY BOOKS READ?"

History and Film History

Historical movies (and more generally historical fiction) are, in a sense, subjected to the same criterion as adaptations, that of fidelity;[1] they are, in the many works on the subject,[2] regularly scrutinized for their handling of historical facts and their sensitivity to various interpretations and bones of contention. Although screenwriters and directors are granted a degree of poetic license, their choices are often criticized on both moral and political grounds. In imagining an alternate history, *Inglourious Basterds* actually follows a tradition more common in comics and literature than in film, including famous works such as Philip K. Dick's *Man in the High Castle* (1962), recently adapted into a TV series (Amazon, 2015–), Dave Gibbons and Alan Moore's *Watchmen* (1986–87), made into a movie directed by Zack Snyder in 2009, and Philip Roth's *The Plot against America* (2004); HBO has just announced a new series entitled *Confederate*, set in an alternate reality where the South won the Civil War. The film's release prompted many articles on the political and ideological implications of the film's treatment of history; over half the articles in the collected volume edited by Robert von Dassanowsky, for instance, deal with the issue from a variety of perspectives (philosophical, reception). Viewers were also very much aware that a movie whose plot centers around a movie theater also engages with film history (American, British, French, and German), as well as with the various genres that inform *Inglourious Basterds* (the WWII movie, the Western). The critical reception of *Django Unchained* was even more couched in discussions on the portrayal of slavery in the antebellum South and its political implications, as the chapters from the collected volume edited by Oliver C. Speck prove.

Inglourious Basterds not only anticipates, but also raises these questions and encourages such connections, as the above quote from Colonel Hans Landa suggests. Rewriting history, Landa implies, is essentially a moral question. In this case, Aldo Raine, Smithson Utivitch, and the US government must choose between signing a Faustian contract with the film's archvillain, the ignoble Jew Hunter, or torching the Nazi High Command in a movie theater, an event that engages both history and film history. On a metafictional level, the movie is offering the direct descendants of the guerilla teams from earlier WWII mission movies like *The Dirty Dozen* (Robert Aldrich, 1967) and *The Inglorious Bastards* (Enzo G. Castellari, 1978) the chance to actually make a significant difference. Landa's question reflexively comments on the ambiguities of the revenge fantasy that constitutes the film's very premise, with the implication that fantasy does not preclude moral engagement, while reminding audiences that this fantasy is contained within the diegesis and that historical tragedies cannot be altered *a posteriori*.

Focusing exclusively on *Inglourious Basterds*, *Django Unchained*, and *The Hateful Eight*, this chapter identifies a turning point in Tarantino's œuvre that everyone, I believe, noticed immediately, and that his ninth film set in 1969 Los Angeles will probably pursue. But investigating the relationship between fiction, history, and film history will also serve as an entry point into the relationship between metafiction and reality in all of Tarantino's films, and more generally of the political potential of metafiction. I argue that the turn toward historical material renders more explicit concerns that had been central since *Reservoir Dogs*, which will be addressed in the next chapters. In what follows, attention will first be paid to the (mis)representation of history and the ethical implications it raises, then to the political potential of allegory, before attempting to determine whether or not the emphasis on film history constitutes, in effect, a denial of history.

(Mis)representation

That is not to say that the three movies have no basis in history. They do. Actual dates (1941 and 1944 in *Inglourious Basterds* [2:08, 38:05], 1858 in *Django Unchained* [3:40]) and locations (Paris and Piz Palü in *Inglourious Basterds*, Chattanooga, Tennessee, in *The Hateful Eight* [7:40]) are provided. Historical figures are either featured (Churchill, Bormann, Goebbels, Göring, Hitler in *Inglourious Basterds*) or mentioned (Alexandre Dumas in *Django Unchained* [126:31], Lincoln in *The Hateful Eight*); Tarantino even makes use of the little known fact that the French author's father, General

Alex Dumas, was black. Specific historical events are discussed (the Battle of Baton Rouge of 1862 in *The Hateful Eight* [65:25–66:33]) or evoked (the Civil War in *Django Unchained* [3:40]), actual publications depicted (the Nazi newspaper *Der Stürmer* in *Inglourious Basterds* [29:10]). The presence of American Jews in the US Army in *Inglourious Basterds* is wholly justified by the fact that many fought in World War II (over half a million according to Solomon Grayzel[3]). Goebbels's propaganda movie *Stolz der Nation* tells a story very similar to that of WWII hero Audie Murphy, who starred as himself in *To Hell and Back* (Jesse Hibbs, 1955),[4] and actor Daniel Brühl even looks like the US hero/actor. The Mannix Marauders of *The Hateful Eight* recall pro-Confederate partisan rangers (or "bushwhackers") like the notorious Quantrill's Raiders [23:44].[5] The occupations of Django and Major Marquis Warren are absolutely credible, as there were African American cavalry during the Civil War (the Fifth United States Colored Cavalry which first fought in 1864[6]) and far more black cowboys (about a third of all cowboys) than classical Hollywood Westerns have portrayed,[7] including lawmen (like Bass Reeves) and criminals (like Cherokee Bill and Ned Huddleston, aka Isom Dart).[8] Calvin Candie's skull monologue [115:45–119:55] recalls Samuel George Morton's *Crania Americana; or, A Comparative View of the Skulls of Various Aboriginal people of North and South America* (1839).[9] The uniforms used in *Inglourious Basterds* (Lieutenant Archie Hicox's,[10] and General Ed Fenech's, SS officer Major Hellstrom's) and *The Hateful Eight* (the Confederate general Sandy Smithers's) have an air of authenticity, their worn look reinforcing the impression of realism.[11]

And yet the three films strikingly tamper with historical and geographical facts to various degrees. The most radical example, of course, is *Inglourious Basterds*'s reimagining the end of World War II, with most of the Nazi High Command going up in flames in a Parisian movie theater. By identifying 1858 as "Two years before the Civil War" [3:39], *Django Unchained* "begins with an astonishingly huge historical gaffe: a factual error so blatant, obvious, and easy to correct that it almost *has* to be deliberate."[12] The score to Beethoven's "Für Elise," performed on the harp [63:53–65:35], was not published until 1867.[13] Locations are either mispelled (Daughtrey instead of Dougherty, Texas, in *Django Unchained*), transformed (a rock formation, Red Rock, becomes a town in Wyoming in *The Hateful Eight*), or invented (Nadine, France, in *Inglourious Basterds*, Wellenbeck prison camp in West Virginia in *The Hateful Eight*[14]). Invented characters interact with historical figures and play major roles in historical events (General Ed Fennech in *Inglourious Basterds*, Major Marquis Warren, General Sandy Smithers, and Mannix's Marauders in *The Hateful Eight*). *The Hateful Eight* renames the commanding officer (Smithers instead of Major General John C. Breckinbridge) who took part in the Battle of Baton Rouge in August 1862, and even the race of some of the combatants, since the Union only started organizing black regiments in the fall of 1862. And the word "bushwhacker" is used as a synonym of ambusher by Chris Mannix, ironically the very character who deserves the label [26:34]. *Django Unchained* depicts an antebellum South where Mandingo fighting is a hobby like any other (there is no proof that such fights actually took place[15]) and posses resembling the KKK (which was founded in 1865) already existed.

Many viewers, whether fans or critics, have taken note of these inventions, anachronisms, and inaccuracies. Adilifu Nama calls *Django Unchained* a "Gothic fantasy." Most of the authors in the collected volume edited by Robert von Dassanowsky describe *Inglourious Basterds* as a form of fantasy: a "revenge fantasy"[16] for Imke Meyer, Eric Kligerman, and Sharon Willis, an "allohistorical fantasy,"[17] i.e., one that presents an alternate version of history, for von Dassanowsky, who uses the same term to describe *Django Unchained*.[18] Melvyn Stokes, a historian and film historian, describes Tarantino's first Western in similar terms, as "a fantasy of what might have happened rather than what did."[19] For him, "[t]he brutal manner in which Tarantino depicts plantation slavery, however, is much closer to how it was conceived in the lurid fantasies of many abolitionists (few of whom had visited the South) than it may have been to antebellum reality."[20] The allohistorical quality of *Django Unchained* would, in a sense, be justified historically by the lack of knowledge of Northern abolitionists.

The three films are underpinned by a fantasy structure, a strategy that is, according to Hutcheon, typical of covert diegetic metafiction.[21] The inventions, anachronisms, and inaccuracies point to "the very act of imagining the world"[22] and, in so doing, draw attention to the fact that "[a]ny text—realistic or fantastic—uses certain conventions in order to create its own reality."[23] Implicit, here, is the idea that historical fiction remains fiction and is, at least in part, fantasy. But the discussion does not revolve so much around the constructed nature of historical fiction—after all, we live in an age where most scholars accept that history itself is a (set of) construct(s) and narrative(s)—as around the ethical and political implications of these modifications and their legitimacy, so to speak. Michael D. Richardson, who argues around *Inglourious Basterds* without actually analyzing the film or its viewers' reactions, claims that, for the film's defenders, "[b]ecause it makes no pretense to historical accuracy and thus realism, the film is exempted from the normal sort of moral engagement that viewers have."[24] It is probably true that movies—such as *Mississippi Burning* (Alan Parker, 1988), *Glory* (Edward Zwick, 1989), *JFK* (Oliver Stone, 1991), and, more recently, *Lincoln* (Steven

Spielberg, 2012)—that claim historical veracity set themselves up for scrutiny and thus charges of falsification, though producers, cast, and crew will also claim a degree of artistic license for the sake of compelling drama.[25] Yet reading von Dassanowsky's and Speck's collected volumes, it becomes clear that none of the authors who defend the films' politics believe that it is exempted from such concerns; on the contrary, they defend them precisely because they address political and ethical issues, such as justice[26] and responsibility—the industry's for the representations it purveys,[27] the audience's for the entertainment it consumes[28]—through allegorical fantasy.

Allegory

The references to Beethoven and Dumas in *Django Unchained*, for instance, establish analogies that inscribe the film in cultural history [126:31–127:25]. Von Dassanowsky insists on the German bounty hunter's inscription in German Enlightenment ideals, named after the nineteenth century's most famous German American, Carl Schultz, a humanist and democrat whose racial politics were, of course, more ambivalent than that of Tarantino's character.[29] He also reminds us that the German composer was a resolute humanist and an admirer of the French revolution.[30] Schultz's bringing up the French author not only demonstrates the profound ignorance of Calvin Candie, who doesn't even recognize the author from whom he has borrowed the name of a famous character (D'Artagnan) for one of his slaves, and who isn't even aware of the cruel irony that the author's father was the son of a slave; the invocation of the historical figure also stands for history's disapproval of the Southern sadist. And it is not just the disapproval of those who will write and read the history books—in other words, of contemporary audiences who would know better—that Candie could incur, but that of at least some of his contemporaries, Schultz but also Dumas (1802–1870), whose *Three Musketeers* was published in French in 1844 and in English in 1846 (fig. 1). Candie's naming a slave after a famous hero of a French romance also invites comparisons with the end of a famous American novel set in the antebellum South, Mark Twain's *Adventures of Huckleberry Finn* (1884–1885), written by an author who loathed slavery.[31] Both Calvin Candie and Tom Sawyer turn a slave into the double of a romantic hero (the Count of Monte Cristo for Jim) for sheer amusement—Calvin is just as amused by Schultz's suggestion of naming his fighter after a figure of Greek mythology [102:30]—but the outcome for D'Artagnan is degradation (he is thrown to the dogs), whereas Jim has, on the contrary, attained the status of a human being worthy of rescue

Fig. 1: *Django Unchained*: Standing with his back to Calvin Candie's library, Dr. Schultz reveals to the phony Francophile that Alexandre Dumas the writer was black.

Fig. 2: *The Hateful Eight*: After hanging Daisy Domergue, the reconciliation between Major Warren and Chris Mannix is sealed when the white renegade reads the black officer's phony Lincoln letter and admits: "Ole Mary Todd. That's a nice touch."

in the eyes of Tom and especially Huck Finn, and, symbolically at least, of a literary hero as noble as a French nobleman or of a captivity narrative heroine meant to embody white values in the face of racial otherness.[32] If the Basterds, the Jew Hunter, Django, Chris Mannix, John Ruth, and Marquis Warren become legends through their own actions, Candie and his like use mythical names (D'Artagnan, Samson, the Black Hercules) as promotional gimmicks, ultimately seeing them as mere products with an expiration date. Schultz's reference to Dumas thus endows history with the same moral authority as Landa's comment about the history books in *Inglourious Basterds*; the actions of the Mandingo afficionado or of the Jewish American guerilla, though fictitious, are, in effect, cast in the light of history, and viewers are by no means exempt of moral engagement with the film.

The Hateful Eight even thematizes the alteration of history through Major Warren's Lincoln letter—a letter by the president of the United States addressed to a fictitious character that turns out to be a fabrication. This overt metafictional strategy is meant to legitimize Tarantino's approach to history in *The Hateful Eight* and the previous films through a story of illegitimacy that frames the entire narrative. It is first read by John Ruth in Chapter One [16:34–18:55], and then by Chris Mannix in the final chapter (fig. 2) [160:42–163:14]. The letter is the means by which Ruth and Warren seal their Hawksian partnership; it points back to a previous meeting where Ruth was already allowed to see it. Reading it anew, Ruth is visibly moved, shaking his head and looking up at Warren appreciatively as he repeats: "Ole Mary Todd." Daisy's display of contempt for Lincoln and Warren when she spits on the letter provokes momentary discord, but the two Northerners are quickly reunited against the Southern dame and the rebel renegade they meet in Chapter Two. Ruth's disappointment is crushing when Chris Mannix, at the dinner table, bullies Warren into admitting the letter is "horseshit" [80:09–82:21]. The issue is then the reason for the fabrication.

> RUTH: Well, I guess it's true what they say about you people: Can't trust a fuckin' word comes out of your mouth.
> WARREN: What's the matter, John Ruth? I hurt your feelings?
> RUTH: As a matter of fact—you did.
> WARREN: (*sighs*) "I know—I'm the only black son of a bitch you ever conversed with, so I'm gonna cut you some slack. But you got no *idea* what it's like being a black man facin' down America. Only time black folks is safe—is when white folks is disarmed. And this letter—had the desired effect—of disarmin' white folks.
> RUTH: Call it what you want. I call it a dirty fuckin' trick.
> WARREN: You wanna know why I lie—about somethin' like that, white man? It got me on that stagecoach, didn't it? [82:48–84:03]

When Ruth initially puts the lie down to Warren's race, the latter counters that it is a matter not of race but of survival in a racist world. The fabrication is justified politically and historically, and testifies to US race relations after the Civil War, and perhaps even to this day, as Warren's phrase "a black man facin' down America" suggests. It has actual effects on its readers, and can unite blacks and whites or divide Northerners and Southerners. For what Warren strives to get across to Ruth is that it is not the letter itself that should unite them but the universal values it conveys—that of friendship between a black man and a white man, a common man and a president, a friendship that transcends race and class. It is the meaning of the letter, not the letter as a fetish object, that should count. Ruth is not given the chance to understand this as he dies shortly after, but another white character does—ironically, the very character who outed Warren in the first place. As they lay dying, Mannix asks to read the Lincoln letter. The letter now confirms a bond established between a white man and a black man who were politically at odds, yet have ultimately come together across common values of justice and loyalty (though the righteousness of such justice is qualified, as we shall see in chapter 8). No longer a fetish, the letter's power to symbolize racial reconciliation is reinforced. Like Ruth, Mannix appreciates the final sentence: "'Ole Mary Todd.' That's a nice touch." But unlike Ruth, it is Warren's wording, not Lincoln's, that he is praising.

The Hateful Eight thus ends on a compliment paid to Warren's talents of pastiche, making him a screenwriter-like figure similar to Tarantino. In so doing, it invites viewers to consider the implications of the historical modifications made in all of Tarantino's films. Some viewers took issue with the Mandingo fighting in *Django Unchained*, Gregory Desilet seeing it as proof that Tarantino "has no interest in portraying the real violence done against slaves."[33] For Nama, however, it is justified as a "racial metaphor" not only for slavery—"the Mandingo fight perfectly articulates the fusion of dread and delight, abjection and desire that underscores the appetite for violence and erotic sadism that was black enslavement"[34]—but it is also "a potent signifier of the relationships between black professional athletes and team owners, a vast majority of whom are white men."[35] Kate E. Temoney seconds this view: "[t]his counterfact conveys a 'truth' about the sadistic practices of the slave trade in a manner that no singular depiction of an actual abuse could—the utter dehumanization, the violence, and the implication of victims in their own victimization."[36] Dumas's disapproval of Candie is not just history's disapproval of slavery—it is moral outrage at racial exploitation in any day and age. Nama goes so far as to opine that, because of the allegorical connections made possible by fantasy, "*Django Unchained* works on a broader ideological scale than does *12 Years a Slave*" (Steve McQueen, 2013).

In *Inglourious Basterds*, the invention of an unlikely character like Hugo Stiglitz, a German who loathes Nazis, can be analyzed in a similar fashion. His brand of lone vigilantism reflects less the well-documented German resistance to Nazism, which mainly involved a "strategy of conspiracy and insurrection,"[37] as, perhaps, the repugnance of subsequent generations of Germans to that period; according to Brad Pitt and Tarantino, the German-born actor Til Schweiger only agreed to don a Nazi uniform to play Stiglitz, something he had refused to do in other films, because his character killed Nazis.[38] Kligerman shows that a mere detail, such as Aldo Raine's scar, which a series of close-ups draw attention to when he is first introduced [21:36], can take the political allegory outside the film's historical range: "[t]he mark of the scar on the neck of a southerner who is fighting injustice in Europe points to a possible backstory of his similar actions in America."[39] A descendant of the Apache, Raine, whose scar recalls that of Glyn McLyntock in *Bend of the River* (Universal, Anthony Mann, 1952) and of the heros of *The Great Silence* (Sergio Corbucci, 1968) and *Hang 'Em High* (Ted Post, 1968), is the vengeful ghost of American history: the racially impure version of the Western town-tamer and its combat movie equivalent, such as the guerilla leader embodied by John Wayne in the Vietnam War propaganda movie *The Green Berets* (Kellogg, Wayne, and LeRoy, 1968). A more obvious example is Shosanna's last name which, by referring to the famous trial of a French Jew, Alfred Dreyfus,[40] whom the French writer Émile Zola defended in an 1898 article denouncing anti-Semitism in the military, implies that the heroine's act is directed at anti-Semitism in general, not just in Nazi Germany and Occupied France; note that the owner of the Louisiane sides with the Nazi soldiers in the shoot-out. The entire film thus reaches far beyond the history of World War II. Kligerman's conclusion on *Inglourious Basterds* recalls Nama's analysis of *Django Unchained*: "Despite the fairy tale-like opening, *Inglourious Basterds* is steeped in history; the Jewish extermination is juxtaposed to other instances of American and French historical violence including the colonization of the West, the genocide of Native Americans, the history of racism and slavery, oblique references to the Vietnam War and the current war on terror."[41] Like Nama, I would argue that these juxtapositions—or, more precisely, analogies—are, in effect, produced *by* and not "despite" the fantasy.

The political potential of the allegorical allohistorical fantasy is thematized in *Inglourious Basterds* when the Nazi soldiers in the Louisiane tavern play a version of the game "Who Am I?" [72:17–73:22, 83:36–87:19]. When Hellstrom has finally guessed the name on his forehead, he cannot resist asking a question he knows to be false, given that the answer can only be the name of a person: "When I arrived in America was I displayed in chains? [. . .] Am I the story of the Negro in America? [. . .] Well, then, I must be King Kong" (fig. 3). Hellstrom provides an interpretation of the 1933 RKO movie as an allegory of the Middle Passage[42] that has become commonplace today.[43] The irony, of course, is that it takes a foreigner to provide a political reading of a Hollywood movie,[44] and one who, no doubt, approves of the ideology that inferior races can be enslaved. As Nama argues, the scene targets not just Nazism—an enemy the film takes for granted—but American racism, which is constructed as its double. The reference, Nama concludes, invites the viewer to consider a "hidden meaning" to the film

Fig. 3: *Inglourious Basterds*: During a game of "Who Am I?" Major Hellstrom proposes, "Am I the story of the Negro in America?" before revealing the name of the character on his forehead.

that would make it a racial allegory, more specifically that "the pathology of German Nazism is the ideological cousin to American racism."[45] This is effected in a scene where Americans are entirely absent (with the exception of the British Hicox, the characters are all French or German). In other words, no American character is there to react to Hellstrom's interpretation, to see their nation's racial history—slavery and the destruction of Native Americans—reflected in German history. This, I would argue, furthers the racial allegory by including the denial of racism; it is significant that the Basterds do not include an African American character, even though their filmic models do (the characters of Robert Jefferson in *The Dirty Dozen*, Sergeant Doc McGee in *The Green Berets*, and Private Fred Canfield in *The Inglorious Bastards*). But the game, like the Lincoln letter, also asserts the artistic right to resort to allegory, and thus to tamper with historical facts; significantly, the characters give each other names of famous historical (Genghis Kahn, Mata Hari, Beethoven, G. W. Pabst, Marco Polo, Brigitte Horney) and fictional (Winnetou,[46] King Kong) figures. In Nama's words, "the reference to *King Kong* does double duty as racial analogy and as an analogy"; "the comments in *Inglorious Basterds* concerning *King Kong* as a whole articulate and represent allegorical meaning that operates beyond the strict narrative and plot devices."[47] The reference to Winnetou builds on this by evoking the figure of the "noble savage," an embodiment of universal human goodness often racially encoded as white in classical Hollywood cinema.[48] The game thus functions like the Lincoln letter by defending the political potential of historical allegory and deterritorialization (King Kong comes from Skull Island, and the character of Winnetou was invented by the German author Karl May) in general.

Engaging with History through Film History

Many of the inventions in Tarantino's three historical allegories are borrowed from cinema, as has been noted by fans, cinephiles, and scholars. Most of the main characters of *Django Unchained* are named after movie characters: Django after the hero of the eponymous 1965 film and the sequels and variations that followed, including *Sukiyaki Western Django* (Takasi Miike, 2007) featuring Tarantino himself; Broomhilda von Shaft after the hero of Gordon Parks's blaxploitation-influenced 1971 MGM production; Stephen after the protagonist (also a butler) of *The Remains of the Day* (James Ivory, 1993, based on the 1989 novel by Kazuo Ishiguro). Tarantino may also have had in mind the German sergeant in *Hogan's Heroes* (CBS, 1965–71) for Schultz. Some characters are named after actors and industry people: Marquis Warren in *The Hateful Eight* has for namesake the creator of the Western TV show *The Virginian* (NBC, 1962–71),[49] who also wrote and directed the satirical Western *Arrowhead* (1953), General Ed Fennech in *Inglourious Basterds*, the French actress Edwige Fenech, who played in a variety of Italian and German exploitation films and, more recently, *Hostel: Part II* (Eli Roth, 2007), the executive producer of which was Tarantino.[50] Goebbels's propaganda movie *Stolz der Nation* sounds awfully like *The Birth of a Nation* (D. W. Griffith, 1915), as Greg M. Colón Semenza has cleverly noticed.[51] The inglourious Basterds are the heirs of the 1967 *Dirty Dozen*[52] and the rogue American soldiers of Castellari's 1978 film, while Hitler's taste for grandeur—he is introduced standing next to a huge map of Europe, as an artist works on a giant portrait of the Führer, in a room with tall windows [24:12–26:00]—conjures memories of Chaplin's 1940 Great Dictator climbing up the curtains and playing with the globe.[53] Django and Warren are modeled on the bounty hunters of blaxploitation movies starring Fred Williamson, including *The Legend of Nigger Charley* (Martin Goldman, 1972), *The Soul of Nigger Charley* (Larry G. Spangler, 1973), and *Boss Nigger* (Jack Arnold, 1975),[54] and the Columbia production *Buck and the Preacher* (Sidney Poitier and Joseph Sargent, 1972) and the Warner Bros. production *Blazing Saddles* (Mel Brooks, 1974),[55] while Stephen, "the consummate Uncle Tom,"[56] is a dark version of the figure that fixed representations of African American men in Hollywood cinema until the 1960s.[57] In *Django Unchained*, the Mandingo fighting comes from Richard Fleischer's 1975 *Mandingo*,[58] which is often mistakenly included in the blaxploitation cycle though it is actually a Paramount production, while the lynch mob scene, which opens on the long shots of the torch-bearing riders, accompanied by Verdi's "Dies Irae (Requiem)," refers to the finale of *The Birth of a Nation* where the Klan ride to the rescue to the sound of Wagner's "Ride of the Valkyries" [41:07–41:49].⁵⁹

These references are more than just playful nods to possible influences. Through them, Tarantino, Kligerman says, "leads us through a history comprised of both high and 'low' cinema," studio productions and exploitation, art and mainstream cinema, "where we become witness to the condensation of filmic history."⁶⁰ Secondly, they reflexively draw attention to the world-building process—overtly when the references are explicitly named, covertly when the source serves as an underlying model—and thus participate in the metafictional discourse. Third, they invite viewers to explore and make meaning of these connections. The transfilmicity thus established could, in effect, be deemed solipsistic, restricting all engagement to engagement with cinema, and yet, because the films referred to often belong to genres like the Western, the war movie, and the historical drama, most of these connections actively problematize the relationship between film and history. Scholars writing on *Inglourious Basterds* have insisted on the way the movie engages with the politics of the WWII movie; Imke Meyer, for instance, argues that the movie demonstrates that Hollywood has exploited the Nazi as "a shorthand for Absolute Evil,"⁶¹ Kligerman that the pleasure we may derive from watching the violence inflicted on the Nazi characters in *Inglourious Basterds* aligns us with both the Basterds, whose sole entertainment is brain-bashing, and with the Nazis watching American soldiers fall in a propaganda film.⁶²

Django Unchained engages in a similar way with romanticized Hollywood representations of the South, by portraying the Southern Belle as a sex trafficker and blowing up the beautiful house of Southern movies.⁶³ It assaults in particular *The Birth of a Nation*, which *Inglourious Basterds* designates as an American propaganda movie, as Semenza has argued,⁶⁴ by drawing attention to the hold Griffith's movie had on cultural representations of the South (the Southern house, the Southern Belle) and race relations for many years.⁶⁵ Not only does the film make a mockery of the hooded, racist lynch mob in the scene where they significantly bicker about their masks, defusing their potential to ennoble or terrify, but it also suggests that we cannot imagine the South without the KKK, and that Hollywood is as guilty of exploiting the power of this imagery as it is of exploiting the figure of the Nazi. The two references on which the character of Stephen is modeled interact in a highly significant manner. Uncle Tom and Ishiguro's Stephens are both accomplices, to varying degrees of course, of their masters' crimes; Uncle Tom, as Nama reminds us, is "a derisive and colloquial title African Americans have used to define a black person who despises black people and acquiesces to the whims and wishes of whites for material gain and a sense of self-worth,"⁶⁶ while in *The Remains of the Day*, Stevens is ultimately guilty of devotion to Lord Darlington, a proponent of fascism in Great Britain. As an active accomplice, Candie's Stephen is the excessive merger of the two, the embodiment of the figure's culpability, and thus of the white people who created it, in the eyes of cultural history.

The Hateful Eight also engages with *The Birth of a Nation*, although it seems to have escaped notice. Warren and Smithers's discussion about the Battle of Baton Rouge brings out the tensions, notably racial, at the heart of the Civil War. This leads the British character, Oswaldo Mobray, to intervene: "I know Americans aren't apt—to let a little thing like unconditional surrender get in the way of a good war. But I strongly suggest we don't restage the Battle of Baton Rouge" [66:50]. And yet the conflict is exactly what *The Hateful Eight* stages without, pointedly, reproducing an actual battle, but, rather, its coda. And it does so by expanding on the finale of none other than *The Birth of a Nation*, in a similar manner as *Reservoir Dogs* expands on that of *City on Fire* (1987). Minnie's Haberdashery becomes the site of the reenactment of the Civil War just like the Northern soldiers' cabin in Griffith's movie. It all starts when Mobray suggests they "divide Minnie's in half—the Northern side—and the Southern side" [67:45]. In so doing, the Englishman deviously turns the clock of history, asserts authority over American space, and allows the national quarrel to be embodied spatially. Warren will nonetheless revisit the Battle of Baton Rouge when provoking General Smithers in a duel and killing him, symbolically putting a conclusion to the war; in a sense, Warren, like the Basterds, seizes the opportunity to rewrite history. This is facilitated by the fact that, unlike the 1915 cabin, Minnie's is a black space. After the death of John Ruth, a new alliance is formed between the Northern black man, Warren, and the Southern white man, Mannix. The final chapter, "Black Man, White Hell," thus represents the inverted reflection of the end of *The Birth of a Nation*. The Southern woman, like Oswaldo who had come to save her, fans the fire of Civil War tensions by trying to convince the former renegade that his future depends on preserving Confederate values, that the white woman, as the symbol of those values, must be protected at all costs, and that the black man, the absolute threat to the woman and the values she incarnates, must be killed. If Daisy Domergue represents the diabolical double of Elsie Stoneman, symbolically at least, her function is exactly the same: preserving the woman means preserving the nation which, in *The Birth of a Nation*, implicitly means preserving Southern values. Tarantino thus does with the figure of the Southern lady—who, in the person of Lara Lee Candie-Fitzwilly, is more expediently eliminated in the previous movie [157:49]—what he does with the figure of Uncle Tom in *Django Unchained*;

he reveals, through violent excess, its complicity in the cultural history of black representations as a white fabrication.

Some of the criticism leveled against *Inglourious Basterds* and *Django Unchained* involved assumptions that, as allohistories filled with references to other films, they were more interested in engaging with film history than with history. In the aptly named "'Fire!' in a Crowded Theater: Liquidating History in *Inglourious Basterds*," Sharon Willis says:

> Nor can irony screen out collective memory and historical trauma in the perverse intersections of fantasy and history that *Inglourious Basterds* produces through its cinematic citations. In this cinephile world, film's only referent is itself; its own film archive displaces History. Despite its fascination with historical detail, the central referent of *Inglourious Basterds* seems to be the auteur's own œuvre, from *Reservoir Dogs* to the *Kill Bill* franchise. Its fantasy of film's intervention in material history finally projects the director's fantasy of making his mark within History reduced to *film* history, like Shosanna, inserting his own footage into its unfolding.[67]

Though I disagree with her conclusion, I follow Willis on several points. Shosanna's act of cutting into a propaganda film and using celluloid to destroy the Nazi is, in effect, a thematization of *Inglourious Basterds* as allohistory, and thus an instance of overt diegetic metafiction; that it is fiction that is empowered is made clear in that the documentary-like scene on celluloid combustion has Tarantino regular Samuel L. Jackson posing as an expert speaking in voice-over, over a clip from *Sabotage* (Alfred Hitchcock, 1937) (fig. 4) [62:35–62:54]. Tarantino, like many filmmakers and artists past and present, refers to his other works in an attempt to construct an œuvre; this runs the risk of solipsism, as Kligerman, though less critical, warns that "we cannot overlook the risks that this archive poses for the critic/analyst of the film, whereby the text entraps us in a hermeneutic labyrinth."[68] However, none of these arguments entails that an allohistorical approach precludes engagement with history, as we have seen above, much less that such works are "perverse" per se. I would reframe the usage of the verb "displace" by keeping in mind that displacement, like its rhetorical equivalents the metonymy and synecdoche, implies an actual connection, whether spatial, temporal, or causal. If film history "displaces" history, then it neither blots out history nor constitutes a denial of history, but is an integral part of it. In Semenza's words, "[r]ather than positioning itself as an alternate history representation of reality, *Inglourious Basterds* celebrates its situatedness in a

Fig. 4: *Inglourious Basterds*: As Shosanna reveals her plan to her lover Marcel, a documentary-like sequence featuring Samuel Jackson in voice-over utilizes a clip from a fiction film—*Sabotage* (Hitchcock, 1936)—as proof of the flammability of celluloid, endowing it with an archive effect.

massive *textual* tradition which nonetheless has contributed directly to the ways the atrocities of the 1940s are understood and narrated today."[69]

The "exhilarating fantasy" that "film becomes a literal weapon,"[70] illustrated at the end of *Inglourious Basterds*, is not really Tarantino's, as Willis seems to suggest. Rather, the idea is part and parcel of the (film) history of World War II, when the British, Americans, Germans, and Italians made propaganda films in order to both rally their troops to a cause and promote their values abroad.[71] This cultural and ideological war is explained by Archie Hicox, whose name recalls that of a British filmmaker (Alfred Hitchcock) who returned to Great Britain in 1944 to make two propaganda films, *Bon Voyage* and *Aventure Malgache*, funded by the British Ministry of Information. When questioned on his knowledge of German cinema during the Third Reich, Hicox explains that "Goebbels considers the films he's making to be the beginning of a new era in German cinema. An alternative to what he considers the Jewish-German intellectual cinema of the 20s, and the Jewish-controlled dogma of Hollywood" [66:27]. Goebbels, according to Hicox, sees his project as participating in transnational film history and, more largely, in racial history, as the common denominator (Jews and Jewishness) indicates. Shosanna's is exactly the type of movie Goebbels is combating: directed by a black man and starring a Jewish woman, the film, which employs aesthetics indebted to German Expressionism (especially Fritz Lang), Soviet Cinema, also recalls another giant face in a Hollywood film, that of the 1939 *Wizard of Oz*[72]—a testament to the importance of Jews in the transnational history of cinema. As an industry and as a cultural product, cinema is thus steeped in ideology and inscribed in history. Framed by Hicox's comments, Shosanna's movie merely literalizes a view inscribed in history and that remains pertinent in a day and age when films, whether nonfiction or fiction as Hicox's name recalls, are still meant to export ideologies, and videos posted online are used as weapons.

Finally, *Inglourious Basterds* attempts to conciliate two competing ontological views of film that are very much relevant to contemporary debates in film and media studies. Celluloid is the actual weapon, and Shosanna's plot is a film historian's nightmare, but the audience in the movie theater never really knows what hit them; from their perspective, they are being attacked by the two machine-gun-wielding Basterds and the giant face on screen, a face that lives on, projected on the rising smoke when the screen has been consumed, becoming spectral. *Inglourious Basterds* aims at putting an end to the debate and encouraging us to accept the paradox that film is both material and transcendent, real and spectral, archive and memory. It is, of course, Tarantino's own view of the medium that *Inglourious Basterds* is defending, the view of a cinephile who delights as much in his movie-watching memories as in the technology of cinema.

For all their outrageous play with historical facts, *Inglourious Basterds*, *Django Unchained*, and *The Hateful Eight* do not seek exemption from either moral engagement or engagement with history. As allohistories, they are underpinned by a fantasy structure, a strategy Hutcheon identifies as typical of covert diegetic metafiction, yet history remains associated with a sense of perspective, notably moral. *Inglourious Basterds* and *The Hateful Eight* resort to the overt metafictional device of thematizing the alteration of history, inviting viewers to consider the reasons for such modifications in relation to a specific context, and to delve for hidden meanings and subtexts. All three films celebrate the ethical and political potential of allegory and metaphor, both of which enable, through analogy, to broaden the historical and geographical scope beyond the represented and its context. Many of the misrepresentations are borrowed from other films or from film genres. Not only do they reinforce the fictional status of the work, as overt and covert diegetic strategies that draw attention to the world-building process, but they systematically invite viewers to establish connections and attempt to interpret them, as comments on the influence of specific films (*Django Unchained*, *The Hateful Eight*), the history of a film genre (*Inglourious Basterds*), Hollywood and transnational film history (*Inglourious Basterds*, *Django Unchained*, *The Hateful Eight*), and even on historical conceptions of the ontology of the film medium (*Inglourious Basterds*).

The films' engagement with historical material brings to the fore two central tenets of Tarantino's work that, as we shall see, are also true of his previous work, albeit less explicitly so. Tarantino's metafictional films are all grounded in a fantasy structure. First, like the historical movies, *Reservoir Dogs*, *Pulp Fiction*, *Jackie Brown*, and *Death Proof* are set in actual places (LA, Tokyo, Austin, Texas, and Lebanon, Tennessee), though some (Tokyo and Lebanon)[73] are completely fabricated. The mix of fashions (the clothing in the first three feature films) and technologies (1970s cars and cell phones in *Death Proof*)[74] confers a sense of timelessness that seems to make them ahistorical on the surface. Like the modifications in the historical films, Tarantino's invented brand names—Big Kahuna burgers (*Reservoir Dogs*, *Pulp Fiction*, *Death Proof*), Red Apple Cigarettes (*Pulp Fiction*, *Kill Bill*, *The Hateful Eight*)—overtly draw attention to the building blocks of a diegetic world that unites all his films. Second, the films do not just refer to other films, but inscribe themselves within film history and, more generally, cultural history, an endeavor that is not solipsistic because it taps into the metonymical relationship between cultural history and history. The three films thus provide both a methodology by which to read his previous films and a defense of metafictional cinema as ethically and politically engaged with real-world concerns. The Lincoln letter, for instance, looks back and comments on the Ezekiel 25:17 speeches in *Pulp Fiction*, also delivered by Samuel Jackson who also takes on the role of director.[75] While Kelly Ritter locates Jules's qualified epiphany as a failure of language "to truly transform identity,"[76] notably due to the fact that the protagonist believes his version is authentic, her comparing Jules's pastiches to "two original" versions of the passage[77] undermines her essentialist conclusion, not to mention her postmodernist framework. *Pulp Fiction* is by no means mourning the "original" (after all, the speech is lifted from a Sonny Chiba picture), but celebrating, rather, the transformative power of language, rhetorics, and performance.

CHAPTER TWO

"BLACK MAN, WHITE HELL"

Identity Politics Vol. 1: Race and Ethnicity

Tarantino's films were political long before *Inglourious Basterds*, and it is the purpose of the two chapters that follow to investigate the degree to which they engage with contemporary issues of identity politics. The title of the final chapter of *The Hateful Eight* is a clear statement of intent: its chiasmic structure establishes a dialectical relationship and suggests a binary worldview; it announces that race, which has already been shown to be divisive, will be the decisive issue in the outcome; it constructs the character of Warren as the hero in this snowy Western horror movie, making him the double of R. J. MacReady, the white hero of *The Thing* (John Carpenter, 1982), rather than that of MacReady's black sidekick Childs; it aligns the white characters with the hostile environment outside; finally, it could almost have been an alternative title for Tarantino's previous movie *Django Unchained* and, albeit less obviously, for *Reservoir Dogs*, a film Tarantino refers to as his first version of *The Thing* (1982),[1] where the "white hell"—the warehouse recalling, as Thomas Beltzer has suggested,[2] Sartre's vision of hell in *No Exit* (1943)—has been created by a black police officer named Holdaway. This deceptively simple title suggests that, even when couched in a clear dichotomy, the racial politics of cinematic representations are complex, layered, and grounded in a history of such representations.

This chapter builds on Adilifu Nama's excellent book *Race on the QT*. This is especially the case of the first two subparts; the last two explore linguistic and formal features that have been largely unattended, notably the use of the n-word that has, to my knowledge, only been studied recently by Keith Allan in *Pulp Fiction*.[3] Like critic Stanley Crouch, Nama sees Tarantino as "a complex screenwriter and director who questions America's traditional notions of race, ethnicity, and gender."[4] Race is an underlying concern of all his films, and the venues explored (the mundanity of white racism, its sadism, racial self-loathing, etc.) are varied. The treatment of race should not be reduced to its relation to blaxploitation; in many ways, it pursues the work of New Hollywood filmmakers like Francis Ford Coppola and Martin Scorsese.[5] Nama's insightful analyses of narrative, characterization, and symbols prove that the treatment of race is not just a gimmick; it underpins the narrative and often proposes complex subtexts. Nama concludes that Tarantino's films ultimately have something to say about the real world, as they "resonate with established and emerging discourses concerning race in America."[6]

I have chosen to focus on race, ethnicity, gender, and sexuality because they are the aspects the films pay attention to most, though we shall see that they are largely steeped in class and economics as well. For one who, like myself, adheres to a view of identity as a complex "crossroads,"[7] this structure is, I admit, a bit of a letdown, not only because it appears to deny the way various aspects of identity intersect, but also because Tarantino's films repeatedly insist on these intersections. But my analyses will ultimately slip through the confines of composition, as questions of gender will repeatedly crop up in chapter 2, as will questions of race in chapter 3. Moreover, I have designed the chapters so that their subparts echo each other, and I hope the reader will find it stimulating to go back and forth between the subparts of each chapter. Each chapter opens with an investigation of how identity politics are dependent on film genre conventions that are gendered, racialized, and so forth. These are followed by studies of power relations within the diegesis, with particular attention to narrative structure and character arcs. The third subparts propose analyses of racial, racist, gendered, and sexist words and phrases in order to assess whether these occurrences are gratuitous, as some critics have contended,[8] or, on the contrary, develop a complex metadiscourse on identity politics. The final subparts focus on how bodies are represented, with special attention to costume, lighting, camerawork, and editing.

My basic argument is that Tarantino's cinematic metafictions are by no means solipsistic; because they are layered, their analysis and interpretation leads the viewer to work her/his way, spiral-like, outward to consider the "real" world implications of these representations. The films reflect on genre films, on Hollywood and exploitation films, and on Tarantino's own films, on cinema as an an institution with a history, and more generally on the cultural history of representations. It is this awareness of representation that, I would argue, inscribes Tarantino's films in the postmodernist and poststructuralist views of our time, in particular those made popular by theories of constructivism.

Some have accused these films of cynicism,[9] of whitewashing history,[10] or of promoting post-racial and post-feminist views.[11] Yet in these films, race, ethnicity, gender, class, masculinity, femininity, nationality, and regional identity are all represented as social constructs caught up in normative discourses and practices that have a history and a context. In these films, the various facets of identity intersect in various ways, and there is no aspect that is universally more essential than another, though Tarantino seems to find some more engaging than others. In these films, all characters are, as imagined subjects, sites where the multiple dimensions of identity converge. In these films, race and gender are intertwined with the treatment of film genre, all the more so as these genres—the heist movie, the gangster movie, the horror movie, the car movie, the war movie, the Western—have long been dominated by white males. As forms of normative discourses and practices, genre conventions function like the "regulatory norms of 'sex'" described by Judith Butler: they "work in a performative fashion to constitute the materiality of bodies and, more specifically, to materialize the body's sex, to materialize sexual difference in the service of the consolidation of the heterosexual imperative."[12] Consequently, if these positions appear to be fixed, they are only so symbolically and discursively, not biologically (biology being yet another construct). Destabilizing these positions can thus produce gender and race trouble, and this is something Tarantino has sought to do quite deliberately by unpacking these terms. I argue that these inversions are not just playful. They demonstrate that patriarchy and racism still carry weight in contemporary representations, and thus in contemporary society, and that we have yet to proceed to a post-gender, post-racial world, one that, at this stage, remains a possibility rather than a reality.

Race and Ethnicity/Genre

For a film released in the early 1990s, the quasi-absence of minority characters in *Reservoir Dogs* is conspicuous. The film's heist plot is centered on a group of white thieves, and all the cops glimpsed in the flashbacks are white. The only character from a racial or ethnic minority appears in the Commode Story flashback: Holdaway, the police officer who has trained Freddy Newandyke in the art of working undercover and whom Freddy reports to. The narrative structure thus delays the revelation that the all-white plot has been compromised by a black man. This leads Nama to conclude that *Reservoir Dogs* "has more in common with the Blaxploitation, racial revenge narratives [...] than it does with the 1950s film *noir*, gangster flicks Tarantino's first film invites comparison to."[13] More precisely, the all-white *noir* narrative is, on a metafictional level, undermined by the blaxploitation narrative, embodied respectively by the two masterminds: Joe Cabot and Holdaway.

Pulp Fiction pursues and expands the strategy whereby characters stand for specific genres or cinemas: Jules[14] and Marsellus recall blaxploitation; Mia, *noir*; Butch, the boxing movie; Captain Koons, the war movie; Fabienne, the French New Wave. Some characters even seem to have stepped right out of specific films: Jules and Vincent out of *The Killers* (Universal, Siodmak, 1946);[15] Vincent, *Saturday Night Fever* (John Badham, 1977);[16] Maynard and Zed, *The Pawnbroker*[17] (Sidney Lumet, 1964) and *Deliverance* (1972); the Wolf, *Nikita* (1990).[18] All these strands are held together by one genre that constitutes the main framework—the gangster movie—and that is associated with a black man, Marsellus, "a figure of power and prestige without peer in American cinema,"[19] who rules over black and white alike. In the world of *Pulp Fiction*, Marsellus is the equivalent of Joe Cabot in *Reservoir Dogs*, only this time the extent of the gangster's power is, as we shall see, put to the test not just by another character (Butch) but by chance. Structurally, the film is framed by another black character, Jules, whose arc opens and concludes it. As a figure who, with his jerry curls and three-piece suit, initially conflates two genres and periods (1950s *noir* and 1970s blaxploitation) that were opposed in *Reservoir Dogs*, Jules confirms his potential to unsettle racialized conventions through generic hybridity when he opts for a new trajectory inspired by Kwai Chang Caine from the TV series *Kung Fu* (ABC, 1972–75), an ethnically mixed character played by a white actor. This shift is enabled, paradoxically, by the very genre that seemed to impose a monolithic definition on him: blaxploitation. Jules's association with this cycle, which also produced Westerns and martial arts films, legitimizes the change to another genre and another medium. Blaxploitation, by token of its generic diversity, represents, *Pulp Fiction* seems to contend, a previous experiment in modifying the racialized terms of established Hollywood genres.

Jackie Brown also taps into blaxploitation in order to adapt Elmore Leonard's novel, though its generic terms are largely inherited from the novel. Changing the female protagonist's race from white to black and casting blaxploitation star Pam Grier in the lead role are central to how the film's racial and gender politics are articulated to film genre and film history. First, the racist fear (i.e., the threat a black man poses to a white woman) underlying the novel is defused. Second, Jackie and Max's romance becomes the sort of interracial relationship blaxploitation movies refrained from portraying, though black men with white women have sometimes been depicted.[20] Third, the black woman is put in the position of the mastermind, like the racist Joe

Fig. 5.1: *Jackie Brown*: Resembling the 1974 Foxy Brown, Jackie (in low angle) dominates . . .

Fig. 5.2: *Jackie Brown*: . . . the gangster (in high angle) who tried to strangle her moments before.

Cabot in *Reservoir Dogs*. Finally, the confrontation between Jackie and Ordell opposes the two staple characters of blaxploitation—the female avenger and the male criminal[21]—with some variation: Jackie is getting back not just at Ordell for exploiting her but at life, and she is not avenging a lover or family member but is acting exclusively in her own interest. The face-off scene in which Jackie points a gun at Ordell, who had just tried to strangle her in her own living room [47:20–53:14], can be seen as a reimagining of the scene in *Foxy Brown* (Jack Hill, 1974) where the heroine barges in her brother's living room to scold him for having played a part in her lover's death (fig. 5.1–5.2). It suggests that *Jackie Brown* is endeavoring to shed the Hollywood stereotypes of the Mammy and the hypersexual black woman that persisted in blaxploitation.[22] Clearly, the homage to blaxploitation does not preclude a desire to revise the genre's limitations.

Kill Bill functions very much like *Pulp Fiction* and *Jackie Brown*. The characters are closely bound to specific genres or even movies: Budd wears a cowboy hat, Elle Driver and O-Ren resemble the protagonists of *Thriller: They Call Her One Eye* (Vibenius, 1973) (fig. 14) and *Lady Snowblood* (Toshiya Fujita, 1973), Gogo Yurabi actress Chiaki Kuriyama's character in *Battle Royale* (Kinji Fukasaku, 2000), while Pai Mei is a recurring character in the Shaw Brothers kung fu films of the 1970s; Tarantino even stated that "[t]here was an aspect of The Bride not just fighting through her death list, she was fighting through the whole history of exploitation cinema, with every character on that list representing a different genre."[23] The overarching framework is provided by two TV series—*Kung Fu* and *Charlie's Angels* (ABC, 1976–81)—associated with Bill. A cowboy-boot-sporting martials arts expert, the male villain controls a multinational, multiracial group of predominantly female elite assassins; the casting of David Carradine reinforces the link to the hypotext, with Bill even playing the flute around a fire in *Vol. 2* [39:24–44:00].[24] Beatrix is, however, endowed with the same transformative potential as Jules in *Pulp Fiction*, a potential that is grounded in her embodying a site where various intertexts intersect: as the Bride, she is the Gothic victim, shot in the head, raped in *Vol. 1* and buried alive in *Vol. 2*; she dons Bruce Lee's *Game of Death* (Robert Clouse and Bruce Lee, 1978) outfit in *Vol. 1*, stalks Budd in a ninja outfit in *Vol. 2*, resembles Frank from *Once Upon a Time in the West* (Sergio Leone, 1968) when crossing the desert, and Luc Besson's Nikita in the hotel room flashblack. By going after Bill, the Bride embodies, among other things, the revenge of Bruce Lee on the white actor who was given Lee's part because producers felt that audiences were not yet ready for an Asian hero.[25] Thus, the critique of one of the film's main hypotexts has to do with the history of ethnic and racial representations in cinema and popular culture.

In *Death Proof*, the treatment of race is strictly organized along generic lines that are racialized and gendered. Associated with the teen movie, the female characters form heterogeneous groups, with blacks (Julia, Marcy, Kim), whites (Shanna, Pam, Lanna Frank, Lee) and a white New Zealander (Zoë); Arlene, who dances to the song "Down in Mexico" [39:12], is played by Latin American actress Vanessa Ferlito, while actress Rosario Dawson, who plays Abernathy, is of Irish, Puerto Rican, and Afro-Cuban descent. The racial diversity is reinforced by the presence of Hispanics, blacks, whites, and Asians at Güero's, the Texas Chili Parlor, and the diner [32:57, 76:54]. It is contrasted with the whiteness of the male characters (Bill, Dov, Omar, Warren,

Fig. 6: *Inglourious Basterds*: A pensive Shosanna leans against the eye-shaped window of her movie theater, a double of the spy Bridget von Hammersmark, whose name tops the poster of a German movie outside.

Sheriff McGraw, and the sheriff's son, Jasper). Several critics, myself included, have demonstrated that *Death Proof* proposes a critique of the white male gaze.[26] The film genres associated with Stuntman Mike (the car movie and the slasher) are stringently racialized in the first part of the film. The tables are turned when Mike encounters Kim and Zoë, who, because they are in the same field as he is, compromise the gendered terms of those two genres, first by playing Ship's Mast on the highway, then by pursuing him following his attack. Moreover, the integration of the multiracial Abernathy during the final car chase suggests that becoming a site where various intertexts and film genres meet is not restricted to the stuntwomen but can be shared. *Death Proof* thus functions in part as an application of feminist film theory by undermining the racialized and sexist terms of alleged white male film genres.

Inglourius Basterds inherits its racial terms from the WWII movie. The opponents of the Nazi regime stand for (national, racial, ethnic, gender) diversity. Shosanna carries out her plan with the help of her black French lover Marcel, and though the Basterds lack black members, they form a heterogeneous group of Jews and Gentiles, led by Aldo Raine with Apache blood, and they welcome a German soldier (Hugo Stiglitz), disgusted by his own regime, and work with a German spy, actress Bridget von Hammersmark. Germans are not equated with Nazis, and Nazis are not equated with Germans, as the Austrian SS officer Hans Landa also proves. *Inglourious Basterds* alters the terms of the WWII movie by allowing the Jewish characters to play an active part in the demise of the Third Reich, rejecting, as Imke Meyer has argued, the Manichean dichotomy of much of Hollywood cinema and American popular culture: "Tarantino's revenge fantasy, then, releases Jews from the dead end of eternal victimhood, at the same time that it confronts Hollywood with its instrumentalization of the Holocaust for the mere purpose of 'good' storytelling."[27] Shosanna exemplifies this transformation from potential victim in Chapter One to mastermind, emerging as a directorial figure and actress in Chapter Five, a transformation which, like that of Jules, Beatrix, Kim, and Abernathy, is reflected, on a metafictional level, by her initial association with the McBain children, murdered by Frank, in *Once Upon a Time in the West*, and with French cinema in Chapter Three, by her resemblance to the German spy Bridget von Hammersmark whose name can be seen on the poster outside the window (fig. 6) before Shosanna applies war paint[28] on her cheeks in the opening scene of Chapter Five [105:46–106:52], and finally by her transformation into a cinematographic synthesis of Carl Theodor Dreyer's 1928 Joan of Arc[29] and the 1939 Wizard of Oz (fig. 13.1).[30] Both the Nazis and the Nazi war movie are destroyed by a figure that embodies filmic, national, racial, and gender diversity, suggesting that the political power of cinema lies in the impurity the Nazis attempt to eliminate.

In *Django Unchained* and *The Hateful Eight*, the Western functions as both setting and frame, much like the snowcapped Rockies, a synecdoche of the genre, surrounding Minnie's way station. And like the mountaintops, it is racialized white. The generic framework is upheld not by one character specifically, but by the majority of white characters whose reactions mark the black bounty hunters as unwelcome in this setting/genre; this is dramatized, for instance, in the scene where Django and Schultz arrive in the town of Daughtrey, Texas, and the mostly appalled inhabitants look on [13:07–14:25]. The black man stands out against the whiteness. His integration within the genre is facilitated by the precedents mentioned in chapter 1 and confirmed when Sheriff Gus welcomes him as an equal [57:22]. As in Tarantino's previous films, the protagonist endowed with a transformative potential is a minority character who represents a site of converging intertexts. Both films combine the Western with other genres: *Django Unchained* with the plantation movie, the interracial buddy movie, the mythic quest, and, as Nama has brilliantly demonstrated, the Gothic;[31] and *The Hateful Eight* with the whodunnit, Gothic horror, and the Civil War movie. Like *Pulp Fiction*, *Django Unchained* is indebted to blaxploitation's revisiting of mainstream film genres (the Western, horror, and even the plantation movie). Like *Jackie Brown*, it deconstructs the racist archetypes of a specific Hollywood genre, here the plantation movie, with its Southern Belle and Uncle Tom,[32] a deconstruction that is enabled by the blaxploitation revenge narrative (fig. 7).[33] Django, a slave who has escaped the plantation movie, is at the same time a bounty hunter, the hero of a Gothic romance and Schultz's Siegfried. It is his quest for his wife Broomhilda von Shaft that leads them out of the interracial Western

Fig. 7: *Django Unchained*: Three Southern stereotypes (Stephen as the Uncle Tom, Candie as the Southern gentleman, and Lara Lee as the Southern Belle) stand on the porch of the plantation house.

buddy movie[34] into the Southern Gothic of the plantation, first on a comic mode, then on a darker, almost body horror mode.[35] While the first hour of *The Hateful Eight* is dominated by the presence of the white bounty hunter, John Ruth, Warren steps in to take on the central role, first, when he provokes General Smithers, then when he investigates the deaths of Ruth and O. B., becoming an equivalent of Agatha Christie's Miss Marple and Hercule Poirot, and of Carpenter's R. J. MacReady in *The Thing* (1982), a role played by the same actor (Kurt Russell) who plays Ruth. For the first time, perhaps, a white male protagonist (Sheriff Chris Mannix) is allowed to undergo a positive transformation; significantly, the former Confederate soldier shifts from endorsing General Smithers in the central part of the film, to Warren in the last chapter, thus accepting to become the older black man's sidekick.

Film genre has, from the start, represented the main framework for each one of Tarantino's films, which seems consistent with the director's admission that "[w]hen [he] want[s] to write, [he] figure[s] out what genre and what style [he] want[s] to work in."[36] Characters are associated with specific genres, even specific movies, and this is often reinforced by the casting of actors (Tierney, Travolta, Grier, Carradine, Russell) who invite such connections. Tarantino's material is by no means raw; to the contrary, it is heavily determined and notably racialized. His films recognize that the terms of a given film genre are such, as are Hollywood conventions and, more generally, American cultural representations. On a metafictional level, they criticize the always already racialized and often racist terms of the genres or specific works they reference or pay homage to. But Tarantino's films also work on the assumption that conventions are inscribed in a historical context and can thus be altered. Each film works to unsettle these terms. Sometimes this is achieved quite simply by placing a minority character (Marsellus, Jackie, Beatrix, Shosanna, Warren) in a central position rarely occupied by such characters. Often, the protagonist endowed with the potential to transform (Jules, Beatrix, Abernathy, Shosanna, Django) is both a site of intersectionality in terms of identity politics and film genre or intertexts. Each film, as we shall now see, investigates the dynamics at the heart of race and ethnic relations, the remnants of racism and the potential of minority empowerment.

Power, Racism, and Racialized Relations

"[R]ace—or more specifically racism—is," according to Nama, "the driving undercurent of *Reservoir Dogs*. Racism dictates that Freddy, the naïve and not-so-sure-footed undercover cop, is the central figure of the film, but not its catalyst."[37] For "[t]he ruthless mastermind and hero of the film is Holdaway, not Mr. Orange."[38] It is Holdaway's "precise tutelage about [the heist men's] mannerisms and mindset" that enables the "inexperienced" Freddy "to walk among" them;[39] the black man teaches the white man to be cool enough to infiltrate the group of, ironically, racist white thieves. Freddy is thus Holdaway's pawn just as much as the thieves are Cabot's. The Commode Story chapter constructs the black cop and the racist white gangster as doubles. Both are masters of cool professionalism[40] who, seated across from Freddy—in the diner [62:09] and the nightclub [67:05]—act like teachers, with Holdaway coaching Freddy [64:00], and Cabot the thieves while standing in front of a blackboard [76:38]. As "a cold and calculating—even Machiavellian—law enforcement professional," Holdaway "functions as a symbolic counterweight" to Mr. Pink's equating black with incompetence.[41]

By confining Holdaway to the flashback and abandoning him the moment Freddy receives the phone call that he is in [71:30], and by singling Holdaway out in shots, particularly on top of the building [64:52] and in the vacant yard [66:40], the narration seems bent on "displac[ing]" the black character "to the margins of the film";[42] one could even argue that the establishing shot of the diner serves to distance the show of affection between Freddy and Holdaway [71:50]. The narrative and the narration thus conflict; the first is driven by racial revenge (and, I would argue, by racial and social consciousness), while the second seems, like Cabot's plot, to be grounded in racist tendencies. Yet because these singles also show the black cop framed by the city and the graffiti in the background, he comes to represent a synecdoche of LA's social and racial diversity and, more generally, of the social reality the genre film seems to deny. Indeed, the character also draws attention to the complex relationship between race and class. While the dogs are dressed in "traditional corporate attire,"[43] Holdaway, who sports a headband with the colors of Africa, resembles, as Nama points out, a guerilla fighter "planning the overthrow of a corrupt and capitalist regime."[44] The confrontation between Holdaway and Cabot thus stands for that between the working-class black man and the Man as "big-game capitalist."[45] Nama concludes beautifully:

> Cabot's crooks symbolize the tensions at work in American corporate capitalism and demonstrate how calculating business logic is infused with and operates alongside gender discrimination and racial animosity. [...] The film frankly demonstrates a white racial prejudice that exists not as an overt act of social victimization but as an everyday sensibility and attitude that shapes and informs the contours of white masculine entitlement in contest with gendered or racialized identity.[46]

For Nama, this portrayal of the everyday racism instrumental to the construction of white masculinity is also achieved splendidly in *Pulp Fiction*. The representation of white racists of various social backgrounds—the drug-dealing Lance, the working-class Maynard and Zed, the middle-class Jimmie Dimmick—"signifies the run-of-the-mill, domesticated racism circulating in American society";[47] it also "dramatically disrupts the pleasure that white, oddball characters often offer in Hollywood films" by constructing them as racists.[48]

In *Pulp Fiction*, the equivalent of the "big-game capitalist" Joe Cabot is his racial other, Marsellus Wallace. I pointed out that Wallace's power is compromised not by a person but by chance. However, each chance event is heavily steeped in racial and even racist implications: "Vincent Vega & Marsellus Wallace's Wife" has the black gangster's white wife OD while on a date with a white employee; "The Gold Watch" relates how Butch and Wallace fall in the clutches of two racist white rapists; and "The Bonnie Situation" is created by the accidental death of a young black man. Yet Zed's playing a racist adaptation of "eeny, meeny, miny, moe" to pick their first victim says it all: Zed starts over and over again until he lands on the black man because he wants to rape him first [100:48–101:25]. This moment reflexively draws attention to the nature of chance in the narrative: it is driven by unconscious racist desires that develop a subtext on race in mainstream American cinema. This is evident in the structure of each story. Each episode opens with Wallace proving his power over white people: Brett and the other white students are terrorized then killed by his hitmen, while Marvin is for some reason spared [111:44–113:38]; Vincent has internalized Wallace's power so that he resists the temptation of sleeping with Mia [52:24]; Marsellus toys with Butch when requiring he lose a fight [21:17]. Each occurrence of chance functions as a retaliation against Wallace's power and ultimately galvanizes highly racialized situations: Mia's body is violated by the drugs purchased from a racist white drug dealer who, pointedly, brags that his product is better than that sold by African American pushers (fig. 45) [27:55]; Wallace is raped first; and it is the white hitman who kills the young black man. Each time the black man's power is restored, but not before his body or one under his protection has been violated. If the rape scene is undoubtedly the climax in this racist assault on the black gangster, "The Bonnie Situation" is, I would argue, the climax of chance's assault on black men in general. For "[t]he inordinate time the trio spend literally cleaning away proof of Marvin's existence is a brilliant metaphor for the disposability of young black men."[49]

So *Pulp Fiction* does not only deal with racism explicitly. In a sense, the main bulk of the film is the exact opposite of *Reservoir Dogs*: it is blaxploitation that is this time threatened by the racism of mainstream cinema and culture that wants to put black men back in their place. In Nama's words, "the victimization of a black character who until his rape represented a figure of power and prestige without peer in American cinema invites interpretation that his victimization is symptomatic of a racist film industry."[50] The Chinese box structure of the film thus serves to both contain and counter the racist desires that drive the narrative. Indeed, if the first chance event—the bullets that impossibly spare Jules and Vincent—compromises Wallace's power since he loses a faithful black employee in the process, it is the same event that will lead another black man, Jules, to regenerate and avoid the sort of death that befalls his white partner. "As a result," Nama concludes, "Jules is able to fulfill a role rarely ceded to a black character in mainstream Hollywood movies—a redeemed and empowered figure who lives to the end of the film."[51] Vincent's death at the hands of Butch can be interpreted two ways depending on whether you look back or forward at the narrative: it is the death of Butch's double, another white man subjected to the black gangster, but as the killing of a white man who violated Mia and killed Marvin (both times by accident), it also announces Butch's final decision to turn against the unconscious racist desires that, perhaps, initially drove him. For Nama, "Marsellus' rape and Butch's behavior operate within a critical racial frame that symbolizes and advocates racial reconciliation and mutual respect between blacks and whites."[52] I would argue that the same can be said of Jules's decision to spare Ringo and Yolanda. *Pulp Fiction* depicts how a narrative governed by a powerful black man is threatened by a racist white unconscious, but offers hope through the two characters (Butch and Jules) who make the ethical decision to change their trajectory. The fact that they all go their separate ways, however, seems to cast doubt on the dawning of a post-racial era.

Part of Nama's praise of *Jackie Brown* concerns the character of Ordell Robbie, "the most outstanding and complex version of ominous black criminality to date."[53] A "self-loathing" black man, his "pathological adoration of whiteness" is manifest in his attitude towards his employees, girlfriends, and even his friend Louis.[54] *Jackie Brown* revisits certain racial situations from *Pulp Fiction*; the black gangster enjoys toying with a black woman (Jackie) before attempting to murder her,[55] and views the disposal of black bodies (like Beaumont) as unproblematic:[56] "Hey, you think I'm gonna let a little cheese-eatin' nigger like this fuck that up? You best think again. Before I let that happen, I'll shoot this nigger in the head—and ten niggers look just like him" [27:00]. Nama argues that Ordell's "racial fetishism" includes both his "trophy"[57] girlfriend and his white partner, whom he prizes in spite of Melanie's lack of loyalty and Louis's dimwittedness. Ordell's valuing his "little white surfer girl" over his black girlfriends Simone and Sheronda is translated economically; he has set up Simone and Sheronda in Compton, while Melanie resides in a middle-class beach apartment. Here, another contrast with *Pulp Fiction* is established, as Melanie's white apartment is devoid of the "African art" signifying racial heritage present in the Wallace house.[58] In Ordell's mind, whiteness and blackness are indelibly marked by class, so that climbing the social ladder entails denying black women the possibility to do so; significantly, when all goes to hell, Ordell is forced to hide out at Sheronda's. Thus, after insisting on the existence of white racism in his first two films, *Jackie Brown*, by "constantly signal[ing] that Ordell's commitment to appropriating whiteness is foolhardy and ultimately self-destructive,"[59] sheds light on another destructive aspect of racism: its integration in the psyche of those it oppresses.

This is not to say that Ordell is unaware of race relations—on the contrary, he is very much so—but that his attitude is generally manipulative and cynical. The black gangster plays the race card on several occasions. On both visits to see Max Cherry, Ordell attempts to attract sympathy by describing a world in which black economic power is suspect and justice denies black people the same rights as white people, especially if they are wealthy.[60] Although the claims he makes are founded, Ordell's motives are "transparent, self-serving,"[61] so that the second time around Max reiterates that Ordell is resorting to "white guilt" to avoid paying his deposit [39:21]. Ordell's manipulation of racial brotherhood is also implicit in his making up a story about a "group of Korean" customers he needs Beaumont to help him with [18:40], and grotesquely obvious, as Jackie immediately realizes, when he tries to convince her that "the police start fuckin' with your mind, start pitting black against black, that's how they do," after trying to strangle her [51:28]. The first time he goes to see Max Cherry, Ordell immediately casts doubt on the possibility of interracial friendship when he notices the photo of Max and a black man named Winston on the wall [12:05-12:23]. This picture of the two men standing side by side, smiling, evokes a harmonious interracial relationship (friendship or other), one in which Winston, who is dwarfing Max and has his right arm around his shoulder, by no means occupies an inferior position. By comparing Winston to a "Mandingo" fighter, however, Ordell immediately guesses that the black man is Max's employee, which he gets Max to admit. Max then refuses to answer Ordell as to whether the picture was his "idea." The shift to extreme close-ups indicates that Max has been unsettled by Ordell's implication that the picture is a mere façade targeted at clients, some of whom might be from minority groups, and that the bondsman is just another white man perpetuating the long history of exploiting black bodies.

Ordell's casting doubt on the possibility of interracial friendship, or at least implying that it remains subordinate to economic power, casts a new light on the opening scene in which Ordell is introduced, along with his white girlfriend and white friend; it confirms that they, like Max's photo, are tokens of Ordell's own value. It is not that *Jackie Brown* questions the validity of Ordell's statements on racial inequality in US society; on the contrary, it fully adheres to them, Officer Dargus recognizing, with more condescension than sympathy, that life can be difficult for a middle-aged black woman.[62] But the film does seek to undermine Ordell's cynical view of interracial relationships as necessarily grounded in a master/slave dichotomy. First, Winston's occupying Max's desk suggests that he is not entirely subjected to his employer, while his concern for Max bespeaks of friendship [83:18]. Second, *Jackie Brown* recounts an interracial love story between Jackie and Max who will help her carry out the plot she has masterminded. What the film ultimately demonstrates is that interpersonal relationships may be complicated by racial and gender identity, but they are compromised by individual greed.

In *Kill Bill*, the white assassin's power is so far-reaching that Bill controls the Japanese underworld via his disciple O-Ren Ishii who, as a mix of Japanese, Chinese, and American, symbolizes his hold over all races and nationalities. Bill has effectively colonized one of the countries whose culture he has partially appropriated. The films reveal that Bill has several peers, all of whom are figures of ethnic and racial otherness. *Vol. 1* features Hattori Hanzo, whose talents at making samurai swords are unparalleled and who holds a secret "grudge" against Bill [15:03]. In *Vol. 2*, Bill is revealed, in a flashback, to be inferior, as a martial artist at least, to the demigod Pai Mei [42:13], and Beatrix manages to find out Bill's whereabouts by seeking out another one of his father figures, the suave Mexican gangster Esteban Vihaio [79:30]. All three mentors retain control over their domain. Bill, however, has, like a comic book supervillain, combined the powers they have bestowed on him to conquer the world and gain an economic might that contrasts with their more humble lodgings; he drives a De Tomaso Mangusta [14:36] and boards in a lush suite [84:30]. The Bride's "roaring rampage of revenge" thus leads her to engage with Bill's peers (Hanzo and Vihaio) and colonized subjects (O-Ren, Vernita, Budd, Elle) one by one. Her journey is one that discloses the chronicle of the American capitalist's rise to power. In destroying O-Ren and the Crazy 88, the Bride effectively puts an end to his reign over the Japanese underworld.

Some critics[63] have taken issue with the Bride's race, as it does seem to perpetuate the idea of white appropriation. After all, the white woman has also made hers elements of other cultures and races, including the cool name "Black Mamba" better suited, in Vernita's mind, for a black person [12:40], and she has also used it for economic gain, before becoming a mother at least. For Nama, however,

> the *Kill Bill* franchise differs from numerous American martial arts movies in which benevolent whites adopt Oriental culture and customs with a great deal of success, [. . .] The *Kill Bill* films reject romanticizing white characters as the honorable heirs to or noble practioners of another ethnic/racial group's culture. To the contrary, in the *Kill Bill* franchise, all of the white characters are refreshingly corrupt. In this manner, the appropriation issue that is present throughout the two films is subverted. Whiteness in this instance may co-opt Asian-based martial arts, but the standard Hollywood trope of white moral superiority is diminished. Beatrix Kiddo may be somewhat rehabilitated, but any moral authority is invested in Vernita's daughter Nikki.[64]

The proleptical Chapter One has, then, an ethical function, as the heroine's moral flaw frames her path of revenge; her wrath leads her to murder the sort of woman she could have become, as her three female foes are, regardless of their race, her doubles, equally subjected to the white super-capitalist. The frame is reinforced by the last chapter, which depicts not only the relationship she has been deprived of, but also the life she deprived Vernita and especially the innocent Nikki of. The structure of the film serves to qualify the white heroine's victory, while her journey, as we shall see, is also one in which she pays for the history of white appropriation. If a racist unconscious persists in the narrative, it emanates entirely from the character of Bill, the white male colonizer, who, the film implies, only engages in serious relationships with blondes (Beatrix and Elle).[65]

In *Death Proof*, the groups of girls are, in terms of race relations at least, endowed with post-racial potential. The first group is led by a black woman, Julia, who, according to both Shanna and Pam, has a tendency to bully others, including her friends,[66] and who proves it by subjecting her friend Abernathy to a distasteful prank. By contrast, the power relations in the second group are less determined: Kim is the loud-mouthed driver, Zoë decides the day's activity, and Abernathy talks the stuntgirls into letting her come along before talking Jasper into lending them the car; only the white cheerleader-looking Lee is sacrificed. Nama points out that Zoë's "odd proposal" to be Kim's "back-crackin' slave" [88:10] "plays as a crude race reversal, whereby a white woman will be a black woman's slave."[67] Traces of racist discourse, of course, remain, but unlike Jimmie Dimmick who unashamedly resorts to racist words in front of his friend Jules, Zoë immediately asks Kim for forgiveness after blurting out a misogynistic and racist phrase,[68] while the only female character to utter a frankly racist comment,[69] Pam, the loner who takes off with Mike, is clearly ostracized. The absence of minority male characters is, however, even more radical than in *Reservoir Dogs*. Minority males are relegated to the background—such as the black couple in the diner [74:29]—while the only one with whom the female characters interact, "the Rock," the stage name of African American actor/wrestler Dwayne Johnson, is, like the black women in *Reservoir Dogs*, relegated offscreen and contained within a conversation in a car [57:15–57:51]. Born of a black Canadian father and a mother of Samoan background, Johnson's background is multiethnic, making him Dawson's male double. The fact that the second part of the film opens with a young white woman describing a sexy moment with a black man (whereas Arlene's Nate is white) announces that it will not be a mere repetition of the first. The exclusion of non-white males confirms that the terms of the movie are entirely racialized. The white male gaze is ready and willing to consume female bodies regardless of their race or ethnicty, but denies competition from males from other racial and/or ethnic backgrounds. Driven by a heterosexual white male gaze, the narrative is thus haunted by a racist unconscious.

Django Unchained, as the title suggests, recounts the arc of empowerment of a former slave: Django goes from belonging to Dr. Schultz, to becoming his partner, to being professionally self-reliant. The narrative avoids placing

Django in a subordinate relationship to Schultz by operating a reversal as soon as the second act. If Schultz initially enlists Django as his helper[70] in his search for the Brittle brothers, Django soon becomes both the dispatcher and the hero in his quest for Broomhilda, with Schultz as his helper and donor. The black protagonist does not act as a foil for long; after standing by during Schultz's performance in [12:47–23:36], he takes matters into his own hands on Big Daddy's plantation, identifying the Brittle brothers and killing two out of revenge [32:11–38:00]. The terms of Django and Schultz's relationship are reinforced through characterization. First, though Schultz frees Django, the former slave was by no means submissive to start—he had already rebelled against his former master by marrying the woman he loved[71] and attempting to elope with her. Second, Django is "a natural" at shooting [45:59], and his talent as an actor may have been acquired as a slave, as is suggested through the flashback in which he negotiates with John Brittle [34:00]. Schultz predicts that Django will be called "the fastest gun in the South" [161:33], and by the time they visit Candieland, Django has become even better at being in character than his coach, who shoots Candie down when Django repeatedly refrained from doing so [91:49; 131:01]. Like *Pulp Fiction* and *Jackie Brown*, *Django Unchained* reverses the relationship between white hero and black helper and foil often found in Hollywood films. And like *Jackie Brown*, *Death Proof*, and *Inglourious Basterds*, it celebrates the possibility of interracial relationships.

On a diegetic level, the presence of a black "free man" threatens to tear the Southern social fabric at its seams. The peculiar institution unambiguously grants the plantation owners dominion over black bodies, but power relations are not so simple as black and white, as both the white people and the black slaves are also subjected to a class system. The plantation owners employ white workers, while house slaves, as Django reminds John Brittle, are considered as superior to field slaves [32:58], so Django and Broomhilda's romance also violates this class distinction. In practice, house slaves are sometimes endowed with even greater value. When Candie tells everyone to clear the room, he makes an exception for his slave mistress Sheba [70:29], and Stephen relays his master's orders to the white workers in plain sight [93:10], even counciling his master for whom he seems to represent a father figure [112:48]. The presence of the "free man" adds an extra turn of the screw. Big Daddy is clearly unsettled when Betina, one of his slaves, asks him how she is supposed to treat Django:

> BIG DADDY: Betina, sugar. [...] Django isn't a slave. Django is a free man, you understand? You can't treat him like any of the other

niggas around here cause he ain't *like* any of the other niggas around here. You got it?
BETINA: You want I should treat 'im like white folks?
BIG DADDY: No. That's not what I said.
BETINA: Then I don't know what you want, Big Daddy.
BIG DADDY: Yes. I can see that. Uh . . . Well, what's the name of that peckerwood boy from town that works with the glass, uh? His mama work over at the lumberyard? [. . .] You know Jerry, don't you, sugar?
BETINA: Yessim, Big Daddy.
BIG DADDY: Well, that's it, then. You just treat him like you would Jerry. [30:53]

Ironically, it is the slave master who finds himself admitting that the racial divide is not absolute, thus undermining the very premise of slavery: that one race is essentially inferior to another.

Django's arrival at Candieland proves to be even more disruptive. Not only does he throw a white man off his horse [74:12], advise a wealthy white man [76:50], and sleep and dine in the house with the white people [89:45], but he threatens the position of another black man, Candie's house slave Stephen. Until then, Django's presence has been integrated into the racist discourse, as it has been explicated by Calvin's "exceptional nigger" theory, which is presented in flashback precisely when Django enters this synecdoche of the abject institution [72:59]. Nama's astute remark that "the crude articulation of racial exceptionalism overlaps with [W. E. B.] Du Bois' belief that exceptional African Americans, the best and brightest of the black race, will lead the masses of black folk out of social decay,"[72] suggests that Calvin's theory unwittingly announces the demise of slavery and racial oppression, and is thus debunked by our knowledge of history. But it is subsequently undermined by the narrative itself. Indeed, Calvin's introducing Django to Stephen as "another cheeky black bugger like yourself" [89:10] implies that both the house slave and his master view Stephen as "exceptional" and, more importantly, that an intelligent black individual is by no means "exceptional."[73]

The presence of the "free man" is a threat to the Uncle Tom's more comfortable position, which rests on the oppression of the other slaves whom he governs, because it hints at a different social structure wherein a black person can aspire to be something more than just a house slave. Hence, the final act of the film follows the death of the two white protagonists, Schultz and Candie, and makes way for the face-off between Django and Stephen, confirming the centrality of the black characters. For Nama, both "symbolize, albeit reductively, an ongoing and strident ideological divide within black political discourse over whether accomodationism or militancy is the most effective approach toward gaining racial justice in America."[74] On a metafictional level, then, the complicit house slave, named after the butler in *The Remains of the Day*, represents a racist stereotype of classical Hollywood cinema resenting the blaxploitation cowboy Django. It is Stephen who puts an end to Django's shoot-out by threatening Broomhilda's life [134:50], and it is Stephen who paves the way for the violent racist backlash subsequently inflicted on the black hero, as we shall see. Many critics conclude that the film seems to adhere to the idea that Django is "exceptional";[75] Nama regrets that the potential for black rebellion "is assuaged by the overly subdued performances of the other black slaves that populate the film,"[76] an impression which the opening scene, as we shall see below, qualifies. Yet Django is both right and wrong when he tells Stephen: "But [Calvin] was right about one thing. I am that one nigger in ten thousand" [159:10]. Django is "exceptional" neither because of his talents (Stephen is just as intelligent and just as good an actor), nor because of his attempts to break free (D'Artagnan and Broomhilda do, too): he is one in ten thousand because, regrettably, he is the one in ten thousand who succeeds. So it is not so much the discourse on exceptionalism that can be deplored, since the film ultimately deconstructs it, as Tarantino's decision to follow the action hero on an individual quest.

The Hateful Eight functions as a follow-up to *Django Unchained* because it relates how the Civil War continues to inform human relationships along racial lines even in Wyoming after 1865. We are again introduced to two bounty hunters, one black (Warren), one white (Ruth), but each acts alone. The narrative then dramatizes how allegiances are determined by politics and how politics are determined by racism. While Ruth, a Union sympathizer, is willing to recognize Warren as an equal and make a deal with him [27:10], the Southern renegade Mannix's racism shortly aligns him with Daisy in the stagecoach [27:52–34:59]. If the North governs the stagecoach, race insidiously becomes the dividing line that determines power relations as soon as the characters reach Minnie's way station: Ruth goes inside with his bounty because he's paying for the ride, while his new partner is left to attend the stable with a Mexican man named Bob [37:05–37:32]. The occupation of space is determined by race, with Bob and Warren the last to escape the cold and enter Minnie's [62:36]—ironically, the two characters will find themselves on opposing lines.[77] This is confirmed when, following the dispute between Smithers and Warren, Oswaldo Mobray divides the cabin in two, a moment that rewrites the final scene of *The Birth of a Nation* [66:34]. At the dinner table, the black and white bounty hunter duo is compromised when Mannix gets Warren to admit the Lincoln letter is a fake, prompting Ruth to give in to racist stereotypes: "Well, I guess it's true what they say about you people. Can't trust a fuckin' word comes out of your mouth" [79:59–84:03]. Warren states what is obvious to everyone but Ruth: that race remains the decisive line in human relations in the US. "But you got no *idea* what it's like being a black man facin' down America. Only time black folks is safe—is when white folks is disarmed," he says. Although Warren initially acts as Ruth's sidekick—for instance, when he disarms Joe Gauge [72:57]—he increasingly occupies center stage. Interestingly enough, it is after the Lincoln letter revelation that Warren provokes General Smithers to a duel, as if killing the general and telling the story were his way of getting back at the white characters who mocked him.

With Ruth dead, Warren immediately steps in to disarm Daisy and take his colleague's place [105:37]. A new, tacit contract is established when Warren, repeating Ruth's gesture in the stagecoach, arms the most unlikely of candidates: Chris Mannix [107:16], a man who initially tried to bond with the Confederate General Warren just killed [59:49]. By putting a stop to Warren, Jody Domergue [118:25], who has been hiding under the floorboards, comes to embody the film's racist unconscious avenging itself of the black character who has taken over the plot. In revealing how the racist avenger and his gang eliminated black bodies and their "nigger lover" allies, Chapter Five fulfills the exact same function as "The Commode Story" in *Reservoir Dogs* and is, in terms of storytelling at least, even more redundant, perhaps, for the only true revelation is that Minnie Mink is black [123:07]. Not only does the flashback present a backstory that confirms Warren's worldview—if Minnie is empowered economically and lives in an interracial utopia, racism continues to be a very real threat—but it proposes the negative print of the previous narrative: the deaths of the black characters and their allies make up for the white deaths in the first part of the film. Chapter Six then tests the potential of the new interracial and interregional partnership between Mannix and Warren, with Daisy and her gang calling on race to revive the sense of connivance with Mannix established in Chapter Two [144:27–152:24]. Of course, the bond between Warren and Mannix comes at a price, that of sacrificing the Mexican and especially the woman, suggesting that the logic of identity politics is such that someone will always be excluded in the end (and this may be exactly what identity politics allow us to see).

Race is more than just a central concern in Tarantino's films—it is an organizing principle that, as Nama has argued, informs the films' various layers.[78] While the early films depict how widespread white racism is and how it inhabits the most mundane spaces, almost all seek to undermine figures of white power or superiority (Cabot, Bill, Mike, the Nazis,[79] the slavers, and even Beatrix to some extent) and insist on their racist or imperialist underpinings; they also reveal how racism can be internalized by its victims (Ordell, as well as some of the female characters of *Kill Bill* and *Death Proof*, as we shall see). The films also show an awareness of how economics affect race, and thus of intersections between class and race. Subtextually, some films (*Pulp Fiction*, in particular) are haunted by a racist unconscious, which appears notably in tensions between the narrative and the subtext or the narration, with one undercutting the other. On a metafictional level, the racist unconscious subtext stands for the backlash of mainstream American cinema and culture against representations of empowered minority figures (*Pulp Fiction, Death Proof, Django Unchained, The Hateful Eight*) and interracial camaraderie (*Reservoir Dogs, Django Unchained, The Hateful Eight*) and relationships (*Pulp Fiction*). But if the films of Tarantino direct a revisionist critique of the filmic material they recycle, and more generally of American society, all display faith in the possibility of interracial relationships, a faith that is often carried by the characters endowed with the potential to transform (Freddy and Holdaway, Jules and Butch, Jackie and Max, most of the girls in *Death Proof*, Shosanna and Marcel,[80] Django and Schultz, Warren and Mannix). We will now turn to the racist and racial discourses these relations are steeped in and try to assess to what extent the films deconstruct their uses, thereby adopting a pragmatic view of meaning-making through language.[81]

Racial Rhetoric and the N-word: A Pragmatic Study Vol. 1

The treatment of race in *Reservoir Dogs* is, above all, linguistic. From the outset, the eight gangsters assert their whiteness through racist remarks: Cabot uses the word "coon" [1:16]; Mr. White tells Cabot he is sick of hearing about "Toby the Jap" [2:46]; Eddie evokes the stereotype of the greedy[82] Jew when Mr. Pink refuses to tip [4:38]. The film then includes three scenes where the characters talk about African Americans: in the warehouse when Mr. Pink splits Mr. White and Mr. Blonde up [34:04]; in the Mr. Blonde flashback when Eddie brings up prison rape [37:30]; and in the Commode Story flashback when Mr. Pink, Eddie, and Mr. White discuss the differences between black and white women [73:43].

Mr. Pink's racist "comments[83] belittle black competency and establish black behavior as highly emotional, impulsive, immature, needlessly violent, and self-destructive."[84] It is through this anti-model that Mr. Pink hopes to maintain the ideal of professionalism that he racializes as white. Ironically, these are the very faults Mr. White has identified in the unprofessional psychopath, Mr. Blonde [22:17]. The Mr. Blonde flashback that follows then provides a racist explanation for Mr. Blonde's behavior; he has, as Eddie suggests,[85] been contaminated by African Americans in jail, and his subsequent killing of a "black girl" during the robbery may very well be a racist backlash [22:26]. However, the flashback as a whole, as Nama has brilliantly demonstrated, actually deconstructs the white characters' racist discourse. Grounded in a binary opposition between a "good fellow" like Mr. Blonde and a murderous "jungle bunny," "Cabot's racial rhetoric casts whites as the victims of preferential treatment given to blacks and suggests an American system now at work where reverse racism is normative and good white men are punished."[86] Yet this is ultimately contradicted by Cabot's providing "an effective cover for 'standup' guy Vic Vega to meet the 'gainfully employed' stipulation of his parole without actually working."[87] Nama concludes that "the economic advantages of white male privilege are couched in everyday racist rhetoric even as the film details the absurdity of arguments that construct white racial identity as disadvantaged relative to black folk."[88]

The last discussion about race also occurs in a flashback. Mr. Pink upholds a dichotomy between black and white women that goes beyond the "slight difference" (Mr. White's words) that is skin color: "What a white bitch'll put up with, a black bitch wouldn't put up with for a minute, man. They got a line, and if you *cross* it, they fuck you up." Racial difference is enforced through an assertion of gender and sexual difference; the "line" that cannot be crossed is gendered and implicitly conceived within a heterosexual relationship. These distinctions are reinforced by the use of the n-word, which, in this scene as in the film as a whole, refers exclusively to African American males. This apparently mundane scene portrays the white male characters' striving to uphold strict identity categories, yet losing control of a discussion in which identity politics are revealed to be incredibly complex. What started out as a clear-cut racial opposition soon involves elements of gender, sexuality, and finally class, through the reference to Lady E from "Adorno Heights, the black Beverly Hills." The film's structure is, once again, central, as the flashbacks reveal the shakiness of the racist ground in which their white identities are anchored. As the alias-giving scene confirms, if the white crooks don't want to be black, Cabot avoids the name Mr. Black because it could very well lead to the same kind of unprofessional behavior Mr. Pink associates with African Americans.[89]

Pulp Fiction confirms the central place of racism in the white male's construction of himself. Six of the secondary characters (Pumpkin, Lance,

Captain Koons, Maynard and Zed, and Jimmie Dimmick) spout racist hate words: Lance [27:55], Maynard and Zed [96:48], and Jimmie Dimmick [118:57] use the n-word, Pumpkin [2:18] and Captan Koons [64:43], derogatory words ("gook," "slope") to refer to Asians, and Pumpkin makes an anti-Semitic comment. The presence of such rhetoric in the most mundane of places (a diner, a kitchen, a living room, a pawnshop) suggests, as Nama remarks, that "racial prejudice is as commonplace as the nattyrobes that Lance schleps around in,"[90] "emerg[ing] in everyday domestic settings,"[91] in the US and elsewhere (Pumpkin is British). It also pinpoints the common function of such discourse regardless of how much racial violence it seems to convey. Whether referring to enemies in a difficult war (Koons) or in a racially divided society (Maynard and Zed), liquor-store owners and employees that are making it harder for robbers to make a decent living (Pumpkin), unwelcome competitors on the drug market (Lance) or unwelcome intrusions in one's household (Jimmie), resorting to such language marks the white male subject's attempt to (re)claim a superior position. The circulation of such language in the film also foregrounds the complex ramifications of racism and xenophobia in context. Lance's comment, "Am I a nigger? Are we in Inglewood?" highlights, as Nama notes, "how geography and white privilege intersect,"[92] and thus how social space is racialized (as with the discussion about Lady E. in *Reservoir Dogs*). Nama also explains that the problem with the scene where Jimmie Dimmick uses the n-word three times has to do with the quality of Tarantino's acting.

> Jimmie's use (or misuse) of the n-word clearly resonates with a long history of white supremacy in which the word is a term of dehumanization. [...] Ideologically, however, the exchange between Jimmie and Jules is more than a simple example of bigoted banter; it functions as a powerful articulation of American racism and its erasure of black people.[93]

Casting himself does, however, enable Tarantino to parody the kind of person his opponents have made him out to be: at best, a wannabe black man who thinks being married to a black woman (Bonnie) and friends with a black man (Jules) authorizes him to use the n-word; at worst, an unwitting racist as "dim" as his name "Dimmick" suggests. Nama's interpretation of the scene suggests that the use of the n-word is just the opposite of what it appears to be: gratuitous and self-indulgent.

Contrary to what Sharon Willis has contended, the film does not "cite the word 'nigger' outside a context formed by its enunciative conditions, which include the author's social location, as well as the word's history";[94] its use is always anchored in character and context. Accordingly, the black characters' use of the word is contrasted to the white characters', but it is also contrasted to each other's. Marsellus first uses it when speaking to Butch and Vincent.[95] Here, as Nama notes, "the n-word clearly telegraphs the power to control the actions of others—even white men."[96] In Marsellus's usage, it is deracialized and serves to address or refer to an employee, whether in a condescending or friendly manner.[97] This is confirmed when Marsellus says: "If Butch goes to Indochina, I want a nigga hidin' in a bowl of rice ready to pop a cap in his ass" [70:33]. Given Koons's spiel on the horrors of Vietnam, the association of the n-word and the "bowl of rice" suggests Butch's killer could very well be of the same race as those who tormented his father. When Marsellus threatens Zed, however, it is the context—the fact that Marsellus was raped first by the white "hillbilly"—and his own reference to the racist "'bad nigger' stereotype"[98] ("hard, pipe-hitting") that indicates Zed's torturers will be black [107:05].

Jules initially uses the n-word as a "colloquial descriptive"[99] to designate the "half-black, half-Samoan" Antoine Rockamora, whom he also describes as a "brother," thereby acknowledging the racial bond between them [9:40]. Like Marsellus, he also uses the word to address a subordinate like Marvin[100] [115:06], and by comparison, uses the more acceptable "Negro" when speaking to Marsellus [121:30]. The only time he employs the n-word to refer to white men is when he speaks of Jimmie and Vincent in their absence.[101] I would argue that this occurrence reveals a second stage in Nama's analysis of the erasure of the black body. Not only is Jules's lack of reaction to Jimmie's abuse of the n-word unbelievable, as Nama notices,[102] but by labeling Jimmie and Vincent so, Jules both subordinates them and legitimizes their positions as "White Negroes"[103]—Vincent, as Nama points out, is also an embodiment of "black cool."[104] Furthermore, Jules's subsequent use to refer to Marvin's remains in the car has him using the word in the dehumanizing sense Jimmie used it. On the level of the character, then, Jules's attitude can be analyzed as a form of self-subjection to white racist discourse, but on a more a symbolic level, it points to the contradiction inherent in Jimmie's position, whereby appropriating black masculinity goes hand in hand with dehumanizing African Americans. In the final scene, Pumpkin's racist and anti-Semitic discourse is redirected at him: Jules, a black man who has decided to follow the example of an Asian American character (Kwai Chang Caine) and whose friend Vincent wondered whether he wasn't Jewish [133:46], points a gun at him, and names him after a famous British pop icon ("Ringo"), while giving Honey Bunny a typically African or Latin American name ("Yolanda"). Jules's final reflections make him the site where tensions between racialized and nationalist discourses and a more hopeful interracial entente come in play.

Jackie Brown came under heavy criticism because of the repeated use of the n-word, most notably by Spike Lee.[105] Unlike Tarantino's first two films and *True Romance*, it is used exclusively by the African American characters (once by Jackie, twice by Beaumont, and thirty-five times by Ordell).[106] The n-word is, first and foremost, a characterization device, as Tarantino claims,[107] meant to signify Ordell and Beaumont's belonging to the West Coast gangsta rap culture based in Compton (like Ordell's two other places). But the arms trafficker's excessive use of the word also serves to dramatize the complexity of his own relationship to race. The instances in the opening scene set the stage. Here, the n-word is used to refer to himself, Beaumont, his customers, his business partner Mr. Walker, and African American actor Malik Yoba, star of *New York Undercover* (Fox, 1994–1999) [5:19–10:14]. At this stage, the word seems exclusively reserved for black men, but such a conclusion lies on the assumption that Ordell exclusively works with African Americans, an assumption based on the fact that Walker is a common African American name[108] and on the stereotype of black gang members purchasing machine guns.[109]

This interpretation, though initially confirmed in the subsequent scenes (when Ordell speaks of Winston or talks to Beaumont), is overturned when Ordell uses it to speak of Melanie's eagerness to please men [75:40] and, even before that, to address Louis:

> ORDELL: So we on the same page, then?
> LOUIS: Yeah, I follow.
> ORDELL: My nigga. [27:01]

The use of the word could be read as affectionate, and on one level, it probably is meant to be, but given the fate of the previous character (Beaumont) Ordell addressed in such a manner, it also registers as a threat. The white man has been forewarned; though officially a partner, he is actually just an employee and is thus in the same position as Beaumont (in relation to Ordell) and Winston (in relation to Max). Ordell's use of the n-word thus resembles Marsellus's in *Pulp Fiction* when addressing Vincent. But with the character from *Jackie Brown*, the n-word is not just a signifier of economic and social subordination; it is more fundamentally one of racial self-loathing, as is later confirmed when he kids Jackie that she needs "nigger repellant" to fend off unwanted black men hitting on her [69:56].

The film's excessive use of the n-word is thus Ordell's excessive use of it, and the instances radically diminish beginning in the second act, when Jackie becomes the main focus of the film. Contrary to what Tarantino suggested in early interviews—that repeating the word would sublimate its meaning[110]—what the repetition of the word shows is that, in spite of the apparent resignification[111] of the word as one of racial pride, it remains heavily gendered and connected to relations of power and submission. Jackie's one use of the n-word is thus made to stand out against Ordell's excess and to confirm the meanings it carries. Pointing a gun at Ordell's private parts, she orders him: "Now take your hands from around my throat, *nigga*" [50:53]. The fact that the n-word is only used by black men to address or refer to men, combined with the emphasis Jackie puts on the n-word, indicates, I would argue, that Jackie is imitating the black male's usage of the word and redirecting it at him; she is yet another one of the black employees Ordell couldn't care less about disposing of, and she is also another woman he wouldn't mind subjecting physically. Sensing this, Ordell falls back on the word "black" in order to cancel the gender opposition and call on their racial bond: "See? Police start fuckin' with your mind, start pittin' black against black" [51:27]. But Ordell's call for blackness, as his turning the lights off moments before suggests, is just a cover for the violence with which he treats others, especially other blacks. Far from a celebration of the transgressive use of the n-word, *Jackie Brown* seems to plead for a less heavily burdened language.

The time-setting of Tarantino's subsequent films accounts for the fact that the n-word is stripped of its contemporary usages and used in a blatantly racist fashion. In *Death Proof*, the only exception, the use of racially inflected language is, above all, a characterization strategy. Kim, whom Tarantino describes in the DVD extras as a "female Samuel Jackson,"[112] is the only character to use the n-word. She does so when speaking of men in general and, on one occasion, when addressing her friend Abernathy,[113] so her use of the word is consistent with the fact that the film's main concern is, in effect, gender.[114] However, employing the word in a deracialized fashion ultimately contests the whiteness of the male world depicted; like the discussion about the Rock, it serves as a reminder that there are also black men out there and implies that, in Kim's lingo, Dov, Nate, and Mike would equally be "niggas."

In *Django Unchained* and *The Hateful Eight*, both set in the nineteenth century, the n-word is an unambiguous marker of racism. The vast majority of the white characters—Dicky Speck the slaver [9:46], the anonymous doctor in Daughtrey [13:32], Old Man Carrucan [24:57], Lara Lee [96:41], the LeQuint Dickey Mining Co. employee [148:32], and especially Billy Crash, Big Daddy, and Calvin Candie—use it, and even Schultz is forced to do so in order to pass for someone interested in purchasing slaves [29:18, 91:06]. The word is not just a marker of race; in slavery, it stands at the nexus of race and economics, and the repetition of the phrase "the right nigger" serves as a stark reminder of this [71:50]. Thus, the excessive circulation of the n-word within the film is not only meant to participate in the representation of the racist South, as Tarantino explains,[115] but it also reflects and ultimately comes to signify the circulation of black people as mere commodities.

However, it is also, paradoxically, the circulation of the racist hate word that threatens the strict binary between whites and blacks the racists strive to maintain, including through the use of the word. The term "nigger lover," which Big Daddy associates with Schultz [41:58, 44:36], is proof of the potential to break racial and economic boundaries between black slave and white master on the basis of a strong emotional relationship. Calvin is initially amused at the idea that Schultz might have fallen for Broomhilda: "Well, be careful now, Doctor Schultz. You might've caught yourself a little dose of nigger love. Nigger love's a powerful emotion, boy. [...] It's like a pool of black tar. Once it catches your ass, you caught" [104:09]. Couched in the racist fear of contamination that associates blackness with an addiction or a disease (as in Nice Guy's prison rape fantasy in *Reservoir Dogs*), Calvin's tirade nonetheless hints at the possibility of a strong emotional bond between a black and a white person, including himself, given his own ambiguous relationships with Sheba and especially Stephen. On occasions like these, the use of the n-word works to contradict the fear of miscegenation and racial impurity that the racist framework is grounded in. This is also true of the racist jokes made about the black fighters' names, which produce an irony that undercuts the racist discourse. Calvin says about another one of his fighters, Eskimo Joe: "You never know how these nigger nicknames get started. His name was Joe, maybe one day he said he was cold, you know" [101:26]. The slave fighter's name is an unwitting ode to miscegenation: it evokes another oppressed race, Native Americans, via the first name and the intertexual reference to Mark Twain's Injun Joe, as well as whiteness via the icy environment of the Inuits. More importantly, however, Candie's comment is almost certainly made in bad faith, as the self-proclaimed afficionado of French culture named another one of his fighters after Dumas's hero, D'Artagnan. These names thus hint at the white racist's unconscious desire for miscegenation that surfaces, in accordance with Freudian theory, through humor.[116] Schultz's informing Candie that Dumas was black ironically proves the fantasy to be true. Racial boundaries are taken one step further when a black slave, Stephen, coins the term "Niggerles" after Schultz proposes to name his fighter "the Black Hercules" [102:28], an allusion to *Mandingo*, in which the fighter is also named after a figure of Greek mythology (Agamemnon).[117] The name merges a black slave and a mythical figure, very much like the film itself that makes Django over into a nineteenth-century Siegfried or a black Django. Granted, it is proof that, like his master, Stephen reinforces racist discourses, but it also proves that the black man also has the potential to create a name and a character, and thus announces a time when black Americans will have the freedom to produce works of fiction on a widespread basis.

Of course, the use of the n-word by the black characters testifies to the system's power and how they have internalized its discourses and practices. For instance, by designating Django as such in spite of the fact that the latter was initially presented as a slaver, the slave questioned by the white slavers is merely confirming the protagonist's return to the status of slave [147:27]. In Stephen's case, however, the use of the word is an indication of how he has learnt to profit from the system by maintaining other blacks in the "nigger" category; sensing that his "exceptional" position is under threat, he alternates between the adjective "black" and the n-word when referring to Django [88:18–90:25], even though Candie has presented Schultz's partner as Stephen's double without resorting to the n-word. Django, on the other hand, employs the n-word, first, when explaining the subtleties of the system to Schultz [14:01], detailing notably the various categories—the "field nigger," the "comfort girl," the "black slaver," the "head house nigger" [59:23, 62:11]—and later, much like Schultz, when acting his part, that of the slaver [76:16]. The word is thus clearly identified as being part of a specific cultural discourse, one that might appear alien to a nineteenth-century German and that the hero understands but clearly rejects. Even when Django says the word to Stephen, he is merely throwing it back at him.

> STEPHEN: I count six shots, nigga.
> DJANGO: I count two guns, nigga. [158:33]

By echoing Stephen's words, Django redirects the violence at the slave who profited from the system. It also echoes a previous nondiegetic occurrence: Django's voice in the track "Unchained (The Payback/Untouchable)" saying: "Expect me, nigga, like you expect Jesus to come back. Expect me, nigga. I'm comin,'" even as Django shoots down a large number of white men [134:08]. Integrated within the revenge narrative, the n-word, here, englobes all Django's adversaries whom, with the exception of Stephen, are white. Moreover, it broadens the circulation of the word by evoking a discourse present outside the world depicted in the film, that of contemporary gangsta rap, in which the word can target a variety of people no matter their color. The possibility is also suggested when they first meet Calvin's lawyer, Leonide Moguy. This time, however, Django is in character.

> MOGUY: One could almost say that I was raised to be Calvin's lawyer.
> DJANGO: One could almost say you was a nigger. [63:06]

The former slave insults the lawyer by pointing out what they had in common: they were both raised to be subjected to a master. Django's comments thus threaten the racist dichotomy that grounds slavery, especially since it targets a subject who upholds the very laws of that system, and yet whose last name evokes other races through the reference to *The Jungle Book*. All Django's occurences act as reminders that, historically, the n-word was by no means attached to coolness (as is the case for the black and white characters associated with black cool in *Pulp Fiction*, for instance) but to violent oppression.

The Hateful Eight really drives home the point. The word is unproblematically wielded by the racist white characters from the outset, especially the Southern characters Daisy Domergue, Chris Mannix, and General Sandy Smithers, for whom it operates as a strict categorizing term, as Smithers's use of "Northern niggers" proves [66:30]. Jody's use of the word when referring to victims at Minnie's is informed by this fear of categorial transgression and, more specifically, miscegenation, as it encompasses everything and everyone (including white people) to have been contaminated by black people, and thus contains the contradiction (whiteness) that compromises the dichotomy [133:45]. However, the film complexly distinguishes between the speakers' positions: that is, whether they are speaking as themselves or from somebody else's perspective, expanding on the use by Schultz when acting the part of a slave buyer in *Django Unchained*. This is the case of the Union sympathizer John Ruth who informs Daisy that "the darkies don't like being called niggers no more" [8:33]. Indeed, his subsequent uses of the n-word are always aligned with the perspective of Daisy or Chris Mannix.[118] Oswaldo Mobray also seems to be citing Daisy when using the word [55:22], as if the sophisticated Englishman were not implicated in American race relations, yet his using it again as himself (English Pete) indicates that discrimination is not restricted to the American characters [149:50]. Bob the Mexican also uses the term when provoking Warren [114:45]. Accordingly, Warren's use of racially inflected terms is more varied; if he also uses the n-word when speaking from the perspective of a racist white man spouting racist rhetoric or hunting black people [34:17, 88:20], he speaks of the "colored troopers" butchered by Smithers [66:12] and refers to himself as a "black man" when explaining the Lincoln letter ploy to Ruth [83:10]. Interestingly enough, Mannix's transformation from an archetypal racist ex-Confederate soldier to Warren's ally is highlighted through the use of the n-word. After repeatedly using the n-word to the ex-Union soldier's face [29:22], he proceeds to mockingly address him as "Major Nigger" [65:43], then "Black Major" [80:00], before finally dropping the insult altogether and calling him simply "Major Warren." If the use of "major" is initially mocking, it ultimately replaces the n-word and comes to signify the younger white man's respect for his black peer. Mannix's transformation is complete when he is finally labeled a "nigger lover" by Daisy [144:26], thus becoming the double of Schultz in *Django Unchained*. At the end, his calling Warren a "black bastard" is interpreted as mere play by the major [156:25], whose own use of "white boy" symbolizes that he himself has adopted him as a surrogate son [155:59, 157:24].

The hate words in *Kill Bill* and *Inglourious Basterds* mainly involve Asians and Jews. The few instances in *Kill Bill* prove that racist language is present everywhere but operates within specific cultural modes. Pai Mei, for instance, says he "despise[s] the goddamn Japs" [47:21], no doubt due to the history of conflict between China and Japan, while Budd's mocking use of the word[119] evokes World War II.[120] The most significant moment where racist, xenophobic, and sexist discourses intersect occurs in *Vol. 1*, in the flashback depicting Boss Tanaka's outburst at the yakuza council:

> My father, along with yours, founded this council. And while you laugh like stupid donkeys, they weep in the afterlife [...] over the perversion committed today. [...] I speak of the perversion done to this council, which I love—more than my own children, by electing a Chinese Jap-American half-breed bitch its leader! [59:25]

Although O-Ren punishes Tanaka for his outburst and forbids the other yakuza leaders to "bring[] up either [her] Chinese or American heritage as a negative," the end of *Vol. 1* reveals that she did so not because she rejected such discourses, but on the contrary, because she adhered to them all too much. After wounding the Bride during their showdown, she, in turn, makes a racist comment steeped in essentialist postulates: "Silly Caucasian girl likes to play with samurai swords" [90:22]. This harks back not only to Boss Tanaka's insult, but also to Vernita's bitter remark that she should have been Black Mamba because of her skin color [12:42]—and thus that the Bride has usurped the name just as she usurps the samurai tradition. On one level, she has. But ironically and tragically, in so doing, the minority characters embrace the racial determinism that oppresses them. *Kill Bill* demonstrates that, in spite of cultural specificities (dramatized in *Kill Bill* through the opposition between Japan and China on the one hand, and Asia and the US on the other), such discourses function in a similar fashion all over the world. Grounded in tropes such as blood and skin color, they enable the subject to establish his/her identity by constructing an other as racial/gender/ethnic bastard.

The anti-Semitic rhetoric in *Inglourious Basterds* is grounded in analogy. Landa's comparison of the Jews to "rats" (and the Germans to "eagles") [14:18] announces the disparaging animal analogies established by the anti-Semites. Speaking of the Basterds, Hitler complains: "How much more of these Jew swine must I endure? They butcher my men like they were flies! [...] The Jew degenerate known as the Bear Jew, henceforth, is never to be referred to as the Bear Jew again!" [24:15]. Anti-Semitic rhetoric, here, is set up for deconstruction even as it is hammered—quite literally, with Hitler pounding on a table—by one of its most infamous proponents. The fact that all the Basterds, including Aldo, are assimilated to Jews debunks the biological determinism expounded by Landa and more generally Nazi discourse. The Jews are described as pests ("Judenschwein" [24:15]) by Nazi discourse, but their victims are placed even lower on the animal scale. Hitler's final order proves that, in constructing their legend, the Basterds have resignified the animalistic discourse by naming their prime executioner after a threatening but noble animal. The Nazis' use of the French "nègre" (by Landa [58:24]) and the German "Neger"[121] (by Hellstrom [86:57])—and their associating blacks with animality—implicit in Goebbels's emphasis on black athletes' physicality [48:29], explicit in Hellstrom's comparing the story of King Kong to the story of the African slaves [86:56]—suggests, as we have seen, that the film is also drawing an analogy between Nazism and American racism. The absurdity of Nazi ideology is further undermined when Hitler adopts the position of the victim, using a verb that evokes William Faulkner's famous two-word sentence ("They endured") to describe the history of the African American characters in *The Sound and the Fury* (1929). The execution scene that follows is an inversion of both Hollywood representations of Nazis and Nazi rhetoric, with Sergeant Rachtman, who insults Aldo and his "Jew dogs," remaining heroically dignified until he gets beatean to death by the Bear Jew [32:57–34:07]. Ironically, the Nazi officer's name contains the seeds of his own destruction; the English pronunciation of "Racht" sounds like "rat" (or the German equivalent "Ratte"), while the the verb "rächen" means "revenge" in German.

The use of racial and racist rhetoric in the films of Tarantino is anything but gratuitous. It is grounded in the pragmatic view that meaning depends on the uses people make of language, and thus that its meaning changes depending on the context or the speaker. What Keith Allan says of the use of the n-word in *Pulp Fiction* can be generalized to the use of hate speech in all Tarantino's feature films: "The lexical form of a language expression such as nigger does not itself constitute a slur, it is its perlocutionary effect—in the light of the co-text together with the situation of its utterance and reception—that decides whether or not it discredits, slights, smears, stains, besmirches or sullies who it is applied to."[122]

The use of such language serves, first and foremost, the characterization. It also underlines the mundanity of racist rhetoric, not just in the antebellum South or Nazi Germany, but in contemporary Los Angeles. Specific usages are grounded in specific contexts that are determined by culture and history, but whether in the US, Asia, or Europe, they generally enable the subject to violently assert his/her identity in relation to a stigmatized other (any minority group in *Reservoir Dogs*, other black men in *Jackie Brown*, the Japanese yakuzas in *Kill Bill Vol. 1*, men in *Death Proof*). Tarantino's films demonstrate that racist rhetoric is universally present but that its forms are specifically local. Though on the surface they seem to accept the idea that the n-word is acceptable among blacks, they reveal how it often serves to submit the addressee or referent socially and/or racially; as a word that is quasi-exclusively used to refer to men, it is not just about race, but about class and gender as well. Sometimes the violence of the word is made apparent when it is redirected at its prime user (Jackie at Ordell, Django at Stephen). Overall, the circulation of racist rhetoric serves to undermine (and not reinforce) the racist discourse, which is often based on some form of biological essentialism, revealing it to be untenable (the animal analogies in *Inglourious Basterds*) and to mask unconscious desires (miscegenation in *Django Unchained*) or fears (racial self-loathing in *Jackie Brown*). Far from celebrating an unproblematic usage of the n-word, Tarantino's first movies use it to foreground and undercut the ambiguous position of the white and the black male subjects' attitudes toward a blackness that it is desirable both to appropriate and reject. Thus, Tarantino's statements in interviews that "any word as powerful as the n-word needs to be shouted out" to defuse its potency is misleading, especially since he is reluctant to use the word himself;[123] it is not so much that a more liberal use of the word will free us from the violence it carries (Ordell Robbie is proof of the contrary), but rather that its circulation in a work of fiction can enable us to observe its contradictions and its power to position the subject and the other and fashion her/his body, as the contested Jimmie Dimmick scene in *Pulp Fiction* demonstrates on a metafictional level. It is to the racial body that we now turn our attention.

Black Bodies, White Bodies, Jewish Faces

For all their graphic violence, Tarantino's first films are actually fairly prudish and avoid visually exploring the racialized body in favor of discourse. In *Reservoir Dogs* and *Jackie Brown*, sexy, more so even than cool,[124] is associated with the black male characters, who are slightly more eroticized than their white counterparts, with Holdaway [67:39], Ordell [4:21, 62:35, 75:16, 91:46, 130:50], and Beaumont [15:52] displaying their chests.[125] In *Pulp Fiction*, the black bodies are initially terrifying: Jules (often in low angle) looms over Brett and his friends before executing them (fig. 60.1) [14:36], while Marsellus, as we shall see in the next chapter, is constructed as a quasi-omnipotent patriarch. The racist unconscious subsequently assaults black bodies, as we have seen, but this underlying narrative is tempered by the way these scenes are depicted by the narration. The rape of Marsellus Wallace occurs behind closed doors and, though it can be heard, is partially drowned out by the music [98:12–100:52]. When Butch finally enters the room, the rape is maintained in the dark—only the men's shirts are lit—and at a distance—in a long shot utilizing frame-within-the-frame composition—and is then reflected in the sadistic pleasure on Maynard's face in frontal close-up [110:54]; Marsellus is only shown in a lateral medium close-up when he notices Butch creeping up on Maynard, so that he is depicted as a subject and not an object of the gaze [101:02]. Having failed to overturn Marsellus and Jules, the racist unconscious takes it out on a secondary character. The killing of Marvin is represented metonymically: the gunshot links the frontal medium close-up of Vincent talking to the frontal medium shot of the rear window sprayed with blood [106:03]; before this, Marvin is not even entitled to his own shot and appears out of focus in the frontal close-up of his soon-to-be killer (fig. 8) [115:24]. Visually, then, the black male body has disappeared, leaving only a "mess" of blood and gore that requires cleaning up. The elliptical editing works not so much to censor the violence as to visualize the African American male subject's erasure from the film.

Given the time-setting, there would appear to be nothing unconscious about the racist violence in Tarantino's two Westerns. For Nama, *Django Unchained* is "deadly serious" when it comes to representing the violence of slavery.[126] The opening credits reprise the contrast from Corbucci's 1966 film between the lighthearted rhythm of the song and the hero's tragic situation, only this Django is presented as one slave among many. The slaves' bodies are both muscular and scarred, fetishized by medium close-ups that highlight their glistening, sweaty skin [0:59–1:29]. They are wounded but not weak, and it is the chains that are making them shuffle along—and that are keeping

Fig. 8: *Pulp Fiction*: Moments before his death, Marvin appears out of focus in the background, as Vincent contests that they witnessed a miracle.

Django down, as the title suggests. This is confirmed in the medium backshot of Django ridding himself of his blanket (fig. 9), which echoes the opening backshot of the slaves: the scars on his back are yet again displayed, but the use of slow motion and the sound effect resembling a burner lighting up emphasize his physical strength and grace [9:37]. The subsequent backshot of the other slaves similarly casting off their blankets as they home in on the slaver suggests that they equally share these qualities [12:07]. The opening scene thus tempers the view that the black rebellion potential "is assuaged by the overly subdued performances of the other black slaves that populate the film";[127] it is the mythical heroic bent of the narrative that, in effect, turns away from the potential announced in the opening scene.

During the film's first hour, the physical horrors of slavery are contained by the flashbacks of Django's past at Old Man Carrucan's [24:43–25:26; 32:57–34:14] and by the two close-ups of the terrified slave (Little Jody) Django prevents John Brittle from whipping [35:01]. Django has become a "spectre of retribution," as signaled by his reflection in a mirror glimpsed by Little Jody[128] [36:01]. Only the hero's scar serves as a reminder of his mortality. The film takes a Gothic turn towards "body horror,"[129] as Nama has argued, with the introduction of the Mandingo expert, Calvin Candie. If Django remains for some time preserved, a quasi-untouchable spectre capable of traversing the white Southern hell, the black bodies around him are consistently violated and humiliated: Big Fred and Luigi are forced to fight to the death (fig. 66) [63:45–66:57]; D'Artagnan is torn to pieces by a pack of dogs [83:42–84:03]; and Broomhilda is stored naked in a hot box before being offered to a guest for the night [94:07–94:42; 95:47]. All trace of humor has disappeared, as Nama has noted: "The absurdist ambiance established earlier in the film with bungling Klansmen, anachronistic background rap music, and witty punch

Fig. 9: *Django Unchained*: Freed by Dr. Schultz, Django casts off his blanket, revealing his scarred back in slow motion.

lines delivered by Django is shattered by shrieks of a black man clawed and bitten to death by dogs."[130] The change in tone is visible in the color scheme, which becomes darker.[131] The violence inflicted on the slaves is emphasized by the use of fetishizing close shots of glistening black skin, slow motion in the D'Artagnan scene, and a quick zoom-in that mimics the water dumped on Broomhilda. Thus, the film resorts to the same techniques to highlight both the power and the vulnerabilty of these bodies; for instance, the glistening skin is, on the diegetic level, produced by the exploitation of their bodies, but visually its radiance aligns them with beauty and health. The close-ups are actually few and, as in the rape scene in *Pulp Fiction*, juxtaposed with shots of the sadistic white spectators, e.g., the low-angle medium full shot over D'Artagnan's legs of the white people cheering [84:02]. As we shall see in the next chapter, all these scenes are sexually charged.

The Mandingo is an apt metaphor that slavery begins and ends with the denial of a person's sovereignty over his/her body. This is conveyed visually, as it is hard to distinguish blood and skin in the dark reddish brown room where Big Fred and Luigi fight; the body of the slave is bloody and scarred because it is not her/his own. It is not Big Fred who murders Luigi, but Candie who uses Fred like the hammer he orders him to wield to finish off Luigi. The Mandingo fight is just the excessive expression of bodily subjection under slavery that is evoked in more mundane situations, such as Lil Raj Brittle's repeating to Little Jody: "You'd better give me that arm" [35:01] or Candie's telling Stephen to "wheel" Broomhilda out of the hot box and into a German's guest bed, Candie's very words being literally enacted moments later [92:37]. The climax of this denial of personhood, I would argue, is reached when Candie destroys the skull of a former slave, Ben, who "took care" of his grandfather, father, and himself [115:04–119:56]. Not only does

Candie aim to demonstrate that the inferiority of blacks is universal,[132] but his desecration of a dead body denies both the respect the dead are entitled to in most cultures and the possibility of the sort of interracial relationship that Django and Schultz enjoy, and that he himself seems to share with Stephen who is pointedly absent during the monologue. The rejection of his own "exceptional" black person theory is, *in fine*, a rebuttal of the other "exceptional" relationships between black and white it could imply. This scene functions like the death of Marvin in *Pulp Fiction*. White racist rage is unleashed in the disposal of a black male body, a rage prompted by a narrative centered on a black bounty hunter who enjoys killing white people for a living. As such, it announces Django's momentary reinstatement to the condition of slave: naked, fetishized, violated, hung upside down or caged like an animal.

It also accounts for the excessive violence perpetrated against white bodies in the shoot-out that has been emphasized by both Tarantino and critics.[133] Following the death of the only decent white man in the film [131:30], the over-the-top shoot-out returns to the white body the violence that has been inflicted against black bodies since the beginning of the film [131:40–134:03]. Django doesn't just kill white men in large numbers (about seventeen). Blown to smithereens, the sanctity of the white bodies is called into question. They become mere shields for Django to hide behind, sites where the distinction between skin, textile, guts, and blood is uncertain, like the bodies of the Mandingo fighters in the eyes of the racists who own them. The black man's face is covered with blood that is not his or another slave's, and that is undisputably the same color as his own. The same formal devices utilized for the slaves (close-ups, slow motion, amplified sounds) are now utilized for the white bodies. The shoot-out functions not just as pure spectacle; it draws attention to the fact that whiteness is not the absence of race or color, and that racial violence can be directed at the white body as it can at any other depending on the context.

The Hateful Eight pursues the assault on the white male body initiated in the final act of *Django Unchained*. Its violation is first enacted discursively and visually through Warren's tale of Smithers's son's death. If the very long shots center on the naked white man stumbling along and finally kneeling before the clothed black man (fig. 70.1), Warren's rhetoric repeatedly fetishizes his own body with the intent of shocking his racist addressee [90:04–93:26].[134] Weighing each word, Warren performatively constitutes his body into a racist's nightmare merely by reiterating its terms ("big" and "black"). Smithers's death announces the fall of other white male bodies, though the film increasingly amps up the gore; in comparison to Smithers's more restrained death scene [104:41], O. B. and Ruth spout blood

[103:45–105:32]. With Jody's intervention, the brutal whiteness that engulfed the white body of Charles Smithers has returned with a vengeance to engulf the black character, just as it destroyed the bodies that occupied the black space that is Minnie's. If the wounds inflicted on Warren, Mannix, and Oswaldo are all depicted in slow motion on cue with explosive sound effects, Chapter Four significantly ends on a medium close-up of the black patriarch now weeping in pain on the floor, his moans filling the soundtrack through the use of a spring reverb [108:29–119:28]. The threatening black body Warren linguistically constituted himself as has been neutralized—at least to some extent. For if Major Warren has become a more vulnerable body in Chapter Six, basically the double of English Pete and Mr. Orange in *Reservoir Dogs*, both played by Tim Roth, he continues to inflict damage on white bodies, shooting Jody in the head in close-up [143:18], English Pete [149:58] and Grouch Douglass in tandem with Mannix [150:09]. Throughout the film, however, the narration counters the racist unconscious underlying the narrative by shying away from depicting the violence inflicted on the black characters, either through camera angle (Warren), a brief shot (Minnie), metonymy (Gemma), or ellipsis (Charly). In *The Hateful Eight*, all white bodies (O. B., Six-Horse Judy [129:54], Sweet Dave [130:08])—and even the Mexican character [117:00]—are made to pay for the racist white unconscious in explicitly violent deaths.

Apart from the dogs fantasizing about Christie Love lookalikes [78:06], black women are absent from Tarantino's first two films, and both Jackie Brown and Vernita Green are characterized as attractive but not hypersexual; this is evidenced in their clothing, notably, with Vernita's casual sportswear [5:47] matching the Bride's yellow jumper more than the stereotypical male fantasy nurse, schoolgirl, and geisha outfits donned by Elle, Gogo, and O-Ren, respectively [20:03, 67:35].[135] Visually, *Death Proof* confirms the idea that the white male gaze subjects all women, but minority women (Arlene, Abernathy, and especially Jungle Julia[136]) do hold pride of place. Nama deplores that Julia "appears unaware of herself as an object of voyeuristic desire," and that the film fails to address her status as sex symbol in a southern white (and, I would add, Mexican-American) city.[137] Julia does not propose a "counter-image,"[138] but, like Elle and O-Ren in *Kill Bill Vol. 1*, packages stereotypical racial and ethnic fantasies: two of the billboards show Julia as a manga geek with pigtails [5:09] and a jungle girl [8:48], the other two as her DJ self [4:39, 15:01]. Her lack of awareness, as we shall see in the next chapter, is central to the film's critique of self-subjection to white patriarchy.

Death Proof does, however, reflexively address the question of black female sex symbols in a white world at the beginning of the second part of the

Fig. 10: *Death Proof*: Abernathy, played by multiracial/ethnic actress Rosario Dawson, shows Lee her photo in *Allure* magazine, erasing her own face in the process.

film when Abernathy, who, while lying on the backseat of Kim's car initially appears to be Julia's "symbolic reincarnation,"[139] goes in a service station to purchase a fashion magazine for her white friend Lee, whose photo is featured in the publication. The camera tracks left, following Abernathy's movement down the aisle, over a series of magazines: an issue of *Tracks* featuring Alicia Keys with the headline "Black Girls Rule!"; one of *Entertainment Weekly* with Jay-Z; issues of *Afro-Dite*, *Ebony*, and *Essence* featuring black women on their covers; followed by issues of *Film Comment*, *Elle*, *Bazaar*, *Allure*, and *People*, all with white women on their covers [63:50]. The tracking shot notes that, outside the music industry, black women are restricted to the pages of African American magazines and that white women still rule the pages of general audience magazines, suggesting that little has changed since the classical Hollywood era evoked in Jack Rabbit Slim's in *Pulp Fiction*, where the lookalikes are all white, while the audience is mixed, including a black couple at a table next to Mia and Vincent's car [36:49]. In so doing, the shot retrospectively sheds light on Julia's situation: the black female DJ is basically the local Alicia Keys or Jay-Z. As such, even her "real" self—her identity as a DJ—is a position allotted to black women in (white) American culture. The tracking shot is followed by a frontal medium shot of Abernathy who, in holding up the magazine for Lee to see, erases her own face (fig. 10). Nothing indicates that Abernathy—who says, in congratulating Lee, "You hot mommy, you!"—is in the least bit aware of this social situation, and the low height clearly indicates that the tracking shot is not a POV shot: it is the narration that comments on the racial politics of media images of women. However, the scene could explain Abernathy's subsequently selling her "hot" white friend off to Jasper as an unconscious act of racial revenge.

Fig. 11: *Kill Bill Vol. 2*: Domineering the low-angle shot, Pai Mei effortlessly subjugates the young Beatrix upon their first meeting.

It is perhaps less obvious that racial revenge is inflicted on another white body in *Kill Bill*, quite paradoxically that of the vengeful heroine. Critics and scholars have reproached *Kill Bill*'s resorting to a white woman to embody Asian revenge on a white man, in a film where she massacres a score of Asians, a black woman, and a few white people.[140] It is possible that the main incentive for having a white woman portray the Bride was to attract a major star like Uma Thurman. However, making the heroine white makes it possible to racialize the violence inflicted on her body, so that the Bride does not just embody yellow revenge—she is also subjected to it. In spite of her talents and swordswomanship, the Bride is regularly shown to be vulnerable; she is on the brink of losing the battle on two occasions in *Vol. 1*, when Gogo is choking her [79:58] and when O-Ren slashes her across the back [94:01], while a flashback in *Vol. 2* relates the "cruel tutelage" of Pai Mei (fig. 11) [50:16–57:33]. In each of these scenes, the camerawork insists on the pain she endures, with extreme close-ups of the chain around her throat [80:05], of her face as she lies in the snow in slow motion, and of her bloody fists. And while the music video montage recounting her training shows her improving, it ends on yet another scene of humiliation. "As a racial signifier," Nama explains, Pai Mei's "punishing instruction symbolizes retribution for white appropriation and cultural encroachment," the film "register[ing] a palpable awareness of, and, most significantly, a simmering hostility toward, white appropriation with the figure of Beatrix as an abused martial arts pupil."[141] On a metafictional level, then, the Bride is constantly being punished—especially by Vernita,[142] who considers her ill-suited for the name Black Mamba, O-Ren, who scolds her for "playing with samurai swords," and Pai Mei, who hates Americans and women—for being a white person guilty, like Bill (and David Carradine), of appropriating the culture of others. The film thus attempts to resolve its

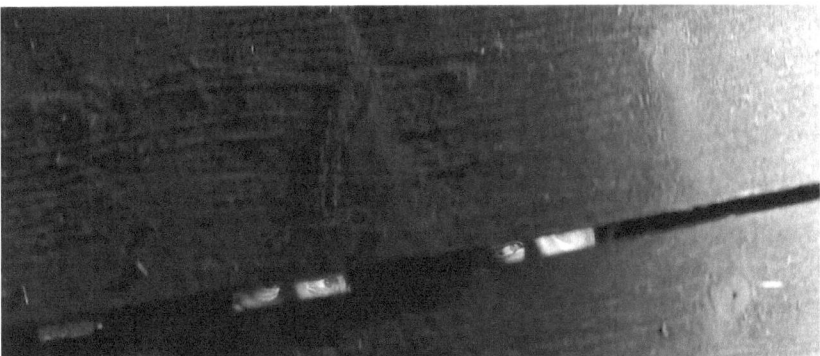

Fig. 12: *Inglourious Basterds*: The Dreyfus family hiding under the floorboards of the LaPadite house.

engagement with cultural appropriation by making the protagonist both the agent and the target of revenge.

Inglourious Basterds has been generally described as a revenge fantasy in which the Jewish characters return the violence on the Nazi characters. I would argue that this revenge is obtained visually and aurally through the body and voice of the Jew. The "revenge of the giant face" goes well beyond the Holocaust. It is not only the revenge of the Jewish face on Nazi Germany that strove to eliminate it effectively and culturally—notably, the heritage of Weimar cinema, of which the mention of G. W. Pabst's *White Hell of Pitz Palu* (1929), rereleased in 1935 with the character played by the Jewish actor Kurt Gerron edited out, stands as a reminder. It is, more generally, the revenge of the Jewish face on Western culture, a face that has a long history of being stigmatized—notably, through grotesque representations.[143] In the opening scene, the members of the Jewish family hiding under the floorboards are glimpsed on two occasions, first, in a descending crane shot that ends on a medium shot of Shosanna and her sibling (fig. 12), which is repeated later in the scene; it is followed by a high-angle shot through the floorboards where only the characters' eyes can be seen [12:33, 14:12]. These shots visualize both the oppression (through the high angle) and the erasure (by the shadows and the floorboards) of the Jewish face; all that remains are the faceless eyes filled with terror, foreshadowing their imminent execution by the Nazi soldiers who fire through the floorboards in high-angle shots [20:02].

The opening of Chapter Five, "Revenge of the Giant Face," recalls the motif of the eyes both visually (the extreme frontal close-up of Shosanna's face) and aurally (the lyrics start with "See these eyes so green"). It is Shosanna's voice that will pronounce the audience's death sentence, and her injunction "to look deep into the face of the Jew who's going to do it" confirms the central role of the gaze (fig. 13.1) [143:18]. In replacing the face of the victorious Nazi soldier Frederick Zoller in frontal close-up, Shosanna's revenge is "an act signifying the re-occupation of cinema and her movie house,"[144] as Kligerman has argued, a reintroduction of the Jewish face in German cinema. In dying, Shosanna's voice and face have become spectral, a metaphor for the revenge of cinema. The scene as a whole replicates Shosanna's editing by proposing close-ups of the faces the Nazis wanted to eliminate in place of the faces of Hitler and Goebbels previously shot in close-up as they enjoyed the movie [142:43]. Sergeant Donowitz is shown firing his machine gun in a series of frontal shots, the series of push-ins from medium close-up to extreme close-up insisting on his face, the slow motion on his physicality [144:47]; the high angles of the opening scene evoking oppression have now been replaced by low angles previously reserved for Landa [20:19]. The revenge of the giant face is also that of other races that have been marginalized by Western culture. Shosanna's announcement is followed by an extreme close-up of her black lover Marcel, at once behind the screen (and thus marginalized) and behind the camera (in the position of directorial control) (fig. 13.2) [143:43]. In other words, the scene contains both a cinematographic metaphor for the face of the other and at least two actual representations of such faces that equally occupy significant positions in the cinematographic apparatus: that of the director (Marcel) and that of the spectator (Donowitz). As such, it suggests that the unique metaphor is not enough. Indeed, it is significant that the actors who get the most attention in this scene are the two Jewish actors (Mélanie Laurent and Eli Roth) and Jacky Ido, who was born in Burkina Faso, in comparison with Omar Doom, who only gets one medium shot [84:13]. In so doing, Tarantino's film admits that, in spite of its fantastical rewriting of history, identity really does matter because it determines the regime of visibility to which one is subjected.

What Oliver C. Speck says of *Django Unchained* is true of all Tarantino's movies: they "provide[] a meta-commentary on the politics of racial representation."[145] The place of race in these films goes far beyond his fondness for blaxploitation. Nor is it limited to the presence of minority characters. Race, ethnicity, and racism are not just topics the films touch on; they are at the heart of these films. Borrowed from film and cultural history, the representations are always re-representations. The films start with a critique of the very material they recycle: genre and Hollywood conventions, and more generally cultural stereotypes. Metafictionally, the films foreground and criticize the racialized and racist terms of the material they are working

Fig. 13.1: *Inglourious Basterds*: Shosanna's Expressionistic image addressing the Nazi audience at the premiere of *Stolz der Nation*: "I have a message for Germany. That you are all going to die. And I want you to look deep into the face of the Jew that is going to do it."

Fig. 13.2: *Inglourious Basterds*: Standing behind the screen ready to set fire to a heap of 35mm film, Marcel simultaneously answers his lover and bids her farewell: "Oui, Shosanna."

with. In reflecting on past representations, they are also reflecting on present representations, and thus on contemporary culture. They testify to an awareness of the historicity of all representations (generic, visual, linguistic). The films show how mundane racism persists, how minority figures (like Julia) are still allotted marginal positions in contemporary culture, how deeply rooted race is in power relations, and how race collides and converges with other aspects of identity, such as class and gender (for instance, in the contemporary usage of the n-word, which can serve to maintain the male addressee in a subordinate position). Race remains decisive (and convenient) for the subject to construct him- or herself in opposition to an other; this can be achieved in particular through the use of hate speech. On the surface, the racial tensions are articulated as conflicts, but they are frequently complicated by undercurrents of violent racism that are far more overt in the films grounded in historical contexts. These tensions are often suggested through discrepancies between several narrative strands or between the narrative and narration. As a whole, Tarantino's films argue that a post-racial era has yet to come, but interracial relationships, often involving characters who have proven capable of positive transformation and represent sites of intersectionality, can and should maintain our faith in it.

This racist unconscious can be directed at black and white (and other) bodies alike, dead or alive. Indeed, Tarantino's films counter the tendency of Western mainstream culture to view white as the absence of race. Visually, the sense of sexy cool that is attached to blackness could be seen as a remnant of racist stereotypes evoking black hypersexuality, but I would argue that, given the reluctance to fetishize the characters' bodies (the girls of *Death Proof* represent an exception) and the emphasis put on the sadistic racist spectator or perpetrator, the depiction of black bodies seeks to celebrate the beauty and power of the black body—thus pursuing the 1960s credo "Black is beautiful"—while acknowledging that African American bodies have been scarred and remain threatened by racist backlashes, even when they ascend to, or gravitate in, positions of power. Valuing minority bodies and faces could thus be a way to counter the denial of bodily sovereignty under slavery, of course, but more generally in social structures where segregation and discrimination persecute them. Yet more proof that Tarantino is by no means an extreme relativist or constructivist: for all the artifice, the allegory is not enough. The faces and bodies of people from minority backgrounds must be shown to counter the history of erasure they have been subjected to. And in this respect, Tarantino's films come close to endorsing a Levinasian ethics whereby the encounter with the face of the other holds pride of place in our acknowledgment of her/his basic humanity.[146] The films' awareness of the complexity of racial representations, of their history, of the racial construction of all bodies, of the multiplicity of identities, of the difficulty of establishing a relationship with an other without excluding someone else, of the necessity and limitations of deconstruction and resignification, prove that they are not instances of shameless white appropriation but problematized engagements with racial politics.

CHAPTER THREE

"THAT'S THE EXCUSE YOU GUYS USE WHENEVER YOU WANT TO EXCLUDE ME FROM SOMETHING"

Identity Politics Vol. 2: Gender (and Sexuality)

Tarantino went from making an all-male film (*Reservoir Dogs*) to a series of female-centered films (*Jackie Brown*, *Kill Bill*, *Death Proof*) and has, with the relative exception of *Django Unchained*, included strong main female characters in all his films since. His biography, no doubt, partly explains this interest: Tarantino was raised by a single mother whose fortitude he admired.[1] In any case, his films evidence an awareness that power relationships are often sexualized and mediated through violence, that genre conventions are gendered, and that gender and sexuality, like race and ethnicity, are constructed through normative discourses and practices. In the above citation from *Death Proof*, Abernathy's response to Kim and Zoë's attempt to leave her out of their plans points to the instability of gender as a discursive category [84:07]. The usage of "guys" to refer to both women and men is so common in contemporary US English as to have become quasi-gender-neutral. And yet, in this case, the usage debunks the male/female binary only to maintain two exclusive and exclusionary categories: the "masculine" stuntgirls (Kim and Zoë) versus the "feminine" make-up artist (Abernathy) and model (Lee). Abernathy's reaction suggests the possibility that female action heroines and Final Girls[2] of the post-femininst era may actually be vessels through which phallocentric discourses, having given up on the male, continue to value, privilege, and uphold the "masculine" whether associated with male or female, with the implication that traditional power structures could, in effect, be perniciously reinstated even in egalitarian discourses and practices.

Many critics and scholars have explored the critique of white masculinity in *Reservoir Dogs* (Taubin 2000) and *Pulp Fiction* (Willis 2000), or attempted to weigh the feminist potential of the female characters of *Kill Bill* (Jordan 2006, Coulthard 2007, Reilly 2007, Lavin 2010), *Death Proof* (Szaniawski 2008, Cervulle 2009, Roche 2010), and *Inglourious Basterds* (Schlipphacke 2012). What has since become apparent is that Tarantino has read feminist film theory; while promoting *Death Proof*, he even stated that Carol Clover's *Men, Women, and Chainsaws* was his favorite work of film criticism.[3] The influence of feminist film theories is, as we shall see, evident as early as *Kill Bill*. Tarantino's feature films take into account and address their main tenets concerning narrative cinema: Laura Mulvey's 1975 thesis that the gaze is gendered male and is often mediated by a male character's gaze in classical films whose male-oriented narratives attempt to alleviate castration anxiety by punishing or fetishizing (through camerawork, lighting, etc.) the female character;[4] Kaja Silverman's observation (1988) that the disembodied voice is likewise gendered male, while the female voice is generally divested of authority or contained; or Carol Clover's demonstration (1992) that the Final Girl, the heroine-victim of the slasher who usually survives, encourages "crossgender identification,"[5] and thus contests the idea that identification is entirely determined by gender (i.e., that a male viewer necessarily relates to a male character). Mulvey's 1984 "Afterthoughts"[6] similarly contends that, in *Duel in the Sun* (King Vidor, 1946), choosing between two male lovers entails, for the heroine (Pearl Chavez), choosing between a classic or a more hybrid model of femininity: the "feminine" wife or the "masculine" cowgirl.

This chapter pursues the argument that Tarantino's cinematic metafictions engage actively with film history and film criticism by reflecting on their own gendered terms as genre films. It works in conjunction with the preceding chapter on race and ethnicity by revisiting the way certain concerns (film genre, power relations, language, the body) intersect on the level of discourse and practice. Attention will be paid, first, to the relation between gender and genre conventions on the macro level (narrative, structure), then to how the plots are often based on an assault on patriarchy, third to the linguistic deconstruction of gender effected through the usage of specific words, and finally to how some of the major concerns of feminist film theories (the gaze, the voice, fetishization, punishment) are taken into account in the figuration of the body. I argue that deconstructing the material his films are based on enables Tarantino to come to terms with genre films and, more generally, cinema, and, in turn, qualify the theories he engages with. In so doing, his cinematic metafictions endeavor to resolve the contradiction between the celebration and the deconstruction of film genre: redeeming it by queering it, so to speak, as is suggested in the quote from *Death Proof* and the film's outcome. The queering—i.e., "the process of making a given set of ideas strange, to destabilize dominant understandings and underlying assumptions"[7]—is, as we shall see, always related to the female protagonist and made conspicuous by the avoidance of homosexuality, except in the violent heterosexual version of homoeroticism.

Gender/Genre

Women are excluded from the main narrative of the heist/buddy movie *Reservoir Dogs*. They are relegated to subordinate roles in the gangster/*noir* parody *Pulp Fiction*: Honey Bunny, Fabienne, and Jody are, respectively, Pumpkin's, Butch's, and Lance's girlfriends; Trudi is just a drug addict hanging out at Lance's place, Esmarelda, a car driver subordinate both in terms of class and ethnicity; and Mia, the only female protagonist, is identified by the title of the first story as "Marsellus Wallace's wife" [20:23]. Most of these female characters correspond to various figures in film *noir*:[8] Mia is a dark temptress;[9] Honey Bunny, a modern-day Bonnie Parker or Annie Laurie Starr; Fabienne, a woman-child who unwittingly gets her man in trouble; and Esmarelda, a ghoul whose seduction of Butch could have taken the narrative in another direction [67:54–72:42]. As in film *noir*, the female characters are central to each of the three stories, even when they are not present: Mia not only tempts Vincent but overdoses; Fabienne forgets Butch's watch at their apartment; and Bonnie, who appears as a silhouette in the foreground of an insert, is the "explosive element" that requires Jules, Vincent, and Jimmie to quickly dispose of Marvin's body [11:00–11:13]. Thus, each story deals with the way a female character complicates an all-male narrative, and in generic terms, with the way *noir* complicates the gangster movie.

This was already the case in *Reservoir Dogs*, a movie that opens with the male characters arguing over Madonna, waitresses, and a song, "The Night the Lights Went Out in Georgia," in which a woman confesses she murdered the male protagonist [0:18–7:24], and where the heist is complicated by Mr. Blonde's killing a female civilian [23:23], Mr. Pink's getting hit by another [20:11], and Mr. Orange's getting shot by yet another [82:54]. On the surface, then, both *Reservoir Dogs* and *Pulp Fiction* seem to relate how female elements threaten a world and a genre that would be more harmonious if all-male. As Larry Dimmick tells Joe Cabot about his former partner Alabama, "You push that woman-man thing too long, and it gets to you after a while" [25:55].

In revisiting a closed-door mystery plot à la *Reservoir Dogs*, *The Hateful Eight* injects the repressed female element in the midst of the male characters in an environment that is itself gendered female—the way station is named after its proprietor Minnie Mink, and O. B.'s frustration at the broken door leads him to call it a "whore" [53:29]. Daisy Domergue is more than just disruptive; she constitutes the premise, the frame, and the catalyst (Chapter Four is entitled "Domergue's Got a Secret"). With Daisy as simultaneously the male and female prisoner of the Western, the Southern Belle of the plantation film and the witch of horror—her bloody face and loose hair conjure up images from *Carrie*[10] (Brian De Palma, 1976), one of Tarantino's favorite movies—the feminine Gothic is not just threatening the masculine Western which *Django Unchained* mainly sought to preserve; it has insidiously merged with it. The focus on race in his first Western seems to have led Tarantino to accept the predominantly male terms of the genre. Both the slaves and the white women are mainly restricted to the plantation as both a locus and a genre: Broomhilda is (mostly) the damsel in distress; Lara Lee, the Southern Belle; Sheba, Calvin Candie's slave mistress, etc. The film reflexively foregrounds its own acceptance of the gendered terms of these genres when it presents the first women onscreen: one is quietly listening to her doctor's instructions on how to cure her illness, while another, dressed in undergarments, looks out a window that frames her [12:51–13:16].[11] Broomhilda is nonetheless a courageous and disruptive element, as her escape attempts with or without Django prove.

Centered on a female protagonist, *Jackie Brown* could be seen as a turning point in Tarantino's filmography, even though the premise originates in Leonard's novel. By making Jackie African American, Tarantino defuses the racial conflict central to the novel in order to emphasize gender tensions among the black protagonists. By taking over an initially male narrative, Jackie is, in some ways, a more radical version of the femme fatales of *Pulp Fiction*. Not only does she thwart Ordell's plans, but she turns the tables on him, first by threatening him at gunpoint in the shadows [50:42], then by snaring him in the plot she has devised, and finally by getting him killed [143:03]. What distinguishes Jackie from the femme fatale is that she assumes authorship of her plan, describing herself as Ordell's "manager" [72:36], and plays a major part in it. In this respect, she resembles heist masterminds Joe Cabot in *Reservoir Dogs* and even more Johnny Clay in *The Killing* (UA, Stanley Kubrick, 1956). Unlike the female characters in *Reservoir Dogs* and *Pulp Fiction*, then, she upsets the male characters' schemes deliberately and decisively. By taking on her perspective from the moment she gets out of jail [40:12], the film refuses to dramatize the narrative as the mere disruption of an all-male plot (and genre) by a female element, but rather as the creation of a female-centered plot. The other female characters, who follow the gendered conventions of the genre (Melanie and Simone are the gangster's molls), also serve to complicate the plot—Simone by running away with the money, Melanie by trying to turn Louis against Ordell and finally provoking him—but they are not alone to do so; the psychopathic Louis is also a crucial element. The character of Jackie Brown is thus at the intersection of several intertexts that associate her with genre characters that are both male and female. The film cannot be reduced to the mere equation female *noir* versus male gangster, or Coffy versus Super Fly. Indeed, *Super Fly* (Gordon Parks Jr., 1972) serves as a hypotext to both Ordell's and Jackie's arcs in that order: Ordell, like the 1972 drug dealer, wants to get $1 million to bail out of town, but Jackie is the one who effects a money exchange (in a changing room instead of an elevator) and is filmed driving around in lateral close-up [102:24]. The *Super Fly* hypotext thus foregrounds the shift from male to female protagonist.

The same can be said of *Kill Bill*. Its novelty is not so much that it is a martial arts movie or an action movie with women in lead roles:[12] its main hypotexts, *Lady Snowblood*[13] and *Charlie's Angels*, are just that. Rather, the Bride, like Jackie Brown, is the point where various references intersect: in the opening credits, she resembles Citizen Kane on his deathbed in Welles's 1941 film [3:54]; Billy Lo from *Game of Death* as she battles the Crazy 88 in her yellow jumper [*Vol. 1* 78:55]; and Frank from *Once Upon a Time in the West* as she crosses the desert haze[14] [*Vol. 2* 61:37]. Like her main adversary, Bill, she is associated with both the Western and the martial arts movie, but her capacity for diversity is far greater, as the allusion to *Citizen Kane* suggests; this is further confirmed by her resembling the Space Sheriff and his offspring, the Power Rangers, who constitute a more diverse group in terms of race and gender, when she looks down at Sofie Fatale in the car trunk [*Vol. 1* 96:04].

Kill Bill, however, enhances the gender conflict by grounding itself in the rape-revenge subgenre. Not only is the narrative driven by the motive stated in the title, but two of the Bride's arch adversaries are intertexually bound to the genre: O-Ren, who witnessed her parents' death as a child, dresses like Yuki Kashima in *Lady Snowblood*, and Elle, whose eye was torn out by Pai Mei, wears an eyepatch like Frigga in *Thriller* (fig. 14). The exploitation subgenre provides a structural underpinning for the gender trouble effected by these characters, its very terms indicating a shift from male rape to female revenge. This structure is also central to the arc of Shosanna Dreyfus in *Inglourious Basterds*, where the use of the music from the rape scene in *The Entity* (Sidney J. Furie, 1982) identifies Shosanna as the female victim of

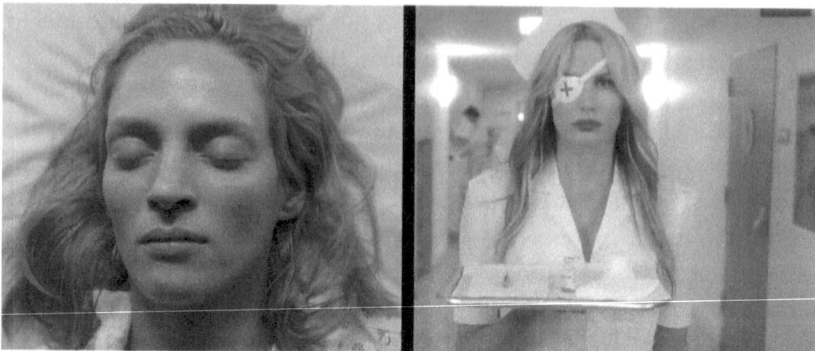

Fig. 14: *Kill Bill Vol. 1*: Elle closes in on the sleeping beauty (the Bride) to finish her off, in a scene that borrows the eyepatch from *Thriller* (Bo Arne Vibernius, 1974) and *Switchblade Sisters* (Jack Hill, 1975), and the split screen and the killer nurse from the trailer of *Black Sunday* (John Frankenheimer, 1977).

a ubiquitous male demon (here, Hans Landa) [53:56], but also underscores how she differs from the character of Carla Moran, who ultimately relies on (predominantly male) scientists to protect her in the 1982 film. By comparison, Shosanna not only takes matters into her own hands, but by becoming what Michel Chion calls an "acousmatic being [*acousmêtre*]" whose voice evokes omniscience and omnipotence,[15] she takes on the part of Fritz Lang's 1933 *Mabuse* and the 1939 *Wizard of Oz* [144:21], and thus, like the Bride, comes to be a site of national-gender-generic hybridity.

Like *Kill Bill*, *Death Proof* grounds its play with gender and genre in a rape-revenge structure, though the two parts only roughly correspond to the two terms, as both groups get assaulted and only the second slays the psycho killer: the first part corresponds, then, to rape/murder, the second to rape-revenge. *Death Proof* mixes genres (the car movie, the slasher) that are considered characteristically "male," yet in so doing, it calls into question what exactly we mean by a "male" genre. Car movies, such as those mentioned by Kim, Mike, and Zoë [43:27, 78:20]—*Vanishing Point* (Richard C. Safarian, 1971), *Gone in 60 Seconds* (H. B. Halicki, 1974), *Dirty Mary Crazy Larry* (John Hough, 1974)—are films with guys, for guys, with no or few secondary female characters; even if the female character is important enough to have her name in the title, she remains a woman in a man's world and a destabilizing element at that. As stuntgirl Kim points out, "most girls wouldn't know *Vanishing Point*" [78:28].[16]

It has long been assumed that the slasher's main audience is equally comprised of young men.[17] Diegetically speaking, however, the slasher is not primarily male. If the killer is "usually—but not necessarily—male,"[18] the victims are both male and female, although "even in films in which males and females are killed in roughly even numbers, the lingering images are inevitably female. The death of a male is always swift" and is "more likely to be viewed from a distance."[19] Clover does not just underline the genre's phallocentrism, but seems to imply that its "femaleness" is, paradoxically, what makes it "male": the female heroine is used "as a kind of feint, a front through which the boy can simultaneously experience forbidden desires and disavow them on grounds that the visible actor is, after all, a girl."[20]

Death Proof is also an all-girl hangout movie.[21] Or, more exactly, the film's two parts start out like one, which, as Tarantino points out, is fairly typical of the slasher.[22] Apart from the brief scenes of Mike alone and the McGraws discussing the crime, the only lengthy scenes with any male characters occur at the Texas Chili Parlor, and the only male-only scene is, appropriately, when Dov and Omar go over their strategy to get invited to the girls-only weekend at Lake LBJ [22:48–24:14]. The girls' occupations and subjects of conversation (music, love, booze, marijuana) are similar to those of male characters in all-male hangout films such as *Rio Bravo* or, in its prologue, *Reservoir Dogs*.[23]

Death Proof is a car movie with girls, but this is truly the case only in the second part of the film. In the first part, the genre is exclusively connected to Mike, who mentions the classics of the genre [43:26], while the first group of girls use Shanna's small red Honda to get around—not exactly the "Detroit American muscle car" of Zoë's dreams [76:19]. The second part, however, has Kim and Zoë driving the *Gone in 60 Seconds* Mustang and the *Vanishing Point* Challenger. Though positioned as "girls" in the opening credits, they take on roles (the driver, the rapist, the killer) the genres have generally attributed to male characters and reject those (the passenger, the victim) attributed to female chatacters. Their unusual assumption of these roles points to an exceptional precedent that *Death Proof* alludes to but does not cite: Russ Meyer's 1965 *Faster, Pussycat! Kill! Kill!*, in which a group of go-go dancers on the run race a man and beat him to death.

With a male serial killer and lots of "girls," *Death Proof* is the quintessential slasher. Although Clover says the slasher is "pretechnological" insomuch as the weapons are "personal extensions of the body,"[24] Mike, as Sheriff McGraw underlines, "used a car not a hatchet, but they dead just the same" [53:05]. Tarantino's film refers to many classics of the genre: Mike has the same first name as the killer in *Halloween* (John Carpenter, 1978), while the girls' going to a lake recalls the *Friday the 13th* franchise (1980–2009) [7:24]. The opening credits designate the male killer as the star of the show, "the girls" as interchangeable victims [1:24], an impression reinforced by the film's two-part structure. In this respect, *Death Proof* represents the "ideal" slasher for guys, with the male killer posing no threat whatsoever to the male characters.

Tarantino's reliance on the rape-revenge as an overarching structure is both formal and political; it is this structure that enables gender/genre reversals. Of the three genres *Death Proof* mixes, the treatment of the car movie is the most dependent on this two-stage structure, which makes sense given that the car is the weapon of choice. The hangout movie appears to be the least dependent on the rape-revenge, but as an expansion of a common feature of the slasher, it is integrated within the slasher that then enters in tension with the rape-revenge. Indeed, the transformation of this "ideal" slasher into a rape-revenge, I would argue, confirms Clover's analysis that "the rape-revenge film goes the slasher one better, for rape-revenge films not only have female heroes and male villains, they repeatedly and explicitly articulate feminist politics."[25] *Death Proof* quite deliberately plays with the figure of the heroine-victim as defined by Clover. The first part of the film sets Arlene up as the potential Final Girl—she is even described as such in the screenplay[26]—in a scene [9:11–9:35] that recalls the one where Laurie notices the stalker's car outside her school in *Halloween* (1978). However, Arlene's demise at the end of the first part of the film, and Abernathy, Kim, and Zoë's victory at the end of the second, is more than just a playful subversion of slasher conventions. First, Clover's argument that the final girl "deliver[s] herself into the adult world" is structurally displaced onto the fact that the girls in the first part are less mature than those in the second.[27] Second, Arlene's death is the first stage in the critique of a figure of exception that culminates in the second part of the film when Abernathy, whose name also starts with an "A," turns into a killer as apt as her friends Kim and Zoë. By suggesting that many (if not all) women, including sexually active ones such as this lot, have Final Girl potential, the very idea of such a character is debunked, and with it its function as "surrogate male" to male members of the audience; if one can relate to all three characters, then one can relate to all people regardless of their race and gender.

Tarantino's films have from the start recognized that film genre conventions are gendered and racialized, as we have seen in the previous chapter. What is more interesting is the extent to which they have increasingly engaged with, and attempted to deconstruct and reformulate, those connections. It is not just that the number of female protagonists is greater, but that the female characters go from being disruptive elements in all-male narratives (in *Reservoir Dogs* and *Pulp Fiction*) to central agents that author their plot (from *Jackie Brown* on), from being associated with one genre in particular (*noir* in *Pulp Fiction*) to incarnating the generic hybridity at work in the films, and combining masculine and feminine attributes (from *Jackie Brown* on). This shift is intimately correlated to an increased alignment with the female protagonists in terms of focalization. In *Kill Bill*, *Death Proof*, and *Inglourious Basterds*, it is further grounded in the structure of the rape-revenge that accounts for this turning of tables in matters of gender and agency, enabling a critique of sibling genres and maybe even a reformulation of their terms; reframing according to the rape-revenge paradigm is also a way of inflicting female vengeance on male genres and, more generally, on mainstream cinema. Far from being just a disruptive element within male hegemony, the female element is a potentially creative force—or a destructive one, in the case of Daisy Domergue. The female—or, more precisely, the "feminine"—element is a force that, we shall see, works to destabilize and sometimes even subvert patriarchy and the essentialist discourses and practices that serve to uphold it, thereby driving a narrative that is ultimately that of the demise of the patriarch in charge of the basic setup.

The Patriarch, His Boys, His Girls—and the Matriarch

In *Reservoir Dogs*, the heist—and thus the movie's initial plot—have been masterminded by Joe Cabot. His power is made manifest as early as the prologue, when he treats his employees to breakfast and is, along with his son Eddie, dressed differently than they are [3:53]. His position is confirmed in subsequent conversations, when Mr. White and Mr. Pink meet in the warehouse Cabot designated and decide, at Mr. White's urging, to wait there until their boss has solved the problem [12:00, 35:38]. It is further staged in the flashbacks; the first two show Cabot sitting in a leather armchair at a big desk, framed by huge elephant tusks [25:51, 36:27], the third, wearing a suit in a nightclub [71:00] and standing in front of a blackboard like a teacher and attributing aliases [76:39]. The other thieves all recognize his authority, even when they (Mr. Pink and Mr. Brown) disapprove of the names they have been given [78:17]; the dress code they have presumably been imposed (black suits, white shirts, thin ties, Wayfarer sunglasses) suggests they are to some extent interchangeable employees. Yet as the story of a heist gone wrong, *Reservoir Dogs* is basically the story of the capitalist patriarch's demise. His rule is, in fact, questioned as soon as the prologue and the opening credits. First, Cabot's failing to remember someone's name calls into question his competence in the brains department and even leads Larry Dimmick to confiscate his notebook [1:11]; the film's flashback structure is central in this respect, since it reverses the chronological order by depicting Cabot's ability to name afterwards. Secondly, the opening credits, by including Lawrence Tierney and Chris Penn with the other actors, notably in the long backshot where the title appears, indicate that the men are not Cabot's dogs, but that Cabot, whose name means "mutt" in French, is one of them, too [8:21].

Cabot's employees are nonetheless all surrogate sons, if to varying degrees; Mr. Blonde even describes Mr. Pink and Mr. White as "kids [...] play[ing] rough" before merrily jumping into the brawl [31:40]. Cabot's plan is thus ruined by three inept or treacherous sons, significantly the three who are given flashbacks: Vic Vega the psychopath, Freddy Newandyke the undercover cop, and, more surprisingly, Cabot's old friend Larry Dimmick. Dimmick, in particular, refuses to trust Cabot when the latter states that Mr. Orange "was the only one [he] wasn't 100 percent about" [87:20]. That Dimmick sees himself on equal terms with Cabot is demonstrated in his teasing Cabot in the prologue and in the contrast between the first two flashbacks; while Eddie joins his father and his friend Vic in the second flashback, in the first the older men converse alone about robbery and romance—a choice topic (and an ironic one at that) given that it is Dimmick's emotions that will lead to their demise. Indeed, the problem with Mr. Orange is not just that he is the newbie and the rat; it is the ambiguous nature of his relationship with Dimmick. His real name, Freddy (a name commonly used for both women and men) New-an-dyke, says it all—his presence is not just the infiltration of the cop among the thieves; it is that of the "feminine" in the all-male heist plot, which is why it is particularly appropriate that he gets shot by a woman. Once Dimmick—yet another portmanteau name that combines "dim" and "dick"—realizes his mistake, he weeps and cradles Freddy like a pietà before fulfilling the role of castrating father by killing him [91:27]. The Mexican standoff thus pits the main patriarch ready to punish a false son, against a father/mother/lover[28] who is standing up for his/her adopted child/lover, against the main patriarch's actual son (fig. 15). At stake, then, is an opposition[29] between an essentialist patriarchal relationship and a symbolic, more ambivalent, and possibly homoerotic relationship, one further complicated by the surrogate father-son relationships between the three men pointing the guns in order of succeeding generation: Cabot as surrogate father to Dimmick, Dimmick as surrogate father to Eddie, yet another first name given to both women and men. *Reservoir Dogs* is thus the story of racial, gender, and sexual revenge against the white patriarch.

Pulp Fiction is also dominated by the presence of a patriarch associated with a specific film genre, this time the gangster movie. As the "god of this world,"[30] Marsellus is the instigator of each plot, the "hub"[31] of the narrative: Jules and Vincent are running an errand for their boss [14:15]; Vincent is asked to take his boss's wife out [13:17, 24:00]; and Butch is told to go down in a boxing match [20:30]. The three stories (the end of "The Bonnie Situation"

Fig. 15: *Reservoir Dogs*: The Mexican standoff between Joe Cabot, Mr. White, and Nice Guy Eddie in the stagey warehouse.

and the beginning of the other two) intersect in Wallace's headquarters in the very first scene of "Vincent Vega & Marsellus Wallace's Wife," where the three male protagonists (Jules, Vincent, and Butch) meet. The "big man," as Jules and Vincent call him [13:20, 23:39], appears in the opening shot as a disembodied voice dictating his terms to Butch;[32] his power is measured by his pawn's silent subjection in the face of a humiliating tirade that the static two-minute-long shot brings out [20:30]. The following shot depicts Marsellus's sheer physicality, a thirty-four-second-long close-up revealing the back of his head and massive shoulders, with Butch, out of focus in the right midground, made insignificant (fig. 16) [22:30]. The two other shots of Marsellus—long shots matched with reverse close-ups of Vincent and Jules, followed by Butch looking at him—keep the head gangster at a respectful distance [23:50, 25:08]. Marsellus is only shot frontally the moment he goes from being a mastermind to a vulnerable participant in someone else's plot, right after Butch runs into him with his car [91:12]; prior to that point, he retains control, even when he finds out Butch has duped him and is again filmed in a lengthy backshot, in the fourth scene of "The Gold Watch," his second appearance in the film [67:14]. The frontal shots after the car assault announce the rape scene where Marsellus is brought down to Butch's level; following the frontal medium long shot of the two men being awakened, the subsequent two-shot from behind no longer signifies power but submission [103:49]. Like Cabot, Marsellus's fallibility is suggested from the start, albeit more discretely and this time visually, through the Band-Aid on the back of his head.

In *Pulp Fiction*, each story recounts how the patriarch loses control, at least momentarily, of his men, wife, and even himself: Mia Wallace momentarily usurps her husband's powers of omniscience and ubiquity when

Fig. 16: *Pulp Fiction*: Marsellus Wallace, whose Band-Aid is the sole mark of his mortality, gives Butch (out of focus in the background) his instructions for the boxing match.

she welcomes Vincent, appearing in a backshot and subjecting her guest to the surveillance technology presumably installed to protect the gangster's house from invasion [31:04]; Vincent's "loyalty" is put to the "test" when he is tempted by Marsellus's wife (fig. 46) [50:25] and he fails at his job as a babysitter when she ODs; Butch betrays his employer before finally saving him; and Jules decides to abandon his gangster ways and start a new life. The protagonists who survive are those who decide to free themselves from Marsellus's hold and author their own fates.[33] Butch's trajectory is more classically Oedipal. The boxer ironically falls into the jaws of the bad surrogate father by going back for his father's gold watch. His redemption stems from his capacity to forsake a simplistic good/bad father opposition (as well as white man/black man) and recognize in his common ordeal with Marsellus that of Koons and his father in Vietnam.[34] In other words, saving the gangster becomes a chance to save the father, who died in the war with a watch in his rectum. Butch, whose first name evokes a potential femininity and queerness,[35] thus succeeds in reframing what seemed to be a clear-cut dichotomy.

Unlike Butch, Jules does not betray Marsellus, but by reinterpreting his role as a "shepherd" and choosing to spare Pumpkin and Honey Bunny (the doubles of the young people he shot in the second scene), he turns away from his role as Marsellus's angel of death to embrace a far riskier parental role: "The truth is: you're 'the weak,' and I am 'the tyranny of evil men.' But I'm trying, Ringo—I'm trying *real hard* to be the shepherd" [142:15]. Although, on the surface, the Mexican standoff, reprised from the ending of *Reservoir Dogs*, opposes two couples, as well as male and female, it serves to dramatize the manifold interpretations Jules can now see in his Ezekiel 25:17 monologue, and thus his capacity to resignify what initially appeared as a monolithic discourse but was already an impure interpretation. What Butch effects in practice, Jules does in both practice and discourse.

The subsequent films—*Jackie Brown, Kill Bill, Death Proof*, and even *Inglourious Basterds* to some extent—relate the downfall of a perverse patriarch at the hands of one or several female protagonists. Each title reads like a program: Tarantino's martial arts film explicitly, his horror movie by referring to the murder weapon that ends up being not as infallible as the male psychopath claimed, and *Jackie Brown* by taking on the name of the heroine rather than the villain who dominates the first act. All three seem to suggest that it takes at least one woman to fully bring the patriarch down.

The premise of *Jackie Brown* is fairly similar to that of "The Gold Watch": Ordell, the gangster who exploits "the bitches he got set up" for sex and work [76:18], and even shares Simone and Melanie with his friend Louis [23:37, 75:15], finds himself snared in Jackie's plot. Unlike Marsellus, his demise is irrevocable and ends with his death in the final act. Accordingly, the film doesn't bother to build him up as a powerful figure; although the video "Chick with Guns" depicts the two "objects" he seems to control,[36] and his disembodied voice cuts off the actress as soon as she starts describing a Tec-9 machine gun, the process of "deacousmatization" (whereby the acousmatic being is stripped of its powers) occurs one second after Ordell starts speaking, with a reverse two-shot of Ordell commenting and Louis listening [3:51]. When Louis later tells Ordell's girlfriend Melanie how "impressed" he is with Ordell's knowledge, she retorts that the latter "isn't anymore of a gun expert than" she is [7:16]. Unlike Marsellus,[37] Ordell is not characterized as an omnipotent "acoustic being," and his authority and knowledge are called into question as early as the opening scene, and, what's more, by a female character.

What the reverse shot also reveals is how "feminine" the male viewer/critic/gun expert actually is—his legs are crossed, and he is dressed in a trendy white shirt and shorts. And yet this surface "femininity" is no more foolproof than his alpha-male dominion over his female employees in ensuring his knowledge of, and control over, women.[38] Neither prevent him from getting played by a woman whose plot is centered on effecting a money change, ironically, in the ladies' changing rooms in a department store—and who manages to buy a classy suit (a more "masculine" getup) in the process [105:00]. The changing room remains the locus Ordell fails to see—even with "his" eyes (Louis's and Melanie's) there. It is, on the other hand, with relative ease that Jackie sits in Max's chair in his office, practicing aiming a gun at her foe in her new suit [138:27], then watching Ordell and Max enter the building, in a shot that tracks right to become an over-the-shoulder shot [142:32], putting Jackie in a position reminiscent of Marsellus's vis-à-vis Butch in *Pulp Fiction*. In *Jackie Brown*, the combination of "masculine" and "feminine" features is only productive in the female heroine, not in the male patriarch, announcing the female protagonists of *Kill Bill* and *Death Proof*.

Like Tarantino's other male patriarchs, Bill upholds the film's dominant genres, this time a mix of the martial arts and Western, that is directly correlated to Carradine's famous role in *Kung Fu*. Like Marsellus, Bill first appears as a voice and a physical presence—footsteps, a pair of boots, and a voice delivering a death sentence [*Vol. 1* 0:55], a right hand toying with a sword [*Vol. 1* 22:04], a body standing behind Sofie Fatale caressing her cheek and hair [*Vol. 1* 95:21]—until his face is finally revealed in Chapter Six [*Vol. 2* 5:51]. Like Ordell, Bill exploits his female employees for business and sex. He has a hold over all of them: Vernita has, presumably, been allowed to live the life of mother and wife that Beatrix aspired to [*Vol. 1* 8:23]; Elle has replaced Beatrix as Bill's girlfriend and assassin [*Vol. 1* 23:33]; and O-Ren was, according to the Bride, backed by Bill "financially and philosophically in her Shakespearean in magnitude power struggle with the other yakuza clans over who would rule vice in the city of Tokyo" [*Vol. 1* 56:25], so even the matriarch, who killed the perverse patriarch (Boss Matsumoto) that murdered her family [*Vol. 1* 39:20] and cut off the head of one of the male yakuzas (Boss Tanaka) she governs [*Vol. 1* 60:23], has a patriarchal benefactor above her. The Bride is no exception—she has been trained by at least two patriarchs (Bill and his own master, Pai Mei, who plucked Elle's eye out [*Vol. 2* 74:41]), and relies on the sword-making talents of a third (Hattori Hanzo) and the information of a fourth (Esteban Vihaio) to accomplish her quest.

All Bill's women (Beatrix, Vernita, O-Ren, Elle) wield phallic weapons (knives, swords, rifles)—the Bride and O-Ren, in particular, are characterized as castrating women who chop off heads and limbs. The Bride's possession of Buck's pickup truck resignifies the Pussy Wagon from a space in which an alpha male transports female bodies into the female superheroine's vehicle—significantly, the flashback structure introduces the viewer first to the resignified version [*Vol. 1* 15:16]. The irony is that the Bride's quest for revenge leads her to kill or maim her own doubles (O-Ren, Sofie, Vernita, Elle). On one level, this indicates the female characters' inability to recognize their common subjection to the patriarch and a recognition of the latter as the ultimate foe. From a feminist perspective, both are disappointing attitudes; after all, one interpretation of *Kill Bill* could be that the Bride punishes the other female characters for remaining subjected to Bill in face of the violence he inflicted on her. Yet in relating a succession of epic fights against three worthy adversaries (Vernita, O-Ren, and Elle), the film creates an expectation that it is ultimately unable to fulfill. The confrontation with the patriarch, presented as a demigod in *Vol. 1*,[39] will be chatty, not physical, and the talents he displays in this scene are, above all, "feminine": fixing snacks like Vernita [*Vol. 1* 12:16; *Vol. 2* 88:29–99:51] and sneakily poisoning his adversary like Elle [*Vol. 1* 21:12; *Vol. 2* 66:56, 75:00, 103:20]. Retrospectively, then, Bill's describing the murder of Beatrix as an act of masochism, a psychic structure traditionally gendered "feminine" and that Freud believed to develop from sadism,[40] can be seen not only as the patriarch's attempt to mask his sadism in bad faith, but also as an unconscious admission of his own femininity.

As in *Jackie Brown*, then, the combination of "feminine" and "masculine" features are more productive in the female protagonist than in the male patriarch. Failing to acknowledge the commonality of their experience of oppression (Beatrix is "curious" about, but not particularly sympathetic to, Elle's losing an eye to Pai Mei), some of the female characters do, albeit momentarily, establish another kind of bond: this one based on a child or childhood. Nikki's arrival interrupts Vernita and the Bride's fight to the death [*Vol. 1* 7:13], and Beatrix tells Bill how Karen accepted to abort her mission when Beatrix informed her she was pregnant [*Vol. 2* 108:40]. O-Ren and the Bride even have a goofy exchange as they size each other up, based on a common memory of TV culture: the Trix cereal commercial [*Vol. 1* 78:41], recalling the cereal Vernita was fixing for her daughter, yet another connection made possible thanks to the prolectic Chapter One. These brief moments hint at the common experiences of childhood and motherhood that lie at the heart of the narrative, but that the characters, for the most part, fail to recognize: both the Bride and O-Ren become the doubles of those who murdered their families; believing her child to be dead and her womb to be infertile, the one-track Bride views her relationship to Vernita according to the warrior code and not the code of motherhood she demanded Karen recognize. It is this failure that prevents the DiVAS from uniting against the patriarch.

Death Proof takes *Kill Bill* one step further by proposing to explore female bonding. Like Tarantino's other patriarchs, Stuntman Mike is presented as a gaze (the POV shot in the opening credits [2:14]), a physical presence (the massive car [8:53]), and a voice (when he chuckles [14:22]); like the other patriarchs, his vulnerability is quickly revealed when he uses eyedrops [14:45]. Mike represents the stereotypical "puritanical" and "repressive father-figure" of the slasher,[41] expressing his sexual drive through violence. If his good manners seem to distinguish him from the "boys" the female characters frequently encounter, the film suggests that the other male characters understand or share his violent sexual potential. Shanna's father's quasi-incestuous "tendency to pop up" at the lakehouse to spy on his daughter's girlfriends is enacted

Fig. 17: *Death Proof*: Stuntman Mike appears out of focus in the background to the tune of "Staggolee," an embodiment of Dov's violent desires for Jungle Julia.

by Mike when he stalks the girls repeatedly and pops up at the restaurants they socialize in [9:13, 78:24]. Mike's first appearance shows him devouring a platter of nachos and is followed by Dov and Omar's discussion about how to get Julia, Shanna, and Arlene drunk; the psycho killer's presence, out-of-focus in the left background of the frontal close-up of Dov, incarnates the violent tendencies the young man's aggressive tone just barely contains (fig. 17) [22:28–24:42]. At the end of the first part, Sheriff Earl McGraw lectures his own son on the killer's motives—"Well, I guess to me, it's a sex thing"—only to conclude: "And just because I can't punish old Frankenstein in there for what he's done, I'm gonna tell you like the Lord told John: if he ever does it again, I can be goddamn sure he don't do it in Texas" [54:12–55:47]. The "ineptitude" that characterizes adults in the slasher film[42] is, in *Death Proof*, gendered male and generalized to all male characters. Unconsciously, perhaps, the male characters don't want to stop Mike because he is merely acting out their own unavowed desires.

This leaves the "girls" to bring the perverse patriarch down on their own. The film's two-part structure contrasts the two groups of girls. For all their attitude, the first group of female characters willingly subjects itself to patriarchy. Julia, whose fetishized body is scattered all over Austin on various billboards [4:35, 5:09, 8:48, 15:01], pressures her friend Arlene into acting out a heterosexual male fantasy: performing a lap dance for a secret admirer who turns out to be none other than the psychopath [12:40, 35:10]. The second group initially resembles the first and is presented in a car talking about sex (Lee instead of Arlene) and party substances (marijuana for Julia, alcohol for Abernathy) [57:14]. However, the second group refuses to passively submit to the violence Mike inflicts on them, instead choosing to chase him down. Thus, the first group is punished not so much for their transgressions (the second group is just as permissive), but for subjecting themselves to sexist fantasies, a subjection that is described as potentially fatal ("they look you dead in the eye") in Julia's own scenario [12:45], hence the lack of awareness noted by Nama and discussed in the previous chapter. This lack of awareness of sexual politics is foregrounded when Julia tells Arlene that they must down the shots of Chartreuse offered by "the house," i.e., Warren, played by Tarantino himself: "Hey, them's the rules, baby. Warren says it, we do it!" [18:46]. The sexual undercurrent of the girls' submission to the patriarch—Tarantino's character exclaims: "I love that philosophy: 'Warren says it, we do it! I love it!'"—evokes the figure of the sexually exploitative male director, especially since Warren makes the waitress sit on his lap; it is retrospectively confirmed when Dov and Omar plan on getting them to drink hard liquor to get them in bed. If none of the female characters are outspoken feminists, the two groups propose two different attitudes: Julia's matriarchy is a "feminine" version of patriarchy, while Abernathy, Kim, and Zoë celebrate the pleasures of adopting queer positions. This is why *Death Proof* is only post-feminist on the surface; at heart, it aims to be feminist.[43]

When it comes to undermining patriarchy, Tarantino's more recent films, *Inglourious Basterds* and *The Hateful Eight*, attempt to unite the two approaches (the all-male model and the female-centered plot) of the previous films, the first by associating them, the second by merging them. In *Inglourious Basterds*, it is ultimately an interracial couple, led by the female protagonist, that devises and executes its plot to bring down the Third Reich; Shosanna and Marcel are not shown to have any connections with the French resistance. An orphan indebted not to an adopted patriarch but to an aunt who passed the movie theater down to her [39:44], Shosanna is empowered to the point that she undergoes the opposite trajectory of the male patriarchs of *Pulp Fiction* and *Kill Bill*: in death she becomes an "acousmatic being," more than ever the matriarch of Le Gamaar theater.

The film opens on a confrontation between the "good" father (LaPadite, a Frenchman who hides Jews) and the "bad" father (Landa, aka the Jew Hunter), symbolically, one who produces a childrearing sustenance, milk, the other who greedily gulps it down [5:21].[44] Like Frank, the family slayer employed by a land speculator in *Once Upon a Time in the West*, a comparison that the title of "One Upon a Time ... in Nazi-Occupied France" invites, Landa is a cog in an overarching system: in his case, the Nazi state, headed by Hitler, who is portrayed not as an omnipotent disembodied voice, but as a quasi-hysterical leader in a frontal shot [24:13]. Like Landa, the other protagonists (Lieutenant Aldo Raine and the Basterds, Lieutenant Archie Hicox and Bridget von Hammersmark) also carry out the plots devised by military strategists. However, while the latter effect minimal adaptations to their orders in Chapter Five, Landa goes freelance and decides to "barbecue the whole high command" [148:05]—that is, murder the Nazi fathers. The final confrontation between Raine and Landa replays the opening scene, this time opposing not so much the good father and the bad father, but two sons who acted as castrators. The two officers have in common that they gleefully carry out their duties: Raine carves swastikas on the foreheads of survivors, has dead Nazi soldiers scalped, and officers like Sergeant Rachtman beaten to death [26:18–37:55]; Landa, even on the verge of betraying the Third Reich,[45] pointlessly murders Bridget von Hammersmark, who, as a traitor to the Nazis, is nothing less than his own double[46] [120:37]. By imprinting the mark of Landa's willing subjection to Nazi ideology on his forehead [148:54], Raine, the "good" officer who follows orders up to a point,[47] thwarts the "bad" officer's attempt to deny his heritage and reinvent himself as the destroyer rather than the defender of Nazism.

With eight male protagonists behind closed doors, *The Hateful Eight* revisits the closed all-male world of *Reservoir Dogs*, but introduces a female protagonist that turns out to be more than just a destabilizing element in a setting named after a woman. An object with monetary value, Daisy Domergue is initially the token by which John Ruth asserts himself as the main patriarch. Each chapter establishes, like clockwork, a new relationship between characters or sets of characters. Chapter One: between two patriarchs, the bounty hunters Ruth and Major Marquis Warren. Chapter Two: between the patriarchs and the "son of a gun," Sheriff Chris Mannix. Chapter Three: between Ruth and the strangers (Bob, Oswaldo, Joe Gage), and between the major and a third patriarch, General Sandy Smithers, whose son the major claims he raped and murdered. Chaper Four: following Smithers's and Ruth's deaths, Major Warren, the last patriarch standing, attempts to unmask the conspiring sons. Although the instigator of the plot to free Daisy turns out to be her brother Jody (Chapter Five), his immediate death leads her to try and overturn the only remaining father-son relationship, that between Warren and Mannix (Chapter Six). In this narrative of disclosure, Daisy goes from representing a mere disruptive element (her numerous outbursts and cackles) and an object of exchange (much like Marsellus's briefcase in *Pulp Fiction*)—in other words, a benchmark by which the male characters measure their virility by subjecting her and rival males—to being the perverse matriarch who kills Ruth [105:30] and speedily replaces her brother as the leader of the Jody Domergue Gang [144:27]. The situation whereby a matriarchy underpins—and undermines—patriarchy was foreshadowed by the fact that the way station in which the events unfold

(Minnie's Haberdashery) is gendered female, and by many of the patriarchs' androgynous names (Ruth, Sandy, Jody). Although characterized as a villain, the character of Daisy Domergue, like the "girls" in *Death Proof*, testifies to the violence (physical and verbal) patriarchy inflicts on women. The "witch" is clearly portrayed as a product of a violently misogynistic male environment. Named after the French revolutionary Jean-Baptiste Domergue (1754-1795), she gleefully witnesses—and indirectly effects—the steady demise of the male protagonists and resembles, in this respect, Shosanna, the Basterds, and Django who bring down the Third Reich and Candieland, respectively. The novelty of *The Hateful Eight* is that, more explicitly so than the end of *Kill Bill Vol. 1*, it imagines a matriarchy that is not ideal, but just as perverse as the patriarchy it contests, because it has been perverted by it and made just as hateful.

The films of Tarantino do more than just depict the workings of patriarchy; each narrative is knowingly grounded in a patriarchal structure that the film seeks to subvert as it does the film genres it taps into. Patriarchy is embodied by an alpha male whose omnipotence and omniscience are often conveyed through the voice, the gaze, and sheer physicality (Marsellus, Bill, Mike, Calvin Candie[48]). On a narrative level and on a metafictional one, the basic setup and genre originate in the patriarch.[49] Yet the patriarch is almost always (Schultz may be the exception) represented as flawed from the start, sometimes very much so (Cabot, Ordell, Landa, Hitler). These flaws (a mastermind with a bad memory or a Band-Aid on the back of his head, a voyeur who needs eyedrops) announce the fact that the narratives will relate the patriarch's momentary (Marsellus) or final (Cabot, Ordell, Bill, Mike, Hitler, Ruth, Smithers, and Big Daddy and Calvin Candie in *Django Unchained*) demise at the hands of the men and women he exploited economically and/or physically.[50] The first and most obvious evolution in Tarantino's films from *Jackie Brown* onwards has been the introduction of female protagonists who seek to overturn the patriarch (*Django Unchained* is the exception).[51] This evolution is more precisely one from a disruptive "feminine," and often homoerotic element (hinted at in Freddy's and Butch's names) that unconsciously undermines patriarchy, to a more deliberate female agent, a matriarch (Shosanna, Daisy) who can be endowed with the same powers as the patriarchs of the early films. The shift from a more symbolic to a more direct assault on the patriarch is especially obvious in the way *Death Proof* first repeats *Kill Bill* by punishing the female characters who willingly submit and propagate phallocentric discourses and practices, before proposing an alternative of revolt by teaming up against the oppressor and finding commonality in sheer pleasure rather than motherhood. So far, Tarantino's films seem to uphold the essentialist (but maybe, after all, realistic) view that, in the end, only women can truly bring down patriarchy. That Tarantino's female protagonists seem more successful at combining "masculine" and "feminine" features makes for strong, compelling characters. However, the implication that, in the male character, the "feminine" is ultimately a fatal flaw (Larry Dimmick, Ordell Robbie, Bill, John Ruth) and feminization is synonymous with emasculation (Stuntman Mike),[52] whereas in the female character the "masculine" is always an asset, seems to indicate that remnants of sexism and homophobia govern most of the narratives. In a sense, the female protagonists ultimately serve to rehabilitate "masculinity," reframed as female masculinity, which may explain why the female progatonists seem more successful at combining the two. On the diegetic level, though, the films work hard at deconstructing the gendered language and sexist rhetoric deployed by the characters in order to assert themselves through the violent subjection and/or exclusion of a female and/or feminine other.

Gender Rhetoric and the B-word: A Pragmatic Study Vol. 2

In *Reservoir Dogs*, Mr. Brown's opening analysis of "Like a Virgin" immediately establishes his and the other dogs' identity as heterosexual males in opposition to the "cooze" whose nymphomania is constructed through the iteration of the word "dick" [0:18–2:17]. Throughout the film, the characters refer to both gender and sexual identity mainly through the b-word. Mr. White's using the word "woman" when talking about waitresses in the diner [5:59] and his former partner Alabama [26:05] initially sets him apart from his younger colleagues as a more mature, more "human,"[53] and perhaps more "noble" gangster from a bygone era. Yet his use of the b-word to refer to a hypothetical woman giving him a hard time during a holdup [80:45] is symptomatic of the attitude of many of Tarantino's male characters—the insult serves to discursively contain a threatening female element. This tendency is confirmed in the Commode Story when Mr. Orange complains that his (fictitious) former girlfriend and partner (a double of Mr. White's Alabama) was taking advantage of him, leading him to rebel [66:28]. Given that the story acts as a pass for Freddy to get in with Cabot's team, the implication, here, is that it is compulsory for a male thief to construct himself in opposition to women; this is mirrored in the story within the story narrated by a police officer, who resorts to the b-word to designate another man's "girlfriend" [70:00]. Holdaway's subsequent use of the b-word when talking about Sue Storm of the Fantastic Four [71:20] ironically confirms that, when it comes to gendered discourses, male police officers are little better than the gangsters they infiltrate, so that calling women such names should come quite naturally for Freddy the undercover cop. In the ensuing discussion about the differences between black and white women that occurs in Nice Guy Eddie's car, Mr. Pink and Eddie not only disagree about the matter at hand, but do not use the same words to refer to women: the b-word (three times) and "women" (twice) for Mr. Pink, "woman" for Mr. White [73:43–74:17]. The paradox is that Mr. Pink, the same character who refused to tip the female waitress in the opening scene, is contending that black women are stronger than Mr. White would have it, so that, like Mr. White in the later scene, using the b-word serves to hold in check, at least in discourse, the possibility of female empowerment he is actually evoking.

It is significant that the discursive construction of women occurs in the flashback, for it is, along with racism and homophobia, one of the sediments of the white male gangsters' collective identity, something that enables them to bond as a group before the job, as when they laugh at Cabot's calling Mr. Pink a "faggot" [78:18]. Yet since the film's narrative structure reverses the order of events, at this stage, we already know that the construction of white heterosexual masculinity has failed, for the insults based on the b-word have up to now been targeted at male characters. After Eddie playfully calls Vic a "son of a bitch" in Cabot's office, Vic responds to his friend's suggestion that he would like to have sex with him after his time in jail in the following manner: "It might break you in, Nice Guy, but it'd make you my dog's bitch. [. . .] Eddie, you keep talkin' like a bitch, I'm gonna slap you like a bitch" [38:14–40:25].Here, the b-word serves to characterize homosexual sex as an essentially debasing and violent form of subjection that could compromise the white heterosexual male's integrity; this is confirmed when Vic calls Officer Marvin Nash a "son of a bitch" after slapping him, framing the act of torture as a repetition of his playful bout of wrestling with Eddie [51:41]. With the b-word, inferiority and subjection are posited as analogous to the female, but the fact that a man can also be a "bitch" shows the ease with which the hate word can just as easily serve to subject the female as the male, ultimately proving that the white heterosexual male's subject position is just as discursive as those he constructs as other.

The b-word follows a similar trajectory in *Pulp Fiction*. It is initially associated with the character of Jules, who uses it first when talking about pleasuring women [11:15], then when asking Brett whether he's trying to do Marsellus over [19:00], and finally when telling Pumpkin/Ringo to cool Honey Bunny/Yolanda down [136:40]. The first instance serves to limit the power of a woman whom a prostrate man is pleasuring (and is thus similar to Mr. Pink's and Mr. White's usage); the second confirms the flexibility of the position, while avoiding an overt reference to homosexual sex (and is thus similar to Vic Vega's usage); the third firmly subordinates Yolanda to her boyfriend Ringo (and is thus similar to the Commode Story usage). The final instance represents a desperate effort to shut out the destabilizing female element that, as we have seen, has repeatedly upset the all-male narratives throughout the film. That it is attempted by a character (Jules) who boasted he was the "foot massage master" before admitting he was deprived of meat because his girlfriend was a vegetarian—and thus that he subjects himself to her diet [15:40]—indicates that it was from the start compromised.

The foot massage conversation announces the destabilization produced by the introduction of the female protagonist, Mia Wallace, which is dramatized, notably, through a tension between the words "wife," "girl," and "bitch." It is announced during the conversation between Mia and Vincent at Jack Rabbit Slim's, when Mia asks for a rolled-up cigarette and mockingly calls Vincent a "cowboy," and he retaliates by calling his boss's wife a "cowgirl" [36:25]. The threat of seeing Mia as a "girl" is confirmed when Vincent takes her back home and she starts listening and dancing to a song called "Girl, You'll Be a Woman Soon" [49:03], announcing the potential breaking of the taboo. Ironically, the word will be drained of sexual connotations when Vincent uses it after she has overdosed [52:37],[54] repositioning himself as the babysitter employed by the patriarch. The precariousness of Mia's condition leads to discursive uncertainty regarding her status. On the phone, a panicked Vincent calls Mia a "chick," while Lance uses the b-word and the word "poof" [54:03]. This discursive uncertainty reaches a climax when Vincent drives onto Lance's lawn and tells him: "This fucked-up bitch is Marsellus Wallace's wife" [54:57]. In Lance's house, the instability is reinforced by the presence of a female character, Jody, who initially is of a mind to get rid of "that girl" and gets called the b-word in the process [55:28]. Jody's reaction thus provides an interesting counterexample to Tarantino's male characters—she does not feel the need to contain a threatening female character through the use of a hate word. The male protagonists all do, including the character (Jules) who is the site of a positive transformation from a racial perspective.

Jackie Brown also exposes the extent to which patriarchal discourses fashion women, mainly through the character of Ordell Robbie,[55] who alternates between the words "girl" and "bitch," and uses "woman" quite rarely when referring to, or talking about, the female characters. Initally, Ordell's use of these words seems to abide by the following taxonomy: the b-word would be a signifier charged with violence,[56] "girl"[57] with affection, and "woman" with neutrality. In a film with more female characters than *Reservoir Dogs* and

Pulp Fiction, the degree to which the male protagonist associates one word with a specific character says a lot about the nature of their relationship. The b-word targets Melanie specifically eight times, including to her face as early as the opening scene [9:56]; when Ordell explains her psychology to Louis, he presents it as one of her essential qualities, using the word as a verb after repeating the noun three times.[58] By comparison, Ordell reserves the b-word for Simone [93:49] and Jackie [123:17] after they have betrayed him and does not say it to their faces. The faithful Sheronda, on the other hand, remains a "girl" to the very end [131:25].

Both words, however, have in common a positioning of the female character in a subordinate role. Indeed, when Jackie turns the tables on Ordell and dictates her terms, he first addresses her as "girl" when trying to deceive her—"Oh, come on, girl, you know I was just playing wichoo"[59]—then as "woman" when finally accepting her terms—"Yeah, woman, damn!" [51:12]. The word "woman" is subsequently used to dramatize the fact that Ordell's attempt to get his money out of Mexico, an enterprise in which he relies on Jackie, turns into an all-out gender war. The first instance occurs when Jackie presents her plan and the need for someone to swap the money with her; Ordell answers: "Yeah, I'm thinkin' a woman" [66:17]. When he explains to Jackie how he subtly modified her plan during the test run, he finally discloses the accomplice's identity: "The woman you saw—was my friend Simone. She's the one gonna be receiving the money. I think she oughta see how the shit go down. She a nice woman. You'll *like* her" [92:43]. Finally, once Louis has described how the money exchange ended in Melanie's murder, Ordell concludes: "If you had to do it, then you had to do it, brother ... What we *don't* want is that bitch survivin' on us. Anybody but *that* woman" [121:00]. The term "woman" has evolved with each stage of the plot, going from "a" to "the" to "that," while the identity of the referent has changed since Melanie has replaced Simone. The apparently neutral word has undergone a journey in which it has, in Ordell's discourse, become an equivalent of the word "bitch," notably by the repetition of "that" which not only determines the noun, but allows, much like the b-word, the male enunciator to distance himself from its abject referent. In a sense, the fact that a host of deceitful females seems to be lurking under the alleged neutrality of the word "woman" is fitting retribution for a man who referred to his girlfriends as his "bitches" [76:17].

The Hateful Eight also explores the power of sexist patriarchal discourses, but the presence of a central female villain works to exacerbate it and push it to a breaking point. With the exception of English Pete's British usage of "cunt" to designate Major Warren [150:00], insults are clearly distributed along gender lines: Daisy is the "bitch," while males (Warren, the suspects,

Joe Gage, Jody) or generic groups (the Yankees or citizens of Red Rock) are "sons of bitches" [60:43, 83:10, 109:57, 118:16, 135:35, 149:18]. That the b-word is the common demoninator in most of the profanity uttered throughout the film identifies the abject as gendered female. As in Tarantino's other feature films, the use of words is indicative of the speaker's position. John Ruth, for instance, refers to Daisy as a "pepper" or a "girl" when being friendly [8:35], a "woman" when speaking about her in legal terms[60] [70:46], and a "bitch" when either beating on her [10:40] or designating her as a conspiring criminal [69:19]. This is made patent when Ruth first introduces Daisy to Warren in the stagecoach.

> WARREN: Who's this Daisy Domergue?
> RUTH: A no-damn-good murderin' bitch, that's who.
> WARREN: I can see you ain't got mixed emotions about bringin' a woman to a rope.
> RUTH: By "woman," you mean her? No. I do not have mixed emotions. [...]
> WARREN TO DAISY: But that, little lady—is why they call *him* the Hangman. [13:02–14:00]

Following Daisy's defilement of the Lincoln letter, Warren will follow in Ruth's stead, forbidding her to include herself in a category above her class: "You—ain't no goddamn—lady!" [20:27], systematically using the b-word [105:40, 117:52, 142:14, 146:01, 149:35], except when considering her as a "woman" from his suspects' point of view: "Now what charms this bitch got—make a man brave a blizzard, kill in cold blood? I'm sure I don't know . . . But John Ruth's tryin' to hang your woman. So you kill 'im" [109:25–109:45]. The trajectory of the b-word works in parallel with that of the n-word; opposing factions in Chapter Six will be divided according to whether they use one word or the other. The excessive repetition of the b-word works to violently fashion Daisy as an abject body, as Warren's final plea to Mannix suggests: "You gonna make a deal with this diabolical bitch?" [151:46]. Mannix's alignment with Warren is betrayed by his repetition of the b-word, his tone loading the word with contempt and disgust [144:40, 146:18, 153:43]. Linguistically speaking, misogynistic rhetoric overcomes racist rhetoric when Warren delivers the following sentence: "But there is one thing left we do have a say in. And that's how we kill this bitch" [157:30]. The use of profanity thus serves to dramatize the intricacies of gender, national, and racial tensions, and participates in a metafictional commentary on the difficulty to achieve satisfactory resignification politically speaking.

In *Kill Bill*, the use by Bill and Budd of more respectful language—they refer to the Bride as "that woman"[61]—may be accounted for by the fact that, although they are criminals not far removed from the gangsters of *Reservoir Dogs* and *Pulp Fiction*, unlike the latter, they work alongside strong women. The use of "that" seems to suggest the male enunciators are liguistically keeping the female character at bay because they are aware of how dangerous she is. Logically, then, the male characters who insult the Bride—Buck, the rapist and pimp [*Vol. 1* 27:15], and Ernie, who helps Budd bury her alive [*Vol. 2* 31:51]—are those who do not know what she is capable of and take for granted her inferiority. By calling her a "cunt" after she has defeated him[62]— yet another pathetic attempt to discursively contain a powerful woman—Bill proves that he is no different from Buck and that his previous show of respect was conditional to her being "[his] woman" [*Vol. 2* 109:12]; this lack of consideration was already patent in his brother Budd calling Elle the b-word when talking on the phone with her [*Vol. 2* 27:54]. In practice, Bill and Budd are not that different from their openly misogynistic predecessors.

The novelty in *Kill Bill* lies, then, in the use of gendered hate speech by the female characters. They repeatedly use the b-word in the heat of battle: Vernita, five times [*Vol. 1* 7:06–13:26], the Bride, four times [*Vol. 1* 11:52; *Vol. 2* 75:51, 106:36], Elle, three times [*Vol. 2* 76:47], and O-Ren, once in Japanese [*Vol. 1* 75:41]. The word is yet again associated with violence which it announces or concludes, in keeping with action film conventions. After poisoning Budd, Elle Driver sighs with regret: "That woman deserved better" [*Vol. 2* 69:45], implying that Beatrix merited a more honorable death and adversary, i.e., at the hands of a woman like herself. In so doing, Elle, whose name is the French equivalent of "she," constructs a group of valorous women who abide by a code of honor, in which she includes both Beatrix and herself by opposition to men like the sleazy and sneaky Budd. In so doing, she constructs her gendered identity by resorting to the same exclusionary process as the 1992 dogs, but she has inverted the value system by equating strength with femininity. Elle's comment in *Vol. 2* retrospectively illuminates the Bride's saying of all five Vipers, including Bill and Budd, in *Vol. 1*: "As I lay in the back of Buck's truck trying to will my limbs out of entropy, I could see the faces of the cunts who did this to me—and the dicks responsible" [35:00]. The pause in the sentence, on cue with the low-angle shot of Elle, Vernita, Budd, and O-Ren, allows for Budd to be momentarily included in the word "cunt," an association that is made all the more possible as he is presented as one of the DiVAS,[63] so that, like the b-word in *Reservoir Dogs* and *Pulp Fiction*, when the Bride insults the minister in *Vol. 2*,[64] an insult that is gendered female can be directed at a male character.[65] Significantly, this hesitation occurs when the heroine is in a vehicle belonging to the male character who first uttered the word to position her in abject submission. The Bride's subsequently insulting Bill and Budd with a separate word reinstates gender categories along power lines: the men are "responsible," the women are just executioners. With this in mind, Bill's parting insult can be seen as one last attempt to subject Beatrix by suggesting that she still belongs to the group of "cunts" he commanded and she combated.

Death Proof pursues the logic of *Kill Bill*, but takes it even further. At the Texas Chili Parlor, the language used to address and refer to the female characters divides the male characters into two groups. Dov uses the word "girls" when addressing Shanna [17:06], the b-word when explaining in a fairly aggressive tone to his friend Omar how they are going to get the female characters drunk to take advantage of them [23:21]. Stuntman Mike, by contrast, acts like a more gallant and mature man, describing Jungle Julia as a "striking-looking woman"[66] [29:47] and addressing the female characters as "ladies" [35:04,], significantly right after the latter have decided not to invite Dov and Omar. During the car chase in the second part of the film, however, Mike uses the b-word twice when assaulting Kim, Zoë, and Abernathy with his vehicle [95:34, 97:27], and only reverts to mock-gallantry once he believes he has subdued them, laughing: "Hey! Ladies! *That* was *fun*!" [98:02]. By resorting to the more polite word after raping their vehicle, Mike reveals what underlied his use of the word all along; like Esteban in *Kill Bill Vol. 2*, "lady" was just another word for "bitch."[67]

Like the female characters in *Kill Bill*, those in *Death Proof* use the b-word to talk about and address each other,[68] but the context is different: they do it when dissing each other playfully or occasionally as a frank insult—for instance, when Jungle Julia badmouths Pam [25:09]. Their use of it is thus similar to that of the n-word by some African Americans: the appropriation and resignification of a hate word serves to construct a sense of sisterhood. This potential is, however, tempered by the fact that not all the female characters utter it. Kim, Zoë, Abernathy, and Julia are the characters that use it the most (Kim, sixteen times; Zoë, four; the other two, three times each); Shanna only says it twice, Arlene and Lee not at all. The use of the word is thus intimately correlated to a character's power: Kim, Zoë, and Julia are the bossy characters, Arlene and Lee those whom their friends sacrifice. In this respect as well, the second group compares somewhat favorably to the first; whereas Julia's use of the b-word reflects her tyranny over her friends and is thus an instrument of subjection, its use by the three characters who slay Mike mirrors their empowerment as a group.

It also effectively destablizes gender norms. When Zoë tells the others that she would like to drive the *Vanishing Point* Challenger, she concludes: "If I can get this guy to let me drive it without him, I will blow the *doors* off that bitch!" [78:12]. Like the stereotypical male car aficionado, she feminizes the car, but a previous line reveals that she does so as both a man and a woman: "I want to drive a Dodge Challenger, fuck me swinging, balls out!" [76:21]. If "fuck me swinging" expresses amazement and "balls out"[69] the idea of driving fast, taken literally, the former places Zoë in a female position, the latter in a male position. The two are then conflated when, playing Ship's Mast, Zoë rides spread-eagled on the hood of the car, undermining the game's name (which phallicizes the player's body) [91:26]. Zoë's discourse announces what she does in practice: combine what are considered stereotypically "feminine" and "masculine" attributes. Kim's everyday usage of the word is also endowed with political potential when she constructs herself both in discourse and practice as the male killer's double by ramming him off the road: "Oh, don't like it up the ass, do ya, you redneck lunatic bastard! Oh yeah, bitch, I'm gonna bust a nut up in this bitch right now! I'm the horniest motherfucker on the road!" [102:37]. Not only does she redirect the violence-laden hate speech at the male character, but she positions him in both male and female positions in discourse and practice, invoking the same kind of homophobia that underpinned white heterosexual masculinity in *Reservoir Dogs*.

Death Proof further shows how contemporary American vernacular enables this blurring of gender lines when an individual says "guys" to address two or more people regardless of their gender. In all five instances where a female character uses the idiom, she does so to distinguish between herself and the other members of the group: Arlene when trying to break up a "fight" between Julia and Shanna [4:10]; Abernathy when she acknowledges that her friends think Cecil is "likeable" even if he cheated on her [69:48]; Zoë when she wants Lee and Abernathy to stay with Jasper as "collateral" [83:25]; and Abernathy twice when she feels "exclude[d]" from the "posse" she is supposed to form with Kim and Zoë [84:05]. Each instance is related to the idea of friendship, thus linking the semantic "gender trouble" to the generic "gender trouble" of a hangout movie with girls. Its being used more frequently in the second half of the movie participates in the construction of the three Final Girls as subversive "masculine-feminine" hybrids, as opposed to the first group who subject themselves to patriarchy. However, each instance also has the speaker using the phrase to extract herself from the group she heretofore belonged to. So although discrimination does not, here, operate along gender lines, it is nevertheless expressed thanks to an idiom that conveys the idea of gender difference. This function of the phrase is most apparent when used by a male character. "Look," Nate says to Arlene, "I know you guys are going to Lake LBJ and we can't come . . . I want to make out!" [21:33]. Ironically, he uses it to distinguish the girls from the guys who are excluded, confirming Eli Roth's joke that the latter are the girls' "bitches."[70] Arlene's telling Nate to "stop with the whine" constitutes him as a "mum" in her eyes, like Abernathy in Zoë's [83:59]. Exclusion is thus expressed in terms of gender, with the "guys" being the excluding group, the "girls" the excluded.

The importance of language in identity construction is emphasized as early as *Reservoir Dogs*, and as soon as the prologue when it comes to gender. Tarantino's dialogues pay as much attention to the part played by language in the construction of sexual and gender identity as racial and ethnic identity, and sometimes foreground the way they intersect. The main evolution in the treatment is directly correlated to the introduction of female protagonists as targets of such discourse in *Pulp Fiction* and *The Hateful Eight*, and as enunciators in *Jackie Brown*, and especially *Kill Bill* and *Death Proof*. A shift is thus operated regarding the level on which the film's gender politics are addressed, and thus regarding their visibility. While the female characters' use of language can have subversive potential, the potential is entirely the film's own when it deconstructs the male characters' misogynistic and homophobic use of language. For what the circulation of such words reveals is both their part in constructing the identity of the subject and the other, and the semantic instability that allows for deconstruction and subversion. Contrary to what the dictionary entry that opens *Pulp Fiction* might suggest, Tarantino's approach to language is pragmatic: his films insist on the varied uses of words and on their meanings in context. These circulations can sometimes be dramatized through the arcs of the characters (Mr. White in *Reservoir Dogs*, Jules in *Pulp Fiction*, Ordell in *Jackie Brown*, Bill in *Kill Bill*). Surface oppositions between hate speech and polite words ("girl," "lady," "woman" versus "bitch," "cunt," etc.) are undermined to reveal the gender and sexual violence underlying apparently neutral or even benelovent words ("woman" in *Jackie Brown*, "lady" in *Death Proof*, "Mademoiselle" or "Fräulein" in *Inglourious Basterds*).[71] In the end, the use of words ultimately says more about the male subject's social and/or racial[72] background than about his attitude toward women. Tarantino's portrayal of male film types reveals them to be quasi-universally sexist because the construction of their masculinity depends on the rejection of what is perceived as abject femininity and homosexuality. The only exceptions are Max Cherry in *Jackie Brown*, and Django and Doctor Schultz in *Django Unchained*. Schultz is more than just polite to Broomhilda von Shaft;[73] by informing her that she is now "a free woman" [123:00], after referring to her as Django's "lady love" [48:44] and addressing her as "Fräulein" [93:20], he recognizes that she is a free agent no longer subjected to slavery and even to Django and Schultz's more benevolent form of patriarchy.[74] Resignification is, thus, effected mainly in the utterances of the female characters, either by altering the emotional charge or the target of a gendered hate word (such as the b-word in *Death Proof*), but within certain limitations, for like the n-word, such words also perpetuate a relationship of domination-submission underlying the surface use (*Death Proof* is a case in point). It remains to be explored to what extent the representation of bodies equally participates in the destabilization of normative patriarchal discourses and practices.

Male Bodies, Female Bodies, Fetishization, and Punishment

Tarantino's films address Mulvey's thesis concerning the fetishizing and/or voyeuristic male gaze of mainstream cinema conjointly with an attention to a fetishization of genre icons that uphold traditional masculinity and femininity. As genre icons with their compulsory getup and paraphernalia, all the characters are potential fetishes. This is especially the case of the male characters of *Reservoir Dogs*, *Pulp Fiction*, *Django Unchained*, *Inglourious Basterds*, and *The Hateful Eight*. With their black suits, white shirts, and thin black ties, the dogs, who resemble both Siodmack's killers[75] and the Rat Pack,[76] call on a hard-boiled white[77] masculinity largely indebted to film *noir*. In the opening credits, they are, for a mere minute, portrayed as the epitome of cool and even fetishized through the use of slow motion, which enhances the spectacular quality of their movements by matching their stride to the rhythm of the song [7:37–8:38]. The film then shows them struggling to maintain a professionalism that is synonymous with their appearance and attitude. Mr. White asks Mr. Orange, whose white shirt is now bloody, to be a "tough guy" [11:10], encourages Mr. Pink to "be cool" and "take a break," before splashing water on his own face and combing his hair (fig. 18) [17:16–22:24]. Mr. Orange's wounded body in particular emphasizes the loss of composure, notably in the extreme close-up of his wound when Larry undoes his belt [11:55]. By contrast, Mr. Blonde appears cool as a cucumber when he makes his entrance in the warehouse, leaning against a pole and drinking his soda in a medium full shot [31:50], then head tilted à la James Dean as he slowly takes off his Wayfarers in a three-quarter close-up (fig. 19) [32:05]. The irony, of course, is that the character who embodies the epitome of cool masculinity is the psychopath who murdered a young black woman and will soon torture a young white man.

Fig. 18: *Reservoir Dogs*: After the disastrous robbery, Mr. White regains his composure by taking care of his look.

Fig. 19: *Reservoir Dogs*: Mr. Blonde, the epitome of cool and sadism.

The potential homoeroticism of male-on-male violence is announced, first, by the conflation of wrestling and prison sex when Nice Guy Eddie and Mr. Blonde squabble, their entangled bodies momentarily shot in close-up [39:11], then by the song lyrics ("You promised me the day that you'd quit your boyfriend") that can be heard in the scene where Mr. White, Mr. Pink, and Mr. Blonde beat up and gag the police officer [44:24]. Though Mr. Blonde is clearly the common denominator, these scenes do suggest that other male characters share the potential for deriving homoerotic pleasure from violence. This reaches a climax in the torture scene. The latter is framed by comments where Mr. Blonde makes a mockery of romantic love—"Alone at last," he says, taking off his jacket [50:27]—and then asks the officer after cutting off his ear: "Was that as good for you as it was for me?" [54:44]. The close-up that shows him reaching for his razor blade inside his cowboy boots tilts up to the same kind of three-quarter close-up as when he took off his

Wayfarers, establishing a direct link between his homicidal tendencies and his cool demeanor [52:28]. After watching the other men work the cop over, Mr. Blonde performs a dance of seduction in a POV shot from the cop's perspective that follows an extreme close-up of the victim [53:38]. Mr. Blonde then straddles Officer Marvin Nash to cut off his ear, and the camera tracks left to relegate the act offscreen [54:15], as it will during the execution of Mr. Orange [91:27]. Mr. Blonde then tosses the ear behind him and, frowning with disgust, wipes the blood off on the officer's uniform [54:51]. The gesture that concludes the first part of the torture session harks back to the moment preceding the act when Mr. Blonde examined Mr. Orange's wound [53:30]. The connection between the blood from Freddy Newandyke's belly and that from the police officer's wound suggests that, in the eyes of Mr. Blonde, both imply the abject loss of masculinity—dependent on the uniform associated with the roles (cops and robbers) in a genre film—and, in a patriarchal worldview, the entry into another category: femininity. That is, the category Mr. Orange entered from the moment he answered Mr. White's question "Who's a tough guy?" in a falsetto wail [11:10]. The male genre characters' bodies are thus the site where identity politics are played out. The force of attraction these cool iconic figures exert, the cinematic metafiction reveals, is constituted by the very elements it attempts to repress: femininity, homosexuality, blackness.[78]

The three stories in *Pulp Fiction* also focus on how chance (an overdose, a kidnapping, an accidental murder) leads three sets of genre icons (a heterosexual couple, a boxer and a gangster, and two hitmen) to lose their composure and get sullied. All the characters are fetishized from the outset. Butch, the boxer played by an action movie star, and Marsellus, played by a former boxer, are determined by characteristics typical of 1980s hypermasculinity: hard bodies, with bald heads or crewcuts.[79] Marsellus's body is highlighted in the backshots analyzed above, while Butch's fit body is often bared: in the back of a cab, his skin glistening with sweat after the fight [67:54], and later in the hotel bathroom [77:50]. Impeccably dressed, with hairstyles that recall 1970s blaxploitation and *Saturday Night Fever*, Jules and Vincent are shot in a lengthy three-quarter close-up as they converse in the car [6:55], then in a frontal two-shot in the elevator [10:03]; later, Jules, like Mr. Blonde, cooly drinks a soda from a straw in a low-angle close-up [16:30]. The male protagonists' cool masculinity is akin to the dogs'. Indeed, "The Bonnie Situation" reprises the premise of Tarantino's first film—the two killers bloody their car and matching suits[80] [111:27]—but takes it to comic lengths, as they end up getting hosed down (a fairly benign form of castration) and dressed like the college students they murdered (yet another fairly benign form of punishment) [124:06]. With Tarantino playing Jimmy, the film reflexively points to the director's project of sullying and stripping the genre icons of what makes them such: their clothes and cool demeanor.[81]

The fetishization of genre icons is *mise en abyme* in the Jack Rabbit Slim's scene. The restaurant, as Ortoli has shown, is inhabited by cinematic ghosts: "[T]his horizon of ghosts is the very context of Tarantino's films, a referential backdrop that both contains and stifles the characters, since it places them in a genealogy deprived of original assignation and specific models, with the certainty that they cannot escape their destiny of resembling someone."[82] By entering the restaurant and especially performing on stage, Mia and Vincent become, like the restaurant employees, ghostly replicas viewed from a distance (Vincent of Travolta's famous roles of the 1970s). This potential was announced by the frontal shot that tracked up the glistening hood of Vincent's red Chevrolet before stopping on a two-shot of Vincent and Mia [32:54], suggesting they were already the iconic teen couple of *Grease* (albeit an aging one) in a fancy convertible before they even sat at the Chrysler table in the restaurant [34:58]. Significantly, Mia and Vincent's date ends on an identical frontal two-shot of them in the Chevy, which undoes their status as icons and confirms the reality of their bodies by showing Mia's weary and Vincent's angry faces after the night's events [58:41]. The transformation from genre icon to bodily subject is grounded in two opposing portrayals of drug use. The music video quality of Vincent's joy ride is debunked by the more naturalistic overdose scene. In the first, the heroin injection is eroticized through the combined use of close-ups and a soft focus textures, while the close-ups of Vincent indicate that the drug's pleasurable effect merely reinforces his cool composure; all this is underscored by the surf music drowned in a spring reverb that conjures up the pleasure of dulled senses [29:06–30:12]. Significantly, the music fades out when Mia ODs, suggesting that the party is over [51:59–52:15]; the soundtrack is then made up exclusively of ambient sounds, the shouting and ringing phones standing out against a backdrop of wind and chirping crickets [52:18–58:40]. Extreme close-ups are now used to show the dangers of drug use—the blood running out Mia's nose as she loses consciousness [51:59], the foam oozing out her mouth[83] [52:18]—culminating in the series of extreme close-ups (of Mia's face, the needle, Lance, Vincent, the red mark on her heart, Jody, Vincent), combined with zoom-ins or rack-focusing, during the resuscitation scene [57:57–58:12]. In the end, Mia and Vincent's story is a cautionary tale in which the "feminine" and "masculine" genre icons, sex, drugs, and rock 'n' roll (and even cars for that matter) have all been drained of their erotic potential.

Imprisonment and rape fulfill the same function in "The Gold Watch" as Mia's overdose in the preceding story, that of revealing the bodily subjects

Fig. 20: *Pulp Fiction*: Marsellus and Butch now share a two-shot, as Maynard brings out the Gimp behind the green door.

under the cool iconic surface. The similarity is emphasized by the use of a fade-to-black to mark the turn of events [52:15, 99:41]. The next scene opens on a frontal two-shot of Marsellus and Butch, side by side, on their knees, tied up and wearing black leather ball gags [93:48]. The sexual perversion is contained in the back room, which can be glimpsed in the background of the frontal two-shot and singles of the two victims (fig. 20) [95:37]. It is embodied by the Gimp, a living fetish who sleeps in a box waiting to be taken out, and whom Zed treats like a piece of furniture, tapping his fingers on his head [96:29]. A prisoner like Butch's father, the Gimp is the gold watch's living, perverse double: a fetish of, and a metaphor for, masculinity. Ironically, then, Butch's quest for the patriarchal fetish has led him to become a potential sex object, a double of the Gimp who keeps an eye on him and whose subjection is emphasized in low-angle shots [98:16]. Although the slow-motion full shot of Zed closing the door fetishizes the moment when Marsellus is taken into the back room, and can thus be seen as a manifestation of the racist unconscious underlying the narrative, the narration, as in *Reservoir Dogs*, turns away from the rape that is kept behind closed doors and overheard exclusively on the soundtrack [98:03]. Butch and Marsellus's revenge will return the sexual violence that was inflicted on them, Butch selecting a samurai sword among a series of castrating tools (hammer, bat, chainsaw) [99:40], and Marsellus shooting Zed in the groin [102:03]. Faced with abject sexual violence, the boxer and the gangster now stand united, in a slightly low-angle medium full shot, as twin figures of masculinity, the black and white hero of 1980s Hollywood action movies [102:00]. The apparent salvation of hard-bodied masculinity is, however, tempered by a female undercurrent that contests the power of the penis: Butch's girlfriend Fabienne, who requests "oral pleasure" [79:45], and Jody's claim that piercings can queer the female body, potentially "turning every part of your body into the tip of a penis" [26:25].

In *Django Unchained* and *The Hateful Eight*, the racial violence discussed in the previous chapter is highly sexualized and equated with rape. The 2012 film, as Nama has noted, "insists on highlighting the sado-erotic subjugation of African slaves."[84] The Speck brothers [4:15], the Brittle brothers [33:37], and Billy Crash [135:05, 138:50] all wield phallic objects (rifles, whips, guns, knives) that they direct at female and male bodies alike; the dogs ("Marsha and the bitches") Mr. Stonesipher unleashes on D'Artagnan are avatars of the monstrous-feminine,[85] which is emphasized by the use of slow motion [83:37]. Crash's verbal threat to Django—"Oh, I'm gonna go walking in the moonlight with you"—sounds like a romantic overture, an interpretation confirmed by Django's response: "You wanna hold my hand?" [74:53]. The perverse romance is played out in the scene where Billy comes close to neutering the bounty hunter. It opens with an oblique full shot of Django hanging by his feet from the ceiling, naked, the high-angle and the lighting drawing attention to his feet and testicles [137:30]. A subsequent close-up tracks down his back, the scars a testimony to the numerous whippings he received as a slave, then pivots clockwise to end on a quasi-frontal close-up of his face wearing a mask [137:35], similar to the one Old Man Carrucan made him wear before selling him off [24:59]. This brief moment in which the camerawork, costume, and staging fetishize the hero's body connects his current vulnerability to his past condition and anticipates the sexual violence that awaits him. In many ways, the scene revisits the torture scene in *Reservoir Dogs*. Like Mr. Blonde, who also wore cowboy boots, Billy gracefully struts about, takes off his jacket, rolls up his sleeves, speaks in a soothing tone of voice [138:22]; and like Mr. Blonde, Billy utters phrases one would associate with a more benevolent situation, such as a doctor cooing a patient or a child: "Calm down, now, here it comes" [138:57]. The camerawork and Billy's body language give away his sexual investment in the act of castration: he is framed by Django's legs, first in medium full shot [138:40], then in medium close-up [138:56], and when Billy picks up the blazing knife with his right hand, his left hand is significantly resting on his belt [138:49]. As in *Reservoir Dogs*, however, the narration distances itself from the act by cross-cutting between the characters' faces and utilizing lateral and back long shots to show Billy with his hands on Django's genitals [138:56–139:40].

The pleasure of the white aficionados of Mandingo fighting (Calvin Candie, Amerigo Vessepi, and presumably others) is also shown to be at least partly sexual. Calvin demands his fighter Big Fred act as a castrator, straddling his adversary and gouging out his eyes before finishing him off with a hammer [66:16–66:58]. Calvin then rewards Big Fred with a drink and sexual favors—"You find him a room with a soft bed," he says to Leonide Moguy, "then you bring him up a pony to lick his pole"—in a three-shot where Fred's bloody bare chest is framed by the two clothed white men; Calvin sucks on his cigarette as he looks over Fred's body before stepping up to the fighter and saying almost affectionately: "You enjoy that, boy. You've earned it" [68:13]. Stephen confirms the predominantly sexual nature of white people's fantasies of black bodies when he steps in seconds before Billy neuters Django, even going so far as to suggest that it gets in the way of rationally coming up with effective forms of punishment: "Seem like white folk ain't never had a bright idea in their life is comin' up with all kinds of ways to kill your ass. Now, mind you, most of them ideas had to do with fuckin' with your fun parts" [140:21].

Django's vengeance will lead him, like Marsellus and Butch, to castrate the white men (Billy and another slaver) before killing them, but he does not seem to derive any sexual pleasure from it [152:27, 156:50]. Not so Major Warren who, in *The Hateful Eight*, describes the act of raping and murdering General Smithers's son in graphic terms in order to make the latter draw [87:15]. Warren's sadistic delight in telling the story (his emphasizing the words "pecker," "dingus," "johnson," "big," "warm," and "throat"), and allegedly in doing the deed itself, is emphasized by the fact that the analeptic shots of him laughing as he rapes Charles Dexter are framed by medium close-ups of him smiling at the father [92:25–93:20]. However, it is uncertain whether the story is true, as Sheriff Mannix keeps reminding the general [89:56, 91:10], and whether Warren's sexual pleasure is sincere. Both the tale and his performance are contradicted by the visual distance established by the narration, which only resorts to very long and long shots (fig. 70.1), and, in the end, by the businesslike fashion with which he dispatches the Confederate general, whom he could have just as easily toyed with instead [94:45]. In other words, by playing the part of the sadistic hypersexual black patriarch, Warren may just be giving the racist white man a taste of his own medicine, as the comparison he makes between the rape and the general's treatment of black Union soldiers whose "uniforms" he "chose not to acknowledge" in Baton Rouge suggests [93:47]. In any case, the revulsion the black castrator inspires is sufficiently potent for Jody, the double of the (closet) racist spectator, to aim not just to kill the black man but, like Billy Crash in *Django Unchained*, castrate him, his mixing English and Spanish—"Say adios to your huevos"—recalling that Warren's first victim was American, the second Mexican [118:26]. The narration refuses, however, to cater to the narrative's racist revenge by depicting the act from a vertical high angle.

Fig. 21: *Jackie Brown*: Jackie calmly going to work at LAX in the opening credits, a shot that refers to *The Graduate* (Mike Nichols, 1967).

We have seen that Tarantino's female-centered films are not interested in deconstructing femininity the way the male-centered films deconstruct masculinity; rather, they seek to deconstruct the phallocentric view of femininity and explore the empowerment of the female protagonists. They endeavor to position the latter as subjects of the gaze and the voice, not as passive fetishes or guilty recipients of violence. The opening credits of *Jackie Brown* are, for instance, programmatic in that they announce how the film is going to tap into the persona of Pam Grier [0:22–3:48]. Walking at a steady gait with her chin held high, Jackie is associated with class, cool, determination, energy, self-assurance (fig. 21).[86] The tracking shots are subordinate to her movement which they highlight. The fourth and fifth shots—a low-angle lateral long shot and a low-angle frontal medium full shot—make her stand tall amongst the crowd, emphasizing her steady gait and elegant bearing [2:09–2:25]. Though it maintains the lateral angle, the final close-up seems to contradict the initial medium shot by revealing a more vulnerable side of the character: Jackie's confident look has made way for anxiety because she is running late [2:42–3:33]. By moving from right to left (against the crowd in the fifth shot), the film suggests she is striving to go against the flow of time.

The qualities foregrounded are those that Pam Grier's persona has maintained since the blaxploitation years. They remain tied to physicality, only the focus is no longer on youthful hypersexuality—*Coffy* and *Foxy Brown* feature nude scenes with Grier—but on an aging body. The film refuses to exploit the heroine as a sexual object. By comparison, the other characters are much more fetishized. A variation on the black and/or female entertainer

Fig. 22: *Jackie Brown*: Melanie uses her legs to sow discord between Louis and Ordell.

of classical Hollywood cinema,[87] Simone is introduced "doing her show" for Louis, in an extreme frontal close-up of her face, before later shots reveal her blue glitter dress [23:37]. Even Ordell, as we have seen, shows more skin than Jackie; the fetishization of his body is largely a consequence of the character's stylishness, thus reinforcing his association with "feminine" stereotypes. So the erotic potential of the black body is, to some extent, displaced onto the male villain.

The film's main sex object is, of course, Ordell's white girlfriend Melanie. Throughout the movie, she wears bikini tops, tank tops, and cut-off shorts that display her tan, fit body [62:25, 73:19, 91:42]. Her body is fetishized from the outset in the opening scene, making her a double of the "Chicks with Guns" (dressed in bikinis and seen in close-ups, medium shots, and medium full shots) that is being watched on videotape by Ordell and Louis [4:03]. Her bare knees and feet first appear in a back close-up of Louis and Ordell in which the latter asks her for more ice. She then appears in a medium backshot bringing the two men their drinks, then in a three-quarter medium close-up that foregrounds her face and knees as she lies back on the couch, and finally in a series of frontal close-ups of her feet, toes, and face [5:03–6:10]. By cutting back and forth between these shots of Melanie's body and lateral close-ups of Louis looking at and away from her, the film introduces the gaze of the male character, who is trying hard not to be distracted, while the extreme frontal close-up of Melanie's knowing look at Louis confirms that that is exactly what she is trying to do: use her body to get between the two men, as the subsequent full shot of Louis and Ordell with Melanie's knees in the foreground confirms (fig. 22) [6:59].[88] Later scenes in Melanie's apartment often portray her laying down on the sofa, as if offering her body to Louis [7:02, 64:43, 98:27], which she eventually does [67:55]. In short, Melanie, like Simone, is putting on a show for the male character, in her case in an attempt to get him to betray Ordell.

The fetishization of Melanie's body also participates in the central theme of aging. Although a contrast is established between the white woman's younger body and the older black women's bodies (Jackie and Simone),[89] an opposition that mirrors the higher value Ordell places on white bodies, the film insists that even Melanie is growing old. After Melanie informs Louis she was fourteen in a photo of her in roller skates, the dissolve linking the extreme close-up of the photo and the medium full shot of her behind the counter marks not an ellipsis in the narrative but the symbolic passing of time [65:48]. She may be the same height, as she tells Louis who thought she looked "at least sixteen" in the photo, but she isn't, as Ordell admits to Louis, "as pretty as she used to be" [77:24]. Significantly, the film insists on the theme of aging at the very moment when her body is most exploited. The lateral medium shot of Louis and her having sex facing left recalls Jackie's facing left during the opening credits, the older male partner's heavy panting drawing further attention to the contrast between his age and her youth [68:04].

The correlation between the body and aging is confirmed in the way Jackie Brown is framed. Interestingly enough, the moments where the camera draws closer to her, and thus comes closest to fetishizing her, are often those that depict her awareness of the state of her life and its relation to time: the fifty-two-second-long frontal close-up of Jackie while Mark Dargus reads her file before concluding that she "didn't exatly set the world on fire" [29:07]; the forty-three-second-long zoom-in when she confides to Max that she "ain't got nothing to start over with" [59:34]; the extreme close-up of her asking Max whether he wouldn't be tempted by the money [84:00]; the shot/reverse shots of Jackie, combined with yet another slow zoom-in, sadly examining her reflection before effecting the money exchange in the changing room [105:29]; and the final close-ups (again with track-in or zoom-in) when Jackie and Max part ways [146:35, 147:56, 149:00]. The black and white women, though in appearance opposed notably by the self-loathing gangster, are all embodiments of the passing of time and function—in this respect, like Mr. Orange in *Reservoir Dogs*.

Jackie Brown relates the story of Jackie's attempt to gain some control over her life in spite of her body. Her endeavor to do so is dramatized in her relation to clothing and makeup, no doubt as a reaction to the traumatic loss of control over her body that imprisonment entails.[90] Indeed, the second time we meet Jackie begins like a continuation of the first, with her leaving the airport [27:33]. However, because she gets arrested, she ends up trading one uniform associated with her official job (the stewardess outfit) for another that is a consequence of her illegal activities (the prison suit) [33:50]; when Max invites her for a drink after picking her up at the county jail, she tells him she wants to go to a dark place "because it looks like [she] just got out of jail" [43:32]. In the second act where Jackie concocts her plot, Jackie wears specific clothes for specific occasions: more "feminine" clothes (a blue gown [77:40], a red dress [95:09]) when meeting Ray Nicolette who may "ha[ve] a thing for" her, as Max suggests [81:16]; casual streetwear (a purple jacket [69 :35], a black tank top [79:06]) when meeting Ordell; and even more casual clothes (a white bathrobe [53:34], blue overalls, and a white T-shirt [96:28]) when meeting Max at home. Her outfits reflect her view of her relationships: seducing the detective, meeting the gangster on equal terms (they even wear the same brand of hat [79:06]), and opening herself to Max. Hence, the decisive spot of the money exchange: Jackie's transformation from rags to riches is effected after she trades her uniform for a classy business suit that she will wear through the end of the movie, significantly facing left yet again in her stewardess uniform and looking at a blonde model wearing the suit [104:49]. "I mean you wear that suit to a business meeting and you'll be the badass in the room," the saleswoman says as soon as Jackie steps out of the changing room in the new suit [105:11]; Melanie will also approve of the "nice outfit" [110:26]. Unlike in *Coffy* and *Foxy Brown*, then, Jackie's ability to change outfits does not provide excuses for the film to shamelessly exploit her body, but it does, as in the blaxploitation films, remain a sign of her empowerment.

Shosanna Dreyfus's clothing is used to similar effect in *Inglourious Basterds*, but her empowerment is more radically tragic than Jackie's because it requires her death; it is also less ambiguous, as her plot is not one of personal gain but a heroic feat. In Chapter Three and in the flashback describing the elaboration of her plot, she is portrayed with no makeup, her hair down, and dressed in dark, very casual, almost "masculine" clothes (pants, coat, shirt, hat) [38:28, 41:48, 46:48, 61:34, 107:20], the very opposite of Goebbel's "French interpreter" Francesca Mondino, whom Shosanna pictures, an insert suggests, being exploited sexually [49:31]. Chapter Five opens, however, with a music video sequence that fetishizes her in a series of three push-ins from long shot to close-up: motionless, wearing a red dress, her hair done up very much like Bridget von Hammersmark[91] in Chapter Four, Shosanna has made herself over into a movie star (fig. 6) [105:47–106:29], a Danielle Darieux lookalike, according to Marcel [116:20]. As Sharon Willis beautifully puts it, "[i]n its luxurious fetishization of feminine masquerade, this sequence clearly recalls countless film *noir* femmes fatales."[92] Yet her presence next to the eye-shaped window belies the impression that she is a submissive object of the gaze; on the contrary, she is shown looking over the Nazis unwittingly gathered in the Jewish female space that is her movie theater (unlike Mia Wallace, she is not a usurper) [109:20], before she becomes the giant face looking back at the Nazi audience (fig. 13.1) [143:20]. Shosanna has become the German star/spy's double whose name is visible on a movie poster outside;[93] significantly, it is shortly after von Hammersmark dies that Marcel compares Shosanna to the French movie star. Indeed, Shosanna first appears in elegant matching hat, suit, and skirt [72:27], and at the movie theater in a black hat with white fur and flowers in her hair [111:08], and is associated with two stereotypical fetishes: her lost shoe and the red kiss she imprinted on the napkin she autographed for the newborn Maximilian that is only shown when Landa discovers it, both clues that will give the iconic star away to the SS officer [104:52]. Shosanna is then shown putting on makeup like war paint (red lipstick like Bridget's), in a montage of close-ups that recalls 1980s action hero gearing-up scenes as in *Commando* (Mark L. Lester, 1985), especially as it matches the upbeat rhythm of Bowie's song [106:30–107:18]. Like Jackie's, Shosanna's outfit is part of her plot: the iconic hyper-feminity masks a strong, masculine-feminine individuality, the red she wears symbolizing the blood of her enemies concealed under the desire she inspires in Frederick Zoller. Her final transformation into a giant face, enabled by the black costumes she wears in her and Marcel's film, speaks of a will that is stronger than death; it is also the victory of the disembodied female voice denied by classical cinema over the fetishized female body imposed by it.

Kill Bill relates the story of the patriarch's downfall at the hands of one of his women, a drama of fetishization and punishment that leads to empowerment and that is centered on a battle to control the gaze and the voice, evidencing a clear influence of feminist film studies in the way it paradoxically comments on Oedipal subject positions, as Mark T. Conard (2007) has convincingly shown. Both installments open on the Bride on the brink of death, with a high-angle frontal close-up of her bloody face gazing offscreen at Bill, whose voice dominates the soundtrack [*Vol. 1* 0:59; *Vol. 2* 0:35]. In *Vol. 1*, the gender positions established in the prologue are reinforced by the lateral tracking shot of Bill's cowboy boots that iconize the male character, and by the lateral medium shot of the dead Bride in the opening credits [3:55]. In *Vol. 2*, however, the prologue is followed by a proleptic frontal medium shot of the Bride driving a car and explaining her plan to the viewer; she is still fetishized, as her impeccable hair and makeup and the slow track-in indicate,

Fig. 23: *Kill Bill Vol. 1*: Vernita Green and the Bride strike the pose, as Nikki comes home from school in the background.

but now it is as a genre icon [0:53]. More than just a reminder of the basic premise, then, the repetition of the prologue insists on the transformation the Bride has undergone in *Vol. 1*: she has both fashioned herself and taken charge of the narrative.

Because Chapter One is proleptic, when we next meet the Bride, the transformation has already been effected. The gaze is now associated with the female characters who recognize each other on Vernita's doorstep. The superimpression of the extreme frontal close-up of the Bride gazing at Vernita and her other tormentors draws attention to the difference between her positions as past victim and present aggressor [5:38]. Neither the costumes nor the camerawork sexualize Vernita and the Bride in the subsequent fight scene. On the contrary, they are fetishized as martial arts icons in a lateral medium full shot that highlights their stylized postures (fig. 23) [7:00], in a manner similar to the lateral long shots of the Bride and Pai Mei training side by side in *Vol. 2* [52:59]. In death, Vernita becomes the object of the Bride's gaze, emphasized by the low-angle, but the absence of eyeline match (Vernita's face is shot in a frontal close-up) suggests that the Bride's empowerment is not at the cost of her adversary's fetishization and dehumanization[94] [13:04].

Chapters Two to Five relate how the Bride will reach this state of empowerment. Chapter Two opens, quite humorously, by establishing the equation between the gaze and the male patriarch, through the shot of the sheriff's sunglasses lined up on his dashboard [16:06]. The shot/reverse shots with eyeline match position Sheriff McGraw in the classic role of the gaze, the dead bride in that of the object, stances that are reinforced by the high and low angles [18:02]. In the hospital, the Bride is then subjected to the gaze of a rapist (Buck) and his client, a power relation that is yet again dramatized through the shot/reverse-shot technique and the low-angle two-shot of the men [26:43]. Both times, the Bride awakens and immediately contests the male gaze: by unintentionally spitting in the sheriff's face [18:48], and later by killing her rapists. *Kill Bill* repeats the *Reservoir Dogs* strategy of panning away from the violence so that all we hear are the rapist's screams, only to reveal the exact nature of the act (the Bride is tearing his tongue out) in a subsequent lateral medium close-up [28:14]; the moment of Buck's death is, likewise, fetishized through the use of slow motion, this time in a close-up that tracks down his body before the Bride cuts his ankle in an extreme close-up [29:09]. In the aptly named Pussy Wagon, the Bride proceeds to regain control over her body. While potentially fetishistic, the close-ups and extreme close-ups of the Bride's feet and toes dramatize, as the eyeline match indicates, her endeavor to command her body, her will being metonymically represented through her gaze [32:27]. It is here, Conard argues, that "The Bride begins to transform herself from pussy, the receptable, to cock, the one in charge and in power."[95] The narrative of O-Ren Ishii's past tells a similar story of assumption of the gaze and the power to castrate. Initially, she represents what Clover would call "abject terror personified,"[96] with her wide-open eyes in extreme close-ups as she witnesses the death of her parents from under a bed [33:57, 37:55], but a subsequent extreme frontal close-up reveals eyes filled with the fire of revenge that demand recognition from the patriarch, much like the Bride's on Vernita's doorstep [39:28]. Though she remains subservient to Bill, her command of the gaze and phallic weapons enables her to execute people for a living, as the POV shot through the scope shows [41:35], before taking over the Tokyo underworld where she decapitates a male yakuza who disrespects her [60:23].

The final showdown is framed by the Bride's mastery of the gaze; it is intimately correlated to the phallic Hattori Hanzo swords that act as mirrors to see herself and her adversaries [50:32, 79:13]. The shot/reverse shots of her looking at Sofie Fatale from behind her mask, which frame the scene, underline the change in position: the two driving their vehicles filmed at eye-level [64:15], the Bride looking down at her one-armed messenger in her trunk in high and low angles [96:54]. As for Marsellus, Django, and the Basterds, revenge is equated with castration; the Bride gouges Gogo's eyes [77:07], severs the Crazy 88's limbs [82:31], cuts a boyish swordfighter's sword into bits before spanking him [84:15], and ultimately stands, with her crotch forming a frame-within-the-frame, over Johnny Mo below, in a high-angle long shot [85:20]. For the showdown, all the characters are fetishized as genre icons, the camerawork tracking over their vehicles [62:11] or singling out their *Reservoir Dogs* suits and Kato masks in the music video scene that references the opening credits of Tarantino's first film (fig. 24) [64:48]; slow motion is

Fig. 24: *Kill Bill Vol. 1*: O-Ren, Gogo, Sofie Fatale, and their minions coolly entering the House of Leaves restaurant, in a pastiche of the opening credits of *Reservoir Dogs*.

repeatedly used to emphasize the characters' movements and poses [82:26]. During the final duel, O-Ren moves slowly and gracefully, the fight getting underway only after she daintily slips out of her shoes in close-up [87:52]. Like Vernita but unlike Sofie, O-Ren is not subjected to the gaze of the Bride, who walks away after her foe has fallen [93:14]. At the end of *Vol. 1*, the Bride, Conard argues, has become alienated from femininity.[97]

Kill Bill Vol. 2 relates in parallel her attempt to reclaim her femininity and the patriarch's failure to regain dominion over the Bride, which is foretold in the opening prolepsis. In Chapter Six, she is subjected to her former lover's ambiguous desire; he acknowledges that he is "looking at the most beautiful bride these old eyes have ever seen" [6:51] and asks if he can "watch" the wedding rehearsal before the massacre [12:01]. In Chapter Seven, she is subjected to Budd's frustration at seeing his own status as a genre icon (a cowboy and former assassin) "emasculated"[98] by his boss and a female employee named Rocket (also a blonde) who makes him clean the toilet [18:30]. He immediately discards the black hood that made the Bride a genre icon (this time a ninja [23:14]) to turn her into the horror movie female victim, her hands, feet, bloody face, and eyes (like the young O-Ren) shot in close-up and extreme close-up [29:47, 32:50, 34:50]. In Chapter Eight, Beatrix is subjected to the "cruel tutelage" of Pai Mei, yet though she practices under his watchful eye [52:08, 52:39, 53:09, 53:17, 53:58], and though Bill describes Pai Mei as a misogynist, the power relation between the master and his disciple is not gender-biased—the chapter's second scene proves Bill has been subjected to the same treatment [42:13], while the outcome of her fights with Elle and Bill show that she has been taught techniques (the eye plucking [76:37] and the five-point-palm exploding heart technique [113:46]) the other disciples haven't. With Budd the cowboy gorily dispatched, the female characters (Elle and Beatrix) emerge as the last genre icons standing, alternately fetishized and sullied (Elle's face is stuffed in a toilet) during their battle, most climactically when, like Vernita and O-Ren in *Vol. 1*, they strike the pose, facing each other sword in hand in close-ups that zoom-in and are edited in shot/reverse shots [74:07–76:23]. The enucleation of Elle's remaining eye is "symbolic of her blindness to her servitude to a masculine conception of power, and to Bill, her master."[99]

The final chapter shows two male patriarchs—Bill and Esteban Vihaio, significantly played by the same actor as Sheriff McGraw, the first man to have been assaulted by the resurrected Beatrix—trying to subject her to their voices and gazes, often dramatized in shot/reverse shot [79:44, 98:10]. Conard rightly notes that their fight locates the power in the female: "If the sword has all along symbolized the penis and the power it represents, then the sheath is symbolically the vagina, and consequently the pussy overcomes the cock in this fight, the woman, *as woman*, defeats the man."[100] In the end, Bill at least partly acknowledges Beatrix's power by asking, "How do I look?" He recognizes the talent, look, and judgement of the woman who has brought him down [115:03], but remains a speaking subject. As at the end of Chapter One, Beatrix's empowerment comes at the cost of Bill's "look," i.e., his status as male genre icon, now sullied by the blood in his mouth, but not at the cost of another's selfhood. As Heidi Schlipphacke notes, Beatrix has gone beyond rape-revenge: her "mode of killing her beloved does not attempt to replay the brutal acts of violence committed against her [. . .] Rather, this method of killing performs the internal nature of violence, revealing the pain of loss that all violence causes."[101]

The influence of feminist film theory on *Death Proof* is even more explicit and was acknowledged by Tarantino in interviews. The credits open on a close-up of an anonymous girl's feet on the dashboard as the actresses' names roll: all the "girls" are condensed in this fetishistic representation of a female body part cut off by the frame (fig. 25) [1:10]. However, the presence of a pair of sunglasses on the dashboard to the left, which references Sheriff McGraw's sunglass-cluttered dashboard in *Kill Bill Vol. 1*, is proof that the female characters are equally associated with the gaze. The second shot, which tracks in to follow Julia as she walks away, starts as a high-angle close-up of her feet, then tilts up over her body as, naked but for her underwear, she slips on a T-shirt, pulling her lush mane[102] through the neckline; it then pans right as she lies down on her sofa and lights up a water pipe, in a position similar to Brigitte Bardot in the giant black-and-white poster hung on the wall above her [1:53]. The subsequent close-up of the Jungle Julia doll with the protagonist in the background parodies the fetishization of the DJ's body,

Fig. 25: *Death Proof*: The first shot of the opening credits introduces the feminist film theory notions of fetishization (the bare feet) and the gaze (the sunglasses).

its grotesquely comical features defusing her sexiness, while its inexplicably shaking head seems to mock the voyeuristic viewer [2:09]. Paradoxically, it is an object that seems to be returning the gaze, a parodic substitute of a female sex object.

The fourth shot introduces the anonymous male killer as a gaze in a semi-POV shot through his windshield [2:14]. It is followed by yet another fetishizing close-up of Julia's body, this time with her feet in the foreground and a poster of *Soldier Blue* (Ralph Nelson, 1970) in the background [2:45]. Depicting a naked Indian woman tied up in rope facing a charging cavalry with her back to the viewer, the *Soldier Blue* poster, like that of Bardot, mirrors the fetishization of Julia's body, which is also seen from behind. But the reference to a movie where a female protagonist (Kathy) supporting the Cheyenne against the US Army utlimately leads a male protagonist (Honus) to change his mind about the conflict encourages a reappraisal of the female character's power. If the camera fetishizes Julia, its initial position in the second shot (on the floor) recalls that of her male worshippers. The various camera angles, in effect, suggest very ambiguous power relations. Inserted between the fetishizing shots of Julia's body, the shot through the windshield seems to construct the male gaze as a destructive force directed at the female bodies, yet it is not a POV shot, unlike the shot of Julia's feet. The narration thus calls into question the alignment between camera and character, while at the same time, suggesting that the female character has internalized the male gaze to which she is subjecting herself. A new crane shot moves slowly over Julia's buttocks, back, and head until it tilts down to focus on her two friends, Arlene and Shanna, crossing the street in a high-angle establishing shot that is now practically aligned with Julia's gaze. Following Arlene's announcement that she has "gotta take the world's greatest piss" [2:57], her crotch and

Fig. 26: *Death Proof*: A POV shot of Abernathy and Lee unwittingly dancing the French cancan, as Stuntman Mike takes pictures of them.

feet are subsequently filmed in a low-angle medium shot, followed by three close-ups [3:07]. Like Julia's, Arlene's body is fragmented and fetishized, her face (and thus metonymically her subjectivity) relegated offscreen. What with her hand covering her crotch and cupping nothing, she is a parodic image of Mulvey's "bleeding wound," allegedly capable of provoking castration anxiety in the male viewer. However, just as much as Julia and especially Mike, Arlene is a body whose movement the camera submits to and is, in this respect, empowered.

Clearly, the opening credits announce how self-conscious the film is about the generic and theoretical framework (the slasher has often been described as catering to the male spectator's scopophilia)[103] the devices it exploits are grounded in, to the point of parody. This is confirmed by the end credits which alternate between photos of mannequins, real persons, and the actresses goofing around on set and looking straight at the camera, as if mocking the fetishizing and voyeuristic potential of the camera gaze [109:47]. The rest of the film develops the terms established in the opening credits and eventually resolves them. The male stalker and the camera eye merge in a POV shot through the viewfinder when Mike takes pictures of the second group of girls; by freezing their movements, the photographer aims at annihilating their potentially disruptive movements (fig. 26) [65:33]. The camera gaze, spectator, and maybe even the director[104] are explicitly targeted as the killer's accomplices when Mike grins and stares right at the camera before driving off to kill the girls (fig. 30) [45:00]. Just as the lap dance warms Mike up for murder, the spectator gets to enjoy several gratuitous scenes of the girls dancing. Yet the medium close-up of Julia dancing also reveals Omar, who is compared to Mike in the very scene where his views on Julia are exposed, watching her in the bottom righthand corner [15:23].[105] This shot portrays both the female object of the gaze and the male "bearer of the look" in a variation of the classical Hollywood dance scenes Mulvey had in mind. Another scene of Arlene dancing by herself raises expectations concerning the prize lap dance [28:28]. These expectations would be thwarted were it not for Mike, who derives pleasure from consuming female bodies, notably the parts fetishized in the opening credits: he gets the lap dance [39:12], licks Abernathy's feet sticking out the open window of the car [60:25], and leans over to get a better look at Pam's mangled body, a literal embodiment of "the bearer of the bleeding wound,"[106] the eyeline match aligning the camera with the killer [47:39]. The car crash results in one of Julia's legs getting torn off [51:16], the very body part the film and billboards fetishized. In acting out his sexual and/or sadistic drives directed at the female body, the killer's function seems to be to fulfill the male spectator's desires by proxy, and thus to confirm Mulvey's and Linda Williams's[107] theses.

Death Proof also fulfills another male voyeur fantasy: that of seeing how women act in intimate situations when men are not around. The camera's interest in Arlene's need to relieve herself is echoed in the second part of the film, when Lee tells her friends about her "pervert" boyfriend's fantasy to "watch her pee" [67:11]; the fact that his name (Toolbox) recalls the slasher movie *The Toolbox Murders* (Dennis Donnelly, 1978) confirms the equation the film establishes between the male voyeur and the horror genre. Some scenes are set in intimate locations (Julia's apartment, Shanna's and Kim's cars), but the narration also creates filmic spaces of intimacy. When Julia is shown texting Christian Simonson in a nook of the Texas Chili Parlor, her intimate space is reinforced both visually (she is singled out in a close-up) and aurally (by one of the film's rare instances of non-diegetic music) [17:23]; the scene is "reassuring" because the cocky tomboy reveals a more vulnerable (i.e., "feminine") side of her personality. Yet the moments of intimacy in the second part of the film contest the equation between gender and camera, or gender and space. During the diner scene, for instance, the camera (in close-up) circles around the girls as they talk (fig. 35), creating a gendered space that is reinforced by the presence of the male killer in the background, yet the fact that this space is constructed visually in the same fashion as in the diner scene in *Reservoir Dogs* indicates that it is the presence of the characters that make the gender, not the technique [71:50]; the same can be said of their conversation in the car which uses similar angles as the scene in Nice Guy Eddie's car in *Reservoir Dogs* [66:35]. Yet another moment of intimacy calls into question the viewer's "masculinity," in spite of the equation between male and gaze the film has hammered in. Before the stuntgirls Zoë and Kim play Ship's Mast, the long shot of them kneeling down emphasizes the distance that separates them from viewers who ignore what Kim has in mind when she says she doesn't "wanna do it" [88:23]. This time, however, the spectator (regardless of her/his gender) is potentially excluded not from the "feminine" but from the "masculine" character of their conversation. As such, the position of the spectator unfamiliar with the daredevil game is mirrored in the heretofore more "feminine" Abernathy, the "mum" who was left waiting in the car [83:59].

Abernathy's initiation[108] in stuntperson ways comprises three stages: (1) sacrificing Lee, and thus the ideal icon of white femininity; (2) trading fear for elation; and (3) beating the male stalker to death. The frontal close-up that slowly zooms in to an extreme close-up of her face seems to depict the awakening of Abernathy's "masculinity" [92:05]. Yet this is contradicted by the final outcome, where the use of the freeze-frame fixes the female characters' powerful bodies in action [108:52]. Not only does it echo the photographs taken by Mike—they are fetishized no longer as passive sex objects but as action genre icons—but the use of retro special effects represents a symbolic retaliation against the sophisticated visual effects the first group of girls was subjected to—slow-mo replays that enable the sadistic viewer to enjoy each girl's death in detail, the artificiality of which was highlighted by the fact that each girl seems to be alone in the car when she dies [51:04–51:25]. The final freeze-frames repeat this by highlighting that, like the women in *Faster Pussycat! Kill! Kill!*, the three girls take as much pleasure in beating Mike to death as in playing Ship's Mast. In the first part of the film, the film resorts to jump-cuts meant as homages to both the poor quality of grindhouse projection and the French New Wave, but that also parodically invoke the psychoanalytic thesis that the cut resolves the drama of castration in a "suture."[109] Significantly, the first and last of these jump-cuts involve fetishizing shots of the female characters (Julia [3:27], Arlene [41:58]), as if inflicting violence on the female bodies. Thus, *Death Proof* encourages more than the mere "cross-gender identification" offered by the slasher; it proposes a queer position which, like the finale of *Kill Bill Vol. 2*, celebrates the power of femininity. Abernathy's "feminine" talent for dancing the French cancan ultimately enables her to deliver the coup de grâce (fig. 27) [109:37].

The Hateful Eight describes a similar, albeit more grotesque, metamorphosis in the character of Daisy Domergue from the iconic Southern Dame to the equally iconic Witch. While the narrative dramatizes her transformation into a "diabolical bitch" effected linguistically through the male characters' words, the narration sheds a more ambivalent light on the villain. Daisy is, from the start, subjected to John Ruth's brutal violence—the butt of his gun [10:36], his elbow [14:33]—every time she calls into question his authority,

Fig. 27: *Death Proof*: Abernathy, now one of the stunt people, delivers the coup de grâce thanks to her flexible body.

with the sound of the blows amped up according to action movie conventions. When she looks up as Warren laughs, Daisy, in medium close-up, meets Warren's gaze, licks her bloody mouth, winks, and looks out the window, the white light reflecting off the snow making her "shine"[110] (fig. 28), as actress Jennifer Jason Leigh puts it [14:55–15:39]. While the character's reaction shows that she is much tougher than the "apple blossom" in the song, the tone and title of the White Stripes' song participate in conjuring up the image of a more complex Daisy Domergue. Ironically, it is because Ruth senses the existence of a more "feminine" Daisy, the one singing the ballad, that he falls into the siren's trap after complimenting her on her performance [101:02]. The narration portrays her as an abject witch when, like the title character of *Carrie* (1976), she is sprayed in blood [105:11], but like her predecessor, the "apple blossom" transpires even under the bloody mask, especially in the fetishizing extreme close-up of her smiling affectionately at her brother Jody (fig. 29) [143:03]. The "monstrous-feminine" is just as clearly the product of patriarchal discourses and practices as the Southern lady,[111] as her being chained to the arch-patriarch John Ruth throughout the movie suggests. She is a convenient scapegoat through which masculinity can be affirmed across racial and regional lines, a troublesome element that needs to be both punished and subjected to the sadistic male gaze in a macabre "dance," as Warren puts it [109:41]. If there was any doubt concerning the major's sexual pleasure in the death of Charles Smithers, it is utterly assumed in the hanging of Daisy which he "want[s] to watch," the two men lying breathless and spent after the climax. Far from defending misogyny, *The Hateful Eight* concludes, pessimistically no doubt, that the birth of an interracial nation comes at the cost of rejecting others, be they women, Mexicans, or homosexuals. Indeed, it is hard not to see Daisy as the body through which the two men sublimate

Fig. 28: *The Hateful Eight*: Daisy Domergue, after getting elbowed in the face by Ruth, grins and winks at Warren before licking her bloody mouth.

Fig. 29: *The Hateful Eight*: Daisy smiles at her brother Jody seconds before Warren blows his head off.

their homosexual desires, as in the movies of David Cronenberg,[112] especially since Warren connects both Charles Smithers and Daisy Domergue when he threatens to "pour this whole pot of [poisoned] coffee down that bitch's goddamn throat" [117:53]. It is hard to imagine a world, the film seems to say, where subjecthood can be effected without the violent abjection of an other.

The films of Quentin Tarantino are by no means cynical; they take identity politics very seriously. They are highly self-conscious of the gendered and racialized terms of the film genres they rework, of the history and historiography of representations in film and cultural history. Fashioned from film genre conventions and intertexual references, the characters are presented as genre icons. On the surface, their cool fetishization reeks suspiciously of postmodern nostalgia and straight white male appropriation. By celebrating genre characters as icons through stylization and yet critiquing them—an approach that recalls both the early Godard and Leone, two directors whom Tarantino has aknowledged as major influences—the films seem to be trying to have things both ways, as Gavin Smith noticed early on: "Far from succumbing to easy cynicism, Tarantino achieves the remarkable feat of remaining a genre purist even as his films critique, embarass, and crossbreed genre."[113] This ambivalence toward the source material is as true of Tarantino as it was of Godard and Leone. Yet the iconization of such figures is more than just a reflexive laying bare of the artifice: in highlighting their articiality and thus their constructiveness, it sets them up for deconstruction. The iconization is thus integral to the metafictional discourse. The films actively work to undermine the seductive male figures by sullying them (*Pulp Fiction*) and/or by revealing the misogynistic, racist, and homophobic violence they conceal (all the films). Indeed, the sexual undercurrent of violence is emphasized through images of rape (*Reservoir Dogs, Pulp Fiction, Death Proof, Inglourious Basterds*,[114] *The Hateful Eight*) and castration (*Kill Bill, Inglourious Basterds, Django Unchained, The Hateful Eight*), for the predominantly white male figures have been constructed through the exclusion of various abject figures of otherness in both discourse and practice.

The female and the feminine, in particular, threaten to destabilize the hegemony of patriarchy. This chapter has confirmed the argument made in the previous one: that the films side with the protagonists with the greatest potential to transform and not remain subjected to the same genre conventions, a potential that is often reflected in the characters' changing costumes (Jackie Brown, the Bride, Shosanna, Django). The white male is less ripe for transformation, perhaps, because he has the most to lose—the character of Chris Mannix in *The Hateful Eight* is, in this respect, an interesting development, but it is effected at the expense of the female element. These cinematic metafictions also strive to imagine an alternative to the white male hegemony of genre films. Largely influenced by feminist film theories about the centrality of the male gaze and voice, *Kill Bill* and *Death Proof* interrogate the possibilities of female empowerment; the films warn of the danger of trading the male/female binary for a masculine/feminine that would ultimately safeguard the privileged value of masculinity, a phenomenon I have observed in contemporary horror remakes influenced by post-feminist discourses.[115] They endeavor to imagine a more specifically female form of empowerment that wouldn't be a mere usurpation of male codes. In terms of gender politics, at least, *Death Proof* represents the end point of this project; after proposing a dialectic whereby the gaze is alternately male and female, it avoids the essentialist, albeit parodic conclusion of *Kill Bill Vol. 2* and opts for a queer position whereby the power of the female victors is grounded in a mix of "feminine" and "masculine" qualities.

All this ties in to what Ortoli says about the protagonists' capacity to master the rules of the game: "knowing the rules and excelling in applying them are the main qualities of the Tarantino hero,"[116] for whom "self-creation is re-creation."[117] Mastering these rules does not mean submitting to them; it requires a degree of agency and aims not at perfect imitation but resignification. The deconstruction of genre icons does not just involve a critique of their politics; it is also effected through an emphasis on the mortal body, whether it be wounded (*Reservoir Dogs*, *Pulp Fiction*, *The Hateful Eight*) or aging (*Jackie Brown*), suggesting that hegemonic politics are violently inscribed on the bodies of the excluded, explicitly in the antebellum South, more insidiously for a black working-class woman living in 1990s Los Angeles. What the films ultimately address, then, is the gap between icon and subject, image and body, re-representation and representation (i.e., our constructed identities), in a metafictional dialogue between fictions as cultural constructs.

The films of Quentin Tarantino prove that metafiction need not be ahistorical or apolitical. On the contrary, they espouse a view of film genre and language that is based on the idea that these discourses and practices are not set once and for all, that they vary according to their uses in context, and that they are rife for resignification. In short, it is a view that is resolutely pragmatic and that is very much in tune with contemporary discussions of identity politics. The films prove both the validity of theories of intersectionality by foregrounding the complexities of identity and identity politics. The recognition of the relevance of such theories is—in the case of *The Hateful Eight*, at least—also a recognition of how far we are from achieving an ideal crossroads, the reconciliation of two opposites inevitably entailing a sacrificial scapegoat. The homoerotics of the film's climax point to what I see as the main limitation in the discourses on identity politics in Tarantino's films: their shying away from sexuality. In such a diverse cinematic world, the absence of LGBTQ characters is conspicuous, even if Mark T. Conard suggests that Hattori Hanzo might actually be in a homosexual relationship.[118] And the fact that the combination of feminine and masculine traits is presented as a viable option for the female characters but never for the male characters constitutes male homosexuality as the ultimate other. Clearly, the option is not desirable to the macho characters, and naming Bruce Willis's character in *Pulp Fiction* "Butch" is obviously a nod at his unacknowledged femininity. But it remains uncertain as to whether it is simply a matter of the queer position's being more difficult to attain for the white male heterosexual—a valid argument in a time when white supremacy discourses are particularly ferocious—or whether Tarantino himself is uncomfortable with the subject, just as he is clearly uncomfortable with sex in general.

CHAPTER FOUR

"REVENGE IS NEVER A STRAIGHT LINE"

A Neoformalist Approach Vol. 1: Narrative Structures and Paradigms

Tarantino's storytelling strategies drew immediate attention with his very first film. Writing for the *Sunday Telegraph*, Anne Billson had this to say:

> Essentially, this bloody chamber piece is a heist movie, but debut writer-director Quentin Tarantino (who also plays a minor role) tampers with the chronology and turns it into a post-mortem. We start off with a pre-robbery breakfast, skip to the aftermath of the bungled job, and then—while the survivors are trying to work out what went wrong and whether one of them is an undercover cop—the film fills in vital information via an assortment of flashbacks. This is an ambitious structure, but Tarantino pulls it off with panache.[1]

Emmanuel Levy believes that the complex narrative structure of *Reservoir Dogs* inspired movies like *Bulletproof Heart* (Marke Malone, 1994) and *The Usual Suspects* (Bryan Singer, 1995).[2] In *Film History*, Kristin Thompson and David Bordwell suggest that, though Robert Altman, with *Short Cuts* (1993), had successfully returned to the network narrative form of his earlier film *Nashville* (1975), *Pulp Fiction* was the film that really triggered a trend of more adventurous storytelling in American cinema of the late 1990s, including films like *Magnolia* (P. T. Anderson, 1999) and *Memento* (Christopher Nolan, 2000).[3]

This chapter proposes to analyze the narrative structures of each film in order to identify general trends and evolutions in Tarantino's storytelling strategies. Grounded in a structuralist and neoformalist methodology indebted to Genette, Thompson, and Bordwell, it seeks to go beyond the identification of formal features in order to demonstrate that these structures are not just playful. As the above quote from *Kill Bill Vol. 1* suggests [97:56], they pertain to main themes, and participate in characterization and even the metafictional discourse. Hattori Hanzo's voice-over accounts for the obstacle-filled journey the Bride has undertaken and, in so doing, reflexively justifies the scrambled narrative structure of *Kill Bill* as ultimately underpinning the character's motive and the film's most obvious theme, already present in the title. Uttered by a character named after both a historical samurai and a character from a 1980 Japanese TV series, *Shadow Warriors*, that starred the same actor (Shin'ichi Chiba), the words are also revealing of the complex network of influences that inform Tarantino's films, and particularly, as we shall see, his approach to narrative and narration. Finally, by appearing to comment directly on the images (the Bride is writing her death list in a plane with a sword holder and a very artificial-looking sky in the background) even though the subsequent shot shows they were spoken during her stay in Okinawa before Hanzo ceremoniously handed the sword over to the Bride [102:06], his words draw attention to the artificiality of the narration and thus contribute to laying bare the artifice. This chapter will focus, first, on the use of titles, then on the relationship between the narrative structures and classical and art-cinema paradigms, and finally on the relationship between the actual story (in chronological order) and the narrative—what the Russian formalists called *fabula* and *syuzhet*[4]—with special attention to Tarantino's varied approach to the flashback. The arguments put forth are largely based on analyses of the tables that follow.

Narrative Structures

	RESERVOIR DOGS	
Structure	**Chapter Titles / Timing**	**Events**
Prologue	[0:15–7:46]	Joe Cabot's team meets up in a diner before the heist.
Opening credits	[7:47–9:30]	They head for their cars.
Act 1	[9:31–25:39]	Mr. White, Mr. Orange, and Mr. Pink meet in the warehouse after the heist which has gone wrong. Mr. Pink suspects a rat is among them.
	Mr. White [26:40–28:24]	Mr. White's backstory: a longtime friend of the Cabots, he used to work with a woman named Alabama; Joe Cabot and Mr. White talk about the details of the diamond heist.
Act 2	[28:25–37:55]	Mr. White and Mr. Pink decide to wait in the warehouse till Nice Guy Eddie finds a solution. Mr. Blonde arrives. Mr. White and Mr. Pink initially suspect him, but he clears himself by showing he's taken a police officer hostage.
	Mr. Blonde [37:56–45:42]	Mr. Blonde's backstory: he's just gotten out of jail, is also close to the Cabots, and enthusiastically accepts to take part in the heist.
Act 3	[45:43–63:58]	After beating up the cop, Mr. Pink, Mr. White, and Nice Guy Eddie take off to get rid of the cars. Left alone, Mr. Blonde tortures the hostage and is killed by Mr. Orange who turns out to be an undercover cop.
	The Commode Story [63:59–87:12]	Mr. Orange's backstory, as well as that of the entire operation.
Act 4	[87:13–95:28]	Mr. Pink, Mr. White, and Nice Guy Eddie return, shortly followed by Joe Cabot, who reveals Mr. Orange to be the rat. Knowing that Mr. Orange killed a civilian, Mr. White refuses to believe this. A Mexican standoff ensues: the Cabots die. Mr. White kills Mr. Orange who confesses he's a cop, while the police encircle the warehouse outside. Mr. Pink's fate remains unknown, although it is likely he gets arrested.

PULP FICTION

General Structure	Chapter Titles / Timing	Substructure / Timing	Events
Prologue (end of Story 1)	[0:30–4:49]	Start of Act 4	Pumpkin and Honey Bunny decide to rob a diner.
Opening credits	[4:50–7:05]		
Story 1	[7:06–21:08]	Act 1	Jules and Vincent, two hitmen, kill a group of college students who have tried to outsmart their boss Marsellus Wallace.
Story 2	"Vincent Vega & Marsellus Wallace's Wife" [21:09–60:59]	Act 1 [21:09–34:12]	After dropping off the suitcase at Marsellus Wallace's club, Vincent gets some drugs at his friend Lance's, then picks up Mia Wallace.
		Act 2 [34:12–49:56]	They eat and dance at Jack Rabbit Slim's.
		Act 3 [49:57–54:48]	Vincent takes Mia back home and decides to resist temptation and go home, but she ODs.
		Act 4 [54:49–61:04]	Vincent takes Mia to Lance's, and they manage to save her.
		Epilogue [61:05–63:29]	Vincent and Mia part ways.
Story 3	"The Gold Watch" [63:30–110:38]	Prologue [63:30–68:06]	Captain Koons gives the young Butch Coolidge his dead father's family watch.
		Act 1 [68:07–82:37]	Although Marsellus has ordered him to lose a fight (at the end of Story 1), Butch wins a fight and the money he bet on himself in the process (after Story 2).
		Act 2 [82:38–93:52]	The next morning, Butch realizes his girlfriend Fabienne has left his watch in their apartment and goes back to get it. He kills Vincent there.
		Act 3 [93:53–102:07]	He then runs into Marsellus who chases him, but the two men are then captured by Maynard and Zed, who intend to rape and murder them.

		Act 4 [102:08–109:35]	Butch manages to free himself and decides to save Marsellus. In return, Marsellus grants him a reprieve so long as he leaves LA.
		Epilogue [109:36–110:38]	Butch and Fabienne drive off together.
Story 1	"The Bonnie Situation" [110:39–149:47]	End of Act 1 [110:39–115:10]	Replay of the scene where Jules and Vincent execute Brett and the others from Marvin's point of view.
		Act 2 [115:11–117:07]	Vincent accidentally shoots Marvin in the car. Jules turns to his brother-in-law, Jimmie Dimmick, for help, but Jules's sister Bonnie is coming home soon.
		Act 3 [117:08–133:21]	The Wolf is called in to help them solve the problem. He tells Vincent and Jules how to clean everything up and get rid of the car.
		Act 4 [133:22–149:47]	At the diner from the prologue, Jules decides to change his ways. He starts by sparing Pumpkin and Honey Bunny.

JACKIE BROWN		
Structure	Chapter Titles / Timing	Events
Opening credits	[0:02–3:51]	Jackie, at the airport, late for work.
Act 1	Hermosa Beach, California [3:52–27:32]	Ordell, a gun dealer, goes to bail bondsman Max Cherry to get one of his employees (Beaumont) out of jail and eliminate him so he won't talk.
Act 2	Parking lot, Los Angeles International Airport [27:33–84:14]	Jackie is arrested by Ray Nicolette and Mark Dargus. Feeling threatened by both Ordell and the ATF, she decides to turn the situation to her advantage and comes up with a plot to get Ordell's money.
Act 3	Money exchange trial run. [84:15–98:48]	The characters rehearse Jackie's plot.
	Money exchange for real this time. [98:49–103:24]	The actual exchange is effected and seen from three points of views.
	3:52 p.m. [103:25–109:30]	(1) Jackie buys a suit and warns the cops something went wrong.
	4:12 p.m. [109:31–114:03]	(2) Ordell's team, Louis and Melanie, take off with the wrong bag, and Louis murders Melanie.
	4:04 p.m. [114:04–119:43]	(3) Max takes off with the money.
Act 4	[119:44–144:26]	The aftermath: Ordell escapes after killing Louis. Jackie and Max trap Ordell; Jackie gets Ray to kill Ordell.
Epilogue	Three days later. [144:30–150:13]	Jackie and Max kiss and part ways.

KILL BILL VOL. 1

Structure	Titles	Chronology / Timing	Events
Prologue		[0:40–2:27]	The Bride tries to tell Bill about her child before he shoots her.
Opening Credits		[2:28–5:07]	
Act 1	Chapter One 2	[5:08–16:08]	The Bride visits Vernita Green. They fight but stop when Vernita's daughter comes home. The two propose to end it elsewhere, but Vernita throws a knife at the Bride, who then kills her. We see her cross Vernita's name off a list where O-Ren Ishii's names has already been crossed off.
Act 2	Chapter Two The Blood-Splattered Bride	[16:09–25:12]	On the crime scene, the police realize that the Bride is still alive. Bill sends Elle Driver to the hospital to finish her off, but at the last minute calls it off.
		Four years later. [25:13–35:09]	The Bride wakes up from her coma. She escapes after killing a nurse named Buck, also a rapist who sold her body to other rapists. In Buck's pickup, she then concentrates on regaining control of her legs through willpower.
	Chapter Three The Origin of O-Ren	[34:10–44:04]	The Bride explains that O-Ren is the head of the Tokyo underworld. An anime then tells the story of how O-Ren's parents were murdered before her very eyes and how she went on to avenge their deaths and become an assassin herself. The Bride is then shown getting beaten up by O-Ren and the other members of the DiVAS during the El Paso massacre.
		[44:05–45:01]	The Bride succeeds in wiggling her big toe.
		Thirteen hours later. [45:02–45:13]	The Bride then flies to Okanawa, Japan.

Act 3	Chapter Four The Man from Okinawa	[45:14–58:39]	The Bride visits Hatori Hanzo in order to ask him to make her a sword. He accepts.
Act 4	Chapter Five Showdown at the House of Blue Leaves	[58:40–98:27]	While the Bride as narrator introduces O-Ren's associates, the Bride goes to Tokyo. In the restaurant, the Bride kills or maims the Crazy 88, Go-go, Johnny Mo, and finally O-Ren.
Epilogue		[98:28–103:18]	The Bride spares Sofie Fatale, as a message to Bill and the other Deadly Vipers.
			The Bride is shown writing the list before visiting O-Ren; Budd is shown speaking to Bill, Elle to Budd on the phone, the Bride to Bill before the massacre.

KILL BILL VOL. 2

Structure	Titles	Chronology / Timing	Events
Prologue		[0:14–0:46]	The Bride tries to tell Bill about her child before he shoots her.
		[0:50–1:40]	The Bride informs the viewer that she is driving to meet the last person on her list: Bill.
Act 1	Chapter Six Massacre at Two Pines	[1:58–14:10]	Bill and the Vipers murder everyone at Beatrix's wedding, leaving her as good as dead.
Act 2	Chapter Seven The Lonely Grave of Paula Schultz	[14:14–37:37]	Having been warned of the Bride's intentions by his brother Bill, Budd strikes a deal with Elle Driver to sell her the Bride's Hanzo sword, captures the Bride, and buries her alive.
Act 3	Chapter Eight The Cruel Tutelage of Pai Mei	[37:38–55:11]	After telling her of the kung-fu master, Bill takes Beatrix to his former master Pai Mei, who takes her on as a disciple.
		[55:12–63:06]	Beatrix calls on Pai Mei's lessons to escape the grave.
	Chapter Nine Elle and I	[63:07–74:42]	Elle purchases the Bride's Hanzo sword and kills Budd with a snake. Meanwhile, Beatrix walks to Budd's trailer.
		[74:43–77:54]	Beatrix Kiddo and Elle fight in the trailer; Beatrix plucks Elle's remaining eye out after the latter admits having poisoned Pai Mei.
Act 4	Last Chapter Face to Face	[77:55–117:11]	After visiting Esteban Vihaio to find out Bill's whereabouts, Beatrix fails to surprise Bill, who introduces her to their daughter B. B. Mother and daughter share some quality time before Beatrix and Bill fight.
Epilogue	Next Morning	[117:10–118:54]	Beatrix and B. B. watch TV in a motel room.

DEATH PROOF

General Structure	Chapter Titles / Timing	Substructure / Timing	Events
Opening Credits	[0:55–3:21]		Arlene and Shanna drive to Jungle Julia's. Meanwhile, an invisible driver is on the prowl.
Part 1	The City of Austin, Texas [3:22–55:47]	Act 1 [3:22–14:56]	The three young women hang out in their car and in a Tex-Mex restaurant called Güero's, where Julia reveals to Arlene that she owes the first man to recite a poem to her a lap dance.
		Act 2 [14:57–22:18]	The three girls meet three boys (Dov, Nate, and Omar) at the Texas Chili Parlor, as well as a fourth girl (Lana Frank).
		Act 3 [22:19–41:59]	The stalker, Stuntman Mike, turns up, interacts with the young people, recites the poem to Arlene and wins the lap dance.
		Act 4 [42:00–51:40]	Mike murders one young woman (Pam) in his car and the four others by crashing into their vehicle.
		Epilogue [51:41–55:47]	Sheriff McGraw and his son discuss the serial killer's profile.
Part 2	Lebanon, Tennessee [55:48–109:31]	Act 1 [55:48–71:49]	Three young women (Kim, Abernathy, and Lee) drive around before picking their friend Zoë up at the airport.
		Act 2 [71:50–87:46]	Zoë, a stuntwoman like Kim, wants to live out her dream of driving an American muscle car. They trade their friend Lee for a local man's (Jasper's) *Vanishing Point* Challenger.
		Act 3 [87:47–98:12]	Zoë, Kim, and Abernathy take the car on a drive and are attacked by Mike.
		Act 4 [98:13–109:31]	The tables are turned when the women decide to pursue and kill him.
Credits	[109:32–113:32]		Abernathy is shown delivering the coup de grâce.

INGLOURIOUS BASTERDS

Structure	Chapter Titles / Timing	Events
Opening Credits	[0:00–2:05]	
Act 1, or Prologue & Act 1	Chapter One Once Upon a Time . . . in Nazi-Occupied France [2:06–21:22]	In 1941, Colonel Landa has the Dreyfus family massacred, but one girl (Shosanna) escapes.
	Chapter Two Inglourious Basterds [21:23–37:57]	US Lieutenant Aldo Raine puts together a guerilla team to terrorize the Nazis in Europe. We witness the aftermath of an ambush where they execute Sergeant Rachtman and leave one survivor behind, marking him with a swastika on his forehead in order to become legend. Hitler is beside himself with anger.
Act 2	Chapter Three German Night in Paris [37:58–64:05]	June 1944. Shosanna now runs a movie theater in Paris, with her lover Marcel. She meets a German war hero, Fredrick Zoller, who is attracted to her and suggests the premiere of the propaganda film he's starring in, *Stolz der Nation*, be held in her movie theater. This leads Shosanna to devise a plan.
Act 3	Chapter Four Operation Kino [64:06–105:38]	British intelligence finds out about the premiere and puts together an operation to end the war by offing some of the major Nazi officers. Lieutenant Archie Hicox is sent to meet a double agent, German actress Bridget von Hammersmark, with the Basterds, in order to set up Operation Kino. They are found out by a Nazi officer, Major Hellstrom; Hicox is killed, and Aldo is forced to replace Hicox in Operation Kino. Bridget reveals that Hitler will be attending, and Landa finds her shoe.
Act 4	Chapter Five Revenge of the Giant Face [105:39–145:46]	Landa kills Bridget von Hammersmark, intercepts Aldo, but permits Operation Kino to unfold because he wishes to make a deal with the Allied forces. Meanwhile, Shosanna's plan is carried out, though she does not live to see it succeed as Frederick Zoller murders her first.
Epilogue	[145:47–149:31]	Aldo releases Landa, but only after marking his forehead with a swastika.

138   A Neoformalist Approach Vol. 1: Narrative Structures and Paradigms

DJANGO UNCHAINED

Structure	Title	Substructure / Timing	Events
Credits		[0:23–3:13]	Django and other slaves march in a desert.
Act 1	1858, two years before the Civil War	Scene 1 [3:14–12:46]	Dr. Schultz buys Django and frees the slaves with him.
	Daughtrey, Texas	Scene 2 [12:47–23:36]	Schultz turns out to be a bounty hunter. He kills the town sheriff for a bounty.
		Scene 3 [23:37–26:40]	Schultz asks Django to help him catch the Brittle brothers, and Django tells Schultz about his wife, Broomhilda von Shaft.
Act 2	Tennessee	Scene 1 [26:41–27:59]	Schultz explains the job, while Django selects a costume.
		Scene 2 [28:00–40:26]	Schultz and Django go to Big Daddy's plantation where they kill the Brittle brothers.
		Scene 3 [40:27–46:04]	Schultz and Django are attacked by some KKK-like men, including Big Daddy. Schultz realizes Django's "a natural" with a gun.
Act 3		Scene 1 [46:05–50:35]	Schultz tells Django the story of Broomhilda and Siegfried, then asks Django to be his partner. Schultz intends to help Django in his quest.
		Scene 2 [50:36–58:02]	They work together all winter long. Django learns the job. They kill Smitty Bacall.
Act 4	And after a very cold and very profitable winter, Django and Dr. Schultz came down from the mountains and headed for . . . Mississippi	Scene 1 [58:03–72:12]	Schultz and Django devise a plan to buy Broomhilda from her current owner, Calvin Candie, a man who specializes in Mandingo fighting. They pretend to be interested in that sport in order to be introduced and witness a fight to the death.

		Scene 2 [72:13–85:56]	They journey to Candieland and witness the savage murder of a Mandingo fighter, D'Artagnan.
		Scene 3 [85:57–115:03]	Everything seems to be going according to Schultz and Django's plan, until Candie's house slave Stephen uncovers their true motives.
		Scene 4 [115:04–131:38]	Candie turns the tables on Schultz and Django, forces them to purchase Broomhilda for $10,000, but Schultz loses his cool and dies after killing Candie.
Act 5		Scene 1 [131:39–142:41]	Django fights Candie's men, is captured and then sold off.
	En route to The LeQuint Dickey Mining Co.	Scene 2 [142:32–151:15]	Django escapes the slavers.
		Scene 3 [151:16–164:58]	Django returns to kill the Candie family, their white overseers, and Stephen, and saves Broomhilda.

THE HATEFUL EIGHT

Structure	Chapter Titles / Timing	Events
Opening Credits	[0:30–4:33]	A stagecoach travels through a snowy mountain region in Wyoming.
Act 1	Chapter One Last Stage to Red Rock [4:34–22:01]	Major Marquis Warren, a bounty hunter, is rescued from a storm by another bounty hunter, John Ruth the Hangman, traveling in a stagecoach driven by a man named O. B. Ruth agrees to let Warren in, though he is worried because he suspects someone will try to take his prisoner, a woman named Domergue, from him.
	Chapter Two Son of Gun [22:02–35:02]	The team reluctantly picks up a former Lost Causer militiaman, Chris Mannix, who purports to be the new sheriff of Red Rock.
Act 2	Chapter Three Minnie's Haberdashery [35:03–95:04]	The four men and the prisoner seek refuge in a stagecoach lodge. Curiously, Minnie, the owner, is absent, and a Mexican named Bob is covering for her. Ruth disarms the other patrons: the Red Rock hangman (Oswaldo Mobray), a quiet cowboy (Joe Gage), and a former Confederate general (Sanford Smithers). After admitting his Lincoln letter is a fake at the dinner table, Warren provokes Smithers by claiming he raped and killed his son. Smithers draws and is killed by Warren.
Act 3	Chapter Four Domergue's Got a Secret [95:05–119:30]	Domergue has seen someone slip poison in the coffee. Ruth and O. B. drink it. Mannix is just about to drink some himself when Ruth and O. B. die, coughing up blood. Warren attempts to determine who the culprits are. He kills Bob, whom he is certain murdered Minnie. Joe Gage confesses to the poisoning. Mobray draws a concealed gun. A shoot-out ensues: Mannix and Mobray are wounded, and a man hiding under the floorboards shoots Warren.
	Chapter Five The Four Passengers [119:31–139:56]	"Earlier that morning," Mobray, Gage, Bob, and a fourth man, Jody, kill everyone at Minnie's Haberdashery. Jody is Domergue's brother and intends to rescue her. They wait for Ruth's stagecoach to arrive.
Act 4	Last Chapter Black Man, White Hell [139:57–163:26]	Mannix and Warren kill Jody Domergue and hold the other three at gunpoint. Domergue, Mobray, and Joe Gage call on Warren's racist sentiments and greed to try and get him to turn against Warren. Warren and Mannix kill Gage and Mobray (actually named Grouch Douglass and English Pete), then hang Domergue in Ruth's honor.

Chapters and Titles

The chapters and chapter titles in Tarantino's films fulfill various functions that can be structural, narrative, and metafictional: they delineate the narrative structure, identify the setting and/or characters, announce the action, and point to intertexts. They can be divided into two groups: those that provide basic information concerning the setting and time-setting (*Jackie Brown*, *Death Proof*, and *Django Unchained*) and those that are explicitly identified as the titles of stories (*Pulp Fiction*) or chapters (*Kill Bill*, *Inglourious Basterds*, *The Hateful Eight*, and to a lesser extent *Reservoir Dogs*). The two groups belong to different traditions: the first is a characteristically cinematic convention, while the second invites the viewer to consider the film as a novel[5] or even a magazine. This second approach is less frequent in film, though it has been used in *Salome, Where She Danced* (Universal, Charles Lamont, 1945), which was based on an original story, and more recently, in *The Grand Budapest Hotel* (Wes Anderson, 2014). If the titles in *Pulp Fiction*, like the title of the film, reinforce the literary heritage, it seems to me that the usage of the word "chapter" in *Kill Bill*, *Inglourious Basterds*, and *The Hateful Eight* is meant to draw further attention to their status as fantasies. In fact, on its release, Tarantino described his martial arts movie as the kind of film the characters from his previous films would watch.[6]

The titles and chapters generally announce the films' structures, but they do so to varying degrees. In *Jackie Brown*, *Death Proof* and *Django Unchained*, the time and place indications foreground the narrative structures (and even the micro-structure in the third act of *Jackie Brown*), though not necessarily in the final stages (the fourth act of *Jackie Brown*, the fifth of *Django Unchained*) when the setting remains the same and announcing it would be redundant. The correlation between setting and narrative structure is a general feature of Tarantino's films,[7] as the names of certain chapters indicate (Chapters Four, Five, and Six in *Kill Bill*, Chapters One and Three in *Inglourious Basterds*, Chapters One and Three in *The Hateful Eight*). If the chapters of *Inglourious Basterds* and *The Hateful Eight* somewhat overlap with the films' four-act structures, those of *Kill Bill Vol. 1* and *Vol. 2* announce, as we shall see, the film's epic structure. In *Pulp Fiction*, the titles clearly designate the film's three stories, but they do so only belatedly (twenty minutes into the film), giving the impression that the first two scenes are disconnected skits. In *Reservoir Dogs*, it is not the titles so much as the analeptical chapters themselves that separate each act.

Of course, the chapter titles have more than just a structural function. Like all titles, they are programatic, framing possible interpretations. In *Reservoir*

Dogs, for instance, the first two are named after characters, the third after a made-up story, thus clearly announcing the content of the three analepses: Mr. White and Mr. Blonde are introduced as trusted friends of the Cabots named Larry Dimmick and Vic Vega, while officer Freddy Newandyke used the Commode Story to construct a character that would gain the professional thieves' trust. Moreover, the three chapters also point to an absence: Mr. Pink does not get a chapter of his own, not only because four intercalary chapters would, in effect, have offset the structure of the film, but because he is, as J. P. Telotte notes, the only character in the warehouse "who retains his professional values from beginning to end."[8] In other words, the least authentic character, the one who never breaks character, is not entitled to a chapter any more than the dead Mr. Blue and Mr. Brown—pointedly, his flashback shows him as Mr. Pink after the job. The titles of the three stories in *Pulp Fiction* seem straightforward. Each announces the basic premise that gives way to a critical situation: Mia and Vincent's date leads to temptation, then to her near death; Butch returns home to get the watch and happens on the gangsters; the Bonnie situation is one in a series of events that lead Jules and Vincent to part ways. But the titles also highlight the film's structural unity:[9] each nods at the film's quasi-omnipotent character, Marsellus Wallace, the film's structural "hub."[10] Hence, referring to Mia as his wife emphasizes the fact that the drama has entirely to do with Vincent's reluctance to violate Marsellus's authority;[11] the "Bonnie situation" is what Jules asks Marsellus to resolve; and the quest for the gold watch, significantly a signifier of the father, ends in Butch's being granted immunity from Marsellus, when he had initially planned on having his way with the crime boss entirely.

The titles in *Kill Bill* and *Inglourious Basterds* likewise provide a frame with which to interpret each chapter, first, by announcing the action. If Chapters One and Two of *Inglourious Basterds* propose to present the context and the characters, Chapters Three, Four, and Five announce plot elements: the basic premise, the military operation it prompts, and the final outcome. Like Chapter Two, Chapter Five alludes to characters, albeit indirectly. In other words, the title invites the viewer to see the demise of the Reich as the triumph not of the Allies but of the film created by two individuals: Shosanna and Marcel. *The Hateful Eight* functions in a similar manner—the first, fourth, and sixth chapters evoke the action—but puts more emphasis on the parts played by specific characters (the second, fourth, fifth, and sixth). Though almost all the chapters in *Kill Bill* refer to characters (Chapters One, Two, Three, Four, Seven, Eight, Nine), sometimes indirectly (the last chapter), they also announce the action: "Chapter One: 2" refers to Vernita Green's position on the Bride's list, "Chapter Two: The Blood Splattered Bride" to the event that fuels the main character's drive to kill Bill, "Chapter Eight: The Cruel Tutelage of Pai Mei" to Beatrix's position as Pai Mei's disciple, and "Last Chapter: Face to Face" to the climax. "Chapter Seven: The Lonely Grave of Paula Schultz" ironically includes the name of a dead person who will not be characterized (and who may not even have existed in the diegesis) in order to foreshadow the Bride's situation at the end of the chapter. The film only shows how "lonely" the grave is for the heroine; in other words, Paula Schultz is yet another one of Beatrix Kiddo's avatars, this one created by Budd. In *Kill Bill*, the chapters thus foreground the extent to which the films' narrative structures are organized according to units of action. They sometimes give the viewer a cognitive advantage over the characters;[12] most obviously, "Chapter One: 2" of *Kill Bill Vol. 1* tells us that the Bride will vanquish O-Ren Ishii. This is also the case in *Inglourious Basterds* where the title of Chapter Five promises that Shosanna and Marcel will be successful. By contrast, the titles of the fourth and sixth chapters of *The Hateful Eight* keep the mystery alive.

Displaying the structure of a film calls attention to its constructedness and is thus an overt means of laying bare the artifice. It is especially enhanced by the use of a term (the chapter) that directly evokes another medium (prose fiction), at least until the invention of the DVD. It is further reinforced when the chapter titles point to specific intertexts, genres, or even another medium, creating a new frame of reference. The title of Chapter One of *Inglourious Basterds* refers directly to the film the scene alludes to, *Once Upon a Time in the West*, whose second scene it reimagines, Chapter Two both to the film's title and to the film it borrows its title from. Many chapters in *Kill Bill* reference a specific intertext: "Chapter Four: The Man from Okinawa" evokes Akinori Matsuo's 1978 film starring Shin'ichi Chiba; "Chapter Seven: The Lonely Grave of Paula Schultz," *The Wicked Dreams of Paul Schultz* (George Marshall, 1968);[13] "Chapter Eight: The Cruel Tutelage of Pai Mei," Shaw Brothers movies featuring priest Pai Mei, such as *The Shaolin Avengers* (Cheh Chang, 1976), *Executioners from Shaolin* (Chia-Liang Liu, 1977), and *Clan of the White Lotus* (Lieh Lo, 1980). The word "showdown" in the title of Chapter Five evokes both the Western and the martial arts movie, the word "massacre" in that of Chapter Six, Westerns like *Massacre* (First National, Alan Crosland, 1934) and *Fort Massacre* (UA, Joseph M. Newman, 1958), as well as horror movies like *The Texas Chain Saw Massacre* (Tobe Hooper, 1974) and *The Slumber Party Massacre* (Amy Holden Jones, 1982). Finally, "Chapter Three: The Origin of O-Ren" recalls the comic book medium, announcing the ontological break from photographic images to drawn ones. Including such references in the chapter titles is a clear indication of the importance of intertexts as a structuring element. Like any intertextual reference, these titles depend on viewers to activate them and, therefore, posit various degrees of cinephilia: the more general references or those to famous films are more likely to be identified by first-time audiences than lesser-known films that may require research after the viewing. As we have seen in the introduction, many fans will actively work to investigate these references and share and discuss their findings on websites like wiki.tarantino.info and the Internet Movie Database, thus participating in what Pierre Lévy and Henry Jenkins call collective intelligence.[14]

The various functions of the chapter titles have one thing in common: they are meant to increase the legibility of the film. Viewers are made aware of the structure, specific plot points, intertexts, and even of the way the film proposes to subvert or on the contrary abide by generic conventions. This knowingness is characteristic of metafiction. The singularity of Tarantino's cinematic metafiction has to do with the extent to which it draws on the conventions of a genre specific to another medium—the novel, or, in the case of *Pulp Fiction*, the magazine or short story collection—not so much to reflect on the ontology of the medium, but just to draw attention to the artifice.

Classical, Epic, and Art-Cinema Structures

The tables above show that most of Tarantino's films abide by the four-act structure identified by Thompson and Bordwell in Hollywood and mainstream films, and promoted in the screenwriter manuals they analyze: the plots can be divided into (1) setup, (2) complicating action, (3) development, and (4) climax, with sometimes a prologue and/or an epilogue.[15] *The Hateful Eight* fits this model, with two acts (acts 1 and 3) including two chapters (One and Two, and Four and Five). *Inglorious Basterds* does as well, even though Chapters One and Two can be seen as either two stages of the setup or an extended prologue and a setup. This is even more true of Tarantino's sole adaptation to date, *Jackie Brown*, whose four-act structure does not originate in the source,[16] but was obtained by eliminating subplots featured in the first half of the novel; it is as if the process of adaptation led Tarantino to fall back on a more classical structure. But even the films that have been associated with more complex storytelling, such as *Reservoir Dogs* and *Pulp Fiction*, are also largely founded on the classical Hollywood structure. Tarantino's first film only strays from that model due to the analeptical chapters, especially the third with its complex chronology. And though *Pulp Fiction* may have been seen as an example of what critic Alissa Quart called "hyperlink cinema,"[17] the three stories also adhere to the classical model[18]—this is equally true of the two parts of *Death Proof*. Consequently, *Pulp Fiction* should be seen as a variation on the anthology film with several recurrent characters (Butch, Jules, Vincent, and Marsellus and Mia Wallace) instead of just one (Ted the Bellhop in *Four Rooms*), *Death Proof* as the first and second installments in a slasher film franchise featuring Stuntman Mike.

The films that are the least classical in relation to Hollywood narrative conventions are *Kill Bill* and, more surprisingly perhaps, *Django Unchained*. Tarantino's first Western was actually the film I found the most difficult to analyze in terms of structure. Though I initally considered dividing the film into two parts, it became clear that, unlike *Death Proof* with its two distinct plots, the film was driven by both Django's quest to rescue Broomhilda (introduced as early as the first act) and, as the title of the film announces and as we have seen in chapter 2, the stages of his own development from Dr. Schultz's slave, to his apprentice, equal, and better, and finally to sole hero. In terms of narrative structure, then, the film is largely indebted to the episodic structure of the epic, here organized into five unequal acts. Tarantino may have had in mind one of his favorite films, *The Good, the Bad and the Ugly*, which deliberately integrates elements of the picaresque,[19] is also organized in five acts,[20] and proposes a political commentary on the Western and, more generally, on the representation of war in film.[21]

Kill Bill Vol. 1 is also based on the hero's journey model, a fact the film playfully acknowledges in the scenes where the Bride's plane travels across the map [45:08–45:12; 64:38–64:40]. If Chapter One resembles a lengthy prologue, Chapters Two and Three an equally lengthy setup, and Chapter Five a development (the Bride versus the Crazy 88) and climax (the Bride versus O-Ren Ishii) all in one, each chapter includes complicating actions in the form of obstacles the heroine must overcome (escaping the hospital, regaining control of her legs, convincing Hanzo to give her a sword, vanquishing O-Ren's minions). Forcing the classical Hollywood structure onto the film is misunderstanding it. This, I would contend, is confirmed by comparing the structure of *Kill Bill Vol. 1* to the more classical structure of *Vol. 2*, whose five chapters (the wedding rehearsal massacre; Beatrix buried alive; her escape and slaying of Elle Driver; and finally her defeat of Bill) correspond more readily to the setup-complicating action-development-climax schema. So my above attempt to divide *Vol. 1* into four acts is somewhat forced. Even considering the two *Kill Bill*s as a whole and reorganizing the narrative according to chronology would fail to produce a classical Hollywood narrative structure. If Chapters Six, Two, and Three could make up the prologue and setup—and the last chapter the climax—Chapters One, Four, Five, Seven, and Eight cannot be organized according to complicating action and development. Reorganizing according to chronology merely confirms the episodic structure of *Kill Bill*. Though such a tradition exists, albeit marginally, in Hollywood cinema—the *Indiana Jones* (Steven Spielberg, 1981–2008) films also follow the epic (and serial) model[22] and make similar use of maps to depict the hero's journeys across the globe—*Kill Bill* owes more to martial arts movies, comics, and video games, in which heroes and superheroes challenge a series of foes, usually in the order of increasing adversity,[23] and to nineteenth-century Japanese traditions.[24] *Lady Snowblood*, as viewers have noticed, clearly served as a template for *Kill Bill Vol. 1*—both resort to flashbacks and relate the stages in the heroine's vengeance against a series of foes.[25] In this respect, it is significant that the return to a slightly more classical narrative structure in *Vol. 2* follows the return to American soil and to more classically American genres (the Western and film *noir*).[26]

On the macro level, then, Tarantino's narrative structures are indebted to traditional forms either typical of folktales, myths, and legends (the epic) or of classical Hollywood cinema (the four-act model), which is itself largely indebted to the conventions of nineteenth-century literature. What Tarantino tends to do, however, is expand or compress particular acts. Expanded prologues (that of *Reservoir Dogs*, Chapter One in *Kill Bill Vol. 1*, Chapter One in *Inglourious Basterds*) and climaxes (Chapter Nine in *Kill Bill Vol. 2* and Chapter Five in *Inglourious Basterds* last forty minutes each) are frequent, expanded setups (the first part of "The Bonnie Situation" lasts over fifteen minutes) and developments (Part 1, Act 3 of *Death Proof*, where Stuntman Mike interacts with the girls, lasts twenty minutes, and especially the money exchange in *Jackie Brown*) less so. Accordingly, other stages are contracted, reinforcing the lack of balance: Act 2 of "The Bonnie Situation," with its two complicating actions (the moment of divine intervention and the death of Marvin), lasts a mere two minutes; Part 1, Act 2 of *Death Proof*, when the boys join the girls, a little over seven minutes. Unity of time and space can sometimes give the impression that certain acts have been conflated; for instance, complicating action and development in Part 1 of *Death Proof*, and especially in the finales of Part 2 of *Death Proof* and *Kill Bill Vol. 1*, that seem to merge climax and development. The whole of *Reservoir Dogs*, which is based on the eight-minute-long climax of *City on Fire* (1987), can be seen as an expanded climax or, like Chapter Five of *Kill Bill Vol. 1*, as a merger of development and climax; elements typical of a setup (the cops' and robbers' plans) or complicating action (the heist gone wrong) are either evoked in dialogue or relegated to the flashbacks.

I would argue that the flexibility of Tarantino's narrative structures owes much to both action movies and art cinema, and thus follow Bordwell who suggests that Tarantino's mentors in this department include Sergio Leone and John Woo.[27] It is notable that many of the expanded scenes (in *Jackie Brown*, *Kill Bill*, *Death Proof*, and *Inglourious Basterds*) are action scenes—in other words, scenes we might associate with classical Hollywood narratives. Yet the models for many of these scenes are rarely mainstream Hollywood fare. If the multiple points of views in the money exchange scene in *Jackie Brown* come from Leonard's novel, the film adaptation also recalls the heist scene in *The Killing* (1956). The lengthy car chase scene in *Death Proof* conflates such scenes from the car movies of the 1970s like *Vanishing Point* (1971) and *Dirty Mary Crazy Larry*, and the final confrontation scenes of 1980s slasher franchises like *Friday the 13th*. More obviously, the fight scenes in *Kill Bill* are heavily indebted to the Hong Kong and Japanese films they copiously borrow from.

Alternating between expansion and contraction in the other acts is, however, more typical of art-cinema narration, with its "suppressed gaps" and "delayed" exposition.[28] Tarantino often cites as a major influence Godard's *Band of Outsiders* (1964), a film where the robbery is systematically delayed while the characters indulge in dance and conversation; similar scenes occur in *Reservoir Dogs*, *Pulp Fiction*, and *Death Proof*, and the lengthy second act of "The Gold Watch" is clearly influenced by the famous twenty-four-minute-long bedroom scene in *Breathless* (Jean-Luc Godard, 1960).[29] Another obvious art-cinema feature is the triviality of some of the dialogue.[30] Many of the expanded scenes (the prologue of *Reservoir Dogs*, Jules and Vincent in the second scene of *Pulp Fiction*, the Bride's visit to Hattori Hanzo in *Kill Bill Vol. 1*, Bill's analysis of Superman in *Vol. 2*, the girls' conversations in *Death Proof*) consist of dialogue that does not necessarily serve to advance the plot, as Tarantino himself has recognized.[31] Interestingly enough, Tarantino seems to have abandoned this device since *Death Proof*, a film about which some viewers complained the dialogues were a bit forced and tiresome.[32] His subsequent films, however, still take their time in the dialogue scenes (Chapters One and Four in *Inglourious Basterds*, the whole fourth act of *Django Unchained*, and the whole of *The Hateful Eight*). A third narrative element that can be at least partly attributed to the influence of art-cinema is the weight of chance.[33] Many complicating actions or developments in Tarantino's films are the result of accidents or mistakes. Fred Botting and Scott Wilson, as well as Eve Bertelsen, note that accidents and errors dominate and direct the narratives of *Reservoir Dogs* and *Pulp Fiction*, arguing that the flashback structure of the first emerges from the "unspeakable event" that is the robbery,[34] not to mention that the only reason Mr. White defends Mr. Orange to the end is because the undercover cop accidentally killed a civilian [86:32].

The three stories in *Pulp Fiction* are likewise triggered by chance events: Mia ODs after mistaking Vincent's heroin for cocaine; Fabienne leaves Butch's watch in their apartment; Jules and Vincent miraculously escape being shot to death, and Vincent accidentally kills Marvin in their car.[35] Accidents are also a main narrative feature of the other films. In *Kill Bill*, for example, the Bride's revenge is made possible because she miraculously survives a gunshot in the head and unexpectedly wakes up from a coma. In *Inglourious Basterds*, the young Shosanna Dreyfus miraculously escapes Colonel Landa and his men, while Aldo Raine has to replace Lieutenant Archie Hicox in Operation Kino because not only did a German soldier just happen to be celebrating his birthday in the tavern in which they rendezvous with Bridget von Hammersmark, but Major Hellstrom was also having a drink there, and Hicox makes the fatal mistake of revealing that he counts on his fingers like a British, not a German. And in *The Hateful Eight*, the Domergue gang's plan to free Daisy is complicated by the storm and the presence of both Warren and Mannix.

What all these examples evince, however, is that the trivial and contingent in Tarantino's films are rarely, if ever, entirely disconnected from the narrative. These events are never left dangling; rather, every example of a mistake or accident becomes central in the narrative and prompts character motivation. Pointedly, all Tarantino's protagonists are, in the classical tradition, goal-oriented, whether they are carrying out someone's orders (the dogs, Jules and Vincent, the Basterds, John Ruth), or out to make money (Cabot and the dogs, Butch, Jackie, John Ruth) or rescue a loved one (Django, Jody, and his gang), or out for revenge (the Bride, Shosanna, Django) or just a good time (Stuntman Mike and the girls). As for the apparent triviality of the dialogue, it ultimately serves, as Tarantino himself admits, the characterization, preventing them from being mere genre characters and serving to establish power relations. The prologue of *Reservoir Dogs* is a case in point. It justifies the characters' interest in 1970s music and K-Billy radio, establishes relationships (Joe Cabot asserts his authority by paying for the meal and Mr. White shows how close he is to Cabot by confiscating his address book), and reveals or conceals character: Mr. Pink shows how rigorous and rigid he is, first by summing up Mr. Brown's "Like a Virgin" thesis, then by refusing to tip, while Mr. Orange, the rat who'll spend half the movie bleeding, doesn't say a word; however, by having Mr. Blonde defend Madonna like a "knight,"[36] the scene makes it impossible to foresee his subsequent sadistic behavior and functions like a misleading clue in a mystery. In *Pulp Fiction*, the dialogue between Jules and Vincent before they "get into character" also provides information about the characters (Vincent has just gotten back from Europe, the two men enjoy recreational drugs) and sets the stage for the next story (the foot massage) by establishing how high the stakes are (Antoine was murdered for it). In *Kill Bill Vol. 2*, the Superman parable represents Bill's final attempt to sadistically subject Beatrix (she, like the viewer, has no choice but to listen to him rant on) and fashion her into a "natural born killer," thereby imposing on her an essentialist view of identity. Ultimately, the art-cinema moments are not gratuitous pauses but are systematically integrated in the classical structure. As Jeremy Carr has pointed out, the long moments where nothing happens in *The Hateful Eight*, such as when Mannix and O. B. lay down the line to the toilet [45:38–46:53], ultimately serve to build up the suspense. In this respect, Tarantino's approach to narrative is characteristic of both New Hollywood and US indie cinema in that it does not fully embrace the European art-cinema or the classical Hollywood narrative, but draws on the flexibility of the former to reinvigorate the latter. Tapping into other models—exploitation cinema, Italian Westerns, martial arts movies—is also characteristic of US indie cinema.

Flashbacks, Flashforwards, and Scrambled Chronology

Finally, the tables above show that, despite the attention Tarantino's complex storytelling techniques have garnered, his narratives have become increasingly linear[37] since *Death Proof*, which includes neither flashback nor flashforward. Tarantino reacted strongly against the use of the term "flashback" to describe the Mr. White, Mr. Blonde, and Commode Story segments in *Reservoir Dogs*; for the director, a flashback must be mediated by a protagonist: "Flashbacks [...] come from a personal perspective. These aren't, they're coming from a narrative perspective. They're going back and forth like chapters."[38] In *Flashbacks in Film*, Maureen Turim explains that popular usage does not differentiate the two: "If flashbacks give us images of memory, the personal archives of the past, they also give us images of history, the shared and recorded past"; she further explains that "flashbacks in film often merge the two levels."[39] Gérard Genette's typology of analepses does not take into account the flashback's relationship to the protagonist or narrator either; he distinguishes between external and internal analepses depending on whether the analepsis interferes with the main narrative, then between internal heterodiegetic and homodiegetic analepses based on their connection to the previous narrative, and finally between completive and repeating analepses depending on whether they provide information the narrative had previously omitted or merely add to an episode.[40] Tarantino's more restrictive definition does, however, illuminate his own pratice, so that the flashbacks in his films can be divided into three categories: mediated, unmediated, and ambiguous flashbacks.

(1) Flashbacks mediated by memory or storytelling

Examples include Mr. Pink's escape in the first act of *Reservoir Dogs* [20:33–21:42]; Shosanna's recognition of Colonel Landa's voice at the restaurant in *Inglourious Basterds* [54:15–54:20], Hugo Stizglitz's memories of being whipped [84:48–84:55], and Landa's planting the dynamite in Hitler and Goebbels's opera box [134:30–134:45]; the flashes of the heroin injection while Vincent Vega drives in *Pulp Fiction* [29:06–29:56]; Warren's description of the humiliating ordeal he subjected General Smithers's son to in *The Hateful Eight*; in *Jackie Brown*, Max's account of the events that led to his decision to retire [82:56–83:01, 83:19–83:27], his remembering his phone call with Jackie [88:36–88:58], and Jackie's of her dinner with Ray Nicolette [95:09–96:27]; Django's account of the decision to sell him and Broomhilda [24:42–25:26], his memories of meeting her [26:30–26:40] and of escaping with her [32:57–34:14], his recollection of Candie's theories on race [72:58–73:55], and Dr. Schultz's flashes of D'Artagnan's death in *Django Unchained* [124:52–125:09]; the Bride's memories of getting shot [*KB1*, 25:46–26:02], of Buck the rapist [*KB1*, 31:13–31:26], and the members of the DiVAS [*KB1*, 35:23–35:49, 67:06–67:22], her account of her discovery of her pregnancy [*KB2*, 105:08–109:15], and Elle Driver's account of the murder of Pai Mei [*KB2*, 74:46–75:22].[41] The subjective nature of the flashback is often evoked through the classical use of a dissolve (*Jackie Brown, Kill Bill, Inglourious Basterds*) or of a different color scheme (red dominant in *Kill Bill*, white in *Django Unchained*) as markers of distant memories; slow motion (*Kill Bill*) can reinforce the traumatic quality. These flashbacks tend to be short. Inserts can suggest the power of a single traumatic image (Max in *Jackie Brown, Kill Bill, Inglourious Basterds, Django Unchained*), a narrative sequence a character's greater degree of control over these memories: Mr. Pink is the most professional of the remaining team; Jackie Brown controls the plot; Landa gloats over his clever plan; Django manages to take matters into his own hands on Big Daddy's plantation and avoids breaking character even when repeatedly provoked by the violent and racist slavers on the way to Candieland; Major Marquis Warren is attempting to provoke General Sandy Smithers with a narrative that might be a fabrication. In Beatrix's case, however, though her account reveals how she quickly came to terms with her pregnancy, her degree of control is compromised by the fact that Bill's truth serum is possibly forcing the memory out of her.

(2) Unmediated flashbacks, i.e., analepses that originate from the narration

Examples include the Mr. White, Mr. Blonde, and Commode Story segments in *Reservoir Dogs*; the two money exchange scenes from Louis and Melanie's, as well as Max's, point of view; "Chapter Six: Massacre at Two Pines" in *Kill Bill Vol. 2*, which is directly introduced by the Bride in narrative voice-over; the replay of the car accident at the end of the first part of *Death Proof* [51:04–51:26]; the brief flashback where Dr. Schultz concludes that Django will be called "the fastest gun in the South" after watching him practice [161:30–161:40]; and in Chapter Four of *The Hateful Eight*, the brief flashback, accompanied by a voice-over, that shows us Daisy Domergue as she observes the coffee being poisoned [96:39–97:23]. All are clearly marked-out, full-fledged segments, but their relationship to the main narrative is different. This is where Genette's terminology comes in handy. If these flashbacks all have in common that they are unmediated narratives that are clearly set apart, they are used with more variation, perhaps, than the mediated flashbacks, which are either "completive" or "repeating homodiegetic internal analepses." "Massacre at Two Pines," for instance, is a "completive homodiegetic internal analepsis"; it fills the gap in the main narrative left by the "paralepsis" concerning the events at Beatrix's wedding that have been up to now repeatedly conjured up through traumatic images and sounds without a complete account.

The examples from *Jackie Brown*, *Death Proof*, *Django Unchained*, and the first example from *The Hateful Eight* are all "repeating homodiegetic internal analepses." The final flashback of *Django Unchained* confirms that Django has fulfilled the legendary destiny predicted by Dr. Schultz. The flashback that opens "Domergue's Got a Secret" discloses what we and the other characters missed when Warren's provocation of Smithers was drawing all the attention. The second and third money exchange also offer different takes on an event we already witnessed, encouraging us to interpret the scene differently each time; the use of the same music "embodies on the soundtrack the recursive temporal sequencing."[42] Hence, following the Jackie Brown segment which ends on a close-up of her calling for help in a panicked voice, the Melanie and Louis segment promises to show us what went wrong, but by showing us the plan was successful, the Max segment leads us to reinterpret the end of the Jackie segment as part of Jackie's act. If these flashbacks are unmediated and originate exclusively in the narration, they ultimately foreground Jackie's control over the plot.[43] On one level, the repetition of the car accident in *Death Proof* could exemplify Stuntman Mike's mastery of the narrative, but on a more unconscious level, it suggests the sadistic drives both the serial killer and the slasher fan are condemned to repeat mechanically. On a metafictional level, then, all the "repeating analepses" covertly comment on the generic conventions (whether they be those of the Western, mystery, the heist or horror movie) that the films draw upon. Specific techniques (titles in *Jackie Brown*, slow motion in *Death Proof*, the freeze-frame in *The Hateful Eight*) serve to mark out these moments, foregrounding their artificiality and encouraging spectators to view them from a knowing distance. This is further exacerbated, in *The Hateful Eight*, by the voice-over spoken by Tarantino himself, who concludes that this is why the chapter is named "Domergue's Got a Secret." In so doing, the filmmaker, whose voice most viewers would recognize, is not so much commenting on the strategy as drawing attention to the fact that, by Tarantino's eighth film, it has, as a narrative strategy, become trademark Tarantino.

The Mr. White and Mr. Blonde segments in *Reservoir Dogs* are "heterodiegetic internal analepses." They provide background information on a character or some characters before returning unproblematically to the main narrative—unproblematically, of course, because each character is revealed to be a trustworthy friend of the Cabots. Structurally, the Commode Story functions in the same manner, but as the change of title indicates, it plays a greater part in the storytelling; not only does the segment plunge into Freddy Newandyke's background, it involves several layers of time. Internally, this segment is organized in the following manner:

T_0: Freddy meets Holdaway in a diner.
T_{-4}: roof scene.
T_{-3}: Freddy rehearsing at home.
T_{-2}: Freddy rehearsing on stage with Holdaway in the audience.
T_{-1}: Freddy performing for the Cabots and Mr. White // $T_{-1'}$: the fantasy comes to life.
T_0: the diner.
T_{+1}: Nice Guy Eddie, Mr. Pink, and Mr. White pick up Orange.
T_{+2}: Joe Cabot gives them their aliases.
T_{+3}: Mr. White and Mr. Orange rehearsing heist, bonding.
T_{+4}: after the heist, Mr. Brown dies; Mr. White and Mr. Orange escape, but Mr. Orange murders a civilian who shot him.
T_{+5}: Mr. Orange in pain in the car = return to the beginning of Act 1.

"The Commode Story" also adds information concerning the preparation of the heist, making it a mix of two forms of internal analepses: "heterodiegetic" and "completive homodiegetic." It thus dramatizes the weight of the past, which has been building up from the start: each flashback is longer than the previous. By going past its initial starting point (the diner), the background story ultimately unravels the whole story. In so doing, it calls into question the idea that the previous flashbacks provided mere backstory. On the contrary, Mr. White's and Mr. Blonde's fatal flaws are made apparent in the flashbacks: Mr. White's sensitivity in his ungrudging account of Alabama's leaving him; Mr. Blonde's homoerotic relationship to violence in his fight with Nice Guy Eddie. "Chapter Five: The Four Passengers" functions similarly in *The Hateful Eight*. In terms of narrative, it is somewhat redundant because it mainly relates events the viewer could have imagined on her/his own, but the new information it provides is essential to the racial politics of the film; it is only here that we find out that Minnie and her employees are African American, while Smithers's abject racism is confirmed by his accepting to become an accomplice to murder.

(3) Ambiguous flashbacks, i.e., analepses whose sources (a character, the narration) are uncertain

There are two instances in *Kill Bill* and three in *Inglourious Basterds*. In *Kill Bill*, Chapter One and the first part of Chapter Eight function like "heterodiegetic internal analepses," providing background information on a character (O-Ren Ishii and Beatrix) before returning to the main narrative. This is complicated, however, by the usage of a first-person voice-over, which sometimes introduces uncertainty as to whether these flashbacks are motivated psychologically (and thus mediated by the Bride as character), narratively (and thus mediated by the Bride as narrator), or both. This ambiguity makes sense in the case of first-person narration, since the narrator may still be affected by some of the psychological issues that affected her as a character. Interestingly enough, the voice-over first appears in *Vol. 1* to introduce the Bride's second flashback: "As I laid in the back of Buck's truck trying to will my limbs out of entropy, I could see the faces of the cunts who did this to me." The film then alternates between subjective images—a low-angle POV shot of the four Vipers looking down at the Bride (fig. 33)—and objective images—a Polaroid photo of the four from behind facing the church—but links them through dissolves that are, in the film's terms, associated with memory. The usage of a freeze-frame and the titles in yellow letters signal the narration's taking over, paving the way for Chapter Three [35:50–35:57].

Before the film returns to the Bride in the pickup, the voice-over suggests that such images may have been running through the Bride's head: "However, before satisfaction could be mine, first things first" [44:05–44:27]. Here, then, the "heterodiegetic internal analepsis" is prompted and thus framed by psychological causality, which is then contradicted by the content of the flashback: the Polaroid was taken by an unknown photographer, possibly Bill (though very unlikely), but undoubtedly not the Bride. Chapter Eight in *Vol. 2* functions in a similar fashion, minus the voice-over. This chapter is introduced by a fade to black of Beatrix in the coffin, and returns to her when she starts punching the coffin lid, suggesting that the character was, in fact, thinking about Pai Mei's lessons. In so doing, Chapters Three and Eight, whose titles both refer to the content of the flashback, establish a structural symmetry between the two installments: both occupy third place, and both have to do with the heroine's finding strength and motivation to be reborn in a film that "tells the story of perpetual (re)birth."[44] These scenes remain ambiguous, nonetheless, because if the use of anime in Chapter Three and of a whitish cinematography in the Pai Mei flashback function, in effect, like markers of subjectivity, the linear narrative structure of these episodes is clearly meant to provide the viewer with a backstory and not to reproduce the workings of the Bride's memory.

Inglourious Basterds features a similar moment of uncertainty in Chapter Four when Adolf Hitler announces that he will be attending the premiere to boost morale [101:14]. Inserted within Bridget von Hammersmark's and the Basterds' conversation, the shot stands for the information Bridget has given the others verbally. In other words, we are being shown either what the characters imagined happened based on the German double agent's account or what really happened, in which case the narration is the source; the absence of a linking device like a dissolve leaves this question open.[45] More interesting still is the temporal fallacy the second scene of Chapter Two is grounded in. The Basterds' disposal of Sergeant Rachtman is presented through the story of the escaped Private Butz, yet in the middle of this scene, the backstory of how Sergeant Hugo Stiglitz became a Basterd is narrated by an omniscient voice-over [28:22–30:18]. Here, a "heterodiegetic internal analepsis" occurs within a "completive homodiegetic internal analepsis." Paradoxically, the extradiegetic narrator intervenes in the intradiegetic narrator's narrative, so that what appears structurally as a second intradiegetic narrative because of the Chinese box structure is actually an extradiegetic parenthesis. The reason it feels like a violation is that, not only is the third-person omniscient narrator fairly rare in fiction films, but unlike the Bride whose voice as narrator precedes the flashback, this first instance of the voice-over occurs simultaneously. In terms of narration, then, by laying bare the artifice, this flashback establishes distance, notably regarding the violent execution of Sergeant Rachtman that follows. But it also functions as a *mise en abyme* of the flashback it is contained within; like Hugo Stiglitz, whose flashback significantly opens with a close-up of his face on a German newspaper, the Basterds have become the stuff of legend through storytelling.[46] The main flashback confirms, then, that Lieutenant Aldo Raine and his men have achieved the renown they were hoping for.

Flashforwards and the case of Pulp Fiction

Kill Bill is the only film to resort to flashforwards (or what Genette calls "prolepses"). Two occur at the beginning of each film: "Chapter One: 2"[47] and the short prologue of *Vol. 2*. They have very similar functions: one informs the viewer that the Bride has already defeated O-Ren, the second that Budd and Elle Driver are out of the way. In so doing, they eliminate some suspense and thwart viewer expectations based on the conventions of martial art movies: in *Vol. 1*, the big boss (O-Ren) has already been killed, and in *Vol. 2*, he (Bill) is already the last remaining opponent. Yet the scrambled chronology turns the Bride's trajectory into a symbolic one. *Kill Bill* opens with the Bride murdering a mother with a child roughly the age hers would have been, and closes on Beatrix murdering the father and regaining possession of her own child. By killing Vernita, the Bride is killing the person she could have been.[48] The connection[49] is reinforced by the fact that the proleptical chapter that opens *Vol. 1* also establishes a structural symmetry with the analeptical chapter that opens *Vol. 2*—both depict a violent assault on a mother. The story justifies the Bride's seeking out O-Ren first in that the Tokyo crime lord was the only Viper that was easy to find and that the Bride needed to go to Japan to get a sword in the first place. But I would argue that, in generic terms, starting with O-Ren and her minions may also be a necessary stage in order for the Bride to become a killing machine capable of murdering Vernita. This is confirmed by the brief flashforwards at the end of *Vol. 1*, which are mixed with images of the Bride writing her list, and flashbacks of the Bride speaking to Sofie Fatale, and of Hattori Hanzo speaking about revenge. These flashforwards do more than just announce *Vol. 2*. Like the flashback in Chapter Two of *Inglourious Basterds*, they prove that the Bride's accomplishments—her vanquishing O-Ren and the Crazy 88—have now become the subject of conversation (between Bill and Sofie, and Bill and Budd) and, in a sense, the stuff of legend. Thus, the symbolical function of the proleptical chapter of *Vol. 1* is, in effect, twofold: it establishes two interweaving arcs, one Oedipal (the family) and one heroic (the revenge).

A study of order in *Pulp Fiction*, I feel, confirms my contention that the film should be viewed as a variation on the anthology film.[50] Considering the film as an example of "hyperlink cinema" would lead to view the handling of time in either one of these three fashions:

(1) if the prologue is T_0, then the second scene is a flashback, "Vincent Vega & Marsellus Wallace's Wife" and "The Gold Watch" are proleptic, and "The Bonnie Situation" opens with a "repeating analepsis" before pursuing the flashback of the second scene and returning to the prologue.
(2) if the second scene is T_0, then the prologue is a prolepsis, "Vincent Vega & Marsellus Wallace's Wife" and "The Gold Watch" are also proleptic, and the film returns to the main timeline via a "repeating analepsis."
(3) if "Vincent Vega & Marsellus Wallace's Wife" is T_0, a case which could be argued because of the use of a title, then that story and "The Gold Watch" are paradoxically contained by a flashback, "The Bonnie Situation," which includes its own prolepsis (the prologue) as well as two "repeating analepses" (the shoot-out and the robbery).

The first two accounts are not satisfactory; taking the prologue or the first scene as a basis for a consideration of time tends to minimize the importance of the other stories in terms of structure. The fact that the title of Story 1 is given after those of Stories 2 and 3 is an indication that it does not take precedence over the other two. Moreover, though Story 1 serves as a frame for the other two stories, it is also informed by Story 2 as the epilogue of "The Bonnie Situation" (Jules and Vincent's return to Marsellus's club) is contained within the first act of "Vincent Vega & Marsellus Wallace's Wife" [21:15–26:23]. The third account is more convincing. First, the opening scene of "Vincent Vega & Marsellus Wallace's Wife" acts as a prologue to "The Gold Watch," an epilogue to "The Bonnie Situation," and the beginning of "Vincent Vega & Marsellus Wallace's Wife"—and in that order; in a manner of speaking, it is both the beginning and the end of *Pulp Fiction*. This account also has the advantage of recognizing the fact that "The Bonnie Situation" as a whole operates as a frame, and that it is the only story for which *fabula* and *syuzhet* differ. These arguments stand if one considers *Pulp Fiction* as a scambled anthology film. The added advantage in taking the three stories as units is that it acknowleges that the *fabulas* can be organized in basic chronological order, and the active role viewers play in so doing.

The structure of *Pulp Fiction* is by no means a gimmick and is highly relevant thematically, as it orders the way we are made to view each character's arc. Indeed, the movie is about people who are subjected to the power of one man, Marsellus Wallace, and who either remain subjected (Mia and Vincent) or find a way out (Butch and Jules).[51] The stories have been ordered in such a fashion as to celebrate the possibility of escape and redemption, and thus to undermine Marsellus's authority. "The Bonnie Situation" serves as a frame because Jules's trajectory takes him from being like Vincent to being like Butch. Symbolically, then, it is no accident that the opposition between Butch and Vincent is dramatized when they meet at the beginning of "Vincent Vega & Marsellus Wallace's Wife" [24:40] and ends with Butch killing Vincent in "The Gold Watch" [87:55]. The arc of Vincent, a character who may be touched by his experience with Mia but not enough to change his ways and achieve redemption,[52] is "entirely encompassed by" structure.[53] Although Vincent is clearly the main character in terms of plot, the structure, as Randall E. Auxier has astutely argued, encourages us to consider each character with equal importance.[54] Moreover, it is because *Pulp Fiction* is organized according to Jules's trajectory that it begins and ends with "The Bonnie Situation." The intent to foreground Jules's trajectory retrospectively explains the use of the prolepsis in the diner: the prologue presents the two characters (Pumpkin and Honey Bunny) the reformed Jules will spare before showing us the characters (Brett and his friends) Jules the hitman will execute. Dramatically and thematically, then, the film opens with the promise of violence and successfully—and quite unexpectedly—defuses the Mexican standoff audiences familiar with *Reservoir Dogs* probably expected.[55] The film's rejection of chronological order is also required symbolically; in terms of *fabula*, Jules's redemption has to occur before "The Gold Watch" because Vincent is killed by Butch, but in terms of *syuzhet* it must take place after "The Gold Watch" because Jules's redemption must occur both after Vincent's death and Butch's success.

What seems to be systematically at stake in Tarantino's handling of narrative order is the question of control and authority. Flashbacks can underline a character's control over her/his narrative arc (Mr. Orange, Jackie, Warren) or establish a contrast between two moments—for instance, a traumatic past and a character's greater degree of control in the present (the Bride, Django). Flashforwards, "repeating analepses," and scrambled structures foreground the artifice of storytelling and, by varying the quantity of information provided, require that viewers actively participate in the construction of the fiction. This can be seen as a form of manipulation, and thus as an assertion of the authority of the narration (and even the filmmaker), but it can also be seen as an invitation to share in the construction of the fiction, and not to fully trust the narration and call into question its authority. This, I would argue, is clearly the case of the ambiguous flashbacks in *Inglourious Basterds*, which, by drawing attention to the film's mythmaking and rewriting of history, remind us, as we have seen in chapter 1, that we should also be aware of the authority of the writers of official history. Many viewers believe it to be the case of the flashback where Warren violates Sandy Smithers in *The Hateful Eight*.

In nine feature films, Tarantino's handling of narrative structure has been fairly consistent, as the use of the same font (Bookman Medium)[56] for the chapter titles of *Kill Bill*, *Inglourious Basterds*, and *The Hateful Eight* indicates. This chapter has demonstrated that the simplicity or complexity of the overarching structure is always instrumental to characterization and narrative, and to the symbolic, political, and metafictional concerns of each film. In other words, Tarantino's chief concern is not formalist—it is, above all, how to best tell a story. The extent to which the films have been thought out are proof of the care he puts into each screenplay.

Whether they invoke a literary or a more cinematic tradition, the titles always fulfill a structural function. The chapter or story titles add a more overt frame of interpretation grounded in genre conventions and specific intertexts, contributing to the films' metafictional discourses by foregrounding the artifice on various levels (the story, the narrative structure, and even the narration). Tarantino has also stuck to his own distinction between mediated and unmediated flashbacks to finally violate that logic in *Kill Bill* and especially *Inglourious Basterds*, thereby laying bare the convention the films are tapping into. If the films have always relied on viewers to play an active role in piecing them together, the chapter titles and the flashbacks have increasingly drawn attention to this part of the fiction-making process. One evolution has to do with the extent to which the more recent films increasingly draw attention to Tarantino's directorial signatures, and thus to his approach to filmmaking. In typical art-cinema tradition, what Bordwell calls the "intrinsic norms"[57] gradually established across his œuvre (in this case, the body of films) are subsequently violated. It remains to be seen whether this is also the case in terms of narration.

The narrative structures proper evince a debt to both the classical and art-cinema paradigms. So the main and most obvious evolution in Tarantino's approach to narrative—their increasing linearity following *Kill Bill*—should not be taken as an indication of increasing classicism. With the exception of *Kill Bill* and *Django Unchained*, which follow an episodic quest structure characteristic of the epic, already present in the films (*Lady Snowblood* and especially *The Good, the Bad and the Ugly*) the three movies are indebted to, all the films or stories are organized according to the four-act structure typical of the classical Hollywood narrative. The internal structures of each act, however, are flexible and participate in a dynamics of delay and ellipsis typical of art-cinema. Triviality and chance are assimilated within narratives governed by goal-oriented characters. In other words, Tarantino's films usually rely on a classical structure within which they integrate an art-cinema approach. To put it another way, they are essentially classical films subjected to an art-cinema treatment.[58] Again, Tarantino's debt to both Godard and Leone is crucial. More generally, though, his films pursue the ambition of the New Hollywood filmmakers of "creat[ing] something like European arts films,"[59] and it is in this respect that Tarantino also epitomizes some of the ambitions of US independent cinema of the 1980s and 1990s.[60] The next chapter will attempt to determine whether the narration likewise blends the classical and art-cinema paradigms, thus raising the question as to whether they shouldn't be considered in their relation to each other instead of systematically opposed. In the end, the films, as we have seen, work to undermine the authority of the classical model and of Tarantino's own art-cinema signature.

CHAPTER FIVE

"EVERYTHING'S THE SAME EXCEPT FOR ONE CHANGE"

A Neoformalist Approach Vol. 2: Narration and Style

Although the cinematography and editing of his films have often been praised—*Pulp Fiction* was nominated in the categories Best Cinematography (Andrzej Sekula) and Best Editing (Sally Menke) at the BAFTA Awards, *Inglourious Basterds* for Directing, Cinematography (Robert Richardson), and Film Editing (Menke) at the Academy Awards, and *Django Unchained* and *The Hateful Eight* for Best Cinematography (Richardson) at the Academy Awards—there have been few analyses of their aesthetics, apart from those proposed by Ortoli in his book, and case studies of *Inglourious Basterds* and *Kill Bill* by, respectively, Chris Fujiawara (2012) and myself (2014). This chapter ambitions to define the Tarantino style and assess its role in the production of metafictional discourses.

The line from *Jackie Brown* in which Jackie speaks of the real money exchange after the trial run is significant because it connects plot and style. The "change" she has in mind is narrative (the amount of money) [96:25]; Ordell will practically repeat the line (he says "except one little difference") when talking about another plot change (the replacement of Simone with Melanie) [97:56]. But in the interval, a scene with Jackie and Max discloses that, while in the changing room, she is going to change into the business suit that symbolizes her transformation into a "badass" success story [97:42]. The line neatly encapsulates Tarantino's approach to film genre and style. His films are grounded in genre conventions, and thus in repetition, but their individuality shows through in the violations of those conventions, as well as in the intrinsic norms established in each film and across the body of his work. Like "the little differences" between the US and Europe that Vincent noticed during his stay abroad [7:48], and that Ordell's variation on Jackie's line recalls, it is these violations that make up the specificity of Tarantino's films. And like the lines from *Pulp Fiction* and *Jackie Brown*, they are reflexive and largely participate in the films' metafictional discourses on film genre and cinema in general. Tarantino's films, like Jackie's plot and European burgers, are indebted to a model, which they mimic to counter both aesthetically and politically, thereby calling into question the very notion of an original, as in Vincent's remark that constructs the New World as a model for the Old Continent from which it originated historically.[1]

This chapter pursues the neoformalist approach adopted in the preceding chapter and seeks to further determine Tarantino's place in the history of film aesthetics, and his relationship to classical, contemporary, and art cinema. Largely indebted to the writings of Bordwell and Thompson, it analyzes how the films relate to the extrinsic norms of the film genres they rework, how they produce their own intrinsic norms and how they ultimately play with the two. It foregrounds the various functions of these devices, that can be dramatic, narrative, and/or metafictional. It progresses from a general overview of the Tarantino style by focusing on the body of his work, before studying a certain number of signature devices, starting with the famous low-angle shot from the trunk, and finally the specific color schemes and devices utilized in each film.

Classical Narration, Intensified Continuity, Art-Cinema Narration

Tarantino's style largely abides by the conventions of classical narration.

- It profits from the whole palette of shot sizes. Examples: the scenes relating Mr. White and Mr. Pink's conversation in *Reservoir Dogs* [17:41–26:39] and Beatrix and Bill's conversation in the living room in *Kill Bill Vol. 2* [101:00–109:35] resort to long shots, medium shots, medium close-ups, and close-ups.
- The characters' situation in space is often established through long shots, whether to open a scene or just to identify the characters' position in space in a scene with a lot of movement. Examples of the first: the long shot of Brett and his friends' room when Jules and Vincent step in in *Pulp Fiction* [14:36]; the two full shots when Landa and Lapadite enter the latter's house in *Inglourious Basterds*

[4:27]; the inside of Minnie's Haberdashery in *The Hateful Eight* [37:42]. Examples of the second: two successive long shots during the House of Leaves battle in *Kill Bill Vol. 1* [85:05]; the three-quarter long shot at the end of the basement shoot-out in *Inglourious Basterds* [92:50].

- Close-ups are used sparingly to highlight a character's emotion or a key element, sometimes fetishizing it. Examples: Mia's overdose in *Pulp Fiction* [54:06]; General Sandy Smithers's sorrow and horror when Major Warren tells him how he raped and killed his son in *The Hateful Eight* (fig. 70.3) [81:06]; the components of Elle Driver's nurse outfit in *Kill Bill Vol. 1* [20:53–21:27]; Abernathy's feet hanging out the window of Kim's car before Mike licks them in *Death Proof* [59:56].
- Compositions are centered on the protagonists or elements that are important to the plot. Examples: the dogs during Cabot's pep talk in *Reservoir Dogs* [79:55–83:03]; Julia and her crew talking at the Texas Chili Parlor in *Death Proof* [9:37–14:06]; the heroin Vincent purchases in *Pulp Fiction* [27:17]; Bridget's shoe that Landa finds in the tavern in *Inglourious Basterds* [104:52].
- Camera movements are usually subordinate to the movements of the characters. Examples: the forward tracking shot when Vincent explores Jack Rabbit Slim's in *Pulp Fiction* (fig. 62) [35:10–35:26, 35:37–36:16]; the track-out when Ordell walks around in Del Amo Mall in *Jackie Brown* [80:01–80:22]; the lateral tracking shot of Landa walking up to shake LaPadite's hand in *Inglourious Basterds* [4:02]; the slight pan when Warren and Charles Smithers cross the bridge to keep the characters centered in *The Hateful Eight* [90:33].
- Handheld and Steadicam shots are mainly noticeable when protagonists are on the move or fighting. Examples: Mr. White and Mr. Orange's arrival in the warehouse in *Reservoir Dogs* [11:22–11:51]; the panic in Lance and Jody's apartment when Vincent turns up with an overdosing Mia [57:33–58:55], and Butch's return to his apartment in *Pulp Fiction* [88:30–90:04]; the fights against Vernita and Elle in *Kill Bill* [*Vol. 1* 6:00–7:17; *Vol. 2* 74:42–77:17].
- The pace of the editing is, likewise, indexed on the energy of the scene or film, accelerating in action scenes. Examples: *Death Proof* has an ASL of approximately 7 shots per minute that increases to approximately 18 during the chase scenes; the chatty *The Hateful Eight* an ASL of approximately 5.5 shots per minute that briefly increases to about 1 second/shot during the massacre [129:50–130:12].[2]

- Conversations are mainly filmed utilizing the shot/reverse-shot technique. Examples: Mia and Vincent at the restaurant in *Pulp Fiction* [36:34–47:24]; Jackie Brown and the police in Dargus's office [30:07–33:03]; Beatrix and Esteban Vihaio in *Kill Bill Vol. 2* [83:24–87:24]; Mike detailing his career in *Death Proof* [32:39–34:19]; or Stephen and Calvin Candie having a discussion in the library in *Django Unchained* [113:17–113:45].
- Cuts are often governed by eyeline match or match-on-action editing. Examples of the first: in *Jackie Brown* when Max Cherry surveys the scene at the mall to assess the feasibility of Jackie's plan [86:53–88:36]; in *Django Unchained* when Django rides past the cabin [78:42–79:09]; and in *The Hateful Eight* when Major Marquis Warren first enters Minnie's Haberdashery, notices the red candy on the floor, and looks over the patrons [64:16–64:55]. Examples of the second: when Mr. Pink gets hits by a car in *Reservoir Dogs* [21:03–21:12]; when Mike rams Kim's car in *Death Proof* [95:25–95:37]; or when Frederick Zoller breaks into the projection booth in *Inglourious Basterds* [138:55–139:07].

Tarantino's films are not typical of the contemporary Hollywood style termed by Bordwell as "intensified continuity," whose main characteristics are close shots, rapid editing, and mobile cameras (notably handheld).[3] Rather, this style tends to be reserved for specific scenes: walk-and-talks, fight scenes, and music video scenes. The walk-and-talk, a recurrent strategy in contemporary films according to Bordwell,[4] is used in *Pulp Fiction* when Jules and Vincent go to Brett's [9:10–9:29, 11:04–12:41], in *Jackie Brown* when Ordell and Beaumont walk to the gun trafficker's car [18:26–19:06], and later when Louis and Melanie are heading away and back to the car [109:36–109:52, 112:17–113:03], in *Kill Bill Vol. 1* and *Death Proof* when Sheriff McGraw and his son discuss crimes [17:20–18:08, 53:15–55:47], and more briefly in *Django Unchained* when Betina takes Django on a tour of Big Daddy's plantation [31:44–32:11]. All these scenes contrast the leisurely pace of the lateral or backward tracking shot, depicting either small talk (Jules and Vincent, Betina and Django), cool professionalism (Ordell and Beaumont, the McGraws) when talking about crime, with the violence of the murder that has just been, or is about to be, committed—in the case of Melanie and Louis, the effect is the exact opposite, the quick pace of the shot echoing Louis's stress and foreshadowing the outcome. The camera's subservience to the character and her/his rhythm is meant to highlight the latter's authority (Jules and Vincent, Ordell, the McGraws) or lack thereof (Louis, but also Betina when Django cuts the walk-and-talk short by asking her about the Brittle brothers). The similar shots of the McGraws in two consecutive movies emphasize the artifice of the situation and contribute to the metafictional discourse on the genderedness of film genre conventions, especially in *Death Proof* where the sheriff analyzes Mike's pathology according to a model that resembles those developed by feminist film critics discussing horror.

The style of most of the fight scenes in *Inglourious Basterds*, *Django Unchained*, *The Hateful Eight*, and especially *Kill Bill* are also fairly characteristic of intensified continuity. The final, seven-minute-long stretch of the House of Green Leaves battle, for instance, averages one shot per second and relies on handheld shots to propose quick pans, yet even in this scene only a quarter of the shots are close-ups or medium close-ups; the majority are medium full shots and medium shots [82:55–89:03]. This is also the case of the *Inglourious Basterds* shoot-out [92:37–2:53] and *The Hateful Eight* massacre [129:50–130:12]; both have an ASL of less than 1 second/shot, with half of the shots being medium full shots or larger. This is even more true of the Candieland shoot-out in *Django Unchained*, with its ASL of 1.6 second/shot[5] and the use of long and medium shots (less of a third of the shots are medium close-ups or close-ups) [131:39–134:03]. Clearly, Tarantino resorts to "intensified continuity" merely as a punctuation device in order to vary and expand the range of the narration—and not limit it as in the films Bordwell discusses—with the quick cutting and camera movements taking on a mimetic function.[6]

The *Django Unchained* scene's music video-like finale is also typical of intensified continuity, a style that has been influenced by television and music videos.[7] In fact, each film has at least one music video scene—that is, a scene where the soundtrack is entirely dominated by the music: "Little Green Bag" in *Reservoir Dogs* [7:57–9:00], "Bullwinkle Part II" in *Pulp Fiction* [30:14–31:20], "Across 110th Street" in *Jackie Brown* [0:22–3:49], "Battle Without Honor or Humanity" in *Kill Bill Vol. 1* [67:34–68:45], "About Her" in *Kill Bill Vol. 2* [97:46–100:14], "Down in Mexico" in *Death Proof* [39:11–42:00], "Cat People (Putting out the Fire)" in *Inglourious Basterds* [105:46–109:36], "Unchained (The Payback/Untouchable)" in *Django Unchained* [133:21–134:13], and "Apple Blossom" in *The Hateful Eight* [15:04–16:08]. These scenes are as compulsory in a Tarantino film as the violent action scenes, something viewers have come to expect. Yet with the exception of the "Battle Without Honor or Humanity" scene that clearly recalls the opening credits of *Reservoir Dogs*, the music video scenes are as varied as music videos themselves. Shots can be primarily close shots (*Reservoir Dogs*, *Pulp Fiction*), a mix of shot sizes (*Jackie Brown*, *Kill Bill Vol. 2*, *Death Proof*, *Inglourious Basterds*, *Django Unchained*), or can shift from the first to the second within the same scene (*Kill Bill Vol. 1*, *The Hateful Eight*). ASL can be short (2 seconds/shot in *Django Unchained*, 2.3 in *Kill Bill Vol. 1*, 4.8 in *Inglourious Basterds*), long (6.3 seconds/shot in *Reservoir Dogs*, 7.3 in *Pulp Fiction*, 9.4 in *Death Proof*), and even very long (12.3 seconds/shot in *Kill Bill Vol. 2*, 16 in *The Hateful Eight*, 23 in *Jackie Brown*); the pacing can be slow (*Reservoir Dogs*, *Pulp Fiction*) and can even be broken by resorting to slow motion (*Kill Bill Vol. 1*, *Django Unchained*).

The function of these scenes is just as varied as their aesthetics. The majority serve to introduce either the movie (*Reservoir Dogs*, *Jackie Brown*) or a scene (*Pulp Fiction*, *Kill Bill Vol. 1*, *Inglourious Basterds*). They can pursue the narrative (*Death Proof*, *Django Unchained*, *The Hateful Eight*), provide an intimate pause (*Pulp Fiction*, *Kill Bill Vol. 2*), or shift from the first to the second (*Inglourious Basterds*). Like the action scenes, the music video scenes are foregrounded moments in which the music video aesthetics associated with "intensified continuity" take over the narration just as the music takes over the soundtrack. This foregrounding, which draws attention to the music video scene as such, can be reinforced visually by stylistic options that momentarily break the film's aesthetics: a different texture (*Reservoir Dogs*), the use of soft focus (*Pulp Fiction*), pulsating light (*Kill Bill Vol. 2*), a different color scheme (*Kill Bill Vol. 2*, *Inglourious Basterds*) or slow motion (*Reservoir Dogs*, *Pulp Fiction*, *Kill Bill Vol. 1*, *Django Unchained*).

For the most part, Tarantino's style is not characteristic of contemporary mainstream cinema, and it is only classical up to a certain point. Classical narration, according to Bordwell, relies mainly on the "invisible observer" paradigm.[8] The invisibility can be on occasion violated, but "[t]he foregrounded moment is reabsorbed as an exception";[9] the effect of such violations resides in their sparsity. In the films of Tarantino, devices that disrupt the transparent narration and reflexively draw attention to the film as artefact occur on a regular basis, testifying to the influence of art cinema. Below is a non-exhaustive list of such devices, starting with profilmic ones and moving onto cinematographic ones.

- looks to the camera. They occur in *Jackie Brown* [119:18], *Kill Bill Vol. 2* [0:55–1:45], and *Death Proof* (fig. 30) [45:00].[10] A no-no of classical narration (apart from the musical where the theatrical origin makes them acceptable), the device typically breaks the fourth wall, making the viewer aware of her/his own position. The protagonist's behavior—Max and Mike grinning or the Bride addressing the audience—leaves no room for doubt as to the intentionality of the look. If it appears as just another self-conscious device

Fig. 30: *Death Proof*: Stuntman Mike breaks the fourth wall by grinning at the camera/viewer before driving away to commit murder.

in a film loaded with them in *Kill Bill*, it is especially disturbing in *Jackie Brown* and even *Death Proof* because these films largely abide—at least up to this point—by naturalist conventions; Max's look even has a precedent (when the department store saleswoman looks at the camera) that is justified because it is a POV shot from his perspective [116:48]. With a male character getting in his car either after accomplishing a mission (the shot concludes the money exchange section) or before setting out on one (taking care of his girlfriends), the instances from *Jackie Brown* and *Death Proof* play off each other. In spite of their differences, both acknowledge the viewer's knowledge of, and complicity in, the crime (effected or to come). This is also the case in *Kill Bill Vol. 2*, where the Bride basically informs the audience that Budd and Elle have already been disposed of.

- studio walls. They are visible on three occasions in *Kill Bill*, including when Vernita and the Bride enter the kitchen [*Vol. 1* 9:50–10:11], when the Bride heads for the bathroom in the House of Leaves [*Vol. 1* 71:16–71:25], and when Beatrix crawls out of the coffin [*Vol. 2* 61:36–61:47]. Revealing the studio set breaks the illusion of the diegetic world. It occurs in classical narration in foregrounded moments, such as the famous opening tracking shot of *Scarface* (Hawks, 1932), so the main difference is the frequency with which it occurs in *Kill Bill* and, more importantly, the fact that the film violates its own terms; indeed, if the first instance seems to equate reflexive self-consciousness with the Bride's authority as a narrator, subsequent instances belie the rule. The device is similarly used to celebrate Shosanna's command of space in Chapter Five of

Inglourious Basterds when she descends to meet her guests/future victims, the camera pivoting smoothly as she spins gracefully out of her chair and through the door [109:02-109:16]; it contrasts with the descending tracking shot evoking the Dreyfus family's powerlessness in Chapter One[11] [12:13-12:45].

- maps and models. Maps are used to depict the Bride's flights to Okinawa and to Tokyo in *Kill Bill Vol. 1* [45:08, 64:38]. Recalling similar scenes in the *Indiana Jones* franchise, the gimmick, in typical postmodernist fashion, combines two incompatible worlds by replacing the planet with a map or someone's finger with a plane. The artificiality of the model plane flying in a blood-red sky and of the city of Tokyo in the aerial views is retrospectively highlighted by the more naturalistic terrestrial shots of the city [65:02-65:58]. Unlike LA in Tarantino's previous films, the Tokyo and Japan of *Kill Bill* are clearly marked as inventions.
- blue screens. In *Pulp Fiction*, the screen that can be seen through the rearview mirror of Esmarelda's taxi draws attention to the paradox that the technique did not disrupt narration in the classical era, whereas in contemporary cinema its use is both self-conscious and stylish, and serves to enhance the *noir* atmosphere by calling on the classical device [70:42-73:42]. The many instances in *Kill Bill Vol. 2* function similarly [0:55-1:44, 54:45-55:28, 87:33-87:45], but the special effect is at once more conspicuous (notably because the backdrop alternates between a forest and an abstract red in the Pai Mei training sequence) and less disruptive for the same reason as the look to the camera is less so: because it constitutes just another instance of artificiality in the film.
- writing on the screen. All these instances are mediated by characters: Mia's tracing a square in the air in *Pulp Fiction* [34:30], O-Ren's whimper in *Kill Bill Vol. 1* (fig. 31) [38:04], and Shosanna's and Donowitz and Omar's gazes directed at key figures of the Third Reich in *Inglourious Basterds* [115:47]. Though justified on the narrative level, the shapes and letters draw attention to the two-dimensionality of the screen, thus breaking the referential illusion, for the connection with the character breaks the ontological barrier between the diegetic world and the screen. The three occurrences differ, however, according to their relevance and purpose: the appearance of the square is playful; the arrows and names in *Inglourious Basterds* have a didactic purpose; the "whimper" inscribes the anime in manga culture. The inscription of "whimper" highlights,

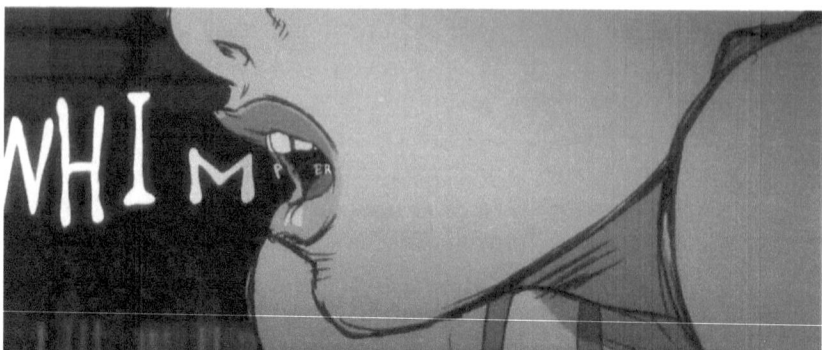

Fig. 31: *Kill Bill Vol.1*: The young O-Ren Ishii letting out a whimper as she witnesses the murder of her father from under a bed, in the anime that recounts her origin story.

of course, the intermediality of a film where one of the characters' backstories is told in animation, but it furthers the artifice by pointing to the inappropriateness of the dialogue; instead of whimpering, the young O-Ren utters a comic book sound effect, annulling all pretense of behavioral realism. The artificiality of an animated *mise an abyme* in a live action film is thus redoubled.

- lens flares. The golden lens flares when Jules and Vincent execute Brett in *Pulp Fiction* not only have a symbolic function, connecting capital—the golden light that shined on Vincent's face when he opened the briefcase [18:02]—and violence [21:00] through the same color; they also endow the scene with a comic book-like aesthetic and emphasize the surface of the screen, in spite of the depth conveyed by the three-quarter positions of the hitmen's bodies.
- modification of the frame size. The use of the device in *Kill Bill Vol. 2*, when the Bride, in close-up, is confined in the back of Budd's pickup, is justified both psychologically and dramatically, as it anticipates an even worse event to come that the sound of people shoveling offscreen gives a clue as to the nature of [31:04–31:55].
- keying and superimposition. They are used to allow us to see a character or an element in spite of a barrier—the bathroom wall in *Kill Bill Vol. 1* [71:38–72:49] and Omar and Donowitz's pants in *Inglourious Basterds* [117:16]. Paradoxically, the barrier is traversed—and further depth is achieved—by tampering with the surface of the image. Much like the writing on screen, the redoubling of the image to increase insight into the diegetic world depth ultimately reveals the two-dimensionality of the image. Paradoxically, narrative transparency—we are cognitively and emotionally aligned

with the characters—is achieved through a see-through effect that violates the transparency of classical narration. *Inglourious Basterds* even demonstrates that, in contemporary cinema, a standard silent-era device like the iris has, like the blue screen of the Hollywood golden age, become a marker of reflexivity.

- conspicuous shots.[12] These are foregrounded either because of their angle (extreme high-angle and/or oblique) and/or because of their distance from the center of attention (very long shots), usually the protagonist(s). Extreme high-angle and/or oblique shots often signal ominous predicaments or outcomes: Butch and Marsellus's imprisonment in Maynard's basement in *Pulp Fiction* [98:04], Vernita's death and the Bride's near death in *Kill Bill Vol. 1* [13:56, 16:16], Django's surrender [137:12]. Some shots can contribute to characterization by playing on stasis and duration: in *Reservoir Dogs*, the medium shot of Freddy pacing back and forth in his apartment while rehearsing, so that he keeps exiting the sides of the frame, seems to suggest that the absence of camera movement stems from his lack of command of his part at this initial stage [68:30–69:25]; in *Pulp Fiction*, the medium shot of Butch listening to Marsellus in the opening scene of "Vincent Vega & Marsellus's Wife" counters the classical norm that privileges the speaker, but, as we have seen, positions the boxer in a subordinate position and constructs Marsellus as a threatening "acousmatic being" [21:15–23:20]. Distance can serve to frame an event or characters in a specific context, with the visual perspective conveying a moral one. It can reflect disapproval by anchoring a crime in a realistic setting—the very long shot of Ordell's van after he kills Louis in *Jackie Brown* [125:26], the very long lateral shot that pans left to follow the cars racing down a hill and ends on an oil drill in the foreground in *Death Proof* [103:20], thereby breaking the exhilarating kinetics of the chase scene, or the vertical high-angle shot of the slaves marching in two opposite directions in *Django Unchained*, which equates the flow of bodies with the slave trade and the state whose name flows in from the right [58:13]. Or the physical distance can foreground the gap between self and role—the very long shots of Mr. White and Mr. Pink trying to regain their composure in the bathroom in *Reservoir Dogs* [17:35–19:07] or of Jules and Vincent cooly talking about foot massages in *Pulp Fiction* [12:46–14:24]; the latter shot even violates the previously established intrinsic norm of the walk-and-talk and makes way for a backshot of Jules and Vincent when they "get into character" before ringing Brett's doorbell, an amusing touch of modesty (given that they're cool killers) that also postpones the action. All in all, such shots rarely compromise the causal logic of classical narration, but they do tap into the conventions of art-cinema narration by introducing delay, reflexively commenting on the situation and sometimes producing irony.

- unmotivated camera movements. By "unmotivated," I mean that they are not aligned with a character's movements; they are, of course, entirely motivated by the narration. They are plentiful in Tarantino's films and are sometimes combined with conspicuous shots. The vast majority of these serve a dramatic purpose: to evoke an emotion, e.g., when the camera tracks out from Dicky Speck's screaming mouth after getting shot by Schultz in *Django Unchained* [7:50]; to introduce a character, e.g., the track-outs in *Reservoir Dogs* (fig. 58) [32:41–33:09], *Kill Bill Vol. 2*[13] [13:51–14:45], and *Inglourious Basterds* [79:19–79:25], which reveal the presence of Mr. Blonde in the foreground watching Mr. White and Mr. Pink argue, the Vipers outside the church, and Major Hellstrom in the tavern cutting in to question Hicox on his accent; to dramatize or herald a dramatic event, e.g., the track-out that shows Ordell moving in to strangle Jackie Brown [49:19], the complex track-out when Django surrenders [137:12]. Camera movements can even foreshadow later events or relationships. In *Jackie Brown*, for instance, the camera pans from Ordell talking on the phone with Beaumont to center on Melanie's feet as she shares her weed with Louis, whom she will later try to turn against her lover [10:19–10:32]. In *Death Proof*, the full shot through the windshield of the Dodge Challenger that pans right to follow Zoë as she moves away from Jasper resembles a POV shot and thus recalls that Mike already has the young women in his sight [79:54–80:06]. In *Kill Bill Vol. 2*, the tracking shot over Bill's samurai sword turns out to be a red herring, as Bill will soon use a gun on Beatrix [101:49]. In *Kill Bill Vol. 1* [20:27–20:44, 68:47–69:12, 70:55–72:48] and *Inglourious Basterds* [110:30, 115:10], complex crane shots are used at the hospital, in the House of Leaves, and the movie theater as a form of omniscient narration that presents a place (the hospital, the House of Leaves, the movie theater), situates the characters (the 5.6.7.8's on stage, the Bride at the bar, the Nazis), follows the movements of various characters (the Bride, the restaurant owners, Sofie Fatale, Shosanna, Landa, Donowitz, and Omar), and generally sets up the action. Briefer camera movements can also disclose important information to the viewer, such as the presence of the Dreyfus family under LaPadite's floorboards [12:18] or the dynamite strapped onto Omar and Donowtiz's shins [117:16]. These shots are particularly conspicuous when they abandon the characters and divert attention from the action. This occurs twice in *Reservoir Dogs*, first when the camera tracks and pans over a bucket and a mop, underlining the heist movie's mundane setting and ironically commenting on the dogs' incapacity to clean up their own mess [17:35].[14] It recurs later when the camera pans away from Mr. Blonde as he straddles Officer Nash to cut off his ear [56:38–57:07]. By centering on the doorway at the top of the ramp in the background, the pan metonymically—and ironically—evokes the hole being inflicted on the police officer. When Mr. Blonde eventually steps back into the shot, the camera tilts down in order to frame him in three-quarter angle, and the narration apparently resumes its subordination to the character's movements; yet instead of panning or cutting through match-on-action in order to follow him as he steps up to the police officer, the camera lingers an extra two seconds on the doorway. This moment recalls the self-censoring devices of classical Hollywood cinema, with the doorway acting both as a signifier of the wound and a dark screen on which the viewer can eventually project an imagined version of the act. The elaborate crane shot which rises from Ordell's car, pans left, and looks down onto the empty lot where the gun trafficker will murder Beaumont in *Jackie Brown* [22:05–23:36], and the track-out to a very long high-angle shot of Donowitz beating Rachtman to death in *Inglourious Basterds* [34:44–34:46], function similarly. Some unmotivated camera movements contribute significantly to the metafictional discourse. For instance, the aforementioned track-out from Dick Speck's face, a horror movie cliché, announces *Django Unchained*'s reframing the Western as Southern Gothic. In *Pulp Fiction*, the camera initially explores Jack Rabbit Slim's with Vincent, then takes off on its own before returning to the protagonist; in so doing, we rediscover Vincent as yet another potential lookalike—ironically, of the actor playing his part [35:25–35:38].

Tarantino's style, unsurprisingly perhaps, is a hybrid one: classicism with an art-house sensibility. All in all, the films abide by the extrinsic conventions of classical narration in that they endeavor to make narrative, space, action, and character motivations clear for viewers. They are less paradigmatic of the contemporary style than one might have expected, making use of the whole palette of shot sizes, alternating between static and mobile shots, varying the pacing, and resorting to the aesthetics of intensified continuity only in specific scenes (walk-and-talk, fight, and music video scenes). The vast array of reflexive devices (looks to the camera, studio walls, blue screens, writing on the screen, conspicuous camera angles, unmotivated camera movement) testifies to Tarantino's debt to art cinema. The films flaunt their artificiality to varying degrees, *Kill Bill Vol. 1* being the apotheosis in this respect, by reminding viewers of the diegesis's status as a profilmic fabrication and of the surface of the screen. Tarantino's brand of self-conscious classical narration—a contradiction in terms since it implies that narration is both transparent and intervening—inscribes his films in the legacy of New Hollywood filmmakers, who, under the influence of the European new waves, "took up an explicit intertexuality" and "selectively applied" "art-cinema devices" to "films which remain firmly grounded in classical genres."[15] The number and frequency of signature devices, as we shall see, confirm the films' high degree of self-consciousness.

Tarantino's Signature Devices

Low-angle shot / high-angle reverse shot

This device is used in all of Tarantino's films except *Django Unchained* and has undoubtedly become his trademark. In Philippe Ortoli's insightful analysis, the reverse shot reveals a deathly space.[16] The low-angle shot frames the actual or potential executioners; though the high-angle reverse shot dramatizes the reactive gaze, it is never a POV shot and is not edited in eyeline match. When the reverse shot reveals a potential victim, we are often aligned with his/her perspective (in *Reservoir Dogs*, *Kill Bill*, and *Inglourious Basterds*, for instance) but never with that of the perpetrator. The terms of the device are masochistic rather than sadistic, as Bill puts it in the prologue of *Kill Bill Vol. 1*. For Ortoli, the insistence on the executioners' desiring gaze[17] makes the device eminently metafilmic: "this shot testifies to a link between the underside of creation, already occupied by other objects, and Tarantino's own execution."[18] The "underside of creation" is, I would add, that of film and cultural history. For Tarantino's trademark is actually borrowed from the opening scene of *The Mack* (Michael Campus, 1973), in which two corrupt white cops have stuffed the protagonist in their trunk. The repeated use of this shot suggests that Tarantino's films are breathing

Fig. 32: *Reservoir Dogs*: A low-angle three-shot of Mr. Blonde, White, and Pink looking down at Officer Marvin Nash, an inversion of a similar shot in *The Mack* (Michael Campus, 1973).

life into the dead objects of cinema, just as they endeavor to revive the film genres and figures of the past. Not only does the repeated use of this motif comment on Tarantino's view of cinema, it also comments on each film in relation to the others.

Reservoir Dogs offers a three-shot of Mr. Blonde showing Mr. White and Mr. Pink the surprise in his trunk: Officer Marvin Nash in reverse shot (fig. 32) [37:38]. The visual reference to *The Mack* reverses the terms of the original scene: we are aligned with the domineering characters, not the potential victim; the police officer is in the trunk; and all the characters are white. The reference to *The Mack* confirms, however, Nama's demonstration that race is a structuring principal in the film. The power relationship the device conveys operates, as in *The Mack*, as a promise of the violence to come. The three-shot is a moment of reconciliation—Mr. White even calls Mr. Blonde "[his] friend"—after the dispute in the warehouse. The "boy in blue" is thus the scapegoat through which the three thieves regain their sense of a common identity, metonymically represented by their clothes. Mr. Blonde has thus restored order after causing chaos in the jewelry store. Accordingly, the device also functions as a dramatic flourish that introduces his chapter.

In *Pulp Fiction*, the two-shot of Vincent and Jules establishes a contrast with both *The Mack* and *Reservoir Dogs* [8:48]. Unlike *The Mack*, the white man and the black man are standing side by side, and the trunk contains weapons, not a victim. The device is also a promise of violence, yet their concern about the number of foes they might be facing and the inappropriateness of their equipment lends a sense of uncertainty, materialized in the absence of a reverse shot: we have no idea who will come to occupy the locus of death—is it Vincent, Jules, or their adversaries? If the tandem initally kills all the white men and spares the black man, Vincent ends up shooting

Marvin by accident, and it is ultimately the latter's corpse that will end up in the trunk [131:02]. The absence of a reverse shot ultimately represents, therefore, a disavowal that the violence will, as in *The Mack*, be racialized and is thus an expression of the racist unconscious that structures the film.

The reprisal of this device in *Jackie Brown*—a two-shot of two black men, Ordell and Beaumont—is also linked to the treatment of race [19:15]. It initially plays on the similarity with *Pulp Fiction*; the reverse shot also contains weapons, which Beaumont (like Jules and Vincent) is to use in service of his employer. This time, however, the potential killer is asked to hide in the trunk in order to "surprise" the Koreans if need be—in other words, to occupy the same position as Mr. Blonde's surprise for Mr. White and Mr. Pink. Ordell's plot functions as a red herring on the racial level. The confrontation appears to pit African Americans versus Koreans, but actually pits black against black, and is thus indicative of Ordell's racial self-loathing. The other main difference—the fact that the scene takes place at night—further draws attention to Ordell's duplicity. Accordingly, a variation of the device is used during the money exchange—this time when Jackie swaps books and cash in the trunk of her car—to foreground Ordell's being bettered by the black woman he attempted to dispose of [103:32].

Kill Bill Vol. 1 also adjusts the trunk scene to its thematic concerns; here, both characters are women (the Bride and Sofie Fatale), and the low-angle shot is a single of the Bride [98:37–98:40, 100:00–100:28, 101:02–101:45]. Although only women are present, Sofie's body is actually used as a means of communication with the abject patriarch, Bill. The device evokes both the violence effected (Sofie's severed arm) and the promise of violence to come, both diegetically (the Bride asks Sofie to deliver her message) and for the viewer anticipating the next installment. Not only does the device emphasize the Bride's physical power, but its framing the epilogue underlines her control over the narration. The device echoes the low-angle four-shot—a POV shot from the dying Bride's perspective of her tormentors (Elle, Vernita, Budd, and O-Ren) standing over her in the church [35:10] that is quasi-identical to a shot in *Lady Snowblood*—in which Bill's presence is also figured by his very absence: he ordered the execution, and the DiVAS are standing in for him (fig. 33). The arc of vengeance has inverted the positions, with the victim now the victimizer, Lady Snowblood now one of the dogs from Tarantino's 1992 film or one of the cops from *The Mack*. The tables are turned once again in *Vol. 2*, when Ernie and Budd stand over the Bride and make misogynistic comments [33:05]. The repetition of these shots in *Kill Bill* foregrounds the spiral of violence the revenge narrative is caught up in.

Fig. 33: *Kill Bill Vol. 1*: The low-angle four-shot of the DiVAS looking down at the Bride, an allusion to *Lady Snowblood* (Toshiya Fujita, 1973), *The Mack*, and Tarantino's previous films.

Death Proof reprises the device just once, when Kim and Zoë admire the engine of the Dodge Challenger [79:42]. It contrasts with all the instances in Tarantino's previous films: emphasis is put on interracial friendship and the promise of fun to come. Or rather, only the viewer is aware of the underlying promise of male violence, as the movie the car is from (*Vanishing Point*) has already been mentioned by Mike [43:28], and the device echoes the low-angle medium close-up of Mike looking down at the dying Pam with his engine running [47:30]. The two stuntwomen are thus constructed as the positive doubles and worthy rivals of the psycho killer.

Like *Kill Bill*, *Inglourious Basterds* proposes a variation of this device minus the trunk. These occur twice [37:43, 149:20]. The device is yet again linked to racial discrimination; it is used when Aldo Raine carves swastikas on the foreheads of Nazis. This draws attention to the fact that the device is always linked to punishment. Its metafilmic function is foregrounded due to its position at the end of the chapter that has the same name as the movie, and at the end of the movie. Donowitz's praise to Aldo—"You know, Lieutenant, you're getting pretty good at that"—points to the repetition of the motif both within the film and Tarantino's body of work, while Aldo's own self-congratulatory remark, "I think this just might be my masterpiece"—the last line in the last shot of the film, immediately preceding the end credits which open with *Written and Directed by Quentin Tarantino*—reinforces the metonymical link between Aldo's gesture and Tarantino's film noted by several critics.[19] *Inglourious Basterds* thus insists on the extent to which the device has become Tarantino's signature just as the carving is Aldo's signature in the film. Both signatures are, pointedly, imitations (of the Nazi insignia, of the shot from *The Mack*), but both aim at resignification of the moral and political (the pride of being a Nazi rewritten as shame; the racial and gender inversions analyzed above).

Raine's conclusion seemed to be confirmed by the fact that neither *Django Unchained* nor *The Hateful Eight* feature the trademark shot. However, Tarantino's eighth feature film recycles the very similar shot from *Lady Snowblood* and *Kill Bill Vol. 1*, when Jody instructs Oswaldo Mobray, Bob, and Joe Gage before hiding in the basement [137:30]. The power relation generally associated with the device has been reversed: the executioners are shot in low angle, while the high-angle reverse shot frames he who is in command. Appropriately, however, given that the movie is a murder mystery, the device is used as an omen: Jody's occupying the space of death inevitably anticipates his own, as he will not come out of the basement alive, shot down by Major Warren, who had previously occupied a Tarantinian low-angle medium shot when exploding Bob's head [117:13].

Tarantino's trademark shot evinces a view of creation as re-creation, and thus a faith that resurrection lies in the revisiting of dead material. In so doing, it invites us to interpret his films by comparing devices that are borrowed from existing films and repeated from one film to the next and sometimes even within a given film. The poetics, politics, and ethics of the films lie in the variations. It is other such devices, perhaps less obvious ones, that we will now explore.

Circling camera during conversation

Another early stylistic device, from the prologue of *Reservoir Dogs*, that is reprised in Tarantino's later films is the circling camera to capture a conversation [0:27–4:03]. Its inspiration is probably the tense lunch scene between the sisters in *Hannah and Her Sisters* (Woody Allen, 1986). The technique has several functions. First, by tracking around the speakers, it creates a circle of intimacy, cutting them off from the other patrons in the diner; this is reinforced by the push-in from medium shot to medium close-up. Second, the continuous movement positions the characters all on par, emphasizing their identical black backs out of focus in the foreground and their black suits, white shirts, and black ties. If, initially, the character played by Tarantino seems more important because he is talking, this is subsequently countered when he gets interrupted and the conversation gets sidetracked, and confirmed by the film when he only reappears to die [85:14]. Though the camera centers on him when he regains control of the conversation, he is yet again interrupted, this time by the man who will turn out to be the real mastermind, Joe Cabot. The circling camera is replaced by shot/reverse

Fig. 34: *Reservoir Dogs*: The camera circles round the dogs as they converse, creating a sense of intimacy as in *Hannah and Her Sisters* (Woody Allen, 1986).

shots[20] as Cabot and Mr. White, the two patriarchs, bicker. This occurs again at the end when the characters argue and debate over tipping. Third, the technique mimics the energy of the scene, an energy that is entirely verbal since the characters are all seated. The moment the characters stray from the main topic, the smooth rhythm conveyed by the tracking shot is broken in a series of wipe-bys, and the direction is even violated by a pan to the right that ends in a medium close-up of Mr. Brown asking: "What the fuck was I talking about?" (fig. 34) Finally, the parallel with the scene from *Hannah and Her Sisters* invites certain comparisons—an intimate conversation between sisters that turns sour makes way for a superficial meeting between thieves in which they must, unlike the sisters, avoid honesty or the disclosure of their true selves for professional/genre reasons.

The circling camera is used in a similar scene in *Death Proof*, when the second group of girls are in the diner [71:50–79:06]. The presence of an all-female group points back to the source for *Reservoir Dogs*, especially since Zoë, like Holly, shares her ambitions with the others, yet hers is presented as a less profound ambition that ultimately resembles that of a genre character and thus connects the female group to the 1992 dogs. The technique's functions are the same: creating intimacy, establishing power relations, conveying rhythm. However, framed as an allusion, it prompts a metafictional interpretation by inviting comparisons between the two scenes. The tracking shot starts circling counterclockwise and suddenly pauses on Abernathy before moving clockwise (fig. 35), suggesting that the scene will not be a mere repetition of *Reservoir Dogs*'s prologue and that attention must be paid to the little differences: (1) the girls are not all dressed the same; (2) instead of talking about sex and money, they are sharing information about themselves (this is consistent with the fact that the dogs were aliases forbidden to reveal their

Fig. 35: *Death Proof*: The camera circles around the four women, but changes direction to mark a difference with *Reservoir Dogs*.

true identities); (3) the audience is attentive to the speaker, whom the camera centers on (Abernathy, then Zoë, Abernathy again, then Lee, Kim); and (4) the camerawork is subordinate to the conversation and is thus not rigidly locked into a movement; the camera also tracks in and out, and focus is also less rigid than in *Reservoir Dogs*, as this time it alternates between the women in the background and in the foreground. When the girls make fun of each other (Lee's gullibility) or argue (about guns, for instance), the camera merely pauses. This time, the circling movement is broken when Zoë brings up her dream of driving a car—that is to say, when the narrative returns to the plot—and it starts again when the characters talk about car movies. The use of the device in *Death Proof* serves to comment on the prologue from *Reservoir Dogs*, confirming how central the opposition between the two patriarchs, Cabot and Mr. White, is. But it also serves to distinguish the second group of girls from the first. The earlier all-girl scene at Güero's resorts exclusively to shot/reverse shots with eyeline match, with Jungle Julia representing the hub [9:37–14:06]. The use of the circling camera thus presents Abernathy, Kim, Lee, and Zoë as an alternative to the all-male group of *Reservoir Dogs* and to the all-girl posse in Austin, whom Julia subjects to the male gaze.

The circling camera is used twice in *Inglourious Basterds*, first during the Nazis' small talk about African American athletes in the restaurant [48:28–48:41, 50:17–50:50], then when Landa and von Hammersmark converse in the hall of the movie theater [111:20–112:02]. As in the previous films, it creates a circle of intimacy and energizes what (to the Nazis, and to Bridget and the Basterds, at least) seems to be harmless banter. In the final instance, the camera, as in *Death Proof*, centers on the two speakers (von Hammersmark and Landa), highlighting how inept the Basterds are in this context. Its disruption and replacement, in the narration, by shot/reverse shots is effected when Shosanna arrives and becomes the main topic of the conversation, and when Landa bursts out laughing, filling the other characters with alarm. The repetition of the device thus draws a parallel between the two enemies (and yet main instigators) of the demise of the Third Reich.

By contrast, in *Django Unchained*, the use of the technique insists on the authority of the teller, as Django explains his plan to the white slavers; the tracking shot is centered on the face of the black man who is doing all the talking [145:07–146:18]. Conversely, in *The Hateful Eight*, the camera circling around John Ruth, Daisy Domergue, O. B., and Major Warren focuses less and less on Ruth, as if to mock his paranoid belief in a plot to free Domergue [68:34–70:17]. The circling camera thus serves as a barometer of narrative control, indicating a storyteller's power over her/his audience or lack thereof.

Eye-level frontal two-shot portraying interracial or intergender relationship

These compositions are used in all of Tarantino's films from *Pulp Fiction* on. In *Pulp Fiction*, they introduce the characters of Jules and Vincent when they take the elevator in medium close-up (fig. 36) [10:23–11:03], and later when Brett and his friends open the door [14:28]. Similar two-shots relate their undergoing a humiliating plight together in "The Bonnie Situation," with medium close-ups of them in their professional suits before and after they have been soiled by Marvin's blood [113:07, 118:23, 125:44], and later when they stand in their drawers and finally in Jimmy's college student clothes [129:18–131:01, 132:10–132:28]. The black and white hitmen are thus presented on equal footing and constructed as an iconic pair.[21] Accordingly, the change in Butch and Marsellus Wallace's relationship, as they are subjected to the same brutal experience in Maynard's basement, is signaled by two-shots, their newfound proximity heightened by the shot size which goes from medium full shot to medium close-up [97:42, 99:36].

Jackie Brown reprises the frontal two-shot to depict an interracial male friendship as soon as the opening scene, with Ordell and Louis sitting side by side on a couch watching TV [4:21]. The presence of Samuel L. Jackson reinforces the similarity with the shots in *Pulp Fiction*. Yet the composition turns out to be deceptive as the scene soon reveals the two men are by no means on equal terms: Ordell, whose clothing is more stylish and presumably more expensive, is showing off his knowledge of guns; Louis is just listening. Comparing the two-shots in *Pulp Fiction* and *Jackie Brown* thus reveals one of its main functions: it serves to question the terms of a power relationship that is staged as equal. Its repeated and near-exclusive[22] use with Ordell

Fig. 36: *Pulp Fiction*: A two-shot of the interracial pair (Jules and Vincent) in the elevator.

and Louis—at the Cockatoo Inn, for instance [75:25]—comes to signify that Ordell values his white friend more than he does his black employees; the frontal eye-level two-shot is not used with Beaumont and Jackie. When Ordell finally gets rid of Louis, the two-shot from behind reflects not only the gangster's duplicity (he takes both the victim and viewers by surprise since the gun is concealed), but also his reluctance to kill the white man [124:50]. By making the two-shot over into a marker of racial self-loathing, *Jackie Brown* invites us to question the function of the two-shot in *Pulp Fiction*, a movie where the bodies that are violated are those of black men (Marvin and Marsellus).

In Chapter One of *Kill Bill*, the two-shot is used to depict the exact opposite of those in *Pulp Fiction*: interracial enmity between two women, Vernita and the Bride [7:54]. This time, however, it serves to highlight what the two adversaries have in common: both wanted to quit the assassin business and lead "normal" lives as mothers and wives. The composition thus draws attention to the solidarity they fail to reach because of their attachment to the values of honor and revenge rather than love and forgiveness, and ultimately calls into question the validity of the Bride's enterprise.

Death Proof reprises the frontal two-shot to depict an interracial friendship between two women, Kim and Zoë (fig. 37) [82:39]. The terms of the relationship have previously been revealed to us on a comic mode, Zoë having offered to be Kim's "back-cracking slave" to convince her to play Ship's Mast. If it is the white woman who makes the offer to submit, they are, in effect, on equal terms as they have both conceived and accepted these terms. All in all, the two-shots in *Death Proof* suggest that relationships between women can be equally problematic. Indeed, it is repeatedly used in the cars to group the more "feminine" women together—Shanna and Arlene in the

Fig. 37: *Death Proof*: A two-shot of stuntwomen Zoë and Kim facing Abernathy, the "mum."

backseat of Lana Frank's car [49:16], Abernathy and Lee in the backseat of Kim's car [66:37]—while the more "masculine" women are not only more directive (sitting up front) but are also more individualized (through the use of single shots). This puts the subsequent two-shot of Zoë and Kim in a different light. The two stuntgirls are on equal terms as they explain to Abernathy their plot to take the Dodge Challenger on a joy ride on their own—and thus to abandon Abernathy and Lee—recalling a less violent version of the two hitmen shooting Brett in *Pulp Fiction*. By negotiating that she can tag along, Abernathy manages to replace Zoë by Kim's side in a two-shot with Kim in the front passenger seat [94:09]. Thus, the repeated use of the frontal eye-level two-shot confirms that, in *Death Proof*, power relations are determined by the degree of masculinity and femininty more than by race.

The frontal two-shots in *Inglourious Basterds* play on a wide variety of power relations. With the first—the medium shot of Goebbels and his translator [51:57]—the visual appearance of equal terms suggested visually, and reinforced by the fact that the Nazi relies on her linguistically, is immediately undermined by the relation of domination-submission depicted in the subjective insert of the two having sex with the woman on all fours. The next occurrences—the two-shots of Bridget and Hicox, and of Hellstrom and Stiglitz in the tavern—also play on the idea of deception; the German uniforms display a hierarchy that is annulled by the game, and then by the presence of a spy, a traitor, and an Englishman in disguise [82:05–90:31]. Chapter Five offers a variation of this when the Basterds endeavor to infiltrate the movie theater. Bridget attempts to introduce Raine and herself, and Omar and Donowitz, as pairs [113:10–113:25], but Landa sees through the deception, as will the viewer: Raine's white suit marks him out as the hero, the only one to survive and to reappear in a two-shot alongside one of the soldiers in his command

(Private Utivitch) [128:08]. *Inglourious Basterds* thus equally invites viewers to decypher the power relations under a surface equality.

In *Django Unchained*, the succession of two-shots dramatize, in a fairly obvious fashion, the evolution of the relationship between Django and Dr. Schultz, and Django's eventual emancipation from white authority. The first such shots occur when they enter and exit the bar in Daughtrey, Texas. If the two-shot reflects the fact that Schultz does not see black people as inferior, it is nonetheless the experienced bounty hunter who does the killing and the talking [14:26, 21:50]. The next such shot, after they have killed the Brittle brothers at Big Daddy's Plantation, also depicts Schultz doing the talking, but this time both the disciple and his mentor have participated in the killing (fig. 61) [38:28]. The end of Django's apprenticeship is marked by a two-shot of him and Amerigo Vessepi, played by Franco Nero, the 1966 Django, making Jamie Foxx's avatar not so much the copy as an equal version [67:30]. Subsequently, Schultz and Django's maintaining the appearance of racial inequality is visually rendered in a medium shot where the white man faces the camera while the black man stands in profile [71:30]. After Schultz's death, the white man ceases to function as a cover for racial inequality, but the white body becomes a literal cover for the black hero, as is indicated by the two-shot of Django using another man's body for protection (fig. 68) [113:48]. Django's emancipation from white authority is complete when he opposes his foes in singles in the final scene [156:38].

The Hateful Eight proceeds similarly to dramatize the complex interactions between race, gender, and region underlying the narrative. The first two-shot introduces John Ruth and Daisy Domergue when Ruth asks Major Warren: "By 'woman' you mean her?" [13:12], indicating that the question of gender is problematic from the start. The last part of Chapter Two is organized around two-shots of Ruth and Domergue, on the one hand, and Major Warren and Chris Mannix, on the other (fig. 38) [27:46]. The two-shots depict unequal relationships (between a man and a woman, between a black man and a white one) in which the dominant position is occupied by the Unionists who, even more so than Kim and Zoë in *Death Proof*, have established equal terms by making a deal. The two-shots of these couples are reprised at the dinner table in Minnie's Haberdashery [76:36], while two more couples are created: Oswaldo Mobray and Mannix, when Mobray shows Mannix his contract as an executioner [55:21], then at the dinner table [77:45]; and Bob and Warren when they come back from the barn [63:28]. The common denominator between these relationships appears to be race. Bob and Warren are both minority figures, while the alleged hangman questions the alleged Sheriff of

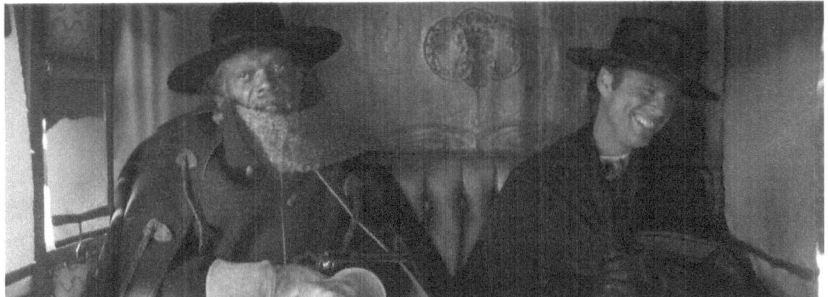

Fig. 38: *The Hateful Eight*: A two-shot of Warren and Mannix, whom initially everything (race, politics) opposes in the stagecoach, sitting across from Daisy and Ruth.

Red Rock about "the bounty hunter's nigger friend in the stable." If Warren immediately distrusts the Mexican, the two-shots of Mobray and Mannix announce the former rebel's role in the last chapter because of his politics. The succession of two-shots thus depicts the transformation of Warren and Mannix's relationship, from one where the black Unionist is in the dominant position—in the stagecoach, but even later when Warren gives him a pistol [107:47]—to one where the Southern renegade willfully sides with the wounded black man on the bed [141:06]. The two-shot thus becomes the site of reconciliation between North and South, black and white. Yet this is at the cost of intergender relationships, which remain grounded in violence until the end, as Domergue endeavors to extirpate herself from Ruth's hold—and thus from the initial two-shot—even in death. The fate of the frontal eye-level two-shot in *The Hateful Eight* confirms what the use of the composition has demonstrated over the body of Tarantino's films: the difficulty of achieving relationships based on equal terms, due to the fact that they are grounded in a history of power relations involving notably race and gender.

Lateral tracking shot following heroine/hero

Jackie Brown opens with a lengthy tracking shot of Jackie going to work while dressed in her airline sterwardess uniform (fig. 21) [0:38–1:52]. By inverting the situation of the film it borrows from—a middle-aged black woman at LAX has replaced a male college student (Ben Braddock) in *The Graduate* (Mike Nichols, 1967)—it draws attention to the central theme of both films: age (growing up in *The Graduate*, growing old in *Jackie Brown*). The leftward movement dramatizes the heroine's struggle against time and her attempt to gain some control over her future. The similar, albeit briefer

Fig. 39: *Kill Bill Vol. 1*: The Bride's arrival in Tokyo, her confident stride recalling that of Jackie Brown.

lateral medium shot used before Jackie goes inside the Del Amo Mall for the money exchange suggests that pretending to subject herself to Ordell's and the police's interests is the price to pay for the change [103:52–103:59]. The borrowing also pinpoints a generation gap in terms of film history: *Jackie Brown* is giving a black actress a chance to star in a New Hollywood film instead of the exploitation films her career was limited to in the 1970s.

The lateral tracking shot of the heroine is reprised in *Kill Bill Vol. 1* when the Bride arrives at the airport in Tokyo (fig. 39) [66:02–66:06], as well as in the opening credits of *Django Unchained* when Django is marching along with the other slaves [1:30–1:43]. Like Jackie, the Bride is shot in a lateral medium shot as she moves left. Unlike Jackie, however, she does not blend in with her environment, but on the contrary, stands out sharply, dressed all in black against a blue then pink background; her movement testifies to her confident resolve to deal with the past—pointedly, she is not carried along by a moving walkway but is striding along. The tracking shot thus contrasts the simplicity of the Bride's one-track trajectory with the complexity of Jackie's plot.

Visually, the lateral tracking shot of Django is the exact opposite: Django moving right, but not of his own accord, so that it is mainly the shot's presence in the opening credits that invites comparisons to *Jackie Brown*. Yet the close-up draws attention to the intensity of his gaze which, combined with the song lyrics ("When there are clouds in the skies and they are gray / You may be sad but remember they'll all soon pass away"), suggests his determination to deal with his past and, like Jackie, take control of his life. These assorted tracking shots endow the characters' movements with ambiguity, highlighting either the regressive nature of their forward momemtum (Jackie, the Bride) or the dynamic potential of their imprisonment (Django).

Split screen

Another technique, the split screen, also makes its first appearance in *Jackie Brown*. It is borrowed from another one of Tarantino's favorite directors, Brian De Palma, who famously used it in *Sisters* (1972) to create suspense by juxtaposing simultaneous events in separate locales. In *Jackie Brown*, the split screen depicts Max's discovery of the gun while Ordell is threatening to kill Jackie in her living room [50:12–50:43]. A cognitive advantage is thus given to the viewer, who is informed of the protagonist's own advantage while being simultaneously aligned with Max in this discovery. Significantly, the split screen ends with the clock of the gun being cocked.

The split screen is used three times in *Kill Bill*: when Elle comes to assassinate the Bride at the hospital (fig. 14) [*Vol. 1* 20:52–21:54]; when the Bride challenges O-Ren at the House of Leaves [*Vol. 1* 73:41]; and when Elle and the Bride simultaneously fall back in Budd's trailer [*Vol. 2* 75:22].[23] The first two instances recall *Jackie Brown*, with the viewer being given a cognitive advantage while one character is shown to be at a disadvantage (the Bride, then O-Ren), precisely at a moment of anticipation (of a murder or a fight). The third instance, by contrast, emphasizes that the two blondes are fighting as equals, and maybe even doubles, as the title of Chapter Nine, "Elle and I," suggests.

In *Inglourious Basterds*, the split screen occurs when the narrator explains how flammable film is (fig. 4) [62:42–62:51]. The viewer is given proof of the validity of Shosanna's plan, and thus an advantage over the unsuspecting Nazis, but the nature of the proof is called into question by the fact that part of it comes from an authority figure in a fiction film, *Sabotage*, directed by the filmmaker who most influenced De Palma. An excerpt from a fiction film is endowed with an archive effect, and thus with the authority of reality, even though it is by no means nonfiction; it is replaced by an image of film burning to prove its point. The split screen ultimately demonstrates that images can be resignified and reinvested with another meaning, that fiction can be given the truth value of nonfiction, and that images can be manipulated by juxtaposing them through composition and/or editing.

Frame-within-frame composition through doorway

The influence of this shot is obviously *The Searchers*,[24] although Ford and others had used it before. Such shots occur three times in *Kill Bill*, when the Bride opens the sliding door onto the Japanese garden [*Vol. 1* 90:15], when she walks out of the church to meet Bill on the porch [*Vol. 2* 5:44], and

Fig. 40: *Kill Bill Vol. 2*: The vengeful Bride exits Budd's trailer like Ethan Edwards at the end of *The Searchers* (John Ford, 1956).

Fig. 41: *Inglourious Basterds*: Hans Landa exits the LaPadite house as Shosanna runs away in the distance.

when she exits Budd's trailer after slaying Elle (fig. 40) [*Vol. 2* 80:44]; once in *Inglourious Basterds*, when Shosanna runs across the field and Landa steps out the door to shoot her down (fig. 41) [20:28]; and three times in *Django Unchained*, when Schultz and Django ride off to do their winter business in a medium backshot [51:17], when Billy Crash walks out of the barn after almost neutering Django [139:45], and when Django returns to deliver Broomhilda from the cabin she was trapped in [154:46].[25] Patrick McGee argues convincingly that the allusion in Chapter Six makes Bill the double of Ethan Edwards, a man who desires to destroy the family he can't possess, although Bill acts out on his desire.[26] But by framing the Bride as killer (Chapters Five and Nine) and the Bride as victim (Chapter Six)—in other words, as both Ethan[27] and Debbie Edwards—the repetition of the shots also foreground the logic of revenge that drives the heroine and the film, while reminding us that Beatrix Kiddo was already an assassin to start with. On a metafictional level, they draw attention to the historical connection between two film genres—the Western and the samurai—and testify to the Bride's capacity to inhabit these diverse genres and spaces, just like her mentor Bill and his model, Kwai Chang Cain.

Heidi Schlipphacke has noted that the shot in *Inglourious Basterds* is an allusion to both *The Searchers* and *Kill Bill*; indeed, like the Bride, Shosanna will seek revenge.[28] William Brown astutely argues that it is by inverting the situation in *The Searchers*—by making Landa step through the door like Ethan—that the film connects American racism and Nazism.[29] The allusion to *The Searchers* is thus meant to conjure up its hero's genocidal tendencies as a negative.

Django Unchained reprises the shot in *The Searchers*, like *Inglourious Basterds*, to evoke the theme of racism and, like *Kill Bill*, to describe the protagonist's trajectory: the first celebrates an interracial relationship that is quite exceptional in a Western; the second aligns the sadistic Billy Crash with Ethan Edwards; and the final shot constructs Django as the shadow of these racist white cowboys—and thus their inverted double who has come to free Broomhilda not from the Indians but from the slavers. Clearly, the recurrent allusion maintains the self-reflexivity of Ford's shot—the protagonist is framed as the iconic figure of a film genre—but insists on the racism associated with the ambiguous icon.

Fast zoom-ins and -outs

The technique is borrowed from the Shaw Brothers productions that *Kill Bill* pays homage to; its use is absolutely consistent in terms of film genre and hypotexts. The effect is expressive, with the violence of the camerawork mimicking the intensity of the sensation and/or emotion, while our attention is forcefully drawn either to a detail (usually someone's eyes) or, less frequently, to the bigger picture. In the first occurrence, at the beginning of Chapter One when Vernita Green opens the door to find the vengeful Bride standing on her doorstep [5:48], the speed of the zoom-in from a medium close-up to an extreme close-up renders the background blurry so that the Bride's eyes garner our undivided attention. The technique establishes a connection between two gazes and two emotions. On the one hand, the zoom-in mimics Vernita's sudden attention, surprise and fear; on the other, it draws us into the Bride's vengeful gaze, as the subsequent flashback confirms.

It is thus the intersubjective quality of the relationship that is foregrounded by the technique. Its functions are dramatic, emotional, and reflexive.[30] Its abundant use in the House of Leaves showdown in *Vol. 1* and the Pai Mei

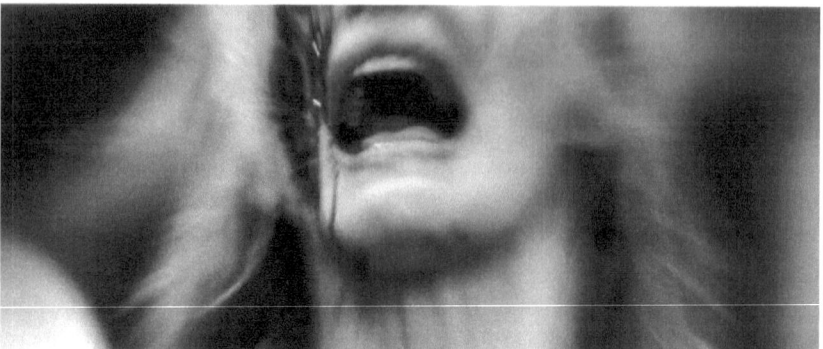

Fig. 42.1: *Kill Bill Vol. 2*: A quick zoom-out . . .

Fig. 42.2: *Kill Bill Vol. 2*: . . . as Pai Mei tears Elle's right eye out of its socket.

flashback in *Vol. 2* is justified by its generic origin. It can be used solely for dramatic effect to evoke a feat—the Bride's leaping off the mezzanine by clinging to a bamboo [*Vol. 1* 84:51]—or introduce a character—Gogo [*Vol. 1* 59:38] or the arrival of Johnny Mo [*Vol. 1* 81:43]. In this case, the technique, often cued to a sound effect, reinforces the fetishization of genre icons. It can also serve to mimic a violent act—when the Bride throws an ax [*Vol. 1* 83:41] or sticks a sword in an adversary's belly offscreen [*Vol. 1* 85:27], or when Pai Mei punches through a board [*Vol. 2* 53:43] or plucks Elle's eye out (fig. 42.1–42.2) [*Vol. 2* 77:58]—or its effect—when the Bride ducks Gogo's ball [*Vol. 1* 79:55] or gets kicked by Johnny Mo [*Vol. 1* 84:21]. In the gut-stabbing or eye-plucking scene, the use of the zoom metonymically evokes the violent act which has either just happened, occurred offscreen, or is soon to happen—the zoom-in on O-Ren's father is accompanied by the sound of a karate chop [*Vol. 1* 36:46]. In this respect, the technique represents violence metonymically and, as such, serves a censoring role.

When associated with a close-up, the technique draws attention to the face as the site of both expression and awareness. It is combined with eyeline match when the Bride notices a table leg with nails jutting out during her fight with Gogo [*Vol. 1* 80:13] or when she stumbles upon Budd's Hanzo sword [*Vol. 2* 77:03]. It is utilized several times to center on the young O-Ren's terror as she hides under the bed and her father attempts to fight off the yakuzas [*Vol. 1* 36:29–36:50]. Its use when the Bride confronts O-Ren before [74:14] and even as [85:07] she fights her minions highlights the fact that the former victim now occupies the same position as the yakuzas who murdered her family; by making O-Ren watch her cut off Sofie's arm, the Bride acts like O-Ren's parents' executioners and thus reminds O-Ren of the trauma in her own past [74:26]. The technique thus reinforces the idea that the two main opponents of *Vol. 1* are connected through the rape-revenge narrative and insists that they are doubles as both victims and killers.

The technique also serves to register surprise, as the Bride's reunions with Vernita and O-Ren show; in *Vol. 2*, it captures Elle's astonishment when she is attacked while stepping out of Budd's trailer [74:43], and later when she sees Beatrix armed with Budd's Hanzo sword [77:17]. All these situations announce the moment when the tables are turned: Beatrix will, in turn, be shocked, first, by the announcement of Pai Mei's death [*Vol. 2* 78:16], and even more by the discovery that B. B. is actually alive [*Vol. 2* 88:30]; ironically, the technique is used twice when Beatrix ends up playing dead for her child [89:40]. I would argue that because the fast zoom is in itself a parodic figure of excess, and because of its repeated use throughout *Kill Bill*, the technique tempers both the physical and emotional violence it expresses, and thus downplays both the graphic and melodramatic potential through parody, an effect that is reinforced by the cartoon and video game sound effects that often accompany it.

The technique is used briefly in *Inglourious Basterds* and more abundantly in *Django Unchained*. The four occurrences in the Louisiane basement shootout scene [92:43–92:49] do more than just mimic acts of violence (carried out by the female Nazi, the French tavern owner, and Wilhelm) or insist on the horror (Marie's screaming face). They also reinforce the connection between the three groups (the Nazis, the French, and the Basterds) established through the editing. In so doing, the technique comments on the scene: all three parties have failed to find a resolution to a complex situation, and this failure leads to the death of the innocent bystander whom both the father and the female Nazi had sworn to protect [75:45]. This is confirmed in the subsequent hostage situation—yet another Mexican standoff—which ends in the death of a new father and thus the birth of an orphan [96:56].

There are fast zooms throughout *Django Unchained*. The technique is used to introduce a notable character—the archvillain Calvin Candie [64:07]; to mimic a violent act—when Schultz draws his gun to shoot Bill Sharp [19:20], Django and Schultz ambush some riders in the snow [56:31], Broomhilda gets splashed in the hot box [94:07], or Django grabs Butch Pooch's gun to kill him [131:39]; to register shock—the Speck brothers' alarm at Schultz's approach [3:55], the tavern owner's surprise at seeing Django[31] [14:40], the two black boys' reaction when they witness John Brittle's death at the hands of Django [36:14], Calvin's astonishment that Schultz would pay for D'Artagnan [82:11], Stephen's horror at the death of his master [131:15]. William Brown posits that the use of the zoom implies "an embodied viewer who does not simply observe, but who also in various respects *feels* the film."[32] The repeated instances serve to comment on the film and the narration. First, they emphasize Django's trajectory from being subservient to Schultz to fully autonomous. Second, they insist on the emotional ambiguities of the various interracial relationships depicted in the film: that a slave (the boys at the window, Stephen) could feel empathy for his master, and that a white man (Schultz) could feel empathy for a slave. Third, they have a reflexive function. In the opening credits, the zooms highlight the film's homage to *Django* (1966), cued first to the word "Django" [1:45], then appearing between the mention of Franco Nero and Luis Bacalov [2:00]; in this case, they even serve to mark a beat and thus to fetishize the music rather than the images. Fourth, they draw a parallel between Django and the Bride as avengers—both are fighting against a white patriarch—but also between the two films. Finally, the use of a technique associated with Hong Kong martial art movies in a movie indebted to both the Italian Western and blaxploitation foregrounds the historical relationship between the three genres: Italian Westerns were very popular in Hong Kong, and martial arts movies were very popular among African American audiences. This, in turn, both justifies and reinforces the similar hybrid aesthetics of *Kill Bill* and *Django Unchained*.

Switching from color to black-and-white to color

Another device that is introduced in *Kill Bill* is the switch from color to black-and-white within the same scene. This device is practically as old as three-strip Technicolor and has regularly served to signal a passage from one world to another, for example in *The Wizard of Oz* (MGM, Victor Fleming et al., 1939). This occurs during the House of Leaves battle [*Vol. 1* 83:09–86:50] and more discretely when the Bride is buried alive [*Vol. 2* 37:37–39:10]. Cued to the heroine's plucking out an adversary's eyeball and her blinking, the change seems to be brought about by the protagonist herself. Yet unlike the blue darkness the scene is plunged into after the restaurant owner switches the lights off [86:53–87:50], the change is not justified diegetically. Nor is it justified subjectively, as the Bride is not being blinded, and it is doubtful that she empathizes with her foe's plight. With these switches, both the Bride and the manager are equated to stage directors, but the Bride's authority is far greater because it is extradiegetic. It also differs from the hotel manager's since it is not inscribed within diegetic causality (the restaurant owner is presumably trying to make it more difficult for the fighters). Rather, the justification for the use of black and white is purely aesthetic; it serves to tone down the graphic violence of the innumerable close-ups of blood spurting that follow by coloring the blood gray (the Japanese theatrical release maintained color throughout), avoid habituation on the spectator's part, and thus maintain interest and engagement during an incredibly long fight scene.[33] It is the Bride's authority over the plasticity of the scene that is highlighted: the composition, the camerawork, and the editing are centered on the heroine, whose movements and yellow jumper stand out amidst the Crazy 88. Yet, in *Vol. 2*, it is the Bride's power that seems to be compromised in the scene that resorts to this device. Indeed, if the change is effected when she turns the flashlight on and off, her position as a character is eminently vulnerable. The switch is, however, justified on several levels: emotional (it heightens the claustrophobic atmosphere), narrative (it recalls her near death in the church), and intertexual (it recalls the allusion to *Citizen Kane* from the opening credits of *Vol. 1*). The narration is thus aligned with the protagonist even when she is at her most vulnerable, the repetition of the device standing for her own capacty to return from the dead.

In *Death Proof*, the switch from color to black-and-white back to color also serves to dramatize a change in the protagonists' power [56:14–62:37]. Cued to Stuntman Mike cutting his engine, the switch initially reflects his control over the film's aesthetics—the next scene shows him photographing the women, the use of a POV shot positioning him as a surrogate director [65:33]. The return to color, however, is triggered not by Mike but by Lee when she purchases a soft drink. Not only is the switch associated with one of Mike's potential victims, but it is not a return to the initial drab grindhouse texture but the introduction of a bright texture more in tune with contemporary teen flicks or TV shows. The passage in black-and-white thus functions as a mere transition between two aesthetics, and the change reflects the male killer's loss of authority over the film. In *Kill Bill* and *Death Proof*, then, the device signals not the passage from one world to another, but from one worldview to another. And by establishing a connection between the character and the screen, it draws attention to the illusory quality of the diegetic world, much like the writing on the screen.

It would seem that most of Tarantino's signature devices come from his early films, especially *Reservoir Dogs* and *Kill Bill*. This implies that Tarantino has very deliberately been establishing his style from the start and that doing so is an ongoing process; it also means that there are no doubt specific devices that may become salient in his next films.[34] Some devices (the low-angle shot/high-angle reverse shot, the two-shot, the fast zoom) are more recurrent than others, which is consistent with the use of these devices to depict specific situations. Most have been lifted directly from specific films (*The Searchers*, *The Graduate*, *The Mack*, *Hannah and Her Sisters*), filmmakers (De Palma), and even production companies (the Shaw Brothers) that are not necessarily Tarantino favorites. Not only does Tarantino wear his influences on his sleeve, but these have been directly integrated into, and have come to be associated with, his personal style. As such, all these devices are, like the low-angle shot/high-angle reverse shot, representative of Tarantino's view of creation as re-creation and resignification. The repetition of these devices serves to constitute the body of his work as a whole not just formally, but by establishing connections and contrasts between each film (its characters and situations) on the narrative, thematic, emotional, and political level. Clearly, viewers are invited to identify these devices, analyze their similarities and differences, and ultimately interpret their meanings. The films of Tarantino are, at least in this respect, characteristic of art-cinema narration, where "[t]he authorial trademark requires that the spectator see this film as fitting into a body of work" and into film history: "full understanding of one film requires a knowledge and a fascination with other films."[35] We shall now see that they are also indebted to art-cinema narration, insofar as each film is conceived as "a distinct formal project" and that "fresh intrinsic norms" vary from film to film.[36]

Intrinsic Rules Specific to Each Film

Color schemes

Reservoir Dogs has a fairly homogeneous color scheme that is predominantly gray, ranging from black to white. The opening scene in the diner immediately sets the tone: the black suits and ties contrast with the dogs' white shirts, the white walls, white fan, and gray windowframes; the red elements (potted plants, menus, ketchup) in the background stand out, while the colorful curtains do not. The tone is set for the rest of the movie: the upholstery of Mr. White's car red is white; in the warehouse, the walls and doors of the main room are a pale blue-gray, while those in the bathroom are white. The gray scheme grounds the film in the *noir* tradition and creates a monochromatic backdrop against which Mr. Orange's red blood and Nice Guy Eddie's blue jacket constrast sharply, marking the latter as a figure of both authority and ridicule—hence the street-level shot that emphasizes the orange balloon trailing behind his car [46:06]. The color scheme is altered in the three analeptical chapters, but not radically so. In the Mr. White and Mr. Blonde chapters, the mahogany walls in Cabot's office border on burgundy, but the men's clothes remain grayish. The Commode Story chapter, however, dramatizes Freddy Newandyke's transformation into Mr. Orange as—paradoxically, given the alias—a loss of color. After the scenes of him rehearsing—in his blue-walled apartment and later against a colorful graffitied wall outside (fig. 57)—his actual performance takes place in a nightclub bathed in red light, the same color that marked him out immediately after the opening credits, until all color is eventually bled out and he is finally incorporated into the *noir* universe.

The color scheme of *Pulp Fiction* is similar to that of *Reservoir Dogs*, with a slightly broader palette, much like the film itself. It is also dominated by various shades of grays (from black to white), and the primary colors of yellow (or, more precisely, gold) and red, as the lettering of the title in the opening credits suggest, are emphasized. The white uplhostery of Jules's car, the white walls of the Wallace house, the Dimmick house, Butch's apartment, and Maynard's pawnshop highlight Marvin's and Vincent's blood, Mia's blood-red lips, Maynard's Confederate flag, and Jimmy's red bathrobe; the red booth seats, ketchup bottle, and Pumpkin's hair stand out in the diner, while Marsellus's club is suffused with red light. Jack Rabbit Slim's, with its wide array of pastel colors (pale blue, purple, cherry red), thus contrasts with the rest of the film, the color scheme setting it apart as a fantasy world within a bleak urban environment. The color gold functions as a thread throughout the movie: the light from Marsellus's briefcase washes over the faces of Vincent in the second scene [17:57] and Honey Bunny in the final one [141:59]; it also suffuses Butch's hotel room after he has duped Marsellus [75:50]. If it is initially associated with Marsellus's economic and quasi-divine power—and later confirmed by his wearing a yellow pullover while he relaxes beside his pool [120:27]—Captain Koons's monologue in the prologue of "The Gold Watch" makes it very clear that gold is the color of hell: the gold watch that lived through World War II and Vietnam inside several soldiers' rectums [65:15]. Accordingly, the basement of Maynard's pawnshop basement is also suffused with a golden light [97:42]. A direct correlation is thereby established between capital and hell, foreshadowed by the fact that the money briefcase's code is 666 [17:55]. In the moral universe of *Pulp Fiction*, gold inevitably leads to the red of blood.

Like Tarantino's other neo-*noir* films, *Jackie Brown* is set in a world of gray tones. Primary colors stand out in Ordell's apartment (red, yellow, and blue), Max's office (red, yellow, and blue), and Jackie's (the red wall, her blue outfit), while the Cockatoo Inn scene is bathed in red light. Blue is the dominant primary color, as is instantly established through the opening shot of Jackie in her blue stewardess's outfit against a blue background (fig. 21): it is the color of Simone's [23:45] and Jackie's [77:59] gowns, the women's prison uniforms [33:44], Melanie's cut-off jean shorts and bikini top [62:25], of the walls and columns in the LAX parking lot [27:33], and the upholstery in Max's car [91:14]. The color blue plays the same part as red in *Reservoir Dogs* and gold in *Pulp Fiction*, establishing the tone of a film about aging by evoking the emotions it is traditionally associated with: nostalgia (for one's youth) and bitterness (about time passing by).[37]

The color scheme reinforces the episodic structure of *Kill Bill*, each scene having its particular look. The prologue is in black-and-white. Chapter One evokes the "normal" life Vernita has integrated with blues and greens (Vernita's outfit, her bright lawn outside), and pastel tones (her green house, the lemon-colored kitchen, the purple furniture and turquoise walls of the living room); the arrival of the bold red and yellow Pussy Wagon disrupts the softer hues, while the Bride's casual outfit (tan jacket, blue jeans) paradoxically stands out because of its drab tones. Chapter Two has one color scheme for each main locus: the discovery of her body takes place in a brownish environment where even the blood looks a brownish red, contrasting with a few dabs of bold colors (the blue gurneys outside, the victims' pink clothes); the red of Elle's lips, eyepatch, and umbrella, and of the rapist's blood, clash with the greenish gray hospital;[38] and the gray parking lot sets off the sharp primary colors of the Bride's blue hospital gown and the Pussy Wagon. The anime of Chapter Three also comprises three main phases: the red blood and yellow fire cut against the blue-gray tones of O-Ren's childhood; O-Ren's life as a professional killer is depicted in bold primary colors (red, green, blue), while the epilogue relating the assassination of the Bride reprises the blue-gray backdrop with red specks of blood and the ghostly white dress of the Bride, confirming that the victim has become the double of those who murdered her parents. Chapter Four depicts the greenish gray world of Hattori Hanzo, allowing the gold and red swords to gleam. Like Chapter Two, Chapter Five proposes one color scheme per locus: primary colors (the orange flames on the wall, Boss Tanaka's blood, the blue ferris wheel, the red light, the Bride's yellow jumpsuit) are emphasized against the darkness of the Tokyo underworld and the city itself; the House of Leaves offers a multicolored space, with a gray center and a different colored background on each side (the blue bar, red hallway, golden alcove, brown mezzanine), allowing the colors red (the blood) and yellow (the manager's tunic, the Bride's jumpsuit, the dresses worn by members of the 5.6.7.8's) to stand out; the duel between O-Ren and the Bride occurs in a blueish gray Japanese garden that contrasts with the Bride's bloody yellow jumper. The brief flashbacks also have their own color schemes (the orange shot of Vernita). The epilogue of *Vol. 1* contrasts different time-spaces, each flashback having its own color scheme: the blue-gray of Sofie Fatale dominated by a reddish Bride, the orange sky outside the plane, the bleached image of Budd in *Vol. 2*.

The episodic color scheme approach is pursued in *Vol. 2*, although the smaller number of locales leaves less room for variation. Chapter Six reprises the black-and-white from the prologue of *Vol. 1*. Chapters Seven and Nine are dominated by the earthen and mineral tones of the desert: the yellowish-brown earth and rock, with some green in the cemetery scene, foregrounding the colors red (Budd's can of beans [15:09], Elle's suitcase [66:11]) and blue (the blue sky [15:14], Budd's Quality Store polo [65:57]); the earthen tones are maintained inside the trailer (where Elle's lipstick hardly stands out [65:44]) and at night with a brownish yellow light—only the red-lit nightclub is really set apart. Chapter Eight, the Pai Mei flashback, is dominated by various shades of dim gray, with the colors blue and green pale in comparison to Pai Mei's blinding whiteness. The last chapter comprises three main locales: Esteban's headquarters, the hotel room where Beatrix faced Karen, and Bill's suite. The first is dominated by a greenish gray that corresponds to the tropical forest environment, the second by variations of gray (from white to black), which contrast with the red and orange (of the rug, wallpaper, and Karen's jacket). The third reprises the pastel colors of Chapter One: the room is white and brown, with dabs of purple (the pillows, the bar) and golden light (from the fire), the walls outside blue, red, and yellow, and the plants green.

The color scheme thus foregrounds the cyclical structure of the Bride's quest: from Vernita's house to Bill's suite, where she will once again kill a parent in the presence of his child. But if the Bride's resolve is patent in her apartness from the color scheme in Chapter One, she is quickly integrated into the color scheme in the last chapter by shedding her black disguise. The color scheme—her blue clothing and B. B.'s pink PJs, and the fact that they are lit in blue and pink in the "About Her" scene, thus merging with their environment—thus draws attention to the fact that, as a mother, she has become Vernita's double. Indeed, the common denominator to the film's various color schemes is that the Bride is always made to stand out except when she is passive (in a coma, dying on the church floor, about to be buried alive, or subjected to Pai Mei's cruel tutelage); her ninja outfit, which enables her to merge with the the darkness when she stalks Budd, ironically anticipates her failure to catch him by surprise. Thus, the color scheme confirms Bill's doubts on the "natural born killer's" ability to integrate the real world [107:00], i.e., to blend in as a bride in a black-and-white world or as a mother in a pastel world.

Death Proof, as we have already seen, has three color schemes: the grayish color scheme of the first part, the black-and-white transition, and the bright color scheme of the second part of the movie. With its drab colors and grainy texture, the first is associated with grindhouse exploitation cinema, while the bold primary colors of the second part of the film, triggered by Lee, the yellow cheerleader, initially signals an entry into the more "feminine" world of the John Hughes movies loved by each of the four female characters [78:46]. The fact that three of the girls get rid of Lee and trade the yellow car with red upholstery for a white one announces the entry into a third world: a hybrid "masculine"-"feminine" one where the three women conquer the gray of the open road while sporting camouflage (Kim) and pink (Abernathy and Zoë) T-shirts.

The color scheme of *Inglourious Basterds* is based on earthen colors: the gray of the weapons, uniforms, and stones (throughout); the green of the grass (Chapter One) and trees (Chapter Two and the end of Chapter Five); and the brown of the wooden door and furniture (Chapter One), of the uniforms and of Hitler's quarters (Chapter Two), of the café and the restaurant (Chapter Three), of the room where Hicox meets Churchill and Fenech, and of Bridget's suit (Chapter Four). These colors are, of course, characteristic of the war movie, but they are especially relevant in Tarantino's film given that much of the action involves outdoor (Chapter Two, the end of Chapter Five) and underground spaces (Chapters One and Four), sometimes lit by a dim golden light. The map in Hitler's quarters initially imposes a clear color code: the Reich in red, Germany's allies in yellow, the conquered lands in orange, and the Allies in brown [24:13]. Yet the color red, set against the film's earthen tones, undergoes an ambiguous trajectory that connects opposing factions: from the Nazi banners (Chapters Two and Five) and the light covering Hitler (Chapter Four) to the curtains in Churchill's quarters (Chapter Four) to finally become the color of Shosanna's revenge (Chapter Five), a potential already expressed by the red seats in the café Shosanna reads in while drinking red wine, and the salmon interior of her movie theater (Chapter Three). Like the flames that engulf the movie theater, the red of violence consumes everything, casting doubt over the glory of the Allies' and the individuals' modes of retaliation.

The color scheme of *Django Unchained* is also based on earthen tones: gray (Schultz's suit, the rocks in the opening credits, and the places Schultz and Django set up camp in), green (Django's khaki jacket, the green fields of Big Daddy's plantation, Smitty Bacall's farm, and Candieland), and brown (the slaves' skin, Calvin's burgundy suit which Django makes his own, the wooden furniture, the earth when Django escapes); the brownish hue is reinforced in the night scenes by the golden light emanating from lamps, fires, torches, and candles. In terms of genre, the earthen tones, as well as the color white (Big Daddy's suit, the lynch mob's hoods, the plantation houses, the snowy mountains), are consistent with both the Western and the plantation film. Two scenes have specific color schemes: the flashbacks of Django and Broomhilda's past as Old Man Carrucan's slaves appear grayer due to the bleached bypass; and the winter interlude is dominated by blue skies and shades of gray. Visually set apart from the rest of the film, these scenes represent the polar opposites of Django's past (as a slave on a plantation) and his future (as a bounty hunter in a Western). Against this backdrop, the color red is yet again made to stand out, as the lettering in the opening credits suggests; even in the dark opening scene, the Speck brothers' red blood glistens when Schultz shoots them. But red is particularly associated with Calvin Candie, whose clothing, living quarters, and carriage are dominated by the color, and who delights in the shedding of his slaves' blood. Other primary colors are made salient by their limited use and are linked to the feminine. The blue of Django's outfit when he visits Candieland echoes that of the dress worn by Broomhilda in the flashback contained in that scene, as well as the purple of Big Daddy's slaves' dresses. By donning the blue outfit, Django comes back to haunt the Brittle brothers as Django, Broomhilda, and the female slaves, both the spectre of slavery and the spirit of the Enlightenment, via the reference to Thomas Gainsborough's 1770 painting,[39] as Robert von Dassanowsky and Margaret Ozierski have astutely noted. In subsequent scenes, pastel colors (the yellow dress Django imagines Broomhilda wearing when he arrives in Candieland, and Lara Lee's pink dress) are used to make the female characters stand out.

The Hateful Eight relies on a color scheme based on shades of blue and gray: the blue of the sky, the white of the snow, the bluish snow at sunset, and the dark blue interior of Minnie's. The richness of the grayish tones is largely permitted by the 70mm film, which is particularly sensitive to variation.[40] The color scheme makes the main protagonist stand out—Major Warren with his red scarf and golden lapels—and largely contributes to the film's atmosphere of mystery and deception, but it also serves to annul oppositions between day and night, inside and outside. Contained within the flashbacks, the pristine white snow and blue skies are framed by the continuous monotony of the grayish sky and the silver blue snow at dusk set up by the film in the opening shots and Chapters One, Two, and Five; ironically, it provides a backdrop for a flashback which may very well be a lie (Major Warren's treatment of Chester Charles Smithers) and for a story of murderous deception (Chapter Five). Thematically, then, the color scheme undermines the binaries—male and female, black and white, North and South, truth and lie—the characters attempt to uphold.

The color schemes of each film propose a set of intrinsic rules, largely contributing to its organic unity. They devolve both from the film genres and the settings—gray for urban neo-*noir*, earthen tones for the Western and the war movie—and operate as a backdrop allowing primary colors to stand out.[41] Unsurprisingly, perhaps, the most recurrent primary color is red, shortly followed by yellow, as the lettering in the opening credits of *Pulp Fiction*, *Jackie Brown*, and *The Hateful Eight* suggest. With the exception of *Kill Bill*, each film has a predominant color scheme, allowing for the foregrounding of specific scenes and locales. Each film emphasizes one or two primary colors, often introduced as early as the opening credits and usually tapping into the emotions, atmospheres, and symbols generally associated with these colors in Western pictorial conventions (the red of violence, the blue of mystery and nostalgia). Insisting on specific colors can establish figurative and thematic connections between characters or factions and/or highlight a dramatic arc; the evolution of a color tells its own version of the story, with political and moral implications. *Kill Bill* may be exceptional because its color schemes reinforce its episodic structure, but, in effect, it confirms Tarantino's very Cavellian approach to color "as packaging, as unifying the worlds of make-believe and of fantasy,"[42] or even as constructing a specific worldview. We shall now examine the intrinsic rules established by each film through camerawork and editing.

Salient devices

The first salient device in *Reservoir Dogs* is the circling camera. We have seen that Tarantino has regularly used this technique in scenes where one character tells others a story. After the prologue, subsequent circling shots

Fig. 43: *Reservoir Dogs*: The camera circles clockwise as Mr. Orange tells the Commode Story to Nice Guy Eddie, Joe Cabot, and Mr. White.

Fig. 44: *Reservoir Dogs*: The camera revolves counterclockwise as Mr. Orange unloads his gun in Mr. Blonde, thus revealing himself to be the rat.

are centered on Mr. Orange telling the Commode Story—in the nightclub (fig. 43) [69:57–70:30] and in the bathroom [71:50–72:12]. The reappearance of the technique in the flashback reveals that, like Mr. Brown and Nice Guy Eddie, Mr. Orange had to tell a story to get in the thieves' all-male world; on a narrative level, the prologue thus demonstrates the use-value of such stories before Holdaway explains it to Freddy in the flashback [66:44]. In *Reservoir Dogs*, other circling shots (all counterclockwise) occur outside storytelling situations: the extreme close-up of Nash gagged [55:57–56:00], the shot where Orange shoots Blonde (fig. 44) [59:55–60:24], and the shot that opens the final act [87:14–87:34]. Unlike the other circling shots that demonstrate Mr. Orange's integration in the gang of thieves, all these shots connect two cops, who are concealing the exact same piece of information: the rat's identity. Used in particularly dramatic moments, they reveal the exact opposite of the storytelling scenes: Freddy's inability to stick to his act.

This is reinforced visually by the fact that the shots move clockwise in the Commode Story and counterclockwise in the warehouse, the latter marking the undoing of the former. The counterclockwise tracking shot is thus turned into a marker of true identity, the clockwise tracking shot into one of duplicity.

The second recurrent device is the slow zoom-in on a character's face. These occur four times: when Mr. White admits to Mr. Pink that he disclosed his identity to Mr. Orange [29:29–30:24]; when Mr. Orange listens to Cabot forbidding the men to talk about their pasts [81:18–81:26]; when Nice Guy Eddie tells Mr. Orange he does not believe his loyal friend Mr. Blonde was the rat [89:34–90:04]; and finally when Mr. White weeps as Mr. Orange reveals his true identity [94:56–95:27]. All four shots register a character's emotion: concern, confidence, anger, sorrow. If only the second zoom-in focuses on Mr. Orange, all four revolve around the character of the undercover cop and are thus centered on the themes of hidden identity and betrayal. Structurally, they emphasize the tragic descent into negative emotions—even Orange's smug look contrasts ironically with what we know of his fate—which accelerates in the final scenes. With the first and last occurrences centered on Mr. White, the older thief—and the film's major star—is made into the film's emotional and dramatic benchmark, and the story's Oedipal dimension is structurally highlighted.

One salient device in *Pulp Fiction* is the use of low angles to frame the characters. The prologue immediately establishes the function of such shots. Throughout their conversation, Pumpkin and Honey Bunny are shot at eye-level; it is only when they stand up to rob the diner that the camera tilts up in a low-angle medium full shot [4:40, 142:23]. The new angle thus distinguishes their professional selves from their true selves. The next scene confirms the rule: Jules and Vincent are shot in fairly eye-level shots as they talk about hash bars, burgers, and Mia Wallace in Jules's car and in the hallway, and appear in low angle when opening the trunk to get their work tools and terrorizing Brett and his friends [8:48, 14:36–21:07]. Established before "Vincent Vega & Marsellus Wallace's Wife," the instrinsic rule equating low angles with professional roles appears to be debunked as early as the second scene: Vincent and Lance are shot in low angle when they talk about the heroin the hitman is purchasing for his own private use, and which comes from Lance's own "private stash" (fig. 45) [27:22]. This usage of the low angle thus appears to invalidate the intrinsic rule. Yet the association between low angle and role-playing is confirmed at Jack Rabbit Slim's when the Marilyn Monroe lookalike peforms the famous *Seven Year Itch* subway grate scene [42:30], and later in the Wallace house when Vincent talks to his reflection

Fig. 45: *Pulp Fiction*: Low-angle shot of Lance selling Vincent heroin from his own "private stash."

Fig. 46: *Pulp Fiction*: Low-angle shot of Vincent in the Wallace bathroom, summoning the wherewithal to pass the test of loyalty, while Mia ODs on his heroin.

in the mirror about the situation being "a moral test of one's self," the very moment when the hitman is torn between his "loyalty" to his employer and his desire for Mia (fig. 46) [51:32]. The confirmation of the rule invites a reinterpretation of the instance in Lance's house. The low angle draws attention to Vincent's dependence on drugs in order to maintain his cool persona, as the subsequent "Bullwinkle Part II" scene demonstrates. The irony at the heart of "Vincent Vega & Marsellus Wallace's Wife" is that it is the drug meant to help the hitman keep his cool that will ultimately create a more significant danger when Mia ODs.

The prologue of "The Gold Watch" further delves into the significance of role-playing and adds another level to it involving gender. Captain Koons is shot in low angle, but this time it is justified by the perspective of Butch the child [64:01]. This scene inscribes the low-angle view of the cool professional in a uniform as a male fantasy, one that contributes early on to the construction of masculinity. Subsequent low-angle shots of the adult Butch prove that he has endeavored to live up to this idealized view of cool, tough masculinity by taking on, first, Marsellus Wallace—the low-angle medium full shot before the boxing match [68:18]—then his whole gang—the low-angle full shot and medium full shot when he realizes he has lost the watch [84:20–86:30]—and finally the rapists, who had also been shot in low angle [99:03], when he handles the sword before saving Marsellus [104:21]. *Pulp Fiction* thus makes a fairly traditional use of the low angle to magnify a power that is gendered male—Honey Bunny is significantly standing on the floor of the diner, while Pumpkin climbs onto his seat—but equates it with a cool professionalism that is epitomized in the character of the highly efficient Wolf, who is first shot in low angle in Jimmy's kitchen in spite of being the shortest of the four men [113:06]. On a metafictional level, the recurrent usage of the low angle draws attention to the part played by cinema in the construction of cool professional personae: all are gendered genre roles lifted from classical genres (*noir*, war movies, boxing movies) or even directly from specific films (*Bonnie and Clyde, Nikita*).

The use of fade-to-blacks to close a scene is equally central to the narration of *Pulp Fiction*. These occur five times in the first story—Marsellus's club scene [26:23], the "Bullwinkle Part II" video scene [31:15], the dance scene [49:55], the overdose scene [54:23], and finally when Vincent leaves the Wallace house for good [63:27]; six times in "The Gold Watch"—Butch's heading for the fight [68:47], when Butch and Fabienne make love [80:19] and then go to bed [82:36], the car accident [94:52], Marsellus getting knocked out by Maynard [97:35], and finally when Butch and Fabienne ride off on Zed's chopper [111:38]; and only once in "The Bonnie Situation"—Jules and Vincent's shower [130:34]—not including the execution scene that precedes the first story [21:07]. *Pulp Fiction* plays on the device's status as both a marker of time and a censoring device in classical Hollywood cinema. The first instance is significant in both respects. First, it creates suspense. What is going to happen to the hitmen and the young black man in the corner of the room? This is also the case in subsequent scenes. Has Mia died from an overdose? Will Butch go down in the fifth as promised? How badly hurt are Marsellus and Butch after the accident, and what is going to happen to them in the pawnshop? Second, the fade-to-black signals the passing of time. Nearly all subsequent fade-to-blacks indicate ellipses, apart from the one that concludes "The Gold Watch" which announces a flashback. By then, however, the technique has already become untrustworthy as a signifier of time; it marks a gap that cannot be measured and, in so doing, disrupts the linear causal logic of the narrative. What is significant is that there seems to be no correlation between the duration of the fade-to-black and the time that has passed or the action depicted: the fade-to-black is just as brief for the execution scene as for Butch and Fabienne riding off; the black screen lasts longer when Jody is speaking or Vincent arriving at the Wallaces' than before Mia and Vincent return home. In *Pulp Fiction*, the fade-to-black turns out to be a marker of subjective time rather than chronological time; in so doing, it contributes to making the film time-image cinema in the Deleuzian sense.[43]

Most instances are connected to three Production Code taboos: violence (the execution, the boxing match, the accident, the pawnshop), sex (Jody's spiel on body piercing, the dance scene, Butch and Fabienne), and drug use (in "Vincent Vega & Marsellus Wallace's Wife"). The first instance partly respects the canonical protocole: Jules and Vincent are shown unloading their guns into Brett, but the narration spares us the graphic vision of his bullet-riddled body. Yet the fade-to-black is not just a tool of censorship; occuring on the medium shot of Jules, it symbolizes the blackness of the killer's soul. The technique will remain a marker of death throughout the film. The next instances occur during frontal close-ups of the protagonists: Butch, who will become an emissary of death, killing an opponent in the ring, shooting Vincent in the toilet, and piercing Maynard with a sword; Vincent, whose path of drugs and crime will lead him to die in a toilet; Mia, who will narrowly miss dying from a drug overdose; Marsellus, who will get run over and beaten up by Butch before being raped by Zed. The second instance, however, is also associated with sex. Because it only affects the image and not the sound (of Jody's voice), it fails as a censoring mechanism: the graphic act is not depicted visually but aurally. The connection between Butch and Jody's voice announces the intimate scenes between the boxer and his girlfriend Fabienne, where the device will, in effect, prevent us from watching the entire sex scene, but only after Fabienne has, pointedly, stated her desire for oral sex. The classical censoring technique has thus been turned into a signifier of intimacy—this was already the case at the end of the dance scene, since we are denied the view of Mia and Vincent as they get closer on their way back home—that does not deny female sexuality. The effect is political, as Jody appears first as the disembodied female voice that classical Hollywood cinema sought to repress (Silverman 1988). It is also comical, as the final instance (the shower scene) confirms. Taken together, then, the first and last fade-to-blacks describe the moral journey of Jules that structures, as we have seen, the entire film: a spiritual journey from darkness and death to purification and rebirth. The fade-to-black has turned out to be just as much a signifier of life as of death: the survival of Mia, Butch and Fabienne, and Jules. If it structures a Christian narrative, the technique, I would argue,

Fig. 47: *Jackie Brown*: Frame-within-the-frame composition as Max watches Jackie exit the prison.

actually suggests an East-Asian worldview of complementary opposites, evoking both positive and negative forces, male violence and female sexuality, as well as death and life.

The story of a woman trying to break free from an arms trafficker and the police, *Jackie Brown* makes repeated use of bars in its compositions in the first and fourth acts: Ordell and Beaumont are seen behind the swimming pool fence as they walk to the car [18:39]; the cell door closes behind Jackie [34:00]; Max and the female prisoner he takes to County are seen from behind bars [39:44]; Max sees Jackie for the first time through bars (fig. 47) [40:36]; the very long shot of Max and Ordell stepping out of the house in Compton is taken over a fence [138:11], while the very long shot of them stepping out of Max's car is taken through the barred windows of Cherry's Bailbonds [142:04]; finally, Max's last glimpse of Jackie is through the very same window (fig. 48.1) [147:59]. The first instance clearly suggests that imprisonment leads straight to death. By framing the narrative structurally, these compositions foreground that the tables have turned on Ordell, with a touch of irony as the gangster believes he is still leading the way—as with Beaumont—even though he is marching to his own death. However, by creating a sense of entrapment and despair, these compositions also reflect Jackie's sense that she is not, as she tells Max, so much trapped by Ordell as by time [60:10]. The final shot thus adds a touch of bitterness to her victory, as there is ultimately no cheating mortality.

Like *Reservoir Dogs*, *Jackie Brown* makes the zoom-in a salient device, but does not seem to refer to the earlier movie in the process. It is used on eight occasions: when Max first meets Jackie [40:43]; when Jackie talks about her

Fig. 48.1: *Jackie Brown*: Frame-within-the-frame composition as Jackie leaves . . .

Fig. 48.2: *Jackie Brown*: . . . and zoom-in on Max wistfully watching her.

life and age [59:40]; when Max figures out Ordell's deception during the trial run [90:03]; when Jackie waits for Melanie in the changing room and looks at her reflection in the mirror [105:36]; when Ordell realizes Jackie's deception [122:52]; when Jackie makes a phone call while waiting for Ordell in Max's office [137:37]; when Ordell lies dead on the floor [144:20]; and when Jackie and Max finally part (fig. 48.2) [146:40]. As in *Reservoir Dogs*, the zoom-in serves to dramatize particularly intense moments involving emotions such as love, melancholy, understanding, and resolve. The shot of the dead Ordell would thus appear as an exception to the intrinsic rule. Yet by inviting us to interpret Ordell's final emotion—surprise and horror, perhaps?—the device highlights that, in a movie about deception, there is no guarantee that what we are reading in a character's expression is not a mere projection. If the zoom-in had up to now appeared to function as a gauge of authentic emotion, its use with the man Jackie deceived ultimately casts some doubt[44] on the sincerity of her claim that she "didn't use" Max in the epilogue [145:25].

Finally, *Jackie Brown* makes striking use of the ellipsis within the same scene on three occasions: when Jackie details her plan to Ordell [53:13], when Melanie and Louis have sex [68:08], and finally when Jackie tries on a suit during the money exchange [105:00]. The function of the device is threefold. First, it is dramatic, creating mystery or comic relief, or endowing the scene with a sense of energy. All three instances engage with the film's major theme of aging: Jackie's plan is meant to give her a chance as a middle-aged black woman, while the sex scene insists on the physical gap between Melanie and Louis who is exhausted by the brief effort. On the narrative level, the first and third instances mark the moment when Jackie takes control of the plot and of her own handling of time, while the second underlines the difference between Jackie and Ordell's other two minions, who fail to team up against Ordell and are late for the money exchange. The fact that the final ellipsis is not marked by a dissolve or an intertitle but is directly introduced via a cut suggests that, by the time Jackie's plot is put into practice, her energy and control even have an impact on the narration.

The most frequent device in *Kill Bill*, one that is not characteristic of Tarantino's films overall, is deep-focus composition, with the use of foreground and background to depict tensions. This norm is immediately established in Chapter One in several instances: the very long shot of the Bride walking up to the house with Nikki's toys in the foreground and the front door where the fight will start in the background (fig. 49) [5:39]; the appearance of Nikki's bus through the window (fig. 23), followed by Nikki next to the front door, with Vernita and the Bride in the foreground [7:31, 7:53]; Nikki standing in the doorway after the Bride has pulled her knife out of her mother [14:00]; and when the Bride sits down in her car and crosses off Vernita's name from her list, with the house in the background [15:26]. These compositions dramatize the tension between professional and personal, and parent and child, that inform the movie as a whole. In Chapter One, they indicate that the Bride's vengeance will discount all other moral concerns, most patently in the shot where she moves out of the way to reveal Nikki in the background. Ironically, the Bride has chosen to deny the special bond between mother and daughter that she will later seek to establish for herself in *Vol. 2*.

Chapter Two pursues the use of layered compositions to portray parent-child relationships—the low-angle two-shot of Sheriff McGraw and his son

Fig. 49: *Kill Bill Vol. 1*: Deep focus highlights the tension between the vengeful Bride in the background and the child she will never have in the foreground.

Earl [19:03]—before introducing a perversion of gender relationships that makes way for violence—the arrival of Buck the rapist, his subsequent death, and the Bride's claiming the Pussy Wagon [27:43, 30:36, 30:54, 32:47]. The anime recounting O-Ren's past in Chapter Three neatly encapsulates all these associations: the father in the foreground trying to save his wife in the background [36:53]; the daughter in the background seeing her dead father's face in the foreground [37:45]; the dead father in the foreground as Boss Matsumoto advances on O-Ren's mother [39:00]; the sword that kills her mother in the foreground [39:33]; O-Ren in the foreground watching her house burn down in the background [40:49]; O-Ren standing over the body of Matsumoto as two of his men burst through the door [42:00]. Positioned after the murder of Vernita and before the House of Leaves showdown, the anime serves as a template for the entire film, the *mise en abyme* putting on display the fact that the live action scenes are influenced by comic book aesthetics. In the first part, the image of the child seeing her dead father recalls the shot of Nikki discovering her dead mother, with the Bride's body replaced by her weapon of choice: a samurai sword. The composition then constructs O-Ren as the double of the Bride when she kills Matsumoto, with the door in the background, their bodies symmetrically inverted (O-Ren is facing left, the Bride right); in Chapter Five, she is portrayed as the double of her father's slayer, in a medium close-up with blood spraying like a geyser in the foreground [63:08]. The repetition of these compositions describes revenge as a cycle whereby the victim becomes the abject killer, and therefore invalidates the righteousness of the Bride's enterprise.

In Chapters Four and Five, layered compositions feature Hattori Hanzo, the Bride, and Hanzo's bald associate [45:59, 50:48, 58:13], and especially O-Ren and her minions—for instance, when the Crazy 88 clown around to amuse their leader [69:13], when the Bride stalks Sofie Fatale in her car [66:28], when she clings to the wall above Gogo [69:46], and when the Bride looks over the bodies of the Crazy 88 [89:37]. This new relationship—that between master and disciple or employee—is presented as a variant of the parent/child relationship. It is also shown to be gendered and racialized in the scene where Tanaka insults O-Ren by invoking their fathers [62:09]. The cycle of violence is pursued as the Bride must kill all O-Ren's minions to get to their leader, even though she invites Gogo to step down [77:39]. The value of loyalty is, therefore, called into question, as O-Ren basically allows all her disciples to die for her, just as Bill allows all his employees to die first. The layered compositions in the final duel between the Bride and O-Ren dramatize the confrontation between two foes who aim to subject the other [90:35, 91:29, 92:07], thereby proving their superiority—O-Ren even insults the Bride like Tanaka insulted her [94:13]—even though the film has constructed them as doubles. The device thus works to counter the narrative, questioning the validity of the values and personal experiences that motivate the avenger.

Another salient technique in *Vol. 1* is the dissolve.[45] They occur on numerous occasions: to introduce the flashback of Vernita beating up the Bride [5:50]; to transition from the Bride's bruised face to her comatose face [19:49]; to allow the camera to enter her hospital room [20:44]; to suggest the causal link between the mosquito bite and the Bride's awakening [25:41]; to introduce the flashback of Buck introducing himself to the sleeping Bride [31:19]; to segue to the low-angle four-shot of the Vipers standing over the Bride [35:09]; to link images in the anime [36:35, 36:39, 36;41, 36:46, 38:35, 39:56, 40:43]; to go from Hanzo watching the Bride to her admiring his swords [51:24]; to introduce the image of the Bride's bruised face when she faces O-Ren [74:16]; to connect the very long shot of Sofie's body outside the hospital to the extreme close-up of her when Bill visits her [99:24]; and finally to introduce the flashforward to *Vol. 2* of Budd stating that the Bride "deserves her revenge" [102:59]. With the exception of the hospital room scenes, the majority of the dissolves function as very classical markers of memory (flashback) and time passing by (ellipsis).[46] This prompts three remarks. First, the flashbacks—Sofie's presence in the church [67:07]—and flashforwards—Elle on the phone [102:47]—are not systematically introduced by dissolves. Second, the flashforward appears as a violation of the intrinsic rule, at least when watching *Vol. 1* for the first time; the flashback structure of *Vol. 2*, which opens on the Bride driving to kill Bill, retrospectively turns *Vol. 1* into a flashback. Third, not all the dissolves are linked to the Bride's own memories; if Chapter Three can be viewed as the Bride's recounting of an event that is common knowledge, the conversation between Bill and Sofie in the epilogue is something she has planned but that she ignores the content of. From a classical marker of time, the dissolve becomes a marker of the narration's tendency to violate its own rules, and thus of the film's artificiality; this accounts for its usage to draw attention to the cut necessary for the camera to penetrate inside the Bride's hospital room.

Vol. 2 pursues the two devices from Vol. 1, particularly the use of layered compositions. The novelty is that these are systematically organized according to gendered oppositions that turn out to be Oedipal and patriarchal. This is consistent with the fact that Bill only reveals his face in Chapter Six. Layered compositions initially depict the Bride's adopted family: Tommy, Beatrix, and their friends seated on the church pews [2:49]. Once Bill steps inside the church, they contrast her new life and her past life, Tommy and Bill, but the Bride's moving from background to foreground to thank Bill and give him one last kiss reveals the Oedipal trappings of the master/disciple relationship: Bill is master, lover, and surrogate father [12:42–12:54]. The perversity of the master and disciple relationship is emphasized throughout Vol. 2. The cruel tutelage of Pai Mei is likewise dramatized in terms of oppositions between foreground and background, that are reinforced by high and low angles: Pai Mei stands in the background dominating Beatrix physically, as when she submits at the end of their fight (fig. 11) [52:09], and/or psychologically, as when she trains [54:53, 55:31]; Elle is similarly relegated to the background when her eye is snatched out (fig. 42.4) [77:57]. These compositions are then associated with the female character who surreptitiously undermines male power, such as Elle, when she baits Budd with the red briefcase in the foreground [66:11] and later examines the Hanzo sword in the background [66:38], or when she stands over Pai Mei whom she has poisoned [78:17].

The return to the family in the last chapter is utterly compromised by the series of perversions we have witnessed. Beatrix discovers the existence of B. B. in a fictitious restaging of the death of Vernita, one where the father lying in the foreground and the daughter in the midground have also been assassinated [88:35, 88:59]. Bill thus stages the family reunion as a bloodbath even more merciless than that of Chapter One, one in which the Bride would, as she explained to Vernita, be "just about even-Steven." Subsequent compositions reveal that this was, indeed, just a sham performance by insisting on Bill's efforts to compose an ideal family portrait,[47] in the shot where daughter and mother are finally reunited [92:26], in the lateral medium shot of him making a sandwich for B. B. (fig. 50) [92:26], and in the long shot of him putting B. B. to bed over Beatrix's shoulder [95:38]. With B. B. in bed, the family show is terminated, and Bill resumes his position of male master and jealous lover by shooting Beatrix and injecting a truth serum in her—when

Fig. 50: *Kill Bill Vol. 2*: Deep focus enables a layered composition that pictures the Oedipal triangle.

he has proved all along to be the arch-deceiver [102:14]. From beginning to end, the layered compositions in *Kill Bill* insistently undermine both the revenge plot and the patriarchal model.

The two devices that are made particularly salient in *Vol. 2* stem from the fact that the second installment is more verbal than the first. The first device, the profile (or American) two-shot, occurs four times: first when Bill and the Bride talk outside the church about her fiancée Tommy [8:13]; then when Beatrix and Elle fight over the Hanzo sword [75:06]; and finally when Beatrix meets B. B. [91:22] and lies down beside her in bed [96:35]. These shots trace the narrative of deception and betrayal: Beatrix unsuspectingly facing her killer, the rival who has replaced her, and the child who has been taken from her womb. The four shots thus dramatize that what stands before the protagonist cannot be taken at face value. B. B.'s and Bill's occupying the left side of the composition puts in relief that the father concealed the existence of the child: B. B. was behind Bill, just as Nikki was concealed behind the Bride's back in Chapter One. The characters' positions in these compositions also invite a host of much darker interpretations: that Beatrix is just as guilty as Bill, and that B. B., who killed her pet goldfish Emilio [93:04], might grow up to become just like her parents.

The second device is the shot/reverse-shot technique. It is classically used to depict discussions. Pointedly, all these discussions involve power relations: between an employer and an employee (Larry Gomez and Budd in Chapter Seven), a master and his disciple (Bill and Beatrix, Pai Mei and Beatrix in Chapter Eight, but also the Bride and Hattori Hanzo in Chapter Four), two lovers (Bill and the Bride in Chapter Six), brothers (Bill and Budd in Chapter Seven), rival disciples (Beatrix and Elle in Chapter Nine) or killers (Budd and the Bride in Chapter Seven, Budd and Elle in Chapter Nine, Beatrix and Karen in the last chapter), a father and a mother (Bill and Beatrix in the last chapter). All these discussions revolve around questions of honor (for one's master), loyalty (to one's employer or brother) and betrayal (of one's master or lover), values that are the moral sediment of martial arts, samurai movies, and Westerns. The face-off between Beatrix and Karen is thus foregrounded because it is not based on the same values. Professionalism is supplanted by what Beatrix describes as raw fear: "I'm the deadliest woman in the world, but right now I'm just scared shitless for my baby" [112:00]. Significantly, it is the only such scene that ends not in violence and subjection, but on a truce. In comparison with the other scenes, and especially with the final confrontation between Bill and Beatrix that frames it, the flashback informs us that Beatrix's power, even at a moment where she appears more vulnerable—lying on the floor, in a high-angle shot, with a gun when her opponent is armed with a rifle—resides in instinct, something which the film's final words seem to confirm ("The lioness has rejoined her cub and all is right in the jungle") [123:59]. It is thanks to this more basic, animal situation that the two opponents step down and attain a form of common identity as women that contrasts with all the other relationships depicted within the film. Paradoxically, then, their more civilized behavior stems not from man-made—i.e., patriarchal—laws but from a universal animal experience.

The jump-cut is the most salient device in *Death Proof*. The technique is used on four occasions in the first part of the movie: when Julia is talking at the very beginning and end of the opening scene [3:21–3:28]; at the end of that same scene when Shanna talks about Lake LBJ [7:15], followed by her car driving past the Jungle Julia billboard [8:52]; at the beginning of the scene at Güero's [9:37–9:39]; and finally at the end of the lap dance scene [41:47]. If the jump-cuts are meant to mimic film skipping in a projector, and thus the poor exhibition conditions of grindhouse films, their intentional use is a tribute to two major influences: Godard and *The Texas Chain Saw Massacre* (1974). As in the films of Godard, the editing technique produces breaks in continuity, and thus constitutes a violation of the extrinsic norms of classical narration, yet their disruptive potential is, in *Death Proof*, limited, as they occur either at the beginning or end of scenes. As in the 1974 mad dinner party scene, they operate like bursts of libidinous energy assaulting the images of women.[48] They thus participate in aligning the narration with the sadistic male gaze. Indeed, the second occurrence lends the impression that Mike has suddenly gotten closer to the girls in time and space, while those that terminate the lap dance scene, though they may be frustrating to some, put an end to the foreplay and precipitate the death scene. In light of this previously established intrinsic norm, the series of jump-cuts at the end of the film, when Abernathy, Kim, and Zoë beat Mike to death, reflect the women's subjecting the male body to the violence the female bodies were subjected to earlier and, ultimately, their taking control of the narration [108:52–109:24]. The editing during the punching bag scene transitions from classical match-on-action to jump-cuts that are further exacerbated by the usage of another device associated with the French New Wave: the freeze-frame.[49] By emphasizing their postures and Mike's beaten face, the latter is a reaction against both the fetishizing shots of the female characters' faces and bodies that permeated the first half of the movie, and the slow motion (combined with match-on-action editing) used during the accident scene that enabled the viewer to sadistically enjoy the destruction of passive female bodies [51:05–51:24]. Both French New Wave techniques are thus put to the service of a feminist attack on the gendered terms of classical narration and exploitation cinema. By invoking the heritage of French art cinema, they legitimize the exploitation material, recalling that the French directors were also working with material (Hollywood genre films) they loved while simultaneously despising its underlying ideology.

Like the gritty color scheme, the lines and blotches that streak across the images are obviously meant to mimic the grindhouse experience. Yet careful attention shows that they also fulfill dramatic, subtextual, and reflexive purposes. Throughout the opening scene, green and white lines flash across the screen as Arlene, Julia, and Shanna bicker [5:30], talk about sex [6:12, 8:08], and their all-girl weekend at the lake [7:30]; some lines even cut through the characters' images, e.g., Shanna's face in close-up [4:20] and Julia's legs before they holler at her poster [8:47]. By contrast, the lines that flash when Mike's car appears at the end of the scene miss it when they cut right through Shanna's car seconds before [8:50]. The pattern is confirmed in subsequent scenes: lines cut through the girls' images [9:07, 9:37, 9:44], notably during Julia's revelation of the lap dance ploy, thus materializing the tension between the characters and foreshadowing ominous events to come [10:10, 10:27, 11:20, 12:12, 12:32, 12:38, 13:38, 13:57]. The violent potential of these lines climaxes in the multiple murder scene—Pam's body is repeatedly crossed by lines as she follows Mike to her death [42:00, 42:44, 42:48, 44:06, 44:12, 44:15, 44:21, 44:26, 44:45, 45:57, 47:59, 45:44, 48:15]. These lines and splotches come to embody the libidinous energy the film directs at its female characters in a parody of the psychoanalytically based feminist readings of the horror genre read by Tarantino. This is confirmed in the epilogue of the Austin story when a line cuts the image of a female nurse [50:50], while another is cued to Sheriff McGraw's comparison of Mike to a giant [53:51] and his statement that Frankenstein's motive is ultimately to "shoot his goo" [55:36]. The reference to a monster made of multiple body parts reflexively highlights the film's palimpsestic quality: the monster (Mike and his death proof car), like the film, is a composite of preexisting material. Using the lines to evoke sexual and violent tension also seems to suggest that the modes of exhibition of grindhouse films may have enhanced their disturbing qualities.

The most salient device in *Inglourious Basterds* is, perhaps, the use of frame-within-the frame composition. Not including *The Searchers* allusion (fig. 41), occurrences abound thoughout the film: when Julie LaPadite looks past a sheet hanging from a clothesline [2:31]; when Landa and LaPadite step inside and Landa's men can be seen through the window [4:47]; when Raine and later Donowitz are framed by the tunnel walls [26:54, 34:05]; when the Basterds break Stiglitz out of prison [29:24]; when Zoller recognizes Shosanna through the café window [41:58]; when Wilhelm fires his machine gun, cornered against a stone archway which presumably leads nowhere [92:50], and later when Raine negotiates from the staircase [96:00]; when Shosanna gazes out her round window on the night of the premiere (fig. 6) [105:47]; when Shosanna and Zoller speak in the doorway of the projection booth [137:53]; and when Raine and Utivitch are taken prisoner in the back of the truck [122:55]. Such compositions magnify Landa in Chapter One and the Basterds in Chapter Two, evoke Zoller's stalking presence in Chapters Three and Five, and dramatize the sense of entrapment in Chapters One, Four, and Five. They also create links between the characters: Landa and the Basterds standing in frames, Landa and Zoller on the threshhold of doors. But in a film whose finale takes place at a premiere, all these compositions obviously anticipate the movie screen in Chapter Five. This is made clear as soon as the opening scene: the occurences put Julie LaPadite in the shoes of the viewers watching Nazis on screen (beyond the sheet or through the window). We are immediately made aware of their cinematic quality; these are movie Nazis, not those of history. *Inglourious Basterds* thus both retains the magnifying power and the reflexive quality of such compositions that make Landa and the Basterds iconic and overtly cinematic. By subsequently making Landa the surrogate viewer when Shosanna runs away, the device also announces the film's program of reversing positions between male/female, Nazi/Jew, and killer/victim. Indeed, the repeated use of these compositions traces Shosanna's evolution from one who is caught in the Nazi gaze to one who returns the gaze on the Nazis trapped in her movie theater; her projected image on the screen not only replaces Zoller's (fig. 13.1) but recalls the Nazi soldiers seen through the LaPadites' window. In *Inglourious Basterds*, power is equated with control of the screen. To be looked at and to be listened to is not to be objectified; rather, it is to claim an audience to a political end (Goebbels's and Hitler's propaganda) or to a lethal one (Shosanna's). Such compositions

Fig. 51: *Inglourious Basterds*: Expressionistic oblique low-angle shot as a Nazi hero (Fredrick Zoller) unknowingly flirts with a Jewish woman (Shosanna).

Fig. 52: *Inglourious Basterds*: Expressionistic oblique low-angle shot as a US soldier topples out of a building in *Stolz der Nation*, shot down by Zoller.

simultaneously celebrate, and warn against, the power of cinema, and thus acknowledge the potential efficacy of propaganda.

Another recurring device that reinforces this metafictional discourse is the Dutch angle. It is used on several occasions: when Donowitz looks down at Rachtman [34:23]; when Shosanna and Zoller first meet outside the cinema (fig. 51) [38:41]; when Aldo sticks his finger in Bridget's wound while questioning her [98:03]; when Landa looks down at Stiglitz's dead body [104:04]; when Bridget unwittingly looks for her shoe in Landa's coat pocket [119:37]; when an American soldier topples out of a window to his death in *Stolz der Nation* (fig. 52) [142:40]. All these instances involve moments that portend bad things to come (pain, death). However, the relationships they dramatize (a Jewish American executing a Nazi, a Nazi hero flirting with a Jew in disguise, an American questioning a German spy, a Nazi looking down at a dead German traitor, a Nazi questioning a German spy) are not only varied; they are reversals of previous instances. Consequently, they contribute to the debunking of the classic dichotomy between the evil Nazi and the good American discussed in chapter 2, and even underline that the male protagonists (Zoller, Aldo, Landa) have in common their sadistic treatment of women. Of course, this sort of framing is, above all, meant as an homage to German Expressionist cinema. Such compositions in *Inglourious Basterds* not only testify to the durable influence of the Weimar era Goebbels's cinema was meant to represent "an alternative to," as Hicox explains to General Fenech [66:26]; they also signify that, in the scope of the film at least, Weimar both frames and inhabits Nazi cinema, just as Shosanna's image will haunt Goebbels's film. Indeed, not only does *Stolz der Nation* reprise techniques of the Weimar era, but it meets with the approval of the film's ideal spectator, Hitler himself, whom a reverse extreme close-up shows to be laughing hysterically at the Dutch shot. Although the Nazi leader is, no doubt, reacting to the profilmic event, his approval encompasses the film's aesthetics, which are also contaminated by influences from Hollywood (*Sergeant York*, Howard Hawks, 1941; *Targets*, Peter Bogdanovich, 1968) and the Soviet Union (*Battleship Potemkine*, Sergei Eisenstein, 1925).[50] The shot thus exemplifies the power and limitations of cinema and, more generally, of aesthetic subversion. If the shot violates the extrinsic rules of government propaganda from the inside, it fails to impede the Nazis' pleasure. Its resistance can only be celebrated by those who recognize the shot and thus the irony.

Another, perhaps less remarkable device, this one not directly linked to a tradition, is the use of the track-in on a character's face. These occur before Landa gets LaPadite to admit he has been sheltering Jews [17:44]; before Landa attempts to shoot down Shosanna as she runs away [20:45]; before the Bear Jew emerges to kill Rachtman [33:26]; when Private Butz reveals the scar carved on his forehead to Hitler [37:38]; when Landa appears at Shosanna's side in the restaurant [55:10] and when he interrogates her [57:59]; when Bridget informs Aldo that Hitler is attending the premiere [100:44]; and finally when Shosanna looks over the balcony at the Nazi audience below [137:44]. The track-in obviously has a dramatic purpose; the increasing proximity to a face is meant to heighten an emotion, whether fear (LaPadite, Shosanna) or dignity (Rachtman). Yet the technique also establishes an equation between knowledge and power or the lack thereof. The situations all involve characters with a secret (LaPadite, Shosanna, Bridget, and even Rachtman, who chooses not to reveal whether or not he killed Jews), and this information can mean the difference between life (LaPadite) and death (Shosanna, Bridget) or not (Rachtman). Thus, the use of the device when

Fig. 53: *Django Unchained*: Pan right as Django and Schultz ride across the snowy mountains.

Fig. 54: *Django Unchained*: Right-to-left tracking shot as Candie's carriage and group ride into Candieland.

Landa aims his gun at Shosanna is not just the moment of horror we initially expect it to be; it is also the mystery of his decision not to fire, which, as we have seen, ironically paves the way for the demise of the Third Reich even before Landa decides to betray it. Like the color red, the repeated use of this device highlights Shosanna's rise to a position of knowledge and power. The exceptional use of the track-in on a scar (instead of a face) is thus absolutely coherent, as it represents the Basterds' rejection of a secret Nazi past. The scar displays what the face would have sought to hide, especially that of a character like Landa whose motives remain unclear.

In accordance with the epic narrative of *Django Unchained*, the camerawork used to depict the lateral movements of characters is made especially significant. Pans occur on several occasions: when Django and Schultz enter Daughtrey [13:07–13:13]; when they trudge through the snow (fig. 53) [51:52–52:13, 56:50–57:09]; when Candie, his men, and his slaves ride into Candieland [72:13–72:19]; when Django rides back to Candieland to save Broomhilda [151:08]. Lateral tracking shots are more frequent: when the slaves shuffle forward in the forest at night [2:54–3:13]; when Django and Schultz ride into Big Daddy's plantation [28:00–28:06]; when Django imagines seeing Broomhilda walking on the side of the road [75:42–75:53] or standing in the field [86:40–86:51]; when Candie's carriage and his men draw closer to Candieland (fig. 54) [85:28–85:38]; and when Django rides back into Candieland after killing the LeQuint Dickey Mining Co. employees [152:46–152:53]. Generally speaking, the movement from left to right or right to left abides by Western pictorial conventions, with the right symbolizing progress (Schultz and Django go west for the winter; Django returns to Candieland to save Broomhilda), the left, a return or regression (Django and Schultz coming down from the mountains at the end of winter; Django's fantasy). Repeated images of Django moving rightward foreground, through comparison with previous instances, his transformation from a slave to a valet to a bounty hunter.

The narration establishes a system, based on film genre conventions, whereby the pan seems to be endowed with its typical Western function of revealing the splendor of the landscapes, the lateral tracking shot with a spectral quality more typical of the Gothic. The Gothic potential is made patent as early as the opening credits, with the nighttime shot of the slaves; it is pursued, as Nama has argued, on a comic mode when Django dons his valet suit.[51] The tracking shot is explicitly associated with the spectral when Django hallucinates Broomhilda, and thus becomes a marker of subjectivity in the process. Combined with the shot/reverse-shot technique, the lateral tracking shot is the visual sign of a hesitation between progress (Django moving right) and regression (Broomhilda moving left), even though, physically, they are moving in the same direction. The contradictory movements are combined moments before the arrival at the Candie plantation house when the camera tracks left as the characters move right, suggesting that the forward momentum is by no means synonymous with progress since the characters are actually entering hell.[52] The Gothic finally culminates when Django returns at dusk, riding leftward with a fire blazing in the background. The system confirms Nama's argument that the Southern Gothic takes over the Western.

Another central device in *Django Unchained* is slow motion, which is often combined with amplified sounds. It is used when Django casts off his blanket [9:37]; when Django looks around Daughtrey as they enter the town [13:04–13:13]; when Django and Schultz kill the Brittle brothers [36:32–38:10]; when Django shoots Big Daddy off his horse [45:41]; when the dogs are unleashed on D'Artagnan [83:42–83:59]; when Stephen looks on in anger as a black man (Django) rides into Candieland [87:20–88:00]; when Broomhilda is taken out of the hot box [93:29–94:42]; when Schultz kills Candie and throughout the gunfight that follows until Django takes off his coat in surrender [131:19–136:58]; and finally when Broomhilda is thrown onto a bed by Candie's men [151:16–151:30]. The use of slow motion in the Western brings to mind, of course, the films of Sam Peckinpah, which influenced the action movie genre, including the Hong Kong martials arts films,[53] that in turn influenced *Kill Bill*.[54] Most of the instances in *Django Unchained* involve scenes of violence, whether that inflicted on the slaves (Django's scarred back, D'Artagnan, and Broomhilda) or that returned to the slavers (the Brittle brothers, Big Daddy, Calvin Candie, and his men). However, the usage in *Django Unchained* testifies to Tarantino's awareness of the debate concerning the aestheticization of violence and its potential glamorization, as we shall see. Indeed, slow motion is not used in the shots depicting violence inflicted directly on black bodies, but in those depicting the dogs and the slavers; by endowing the latter with a sense of fantastic monstrosity, the slow-motion shots heighten the realism and horror of the other shots.[55] Accordingly, there are no slow-mo shots in the Mandingo fight scene. *Django Unchained* does, however, resort to slow motion to emphasize Django's and Schultz's prowess when they shoot their opponents and to celebrate Django's transformation. Significantly, if the film is framed by the shot of Django casting off his blanket (fig. 9) (and thus metonymically his status as slave) and that of him casting off his coat (and thus returning to his status as slave), the final act does without the special effect in the action scenes. Instead, emphasis is put on his speed in the final shoot-outs. Moreover, attention is paid less to his actions than to what he has to say. The use of slow motion until the final act thus highlights Django's transformation from a physical being into a subject of language who can easily rival with—and thus do without—his former teacher, the eloquent Dr. Schultz.

One last salient device in *Django Unchained* is the brief ellipsis within a given scene. Specifically, these occur in seven scenes: three times in the Daughtrey, Texas, scene [14:48, 19:56, 20:15]; twice in the Big Daddy plantation scene [31:38, 32:12]; twice in the lynch mob scene [40:42, 44:26]; once when they meet Calvin Candie at the Cleopatra Club [62:57]; once on their way to Candieland [76:50]; and four times when Django effects his escape from the slavers [144:57, 146:19, 147:38, 148:41]. These abrupt cuts have a jarring effect; by leaping ahead in time, they convey a sense of urgency and energy. They systematically occur in scenes where Django and Schultz are playing roles. They foreground the characters' command over their plots and selves by evincing their control over themselves and others. While the

Fig. 55: *The Hateful Eight*: The snowy hell filmed in glorious Panavision Ultra 70.

"I Got a Name" scene shows Django taking control of his image as a bounty hunter [50:59–51:13], the cuts in the Daughtrey, lynch mob, and escape scenes show the other characters' (the sheriff and the Marshall, Big Daddy and his accomplices, the slavers) unwittingly taking up the roles assigned to them by Django and Schultz. The cuts are the mark of the clockwork mechanism of their plots. They even have a comic effect in the scenes where the overall tone is by no means threatening; Schultz appears very confident in the first, and by the second, we know they are talented schemers. By comparison, the scene where Django and Schultz talk strategy in Candieland is full of tension because it shows the plotters disagreeing under the watchful eye of those they seek to manipulate. Appropriately, it is the last instance before Django's escape from the slavers. The use of the device throughout the film obviously dramatizes Django's capacity to be as good a plotter and actor as Schultz, if not better; if the cut to a medium close-up of Django pushing Betina against a tree shows him reacting emotionally, the escape scene only shows the slavers' falling into his trap.

Of course, the most central device in *The Hateful Eight* involves the highly publicized use of the Panavision 65 with 70mm film stock (fig. 55). Upheld as a means to defend film against digital technology and attract audiences to movie theaters equiped with analog equipment,[56] the technology is also coherent to dramatize the film's subject matter. The rectangular format serves to contrast the opposition between inside and outside. The potential of 70mm film to capture wide-open spaces, like the desert in *Lawrence of Arabia* (David Lean, 1962), for instance, is limited to the opening credits, a few very long shots scattered across the first two chapters, and the subsequent flashbacks (especially the death of Charles Chester Smithers). With the rest of the movie taking place indoors, the Panavision 65 allows the film to take in one half of the cabin in one very long shot. In so doing, it annuls the offscreen, or rather relegates the offscreen to what lies beyond the way station walls. The feeling of claustrophobia—and of being in a self-contained aquarium—is thus reinforced, for there is never any indication that anything is lurking outside in the snowstorm. In this respect, the film sets itself apart from one of its hypotexts, *The Thing* (1982), since the "monster" can only be hiding in plain sight, as there are no corridors or other rooms (or so we are initially led to believe), and there is absolutely no reason to go outside. The mystery lies within, that is, within the characters whose faces, in various close-ups and medium close-ups, the wide-angle lens turns into spaces to explore for the slightest sign or clue, as in the films of Sergio Leone. The presence of Jody under the floorboards thus proves the characters' and the camera's failure to grasp everything. Ironically, the film ultimately underlines that the potential of the technology it seeks to defend remains limited, and that its power has to do with its false promise that wider is actually better. Instead, the film celebrates the Panavision 65's ability to better misdirect our attention, much like all the ballyhoo around the use of 70mm film for a static Western that takes place predominantly indoors and is, in fact, a tale of Gothic horror.

The second recurrent device, rack-focusing, is also imposed by the use of the Panavision 65, which makes deep-focus composition difficult to achieve. Significantly, the first occurs when Chris Mannix witnesses Warren and Ruth shaking hands that they will team up to protect each other's assets, Mannix ironically commenting: "Well, ain't love grand" [27:27]. Later instances occur at Minnie's Haberdashery: Warren examining Bob in the barn until the latter asks if he's calling him a liar [56:48]; John explaining to Warren and O. B. that someone is aiming to free Domergue [69:20]; Mannix getting Warren to admit his Lincoln letter is a fake [79:40]; the coffee pot as the narrator reveals it has been poisoned [96:53]; Daisy playing the guitar while keeping an eye on Ruth whom she knows has drunk the poison (fig. 56.1–56.2) [99:26]; the innocent Judy unwittingly showing the murderers into Minnie's [122:40, 123:25]; Jody and Bob taking their positions to murder Minnie and Sweet Dave [125:01]; Peter telling Gemma to be careful on the ladder [128:49]; Jody's hands when he emerges from the trapdoor [142:46]; the gun under Joe Gage's table as Warren says, "Keep your hands flat on that table" [144:22]; Joe Gage revealing his true name to be Grouch Douglass [147:51]; Warren attempting to kill the arch-deceiver Domergue [150:28]; Mannix negotiating the terms of the deal with Domergue [151:59, 152:26]; Domergue reaching for a machete to kill the two men [155:34]; and finally Mannix's and Major Warren's faces and hands as they hang her [158:30]. By drawing the viewer's attention to key elements or characters suspiciously glancing at each other, rack-focusing is put to the service of classical narration. But like the wide angle, it simultenously points to what we (and the characters) cannot

Fig. 56.1: *The Hateful Eight*: Rack focus on Ruth and O. B. helping themselves to some poison coffee under Daisy's watchful eye . . .

Fig. 56.2: *The Hateful Eight*: . . . back on Daisy as she resumes playing the guitar.

determine: that is, who is worthy of trust. As a visual marker not so much of trust and deception but of hesitation between the two, the technique is essential to the film's aesthetics and heuristics that are part in parcel; it is organized according to an escalation that climaxes twice—right before the multiple murder scene and during the final negotiation between Domergue and Mannix. Accordingly, the first and final occurrences, those that frame the film, dramatize the establishment of a contract, or at least the attempt to do so: Ruth considers Major Warren more trustworthy than Mannix, and Domergue endeavors to convince Mannix to side with her. The technique thus highlights the drama and ethics of trust that are the heart of the movie.

Formal analysis of his films confirms that Tarantino, like many off-Hollywood indie filmmakers, is the direct descendant of the New Hollywood filmmakers. Like their forebears, his films are grounded in classical genres and tap into a wide range of stylistic possibilities in order to optimize storytelling efficacy, while evincing a critical self-awareness more typical of art cinema. His films reprise the aesthetics of specific genres—for instance, the gray color scheme of *noir* (*Reservoir Dogs*, *Pulp Fiction*, *Jackie Brown*) or the more earthen palette of the Western or the war movie (*Inglourious Basterds*, *Django Unchained*). Specific devices are borrowed from specific films (the low-angle shot from the trunk from *The Mack*), filmmakers (slow motion from Peckinpah), national film genres (the fast zoom-in or -out from Shaw Brothers kung-fu movies), or periods of cinema (the fade-to-black as a censoring device in *Pulp Fiction*, the oblique angles of German Expressionism in *Inglourious Basterds*, the jump-cut and freeze-frame from the French New Wave). These devices can even be called on to assimilate two genres (Western and Gothic horror in *Django Unchained* and *The Hateful Eight*) and even two very different conceptions of cinema (grindhouse cinema and French New Wave in *Death Proof*) in the same film. This assimilation exemplifies Tarantino's endeavor to tap into the material made available by all cinemas, high and low, mainstream and marginal, and to celebrate the wealth of diversity in the process, all the while critically pointing out their limitations. Tarantino's loving relationship to cinema, and yet critical view of its past and present, is closer to the early Godard's than either director would probably care to admit.

The repetition of these devices, much like the color schemes of each film, work to construct the scene, the film, and the body of work as a unit integrated in the palimpsest that is cinema. Because they are always recycled, these devices point as much outward (to other films and works) as they do inward. In the films of Tarantino, intrinsic norms are always already extrinsic; more precisely, they are extrinsic norms reworked. Notwithstanding their singular uses within each film, the utilization of these devices is fundamentally metafictional because it produces a discourse on creation: creation is conceived as reprisal with variation, and thus as re-creation, and repetition enables resignification, with political implications. Therein lies the postmodernism of Tarantino—in this awareness that the material of creation is never raw. And it is his reveling in the view that creation is re-re-creation, the copy of a copy, that makes him characteristic of poststructuralist practices of deconstruction and resignification.

If the repeated use of these devices—from film to film but also within each film—has a dramatic and narrative function, contributing to the atmosphere (*The Hateful Eight*) and foregrounding the protagonist's evolution (Freddy Newandyke, Jackie, Django, Mannix), it also largely participates in the films' subtexts on issues of gender and race (*Jackie Brown*, *Django Unchained*, *The Hateful Eight*), and on ethical queries into values such as loyalty and revenge (*Kill Bill*), trust (*The Hateful Eight*), and professionalism (*Reservoir Dogs*, *Pulp*

Fiction, *Kill Bill*). It is at least as much through these devices as through the narrative that these values, which underlie the genres (the crime movie, the rape-revenge movie, the samurai movie, the Western) Tarantino reworks, are debunked. The deployment of these devices is by no means gimmicky, nor is it just form for form's sake. The varied uses, like the intertextual references they sometimes point to, are an invitation to viewers to make meaning of the stories, images, and subtexts.

One constant in Tarantino's films that this study has revealed is the dialectics between the construction and deconstruction of an appearance through the utilization of specific techniques: low-angle shots (*Pulp Fiction*) and fetishizing shots (*Death Proof*) in the first case; layered compositions (*Kill Bill*), the wide angle (*The Hateful Eight*), zoom-ins (*Reservoir Dogs*, *Jackie Brown*) and track-ins (*Inglourious Basterds*) in the second. These techniques foreground an unsuspected yet essential characteristic of cinema and the photographic image: that they draw their power, as well as their vulnerability, from the common belief that seeing is not only believing but knowing. Cinema has the power to construct these appearances, most typically in the form of icons, whether the stars at Jack Rabbit Slim's or Zoller, the hero in a propaganda film. But its power is also its limitation. Although the camera can scrutinize the face, it ultimately fails to see what lies beyond the surface of a master actor like Jackie or Landa, whose faces reveal no more of their mysteries than Ordell's dead face reveals of the afterlife.

CHAPTER SIX

"LOOKIN' BACK ON THE TRACK, GONNA DO IT MY WAY"

The Use of Preexisting Music

The music featured in Tarantino's films has, no doubt, contributed to their success. The soundtracks of *Pulp Fiction*, *Kill Bill Vol. 1*, and *Django Unchained* reached no. 20, no. 45, and no. 53 on the Billboard 200 album chart. Viewers have come to associate songs like "Little Green Bag" (George Baker, 1970), "Misirlou" (Dick Dale and the Del Tones, 1963), "Bang Bang" (Nancy Sinatra, 1966) with *Reservoir Dogs*, *Pulp Fiction*, and *Kill Bill Vol. 1*. The soundtracks further encourage this association by including lines Tarantino and the producers have selected to become "cult," including Tarantino's "Madonna Speech" (Track 8 on the *Reservoir Dogs* soundtrack) and Samuel L. Jackson's rendition of "Ezekiel 25:17" (Track 16 on the *Pulp Fiction* soundtrack).[1] Tarantino has made rediscovering forgotten singles of the 1960s and 1970s, sometimes by one-shot bands or singers, one of his specialties, deliberately constructing his persona as a historian of pop culture, with cinema at the top of the list, closely followed by music, comics, and TV. Bill analyzing Superman in *Kill Bill Vol. 2* or Jungle Julia's occupation as a DJ in *Death Proof* represent, in this respect, stand-ins of the director. Tarantino admits he was encouraged to add music by the Weinsteins,[2] the producers of his films to date, who probably saw it as an opportunity to bank on original motion picture soundtrack sales.

Considering the attention the music gets from audiences and journalists, it has received comparatively little from film critics and scholars. Apart from Ortoli's astute analyses scattered across his book, Robert Miklitsch's excellent piece on "audiophilia" in *Jackie Brown*, Lisa Coulthard's and Miguel

Mera's convincing studies of Morricone's music in *Inglourious Basterds*, and Regina N. Bradley's insightful analysis of the lyrics of two of the rap songs in *Django Unchained*, Ken Garner's excellent "'Would You Like to Hear Some Music?' Music In-and-Out-of-Control in the Films of Quentin Tarantino," published in 2001 before *Kill Bill*, is, to my knowledge, the only in-depth study entirely devoted to music in the films. Distinguishing between three categories of music—nondiegetic music, "incidental diegetic music," and the diegetic music selected by the characters—Garner shows how the music often refers to distinct musical or film genres[3] and is also instrumental in both evoking "the intensity of emotion," e.g., the use of surf music in *Pulp Fiction*,[4] and structuring the narrative, e.g., the use of "Aragon" (Roy Ayers, 1973) in the money exchange scene in *Jackie Brown*.[5] He notes that the main novelty in Tarantino's films is the degree to which the actors' "taking control of the score" is "celebrated," notably by insisting on the process of "selection."[6] Garner concludes that "[t]he potency of these foregrounded music-selection scenes for audiences is not simply a result of their shocking outcomes on screen," but has a lot to do with "dramatizing the dominant music situational-use practices of his youth audience."[7]

This chapter will expand Garner's line of inquiry and attempt to assess the evolution in how Tarantino has handled music since *Jackie Brown*. A few general trends in Tarantino's use of music in his films can be noted. With the exception of the music composed by RZA for *Kill Bill Vol. 1*, Robert Rodriguez for *Kill Bill Vol. 2*, and Ennio Morricone for *The Hateful Eight* and four songs in *Django Unchained*, all the music in Tarantino's films consists of preexisting music. Most of it dates back to the filmmaker's formative years, the 1960s and 1970s, and thus refers to the music, films, and TV shows he grew up with. Tarantino started using pop songs written for films in *Jackie Brown* and orchestral film music, mainly from Italian Westerns and exploitation films, in *Kill Bill*. Since then, the ratio between pop and orchestral music on the one hand, and that between diegetic and nondiegetic music (or what Michel Chion calls screen and pit music[8]) on the other, has, in both cases, increasingly tipped in favor of the second. Of course, these tendencies arise from the genres Tarantino has explored in recent years—the martial arts movie, the war film, and the Western—which provide less opportunities for the characters to perform or listen to recorded music than films set in a contemporary urban setting.

In the past, Tarantino said that he could not work with a composer because he was afraid he would be disappointed with the music and that, seeing the crucial role music plays in a film, he could not risk giving so much power to a single person.[9] Interestingly enough, Tarantino has accepted to give that power only to a friend and collaborator like Rodriguez, or to a mentor like Morricone whose music he had already used in previous films. Like many filmmakers who write their own screenplays, Tarantino begins the process of picking music while he is writing the screenplay. Like many filmmakers, including one of his mentors, Sergio Leone,[10] Tarantino often has the music played on set, sometimes between takes.[11] Thus, Tarantino's modus operandi clearly indicates that the music is not tacked on but, on the contrary, serves to shape the film and is, from the start, an essential ingredient in the creative process. Inevitably, then, a study of music in Tarantino's films calls for an analysis of the relationship between the preexisting music and the film as an "original" work. Relying largely on Michel Chion's terminology, this chapter explores the various functions of preexisting music in Tarantino's films, in terms of narrative, rhythm, tone, and intertextuality, before analyzing the use of original music in *Kill Bill*, *Django Unchained*, and *The Hateful Eight*. I argue that the use of preexisting music largely informs the metafictional discourse on the politics and aesthetics of representation.

Characterization and Narrative

The music in Tarantino's films participates actively in the characterization and the highlighting of character arcs. Some characters are directly engaged with music by bent of their profession—K Billy in *Reservoir Dogs*, Jungle Julia in *Death Proof*—or because the performer's star image is directly connected to music: Pam Grier, whose "Long Time Woman" from *The Big Doll House* (Jack Hill, 1971) is used in *Jackie Brown*, and especially John Travolta, star of *Saturday Night Fever* and *Grease* (Randal Kleiser, 1978). Significantly, half the music in *Pulp Fiction* (eight tracks) is featured in "Vincent Vega & Marsellus Wallace's Wife."

In spite of his love of Morricone's music, Tarantino rarely resorts to the leitmotif-per-character the Italian composer initiated most famously in *The Good, the Bad and the Ugly*.[12] In fact, only *Jackie Brown*, *Kill Bill*, and *Death Proof* make use of leitmotifs; the use of the tracks that accompany Jackie, Ordell, and Max in *Jackie Brown*, the Bride's visions of the Vipers standing over her in the church in *Kill Bill*, and the three groups of characters in *Death Proof* will be analyzed below. Common, however, is the association of a character and a specific song in scenes that sometimes resemble music videos. Examples include Vincent and "Bullwinkle Part II" (The Centurians, 1964) in *Pulp Fiction* [30:08–31:40]; Jackie and "Across 110th Street" (Bobby Wormack, 1972) [0:03–3:47; 148:25–150:12], and Ordell and "Cissy Strut" (The Meters,

1969) [9:23–11:15; 18:26–19:14; 71:15–73:10] in *Jackie Brown*; Shosanna and "Cat People (Putting Out the Fire)" (David Bowie, 1982) in *Inglourious Basterds* [105:39–109:40]; and, most obviously, Django and the song of the same name (Luis Bacalov, 1966) in the opening credits of *Django Unchained* [0:23–3:06]. Sometimes the song is listened to and/or performed by the character: Mr. Blonde singing along to "Stuck in the Middle With You" (Stealers Wheel, 1972) in *Reservoir Dogs* [55:51–59:11]; Mia Wallace singing "Girl, You'll Be a Woman Soon" (Urge Overkill, 1992) in *Pulp Fiction* [51:00–54:18]; Max listening to "Didn't I Blow Your Mind This Time" (The Delfonics, 1969) on his car radio in *Jackie Brown* [53:23]; Elle Driver whistling "Twisted Nerve" (Bernard Hermann, 1968) in *Kill Bill Vol. 1* [20:01–21:45]; and Daisy Domergue singing and playing "Jim Jones at Botany Bay" in *The Hateful Eight* [98:32–102:10].

In most of these cases, the lyrics and sometimes just the title serve to comment on the character and/or situation. The story of lost love related in "Django," for instance, immediately establishes the character's main motivation—finding and delivering his wife Broomhilda von Shaft—while, in *The Hateful Eight*, the lyrics of "Apple Blossom" (The White Stripes, 2000) evoke an innocence Daisy Domergue might have once possessed before toughening up to survive in the harsh world, and that one can glimpse in the beautiful medium close-up of Jennifer Jason Leigh (fig. 28) [15:03–16:08]. More frequently, though, the lyrics comment on the situation, adding a note of humor, pathos, and/or irony. In *Kill Bill*, for instance, the Bride breakdances while severing the Crazy 88's limbs to the line "Nobody can do it like I can" from "Nobody but Me" (The Human Beinz, 1967) [*Vol. 1*, 85:55–86:46], while the words "Well, no one told me about her" from "About Her" (Malcolm Mclaren, 2004) ring out during her alone time with her daughter B. B. [97:46–101:17]. If the lyrics, in the first example, invite us not to take the scene too seriously, they are put to more perverse use in the second. The first line, which is perfectly coherent in narrative terms, is followed by a second line—"the way she lied"—that tells a story of a mother abandoning her child that vastly differs even from Bill's account; the suggestion that wrongs may not be entirely on the father's side casts doubt on the future of this mother-daughter relationship, as well as on the righteousnesss of her vengeance. The use of song lyrics to produce irony is, indeed, a common feature of Tarantino's films. In *Reservoir Dogs*, and this in spite of Tarantino's claims that it's not about the lyrics,[13] Mr. Blonde singing along to "Stuck in the Middle With You" resonates with the sadistic treatment he is inflicting on the policeman—"I'm so scared in case I fall off my chair"—yet the title resounds more ironically given the outcome of the scene, when Mr. Blonde is shot down by Mr. Orange, the undercover cop he was unwittingly "stuck in the middle with."[14] Equally ironic is the usage of "Little Green Bag" associated with all the reservoir dogs in the opening credits, since it also nods at the made-up story Freddy told the thieves to convince them he was one of them.[15]

When several songs are used to accompany a series of scenes, the lyrics can serve to foreground the characters' arc and enrich the subtext. In *Pulp Fiction*, Mia and Vincent dance to "You Never Can Tell" (Chuck Berry, 1964) as if they were the newlyweds mentioned in the lyrics. The use of French— "C'est la vie"—reinforces this connection, since Vincent has just come back from Europe [48:05–49:55]. However, the fact that the couple in the lyrics are described as "teenage lovers" not only refers to the 1970s movies that made Travolta famous, but also suggests a darker subtext: that the two dancers are like children in relation to Mia's husband and Vincent's boss, Marsellus. Thus, in the following scene, the lyrics of "Girl, You'll Be a Woman Soon," which manifest the character's mood by evoking illicit love,[16] fail to announce that Mia and Vincent will make love, but by evoking rebellion vis-à-vis the adult world rather than allegiance to it, as was the case with "You Never Can Tell," they indicate that Mia and Vincent can only become adults if they free themselves from Marsellus's clutches. Mia's failing to make it to the end of the song, coupled with their decision not to pursue their relationship, foreshadow the fact that both characters will, as Ortoli has brilliantly shown,[17] remain subjected to Marsellus's power and to the stereotypes they find themselves trapped in.

If various songs can serve to emphasize an evolution in the narrative, then repeating a song can serve to highlight continuity, and thus a character or a situation's lack of evolution and maybe even symbolic imprisonment. This is the case in *Kill Bill*, where the repetition of the obsessive siren from "Ironside" (Quincy Jones, 1967) underlines the vengeful Bride's one-track mind. A more developed version of this approach had already been used in *Jackie Brown*. Max's listening to "Didn't I Blow Your Mind This Time" repeatedly is not just symptomatic of his infatuation with Jackie; it indicates that, in so doing, he has become a cog in her master plan. Though "Cissy Strut" initially matches the coolness with which Ordell deals with a critical situation like eliminating his former employee Beaumont Livingston, its recurrence with another employee—this time, Jackie—becomes, retrospectively, ironic, since Jackie, a woman at that, has not only escaped Beaumont's fate, but will ultimately best the arms trafficker, making him the "Cissy" of the title. As for Jackie, the return of "Across 110th Street," which, in the opening credits, evoked her struggle to make ends meet, suggests, in conjunction with the sad look on her face, that, if she has walked away with the money, total happiness still eludes her. In *The Hateful Eight*,

"Bestiality" is likewise used to invite comparisons between similar situations [102:39–103:44, 103:55–105:32, 158:03–159:39]. Associated with the deaths by poisoning of Ruth and O. B. and the hanging of Daisy Domergue, it frames the second act as the retribution of the crime, but by drawing attention to the "bestiality" inherent in both situations, it emphasizes that the hateful quality is shared by all those who derive pleasure from the violence: Daisy in the first scene, Warren and Mannix in the second.

The repetition of "Baby It's You" (Smith, 1969) in *Death Proof* offers more variation, the various instances inviting reinterpretation of the situation as a whole: (1) associated with Stuntman Mike, the title ironically points at Arlene and the other girls' being, in the tradition typical of slasher films, the killer's potential girlfriends [8:53–9:01; 9:30–9:34]; (2) associated with the girls dancing, it evokes the romances they are attempting to initiate (Arlene with Omar, and Julia with Christian Simonson), while ironically and tragically foreshadowing the fact that Mike will turn out to be their unwanted boyfriend instead [14:57–16:20]; and (3) associated with Lee singing the song a capella, the title underscores both continuity and difference between the two parts of the film [59:15–60:30]. The girls are dreaming of lovers and stalked by a dangerous man, and Lee is the Lebanon girl who most resembles the Austin girls (and who might even meet a bad fate at the hands of a pervert named Jasper), but Lee is also empowered by her appropriation of the song, anticipating her friends' potential to appropriate the gendered genre conventions of the slasher and the car movie to their advantage.[18] In any case, this notable exception may explain Tarantino's distaste for repeating a song. Compared to an original score or a piece of classical music, the usage of preexisting pop music leaves less room for variation and imposes many limitations, where a leitmotif in a music score or a piece of classical music can provide opportunities for variation.

Tone and Rhythm

Tone and rhythm contribute to what we usually call, perhaps for want of a better word, "mood" or "atmosphere." The tone of a song or a scene can be described as "sad," "funny," "creepy," "energetic," "ironic," and so forth. Tone in music is produced by a combination of pace, velocity, and key, with the arrangements ultimately contributing to the texture and thus to the tone. A major key evokes and possibly produces positive emotions such as joy, a minor key negative emotions such as sadness, while dissonance creates "musical tension."[19] The obvious question concerning tone when studying music in film is, then, whether the tone of the music matches the emotion and tone of the scene. When it does, it is, in Michel Chion's terminology, "empathetic," thus raising the question which character the viewer is meant to relate to in the first place; the music is "anempathetic" when it does not match, and is thus indifferent to, the tone of the scene.[20]

Empathetic music is, generally speaking, more common in film, and Tarantino's films are no exceptions. Examples include: "Bullwinkle Part II" in *Pulp Fiction*, its midtempo beat and tremolo guitar evoking Vincent's heroin high; "The Grand Duel" (Luis Bacalov, 1972) in *Kill Bill Vol. 1*, its slow tempo and wavering trumpet solo in a minor key emphasizing the tragic past of O-Ren whose parents were butchered before her very eyes [34:19–38:00]; "About Her" in *Kill Bill Vol. 2*, its midtempo and melody composed in a minor key matching the bittersweet emotions Beatrix experiences when watching TV with her daughter B. B., whom she believed to be dead; "Paranoia prima" (Morricone, 1971) in *Death Proof*, its atonal guitar melody matching Arlene's unease as she notices Stuntman Mike's car outside both bars [9:08–9:30; 20:23–20:54]; "Norme con ironie" (Morricone, 1970) in *Django Unchained*, its minor key and tonal modulations eliciting an anguish similar to that provoked by Django's memory of Old Man Carrucan's sentence and torture [24:43–25:26]. Empathetic music can be particularly disturbing when it seems to side with a sadistic character. This is the case of both "Stuck in the Middle With You" in *Reservoir Dogs* and "Comanche" (The Revels, 1961) in *Pulp Fiction* [102:06–105:31], the midtempo of the first reflecting Mr. Blonde's cool execution of torture, the fast tempo of the second driven by a hectic sax solo in a major key played using a combination of growl and flutter tongue technique, the rapists' frenzy of pleasure. The use of "Hold Tight" (Dave Dee, Dozy, Beaky, Mick, and Tich, 1966) before the death of Arlene, Julia, Lanna Frank, and Shanna in *Death Proof* initially sides with the girls by contributing to the fun they are having, while, for the spectator in the know, also reflecting Stuntman Mike's murderous rush. Including such lighthearted songs in scenes of violence produces a form of what Chion calls "audiovisual dissonance," i.e., a contradiction between image and sound,[21] that points to the guilty pleasure watching them entails. It is simultaneously an invitation to "hold tight" and enjoy the ride, but because they are aligned with the sadists, it is also a condemnation of such pleasure; Marcus Breen (1996) goes so far as to claim that the Mr. Blonde scene uses music "to heist the audience's own affective alliances," making pop music "complicit in the barbarity" in a manner that recalls some soldiers' use of music on the battlefield. In all three scenes, this alignment is established by emphasizing the spatiality of the music, the songs disappearing or fading out when Mr. Blonde exits the warehouse [57:41–58:20], Butch the cellar [103:08–104:51], or when Mike drives by [50:13–50:40].

Anempathetic music is less frequent in the films of Tarantino, as is true of films in general. Examples include: "Let's Stay Together" (Al Green, 1972) in *Pulp Fiction*, its downtempo beat and mellow romantic melody matching neither Marsellus Wallace's cool when delivering his instructions to Butch nor the humiliation Butch is subjected to [21:06–26:25]; "Strawberry Letter 23" (Brothers Johnson, 1977) in *Jackie Brown*, its smooth, sensual groove framing Ordell's execution of Beaumont [21:18–23:35]; "Nobody But Me" (The Hung Beinz, 1967) and "Bannister Fight" (RZA, 2003) in *Kill Bill Vol. 1*, the first (a rock 'n' roll song) equating the Bride's cutting the limbs off the Crazy 88 to a dance scene, the second (a pastiche of fighting game music) her final face-off with Johnny Yu to a scene in a video game, both drawing attention to the fact that there is nothing realistic about the violence of the scene; "Staggolee" (Pacific Gas & Electric, 1970) in *Death Proof*, its mellow tempo and melody in a major key contributing to make Stuntman Mike look fairly harmless when he first appears [22:25–24:42]; "Un amico" (Morricone, 1973) in *Inglourious Basterds*, the romantic music contrasting with the fact that Shosanna never was in love with Frederick Zoller, whom she has just killed and who has just killed her [140:19–141:48]; "Django" in *Django Unchained*, its compound rhythm and romantic melody inappropriately accompanying the slaves marching in a chain gang; and the ballad "Now You're All Alone" by David Hess, which accompanies the murder of Charly in *The Hateful Eight* [132:00–133:23]. Significantly, all these instances are associated with some form of violence, sometimes psychological (the Marsellus Wallace and Butch scene), most of the time physical. It is important to note that the music's indifference to the situation is actually one of degree: the minor tones of "Un amico,"[22] "Django," and even "Strawberry Letter 23" evoke the compassion at the protagonists' conditions that the rhythm and orchestration seem to deny. This suggests that empathetic and anempathetic music should be not be thought of as a dichotomy but as two poles on a continuum. In all these examples, anempathetic music actually serves to establish a distance both between image and sound, thereby foregrounding the artifice that is the film, and between the fictional violence onscreen and the historical violence (of slavery or Nazism) the cinematic representation (and the previous representations evoked through the use of preexisting music from other such films) is grounded in.

Atmosphere also largely depends on the manner in which the rhythm of the music endows a given scene with a sense of momentum. This concerns mainly the choreography of the actors' bodies, editing, and camera movements. Many scenes have characters moving to the beat of the music by playing the music on set.[23] This is necessarily the case in scenes where characters are performing and it is justified diegetically: Mr. Blonde in *Reservoir Dogs*, Mia and Vincent in *Pulp Fiction*, Simone in *Jackie Brown* [23:36–25:33], Elle Driver in *Kill Bill Vol. 1*, Arlene and Jungle Julia in *Death Proof* [39:10–41:58]; in *Kill Bill Vol. 1*, the Bride, the restaurant owners, and Sofie Fatale even walk to the rhythm of "Woo Hoo," performed on stage by the 5.6.7.8's, whose bass player had initiated the movement [70:55–72:43]. Obviously, it is not justified diegetically in scenes with nondiegetic music—for instance, when Ordell and Beaumont walk to the rhythm of "Cissy Strut" in *Jackie Brown*, when the soldiers march to "White Lightning" (Charles Bernstein, 1973) in *Inglourious Basterds* [25:56–26:28], or when Calvin Candie's hired men's spurs click in time to "Un Monumento" (Morricone, 1967) in *Django Unchained* [155:08–155:34].

More common, perhaps, are effects of contrast where bodies fail to completely match the rhythm of the music or do so only momentarily. Notable examples occur in the opening credits of *Jackie Brown* when Jackie goes from walking to the rhythm of "Across 110th Street" like a cool professional[24] to breaking out in a run; when Shosanna, in *Inglourious Basterds*, returns to the movie theater after meeting the Nazis and goes from not walking to the beat of "Claire's First Appearance" (Jacques Loussier, 1968) to matching it [61:24–63:25]; and in the opening credits of *Django Unchained* where the bodies of Django and the other slaves fail to keep up with the springy rhythm of "Django." All these scenes seem to point to the relationship between the characters and some form of order. Bodies perfectly matching the rhythm of the music reflect situations where the characters have some control or are under someone else's (Beaumont, for instance). Bodies that hesitate reflect a lack of control: Jackie, who appears to be perfectly on time to the music, is actually running late, the conclusion of the scene thus reflecting the struggle to survive described in the lyrics; Shosanna's change in pace may indicate an emotional shift from distress at meeting the Nazis and her family's killer to her resolve to devise a plan; as for Django, as a slave on a chaingang, he is in no position, at this stage in the narrative, to meet the expectations of the hero whose glory is lauded by the lyrics. It is significant that these characters are actually those who are somewhat redeemed in Tarantino's moral universe because, according to Ortoli, they ultimately learn to master the codes,[25] and thus metonymically the moves.

Resorting to slow motion can make bodies match the rhythm of the music. This is the case in the opening credits of *Reservoir Dogs* [7:47–9:55] and in the scene from *Kill Bill Vol. 1* that refers to it, O-Ren and the Crazy 88's arrival at the House of Leaves [67:23–68:44]. In Tarantino's first film, the effect, by making their footsteps correspond to a bar,[26] emphasizes that Joe Cabot's dogs are interchangeable, and thus acts as a manifestation of his power over them; however, it is ironically debunked, as we have seen, by the lyrics and by the fact that the actor who plays the undercover cop is presented last looking right at the camera from behind his sunglasses [8:38]. The scene from *Kill Bill Vol. 1* alternates between shots with and without slow motion, the characters making two paces per bar in the first and walking to the beat in the other shots. Their marching to the beat suggests they are perfectly aligned with, and thus loyal to, their boss O-Ren, yet the title of the track, "Battle Without Honor and Humanity" (Tomoyasu Hotel, 2000), calls into question the very values they embody. The utilization of slow motion reflexively reveals that the bodies are, in effect, filmic icons by insisting on the stereotypical garb of the dogs and the Crazy 88, with suits taken from the killers in Robert Siodmak's 1946 film,[27] masks from *The Green Hornet* (ABC, 1966–67), while Gogo sports a school girl outfit similar to Takako Chigusa in *Battle Royale*, a character played by the same actress.

The music can also organize the rhythm of the camerawork and editing. The slow pace of some tracking shots seems to follow the slow pace of the music. This is the case in the "Cissy Strut" scenes in *Jackie Brown* or in *Kill Bill Vol. 1* when the Bride examines Hattozi Hanzo's swords to the sound of "Wound That Heals" (Salyu, 2001) [50:32–53:10]. Most of the time, the rhythm of the music provides a foundation for the rhythm of the editing, which, in Chion's words, "takes its speed from the rhythm and tempo of the music."[28] Most cuts occur on or around a strong beat, but not systematically on the same one. Scenes where cuts occur on a strong beat (often the first) tap into music video conventions; these include scenes where the music is very obviously present, such as the opening credits of *Reservoir Dogs*. Cuts around beats also rely on the music, but the connection is more loose; for instance, in *Death Proof*, cuts occur on strong beats when "Staggolee" first plays and Mike is shown eating nachos, then around beats when the music fades out during the dialogue between Dov and Nate. Even background music can provide a template for the editing; for instance, in the scene where Jackie and Max have a drink after she has just gotten out of jail, the cuts occur around the beats of "My Touch of Madness" (Jermaine Jackson, 1976) [41:55–45:52].

The usage of preexisting music suggests that it sonically imposes its rhythm on the scene, especially with pop music in which the beat is usually firmly marked by the drums. In this respect, the usage of film music, from *Kill Bill* on, has, no doubt, given Tarantino more leeway in terms of audiovisual rhythm, if only because they offer segments in which the beats are less clearly marked. It also pushes it towards a mannerist style inherited from Leone and, perhaps, the music video. The usage of "The Verdict (Für Elise)" (Morricone, 1966) in the opening scene of *Inglourious Basterds* is a prime example [2:32–3:44]. Coulthard splendidly shows that, if Morricone's music is mainly featured in the first two chapters of *Inglourious Basterds*, the entire score is patterned after the use of Morricone's music in Leone's Westerns, largely contributing to the film's "sonic cohesion":[29]

> the integration of voice, sound effect and music; the irreverent mixing of idioms (popular, avant-garde, classical); the use of music as a foreground, not background element; the sonic referencing of a regular, rhythmic, kinetic movement frequently associated with action and adventure; the frequency of musical interludes that heighten emotion and freeze or extend narrative action.[30]

Yet the idea that the music absolutely determines the rhythm of the film must be qualified. In many cases, the music has been tailored to fit the scenes through alterations of pitch, tempo, and structure. In *Kill Bill Vol. 1*, for instance, the speed of "Don't Let Me Be Misunderstood" (Santa Esmeralda, 1977) has been increased, the pitch raised, the introduction lengthened, and the drums rearranged [91:52–94:00]. Many songs are covers or remixes, as Ortoli has noted:[31] "Misirlou"[32] and "Girl You'll Be a Woman Soon" in *Pulp Fiction*, "Flower of Carnage (Shura No Hana)" (Meiko Kaji, 2003) in *Kill Bill Vol. 1*, "Baby It's You" in *Death Proof*, "The Green Leaves of Summer" (Nick Perito, 1960), "Unchained (The Payback/Untouchable)" (Claudio Cueni, 2012), and "Ain't No Grave (Can Hold My Body Down)" (Johnny Cash, 2003) in *Django Unchained*. Thus, the usage of preexisting music entails a dialectic relationship between the preexisting and the "original" that is at the very core of Tarantino's creative approach: the original material is first fashioned by the preexisting material which is, in turn, fashioned by the new material to become something else.

Genre, Intertexuality, and Politics

Privileging a musical genre is often, as Garner has noted, a question of homage and audiovisual consistency.[33] Whether it be through hip-hop and R&B in *Jackie Brown*, Japanese music in *Kill Bill Vol. 1*, music from horror films in *Death Proof*, French and German songs in *Inglourious Basterds*, or Western music in *Kill Bill Vol. 2* and *Django Unchained*, the films tap into the network of cultural associations the music conjures up in order to reinforce both its world-building and its generic identity, which can be intertwined with questions of national, racial, and gendered identities. Less obvious alliances are sometimes made. For instance, the use of music from Italian Westerns in "The Origin of O-Ren" in *Kill Bill Vol. 1* and in *Inglourious Basterds*, or from horror movies in *Inglourious Basterds*[34] and especially in *The Hateful Eight*, which features the song "Now You're All Alone" from *The Last House on the Left* (Wes Craven, 1972) and Morricone's music from *Exorcist II: The Heretic* (John Boorman, 1977) and *The Thing* (1982). In the second case, referring to a genre different from the films' is a means of evoking emotions (horror, dread, anxiety) specifically associated with it. Dipping into the Italian Western library, however, should not be attributed solely to Tarantino's appreciation of the genre, nor is it merely a matter of drawing attention to the connection between the samurai movie and the Western in *Kill Bill*. Rather, the lyrical music Morricone initiated and Bacalov pursued are meant to bring out the poetic potential of images from lesser cinematic genres. In other words, Tarantino's love of the genre, and thus his use of its music, has a lot to do with these moments where the music adds poetry to otherwise crude images.

The usage of preexisting film music can also establish a direct connection with the film, sometimes even the specific scene, from which it was drawn, inviting intertextual readings that can enrich the metafictional discourses. Examples are numerous from *Kill Bill* on, since approximately half the tracks in *Kill Bill Vol. 1*, one-third in *Kill Bill Vol. 2*, half in *Death Proof*, all but two in *Inglourious Basterds*, and two-thirds in *Django Unchained* were written for, or featured in, films or TV shows. The intertextual networks created by the preexisting songs can vary in complexity.

(1) A preexisting piece of music can indicate a film's hypotext.

The song "Flower of Carnage," at the end of *Kill Bill Vol. 1*, is a cover of the song from *Lady Snowblood*, based on a 1972–73 manga, from which Tarantino's film borrows its tale of a female samurai out for revenge, the look of O-Ren Ishii, and the snowy setting of the duel between O-Ren and the Bride [97:01–99:08]. Similarly, the use of "Django" in the opening credits of *Django Unchained* inscribes the romantic black bounty hunter in a long line of Western heroes featured in films that tapped into the success of Corbucci's 1966 movie. With three tracks ("Eternity," "Bestiality," and "Despair") from Morricone's score for *The Thing* (1982), unused by John Carpenter at the time, *The Hateful Eight* points to one of its main hypotexts more ironically than in the previous examples: both films depict humans trapped indoors in the presence of an unseen evil while a snowstorm rages outside, but John Ruth, the character played by Kurt Russell, who starred in Carpenter's film, will fail to unmask the villains and be one of the first to fall. As for the song "Now You're All Alone," it points to precedents in anempathetic uses of music in *The Last House on the Left* (1972), where it occurs in the early stages of the rape scene, but also to the *Reservoir Dogs* torture scene, also featuring Michael Madsen, as if the later film were revealing the earlier film's influence.

(2) A preexisting piece of music can tap into an actress or actor's "star image."

The music from *The Thing* (1982) taps, more generally, into Kurt Russell's star image, since the characters he portrayed (Snake Plissken, R. J. MacReady, Jack Burton, Wyatt Earp) are usually more successful than Ruth, but in a less complex fashion than in *Jackie Brown* (in which Pam Grier's image as a star is at the heart of the movie). Indeed, in Tarantino's third film, the tracks from *The Big Doll House* ("Long-Time Woman") and especially *Coffy* ("Brawling Broads," "Exotic Dance," "Aragon," "Escape," and "Vittrone's Theme" by Roy Ayers) do more than simply nod to the AIP films directed by Jack Hill that made Grier famous. In the scene where Jackie is put in jail, a twenty-two-year-old Grier can be heard singing "Long Time Woman" while the camera pans left over a tired-looking Jackie, played by the forty-eight-year-old actress, ending in a long shot of her being locked in a cell with several other women [33:41–34:05]. If the song initially suggests that Grier has come full circle in her acting career, drawing attention to the theme of aging that becomes so central to the plot, the parallel is short-lived, for Tarantino's film quickly distances itself from *The Big Doll House* both in terms of narrative—Jackie will be bailed out immediately and will ultimately get away with her crime, whereas Grear is murdered in jail—and approach—though indebted to blaxploitation, *Jackie Brown* makes a point of not sexualizing Grier's body, as we have seen. This is later confirmed by the usage of "Escape" and "Aragon." Although both tracks start in the changing room, the first suggests tension, as a worried Jackie looks for Nicolette and Dargus in the mall, and largely contributes to the feeling that something has gone wrong [106:22–109:29], while the second accompanies Max as he walks out of the mall with the money, and thus celebrates the success of Jackie's plan [118:03–119:00]. The music indicates that, like Coffy, Jackie wins the day,[35] but without having to undress, even in a changing room.

(3) Preexisting music can complexify a film's subtext.

The examples from *Jackie Brown* already testify to this. The music in *Death Proof*, in particular, is key to the subversion of gendered horror movie conventions discussed above. While the title announces Stuntman Mike's ultimate demise, "The Last Race" (Jack Nitzsche) invites comparisons between the opening credits of *Death Proof* and *Village of the Giants* (Bert I. Gordon, 1965), the film in which it was originally used. Indeed, both fetishize youthful bodies, but the 2007 film associates it with the male killer's gaze by crosscutting between shots of the girls and shots of the road seen from his point of view [0:54–3:20]. The use of the music composed by Morricone for Dario Argento's first two films—"Paranoia prima" from *The Cat O'Nine Tails* (1971) and "Unexpected Violence" from *The Bird with the Crystal Plumage* (1970) [65:32–66:30]—draws attention to the fact that the scenes from *Death Proof* reprise those from Argento's films while inverting gender roles. The first instance uses mainly the second half of a piece not used in Argento's film, thus establishing a connection with the earlier film while insisting on the difference. Instead of a blind man failing to identify the killer he had sensed in one of the cars outside, Arlene notices Stuntman Mike's car, suggesting, in the light of slasher conventions, that she is the film's potential Final Girl. Yet this turns out to be a red herring. The end of the Austin part of the film proves that Arlene's awareness was ultimately not enough to save her, while the Lebanon part of the film relates how the three Final Girls manage to slay the killer even though they had been oblivious to his presence before the attack. Unlike previous Final Girls, then, it is the physical strength and talent of the second group of girls that win the day, not their ocular attentiveness. The utilization of "Unexpected Violence" is perfectly symmetrical to that of "Paranoia Prima"—it accompanies Stuntman Mike as he takes pictures of the four girls in the airport parking lot, thus placing him in a similar position as the female killer of Argento's first film.[36] *Death Proof*'s apparently abiding by slasher conventions therefore points to an early instance in which the gaze and the male were not equated. Occurring when Zoë's arrival tips the balance in favor of the tomboys in the group, the scene celebrates physical power in place of ocular power, as Stuntman Mike observes Abernathy showing off her capacity to dance the French cancan, the very move she will use to deliver the *coup de grâce* (fig. 26-27).[37] The use of music in *The Hateful Eight* also participates in the discourse on gendered genre conventions. Including a song from the rape-revenge movie *The Last House on the Left* (1972) and music from *Exorcist II: The Heretic*[38] inscribes the female villain, Daisy Domergue, in a long line of "female monsters" that are victims of the patriarchy they seek to resist.

Many of the musical choices in *Inglourious Basterds* and *Django Unchained* are even more resolutely political. In *Django Unchained*, for instance, Django's putting a symbolic end to antebellum lifestyle by freeing the slaves and killing the slavers and the Southern Belle in the main house at Candieland is, quite ironically, framed by two pieces ("Un monumento" and "Dopo la congiura" by Morricone) from *The Hellbenders* (Sergio Corbucci, 1967), a film about Confederates trying to revive the Confederacy [153:06–155:34; 158:14–159:22]. Much of the music in *Inglourious Basterds*, as Ortoli has pointed out, comes from films that deal with colonialism.[39] By citing *The Alamo* (John Wayne, 1960), *The Battle of Algiers* (Gillo Pontecorvo, 1966), *The Mercenaries* or *Dark of the Sun* (UK/USA, Jack Cardiff, 1968), and *Eastern Condors* (Sammo Hung Kam-Bo, 1987), the film refuses to vilify Germany by indicating that the nations of the Allied forces (France, Great Britain, and the US) have all committed atrocities in other contexts.[40] The link established with the Italian Western in the opening scene, reinforced by "The Verdict," is equally political [2:30–3:40], as many Italian Westerns were haunted by the return of fascism.[41] The images evoke the massacre of the McBain family in the second scene of *Once Upon a Time in the West*, which epitomizes what Ortoli identifies as one of the main themes of the Italian western: the death of innocence.[42] The music from *The Big Gundown* (Sergio Sollima, 1966) is especially potent because, in Sollima's film, "Für Elise" is directly associated with Baron von Schulenberg, a former German officer whose sadistic methods and fetishization of the technology of murder clearly evoke fascist practices.[43] The baron first plays the piece on the piano in a saloon; Morricone's adaptation, "The Verdict," later accompanies the final gunfight pitting the hero Jonathan Corbett against the baron. The combination of these two references is tragic as the "verdict" is aligned not with the hero but with the murderer of innocents. The reversal announces Landa's abject attempt to write himself up as a World War II hero (perhaps the greatest). Like the aforementioned references, this music does more than announce Colonel Landa's arrival and the tragedy to come; it also designates fascism as an ongoing universal threat (in Sollima's Italy), and not just as a freak occurrence in German history. Alluding to this film via its music is also a way of recognizing, on a metafictional level, the potential of genre films to metaphorically reflect on, and sometimes even subtextually engage with, their times.

Tarantino seems as reluctant to use the same music in another film as he is to use the same music in the same film. So far, he has only done so on four[44] occasions and usually with variation: the music Charles Bernstein composed for *White Lightning* (1973) in *Kill Bill Vol. 1*, when the Bride sizes up her remaining adversaries in the House of Leaves [85:31–85:53], and in *Inglourious Basterds*, when the SS come to pick up Shosanna [25:56–26:28]; the theme from "Twisted Nerve" in *Kill Bill Vol. 1* and Abernathy's ring tone in *Death Proof* [63:16–63:22]; and "Für Elise" in *Inglourious Basterds* and *Django Unchained*, where an unnamed woman played by Ashley Toman plays the famous piece on the harp [123:53–125:31]. If the gimmick in *Death Proof* appears mainly as a means for Tarantino to suggest that *Kill Bill* would be the kind of film shown in the world depicted in films like *Jackie Brown* and *Death Proof*, the use of the same music in *Kill Bill* and *Inglourious Basterds* announces Shosanna's potential to become a vigilante of the ilk of the Bride. The relationship established between *Inglorious Basterds* and *Django Unchained* is both aesthetic and political, and largely depends on the contrast between the roles played by Christoph Waltz in both films: Waltz's character is also a hunter, but the sadistic Jew Hunter has made way for a man who is resolutely anti-slavery. The reference to Beethoven in *Django Unchained*, as Robert von Dassanowsky has shown, draws on the composer's politics that informed one of his most famous symphonies; initially dedicating his Eroica symphony (1803–1804) to Napoleon, Beethoven, who adhered to the spirit of the French revolution, changed the title because he was revolted that Napoleon had proclaimed himself emperor.[45] In *Django Unchained*, the music accompanies Dr. Schultz's flashbacks of the slaying of D'Artagnan, which horrified him so, evoking once again the theme of the death of innocents. By demanding that the harpist stop playing, Schultz reacts much like a viewer could react to the use of anempathetic music in a violent and/or cruel scene in a film, including a movie by Tarantino. I do not think this means that Tarantino has necessarily changed his mind about the occasional use of such strategies, but by weaving the political ambiguities of these strategies into his work, he increases the distance I previously argued the anempathetic music served to establish.

For the most part, the music in Tarantino's films fulfills the various functions identified by Chion and other scholars of film music: it comments on the characters and situations, contributes to the atmosphere and rhythm, and allows for contrasts between sound and image, notably when it is anempathetic. Resorting to preexisting film music, no doubt, invites intertextual readings more obviously than more subtle allusions to another work in an original composition (the reprisal of popular melodies and classical themes in classical Hollywood scores, for instance), because even if the music is unknown, the paratext and peritext—the credits, the motion picture soundtrack album, Internet Movie Database, and wiki.tarantino.info—provide viewers with ample information regarding the source. In other words, the signifying power of preexisting music devolves from the fact that it taps directly into the viewers' memories and, more generally, in cultural memory: it is music with baggage. The inevitable constraints of such an aesthetics also produce boundless possibilities. Anahid Kassabian argues that

> [m]ore often, compiled scores offer what I call *affiliating identifications*, and they operate quite differently from composed scores. These ties depend on histories forged outside the film scene, and they allow for a fair bit of mobility within it. If offers of assimilating identifications try to narrow the psychic field, then offers of affiliating identifications open it wide.[46]

The use of preexisting music is thus central to Tarantino's conception of an aesthetics of re-re-creation that is liberating because it is material with which viewers may already be engaged with or may engage with after the fact, thus complicating their experience of the film itself and taking it far beyond the film (for instance, by listening to the soundtrack). Its use implies, then, that the acts of both creation and interpretation are inevitably back-and-forth processes. The filmmaker is left with the freedom to pick the track, then faced with the constraint of adapting his creation to it, before, in turn, adapting the track to his creation. In so doing, the creative act is, as we have seen in chapter 5, conceived in terms of re-creation. Looking back on the opening credits of Tarantino's first film, then, the line from "Little Green Bag" cited in the title of this chapter was already a statement of intent: though relying on preexisting music, Tarantino aims to use it his way. The presence of preexisting music in film also reinforces the back-and-forth process of interpretation, as the viewer is made to consider the relationship between the lyrics and the situation, between the original and the cover, between two songs, between bodies, images and music, between various references, between musical and film genres. If this approach may seem to close off meaning, giving the impression that these films are "closed works," the multitude of associations conjured up seem to confirm Eco's conclusion that there is nothing more open than a closed piece.[47]

A Note on the Use of "Original" Music

To what extent does the use of "original" music change Tarantino's approach? In the case of *Kill Bill*, the pieces composed by RZA and Rodriguez, who also helped Tarantino find music and sometimes even secure the rights,[48] function as fillers. RZA's four tracks—"Crane," "Banister Fight," "Yakuza Oren 1," and "Black Mamba (instrumental)"—resemble music or sound effects from martial arts movies and fighting games, while Rodiguez's, for the most part, pastiche Morricone; note how smoothly "A Fistful of Dollars" (Morricone, 1964) segues into Rodriguez's "Calling the Hateful Bitch," which pursues Morricone's minor key one tone higher, somewhat reprising the melody of "Bang Bang" [28:11–30:55]. This "original" music deliberately imitates the rest of the preexisting material and seeks not to break with it, but rather to prolong its atmosphere and associations. It remains entirely subordinate to the preexisting music.

This is not the case of *Django Unchained*, for which Tarantino did not initially request original songs.[49] Having heard about the film, singer/composer John Legend sent Tarantino a tape of "Who Did That to You?" When they heard that Legend's song would be included in the film, other artists (including Anthony Hamilton who contributed "Freedom") started doing the same, while Rick Ross and Morricone were invited to contribute material ("100 Black Coffins" and the unreleased "Ancora qui"). In other words, following Legend, black artists started appropriating the film as it was being made, so that the original music ended up fashioning the film very much in the same manner as the preexisting music. If the use of the songs remains the same, the fact that Tarantino relinquished some authorial control by accepting these unsolicited collaborations means that he recognized the political and aesthetic importance of these black artists' intention to contribute to the film; it is coherent with his asking producer Reginald Hudlin for input from the start of the project.[50] In "I Like the Way You Rhyme, Boy: Hip Hop Sensibility and Racial Trauma in *Django Unchained*," Regina N. Bradley argues that the anachronistic music does more than contribute to the film's "hip hop sensibility"; it bespeaks of the legacy of slavery in contemporary US culture, providing "a bridge between a (revisionist) slave narrative and contemporary racial violence." Her astute analysis of two tracks in particular, Ross's "100 Black Coffins" and "Unchained (The Payback/Untouchable)," reveals how, together, they participate in a form of unchaining from both the historical context and the hypotext (the 1966 Django's coffin) that, in effect, inscribes the 2012 *Django* in cultural history through association with important figures of black masculinity (Brown, Shakur, Ross) from various periods and backgrounds (New York and LA for Shakur, the South for Brown and Ross). The adhesion to a "hip hop" sensibility is political, then, as well as aesthetic, since it also involves a view of creation as remix or "mashup," as Mera contends.[51]

The view of creation as re-creation is also at the heart of Morricone's "original" score for *The Hateful Eight*. Ironically, the Italian composer earned his first Academy Award for Best Original Score for a film in which there is very little music—approximately 30.5 percent (about 51 minutes) of the runtime including the credits—and only 14.3 percent (roughly 24 minutes) of the music is not preexisting; Morricone's music from *Exorcist II* and, in particular, his unused music for *The Thing* (1982) are especially prominent.[52] In many ways, the original music is used in a similar fashion as in Tarantino's previous movies. It plays a structural function—for instance, at the openings of the first, third, and fifth chapters [4:34–4:46, 35:03–37:30, 119:31–121:48]. Predominantly nondiegetic,[53] it is often triggered or halted by the action; one example is the scene where English Pete and Grouch Douglass go for their guns that ends with Daisy yelling [150:02–152:44]. The music largely determines the pacing of the film: tracks like "Narratore letterario" [119:31–121:48], "I quattro passeggeri" [122:45–124:29], "La musica prima del massacro" [126:22–128:14], and "L'inferno Bianco" [155:03–156:18] play for their entirety; the camera pans slowly to a descending flute melody when Ruth's stagecoach arrives at Minnie's [35:03–37:30]; and cuts occur on the beats when Warren tells the story of Sandy Smithers's rape and death [90:05–93:05], or are effected more brutally, with the music stopping on an offbeat when Warren pauses in his story. Morricone's score creates a portentous atmosphere that owes more to the Gothic than the Western, so that the stagecoach riding alongside a snowy riverbank (depicted in very long shots, including two oblique high-angle tracking shots) recalls images of the coaches heading to Castle Dracula in numerous *Dracula* adaptations [120:34–121:03].

In spite of its sparsity, the music becomes, in effect, a haunting presence. As the titles "Neve" and "L'inferno bianco" ("Snow" and "White Hell" in Italian) indicate, and as is made clear as early as the film's opening shots, the original music is intimately connected to the environment, serving to heighten the contrast between outside and inside (Minnie's and the stagecoach), and bringing out the sublime quality of the snowy mountains and stormy sky. It makes sense, then, that the eruptions of music in the indoor scenes correspond to the violent outbursts: the deaths of General Smithers, Ruth, and O. B., the massacre, and the final confrontations in the last chapter. The major novelty the original score brings is the possibility for the film to play on Morricone's use of leitmotifs: the violin theme is associated with the snowy environment, the bassoon theme with the stagecoach. As variations on the key of E minor, the two themes are sometimes combined—for instance, at the beginning of Chapter Four, with the glockenspiel, a reminiscence of Morricone's Italian Western scores, replacing the strings [96:36–97:31], and especially in Chapter Five. In other words, the leitmotifs are fully integrated into the play on narrative repetition from a different perspective, introduced either by a diegetic narrator (Warren), an omniscient one (Tarantino's own voice-over), or the narration (Chapter Five), something Morricone was fully aware of, as is demonstrated by the very title of one of the variations, "Narratore letterario" ("Literary Narrator" in English). The leitmotifs that characterize the original score are thus both elements of the artifice and self-reflexive markers of it, and are integral to the metafictional discourse on creation as re-creation.

CHAPTER SEVEN

"COME ON, LET'S GET INTO CHARACTER"

Acting and Theatricality

This is the line Jules addresses to Vincent in *Pulp Fiction* to conclude their discussion on the significance of foot massages, moments before they make their dramatic entrance in Brett's apartment [13:37]. The wit and wrath he displays with his future victims then appear as elements of his act leading up to the soliloquy he recites at every execution [20:05]. The line not only equates their jobs with an act and displays the speaker's awareness that being a hitman is just a role, but in so doing, it reflexively draws attention to the fact that Samuel Jackson and John Travolta are themselves interpreting staple genre characters of the kind of fiction the film's title refers to. The thematization of performance lends a sense of theatricality to the scene, which is enhanced by the use of frame-within-the-frame composition, achieved thanks to the doorway they step through following their cue.

The theatricality of Tarantino's films has regularly been noted, including by the director himself.[1] Critics and interviewers have regularly compared *Reservoir Dogs* to a play,[2] a word Tarantino himself has used more recently to describe his eighth feature film,[3] and Agnes Matuska and Eric Kligerman have even described the reflexive strategies deployed in *Kill Bill* and *Inglourious Basterds* as Brechtian.[4] Tarantino's interest in drama has become more obvious in time, with him mentioning attending David Mamet's *China Doll* starring Al Pacino in 2015[5] and even acting in Leonard Foglia's production of Frederick Knott's *Wait Until Dark* in 1998.[6] And yet this aspect of Tarantino's work has received very little critical attention. This chapter is thus meant as an introduction to this complex and uncharted topic.

Scholars of cinematic theatricality have often described it as a particular handling of space and/or a specific acting style.[7] Cinematic theatricality,

Sylvie Bissonnette explains, involves style (frontal static shots)[8] and/or structure (division into acts, delimitation of space).[9] It can be effected, as James Naremore has demonstrated, by integrating theatrical devices into a film; in *Rear Window* (Alfred Hitchcock, 1954), for instance, the curtains raised in the opening credits, the pantomimes of those whom L. B. Jefferies spies on, and the entrances and exits of the main characters.[10] Naremore remarks that even ordinary scenes such as Robert De Niro's entrance in *Mean Streets* (Martin Scorsese, 1973) can be endowed with theatricality.[11] These devices would tend to disrupt the naturalistic tendencies of classical narration and thus effectively contribute to laying bare the artifice of film and even reality; indeed, Timothy Corrigan suggests theatricality in film has evolved into a set of "mechanisms and styles whose artificiality and spatial limitations could expose or critique the false realism of social identities, as well as the commodified realism of movies themselves."[12] If scholars occasionally equate cinematic theatricality and reflexivity,[13] in what follows, the former will be described as a modality of the latter, not a synonym. It remains to be seen whether such devices participate in the elaboration of a metafictional discourse. By paying attention to staging, casting, acting, and its thematization, I show that the theatricality of Tarantino's films serves to frame the films' metafictional discourses on acting, transposing the *theatrum mundi* metaphor to film.

Staging and Theatrical Space

The fact that *Reservoir Dogs* and *The Hateful Eight* are regarded as the most explicitly theatrical of Tarantino's films has largely to do with the degree of "staginess" the settings are endowed with. A few scenes contain actual stages: the graffiti-covered, open-air theater in *Reservoir Dogs* (fig. 57) [69:26–69:56], as well as the stages in the restaurants (Jack Rabbit Slim's and the House of Leaves) in *Pulp Fiction* [47:25–49:52] and *Kill Bill Vol. 1* [68:31–72:28]. But many ordinary places are turned into stages. Much like any no-exit play, *Reservoir Dogs* and *The Hateful Eight* are centered on a single locus, a warehouse and a way station, from which it is either dangerous or practically impossible to leave. The narrative of the 1992 film advances according to the entrances and exits of various characters: first Mr. White and Mr. Orange [11:21], then Mr. Pink [15:21], Mr. Blonde (fig. 58) [33:00], Officer Marvin Nash [46:19], and finally Nice Guy Eddie [47:43]; Nice Guy, Pink, and White leave together [52:22] and return later [87:28], with Joe Cabot arriving shortly after [90:06], until Mr. Pink tries to escape only to find the police waiting for him outside [92:50]. The plot of *The Hateful Eight* really

246 Acting and Theatricality

Fig. 57: *Reservoir Dogs*: Freddy Newandyke rehearses the Commode Story on stage in front of his coach Holdaway.

Fig. 58: *Reservoir Dogs*: Mr. Blonde watches Mr. Pink and Mr. White play rough in the stagey warehouse.

gets underway once each character has been introduced, after John Ruth has gone about the room to interrogate the patrons and size them up [49:10–52:11] and present Daisy and his intentions [70:19–71:53]; the only character to be revealed later, Jody, is conveniently located under the floorboards [118:26], the last place you would think to look, since theaters traditionally reserve the area for prompters.

In the other films, specific spaces are turned into stages for the duration of a scene. In Chapter Five of *Kill Bill Vol. 1*, the House of Leaves becomes the arena for the film's sophisticated fight choreography. The scene opens with O-Ren, Sofie Fatale, Gogo, and their group making a stylish entrance [67:33]; the Bride's presence is revealed to us [69:03], and she then sets the stage for the fight, calls out her opponent [73:36], and neutralizes all but O-Ren, before Johnny Mo and the rest of the Crazy 88 make a surprise appearance (fig. 59) [81:00]. The fighters replace the 5.6.7.8's as the performers,

Fig. 59: *Kill Bill Vol. 1*: The House of Leaves dance floor, now a stage for the Bride's exploits.

and the stage expands with the number of fighters, from the dance floor to the main room in its entirety, to the mezzanine previously reserved for the diegetic spectator (O-Ren), and finally to the private rooms and courtyard, which function as equivalents of backstage and back alley. Even small indoor spaces can be endowed with theatrical potential. In *Pulp Fiction*, Brett's apartment is the stage on which Jules performs his role as sinister hitman, concluding with his famous Ezekiel 25:17 monologue and the final execution (fig. 60.1–60.2) [14:25–21:06], while Jimmie's kitchen is the stage where the Wolf paces around delivering his instructions to Jimmie, Jules, and Vincent [122:41–123:12, 124:00–126:14]. Jules, Vincent, and Wolf make noted entrances. One of Brett's friends, who had been hiding in another room, bursts in, gun ablaze [113:09], albeit to no effect (unlike Jody in *The Hateful Eight*), while the Wolf and the others work against time to prevent such a dramatic entrance from happening, a possibility the narration visualizes in a ten-second-long subjective insert that starts with Bonnie opening the front door [120:47]. "Chapter Four: Operation Kino" in *Inglourious Basterds* contrasts the gigantic empty room where General Fenech briefs Archie Hicox on his mission under Winston Churchill's watchful eye [64:24–69:24], to the cramped underground tavern in which Hicox and the Basterds' uneventful entrance [73:22] is followed by the sinister intrusion of Major Hellstrom, who then crosses the room to join them [79:26].

All these spaces have three things in common: they have doors, offer enough room for movement, and are divided into several sections. What makes these scenes theatrical, however, is that they exploit these features, much in the fashion described by Bissonnette. Most of them start with doors opening and doorways being traversed (Mr. White and Mr. Orange enter the warehouse; Jules and Vincent step inside Brett's and Wolf Jimmie's; O-Ren's

Fig. 60.1: *Pulp Fiction*: Jules performs in Brett's apartment, while Vincent offscreen to the left looks on.

Fig. 60.2: *Pulp Fiction*: Travolta's Method acting contrasts with Jackson's theatrical performance.

gang and the Crazy 88 exit corridors; Archie goes through several doors before meeting Churchill and Fenech); the act of opening and closing doors is exaggerated to the point of parody in Chapter Three of *The Hateful Eight*, where the difficulty of shutting the broken door is turned into both a running gag (the patrons' shouting instructions) and a morbid ritual (nailing the door like a coffin) [37:38, 52:12, 62:35]. Characters pace, stride, strut or dance across and about these rooms (Mr. White, Mr. Pink, Mr. Blonde, and Nice Guy in the warehouse, Jules at Brett's, Wolf at Jimmie's, the Bride in the House of Leaves, Archie and even General Fenech in the meeting room, John Ruth and Major Warren at Minnie's). The rooms are divided into distinct quadrants: in the warehouse, Mr. Orange lies at the foot of the ramp throughout, Mr. Blonde against the post (fig. 58) [33:00], then on the roof of a car near the entrance [47:28], waiting for his turn to perform [52:33]; in Brett's apartment, Vincent takes a position in the kitchen area, while Brett and Jules occupy the center,

Marvin stays next to the front door, and one of Brett's friends rests in a bed against the wall (fig. 60.1); the first fights at the House of Leaves take place on the ground floor under O-Ren's watchful eye [75:24–80:36], the checkered dance floor facilitating the comprehension of moving bodies in space as they fight (fig. 59); during the Operation Kino briefing, Churchill sits at the piano in a corner of the room, and Fenech mainly stands on the other side of the room near the map of France. Again, this is blown up to parodic portions in *The Hateful Eight*, where the division is effected explicitly by Oswaldo Mobray, as we have seen in chapter 1. The division of space can be furthered through the use of the typical dramatic device of having two or more characters step out of earshot of another to have a confidential conversation, sometimes in an adjacent room—a bedroom or bathroom (Mr. White and Mr. Pink [17:36–26:39], Jules and Vincent [117:08–118:22], Wolf and Jimmie [126:14–127:55]) or in a corner (Ruth, O. B., Warren, and Domergue around a small table [68:33–70:17])—with the smaller size reflecting the increased intimacy. Spatial theatricality can also be reinforced by various props that call to mind elements from the theater: stages (obviously), mezzanines, curtains (the red and golden ones in Fenech and Churchill's room), blinds (the yellow ones in Brett's apartment), or norens (in the House of Leaves), as well as tools that are usually concealed backstage or in the rafters, such as the ladders, beams, and chains hanging from the ceiling (in the warehouse and Minnie's).

Outdoor spaces can also be turned into stages. In *Kill Bill Vol. 2*, Pai Mei's domain becomes a ring for Beatrix's test against the kung-fu master [49:41–53:17], while in Chapter Two of *Inglourious Basterds*, the interrogation, torture, and execution of Nazi soldiers take place in an arena-like venue, with the audience on the side and the performers in the middle (fig. 65)—Aldo, his interpreter Wilhelm Wicki, the Nazi prisoners, and Sergeant Donny Donowitz, aka the Bear, who makes a dramatic entrance by strutting out of one in a series of dark tunnels [26:39–37:33]. Many of the outdoor locations in *Django Unchained* are rendered theatrical through staging. The encounter between Schultz and the Speck brothers takes place in a flat clearing in the middle of a forest of barren trees [4:27–12:38], that between Schultz and Sheriff Bill Sharp at an empty street corner [19:34], with the bounty hunter occupying the central position each time; the dead sheriff's blood marks out the center stage area when US Marshall Gill Tatum arrives, humorously drawing attention to the fact that the stage is void and that the star performer is preparing to make his entrance by stepping through the tavern door [20:31]. Big Daddy's house is turned into an outdoor theater when the plantation owner looks down from the balcony (like O-Ren in *Kill Bill Vol. 1*) at Schultz and Django standing in a circle of dirt[14] below [28:22–31:37]. Django's empowerment is then dramatized through the staging, with the former slave stepping off the grass onto an empty brown patch of dirt and leaves, framed by oak trees with Spanish moss hanging down like curtains, to kill John Brittle and whip his brother Raja, before addressing the audience of slaves and inviting them to watch him finish off Little Raja [35:47–37:31].

Tarantino's style largely contributes to the theatrical handling of space. The frequent use of lengthy very long and long shots both constructs the open space as a stage and enables us to identify the various sectors and watch the characters move from one to another. In *Reservoir Dogs*, the scene in which Mr. White and Mr. Pink argue over what to do with Mr. Orange utilizes three long shots [29:06, 30:25, 31:15] and two very long shots [32:28, 33:05], dividing the warehouse into four zones: the central stage, plus three zones on the sidelines (Mr. Orange on the ramp, the table, and Mr. Blonde against the post) (fig. 58) [28:30–33:09]. Similarly, the scene in *The Hateful Eight* where Domergue and Ruth first enter Minnie's offers a series of very long shots, enabling us to discover the patrons' position in space along with the bounty hunter, who immediately moves into the only unoccupied zone (the kitchen) so as to guard his back [37:42, 38:53, 39:03, 39:17, 39:53, 40:06, 40:25]. In *Pulp Fiction*, the establishing shot (a long shot) of Brett's apartment recurs five times in the scene (fig. 60.1) [14:26, 17:20, 18:11, 18:20, 19:14]. The briefing scene in *Inglourious Basterds* comprises thirteen very long shots that neatly delineate three zones, each associated with one of the characters (Hicox near the door, Fenech near the map, Churchill at the piano), while the outdoor execution scene features ten very long shots that clearly separate the performers on stage from the audience around them, the high and low angles reinforcing the boundary between the two.

Frontality, as Naremore, Bissonnette, and Christian Viviani have noted, can also construe a sense of theatricality. In Tarantino's films, this is especially the case in moments where the characters' positions are fixed. This is the case, for instance, in the kitchen and backyard scenes at Jimmie Dimmick's in *Pulp Fiction*, which present Jules and Vincent on one side and Jimmie and Wolf on the other [118:23–120:26, 129:18–131:01], in *Kill Bill Vol. 1*, when the Bride meets Hattori Hanzo [49:29–49:48], and in *Django Unchained*, when Dr. Schultz delivers his spiel and produces his warrants to his audience (fig. 61) [21:51–23:36, 38:28–39:41]. Deep-focus composition can enhance staging in depth—for instance, in the very long shot of Mr. White standing over Mr. Pink with Mr. Blonde standing in medium full shot in the right foreground (fig. 58), or in the long shots of Hicox in the foreground looking back at Churchill in the background. Tarantino occasionally utilizes split-focus thanks to the split diopter made famous by *Blow Out* (Brian De

Fig. 61: *Django Unchained*: Schultz delivers his spiel with some prompting from Django in a frontal two-shot.

Palma, 1981), as in *The Hateful Eight* right before Mannix (in frontal close-up to the left) turns down Domergue's offer as Warren, lying wounded on the bed, looks on (to the right) [152:12], combining frontality (both actors are facing the audience) and distance (the actor in close-up resembles an actor positioned downstage center). The theatrical quality can also be reinforced by frame-within-the-frame composition, thanks to props reminiscent of the theater such as those noted above (the norens, sliding doors, bead curtains in Hanzo's sushi bar) or more mundane elements such as the cupboard doors, posts, windows, walls, and fence in Jimmie's kitchen and backyard in *Pulp Fiction*, or the posts, doors, and trees in *Django Unchained*. In the case of the outdoor scenes, theatricality is often as much a question of composition as of staging, if not more so. In the scene at Jasper's in *Death Proof*, for instance, it is the use of split-focus when Kim steps away from Zoë [82:07], followed by the frontal medium two-shot of Zoë and Kim on one side and the frontal medium full shot of Abernathy on the other [82:39–85:37]—shots long enough to reveal that the three women are standing on a patch of dirt surrounded by a circle of grass—that adds a sense of theatricality to their conversations.

The handling of space in Tarantino's films largely contributes to their theatricality; it concerns the degree to which spaces, whether indoor or outdoor, are rendered stagey, notably through the modalities described by Naremore and Bissonnette. Although it varies from film to film (*Reservoir Dogs* and *The Hateful Eight* are the films in which the handling of space is the most theatrical, *Jackie Brown* and *Death Proof* those in which it is the least) and within each film (specific scenes are more theatrical than others), it is always achieved through a combination of staging and camerawork. A flat, empty, stage-like space, allowing freedom for the actors' movements, can be marked out by various profilmic elements (including elements that directly recall a theater environment). But in order to be fully theatrical, it must be exploited dramatically (the use of doors, actors' movements, the division of space) and enhanced by the camerawork through lengthy, very long and long shots, frontality, and/or deep focus. Cinematic theatricality, as film scholars have noted, is a laying bare of the artifice: it immediately draws attention to the set as fabrication. But its function is also to create a space in which the actors' movements will have free reign, and in this respect, I would argue that Tarantino is highly influenced by Howard Hawks. As is already evident from the examples cited above, the theatrical handling of space in Tarantino's films is not merely aesthetic and reflexive; it serves to frame both the actors' performances and the thematization of acting within the films.

Star Image and Typecasting

Casting plays an integral part in the metafictional discourses of Tarantino's films because of the intertexual relationships it establishes with films and TV shows of the past. Tarantino has often explained how he has specific actors in mind when writing a script, including actors as they appeared in older movies.[15] His passion for film history has led him to cast many of his actors based on their own history, and thus on what Richard Dyer calls a "star image." About her role in *The Hateful Eight*, Jennifer Jason Leigh explained that Tarantino "doesn't just see what you did the last two years and he doesn't think you're not that person you were in [. . .] 1985," when "a lot of times, this town, or this business, really only looks at your last three projects."[16] "[M]ade out of media texts that can be grouped together as promotion, publicity, films and criticism and commentaries,"[17] a "star image," Dyer says, is comprised of a "finite number of meanings"[18] and can change in time. Tarantino's willingness to exploit an actor's star image participates in the films' overall engagement with film and cultural history. In this sense, at least, the stars are used very much like the preexisting music—as material with baggage.

Many, if not all, of the lead roles are cast based on an actor's or actress's previous work. *Reservoir Dogs* draws on the figure of neurotic, vulnerable masculinity[19] Harvey Keitel developed in *Mean Streets*, *Bad Lieutenant* (Abel Ferrara, 1992), and *The Piano* (Jane Campion, 1993); *Pulp Fiction* on John Travolta's status as teenpic star in *Carrie* (1976), *Saturday Night Fever*, and *Grease* (1978), and on Bruce Willis's action movie persona, which exploded with the first two *Die Hard* films (John McTiernan, 1988; Renny Harlin, 1990);[20] *Jackie Brown* on Pam Grier's badass heroines in *Coffy* and *Foxy Brown*; *Kill*

Bill on David Carradine's role in *Kung Fu* and his association with the Western; *Death Proof* on Kurt Russell's cynical heroes in John Carpenter's *Escape from New York* (1981) and *The Thing* (1982). This implies that lead roles are cast at least partly according to type. An "asshole" with a "sweet" side, Butch is, as Tarantino himself acknowledges, very much like the other characters Willis has portrayed in the past;[21] Russell endows Stuntman Mike with the same arrogant humor as Jack Burton in the martial arts fantasy comedy *Big Trouble in Little China* (Carpenter, 1986); the combination of confidence and provincialism Aldo Raine exudes mixes traits from some of Brad Pitt's earlier characters, the slick Rusty Ryan in *Ocean's Eleven* (Steven Soderbergh, 2001) and the silent sociopath Early Grace in *Kalifornia* (Dominic Sena, 1993); and the cool resolve and verbal dexterity of Django recalls Jamie Foxx's roles in *Collateral* (Michael Mann, 2004), *Miami Vice* (Mann, 2006), and *Law Abiding Citizen* (F. Gary Gray, 2009).

Supporting actors, too, are often cast according to their history. In *Reservoir Dogs*, Lawrence Tierney reprises his "sadist brute"[22] act from *Dillinger* (Max Nosseck, 1945) and *Born to Kill* (Robert Wise, 1947). *Pulp Fiction* and *True Romance* tap into Christopher Walken's famous roles as a soldier in *The Deer Hunter* (Michael Cimino, 1978) and a gangster in *King of New York* (Abel Ferrara, 1990). *Kill Bill* harks back to Daryl Hannah as a femme fatale replicant in *Blade Runner* (Ridley Scott, 1982). Tierney's presence in *Reservoir Dogs* announces the theme of the aging actor—he is first introduced having memory problems [2:24]—central to *Pulp Fiction*, *Jackie Brown*, *Kill Bill* (with David Carradine), and *Death Proof* (with Kurt Russell). Walken's cameos simultaneously laud his talent and yet basically confirm that the actor is condemned to endlessly repeating the same supporting roles over and over again. Hannah, as Elle, resurrects the ominous potential of Pris that was repressed in the figure of the innocent blondes she portrayed in *Splash* (Ron Howard, 1984) and *Roxanne* (Fred Schepisi, 1987). In fact, I would argue that the only actors who are really cast against type are Leonardo DiCaprio and Don Johnson in *Django Unchained*, and this was done for the same reason: each actor is or was a sex symbol generally cast in the role of a sympathetic hero, albeit sometimes psychotic in DiCaprio's case (Scorsese's 2010 *Shutter Island* comes to mind). Casting them as plantation owners is a way of insisting on the abjection underlying the sugary charm with which the antebellum South has often been portrayed in Hollywood cinema. The same can be said of Jennifer Jason Leigh in *The Hateful Eight*, whose witchy Daisy Domergue contrasts with her previous roles which were predominantly sympathetic, while combining traits (grumpiness, intelligence, radiance) the actress had expressed in some of her most famous roles in *Short Cuts* (Robert Altman,

Fig. 62: *Pulp Fiction*: Vincent Vega admiring Jack Rabbit Slim's, "a wax museum with a pulse" in which the 1970s John Travolta could easily find his place.

1993), *The Hudsucker Proxy* (Joel and Ethan Coen, 1994), *Kansas City* (Altman, 1996), and *eXistenZ* (David Cronenberg, 1999).

With the exception of DiCaprio, Foxx, Pitt, Willis, and Keitel, whose status in 1991 gave him sufficient leverage to actively support and promote *Reservoir Dogs*,[23] the other stars have in common that their careers were slumping, so that they were remembered more for their past roles and not their current work. Casting these semi-forgotten actors partially according to type endows them with an uncanny aura—they are simultaneously familiar (as stars) and unfamiliar (because of the passing of time and the physical changes), making them cinematic revenants that haunt the films, as Ortoli has demonstrated.[24] "Vincent Vega & Marsellus Wallace's Wife," *Jackie Brown*, *Kill Bill*, and *Death Proof* are largely about these ghostly images. With Carradine in the role of Bill, an older, villainous version of Kwai Chang Caine, the title of Tarantino's fourth film metafictionally frames the film as the vengeance of Bruce Lee's spectre on the actor who took the lead role in *Kung Fu*, originally written for the actor and martial arts expert following the success of *The Green Hornet*, because the producers believed American audiences were not ready for a Chinese American leading man[25]—Thurman even dons the *Game of Death* jumpsuit, as if her valor could only be "measured in relation to the spectre of Bruce Lee."[26] *Death Proof* operates a similar transformation, enhancing the sexist macho side of its star, announced as such in the opening credits, before punishing him for it, as we have seen in chapter 3.

An actual star of the past, and thus a living waxwork, Travolta is the inverted double of the employees at Jack Rabbit Slim's (fig. 62). Vincent's trajectory in *Pulp Fiction* can even be interepreted as Travolta revisiting the evolution of his star image:[27] from cool guy in a teen flick taking a chick out on a date to drug addict with career issues, dramatized as questions of loyalty to Marsellus (and gangsterism) or to Mia (and teen romance).[28] On a metafictional level at least, the death of Vincent Vega ends up being as rejuvenating for Travolta as Jules's epiphany, for it signals the rebirth of the actor's career, which *Pulp Fiction* effectively relaunched. Travolta went on to star in such popular films as *Get Shorty* (Barry Sonnenfeld, 1995) and *Broken Arrow* (John Woo, 1996). This approach is taken even further in *Jackie Brown*. The movie is as much about Pam Grier getting back at an industry that cast her throughout the 1980s—with secondary roles in films like *Tough Enough* (Richard Fleischer, 1983), *The Vindicator* (Jean-Claude Lord, 1986), and *The Package* (Andrew Davis, 1989)[29]—according to a type her aging body, as Jackie tells Max, can no longer fit [58:14–59:12], as it is about Jackie trying to turn her life around. Perhaps the greatest disappointment of *Jackie Brown* is that, in spite of Grier's stellar performance, it did not renew her career as much as *Pulp Fiction* renewed Travolta's, which can, regrettably, be put down to the fact that she is a black woman facing down Hollywood. The film's imperfectly happing ending even seems to regretfully anticipate this likely outcome: Jackie, unlike Vincent, has successfully carried out what she views as her last performance, significantly effected in a changing room, only to leave the film on a melancholy note in the final close-up [149:01], and even Max Cherry's sad look after she leaves can be seen as Forster's tearful farewell to his collaboration with the black actress [148:20].

Tarantino does not so much cast against type as integrate a reflection on typecasting in his films. The early films seem to demonstrate how difficult it is for a star to shed her/his skin and control her/his image. What distinguishes his approach is not so much that he takes into account his actors' star image—most filmmakers do—but the degree to which they participate in the films' metafictional discourses and are sometimes even its main concern.

The metafictional discourse can also be reinforced by the casting of supporting actors who are not primarily actors. It is only fitting that, in *Death Proof*, a movie that relates the girls' revenge over the male killer, one of Stuntman Mike's slayers should be played by an actual stuntperson, Zoë Bell, who ends up slaying the sort of person (an actor) who stands in the limelight in her place and who has, in this case, usurped her role. Larry Bishop in *Kill Bill Vol. 2* and Eli Roth in *Death Proof* and *Inglourious Basterd* are also cast not so much for their talent as for how their real-life status as directors (Bishop's character is even given the same first name) construes meaning. Larry Gomez's debasing Budd in his office mirrors Tarantino's own treatment of the actor who portrayed Mr. Blonde, the epitome of cool, in *Reservoir Dogs*, now made to play a loser. As for Roth, he is always cast in the parts of sadists (Dov whose desires Stuntman Mike acts out, and especially the Bear Jew), provocatively giving fodder to those who believe that the director of *Hostel I* (2005) and *II* (2007) could only be a degenerate in real life.

Tarantino took a lot of flak for his own ambitions as an actor in the early stages of his career,[30] ambitions that were, no doubt, sincere. Once he had become identifiable as a star from *Pulp Fiction* on, each of his cameos became overtly reflexive and served to comment on his function as a director. As Mr. Brown in *Reservoir Dogs*, Tarantino delivers a statement of intent before signing off as an actor and embracing his role as a director. As Jimmie Dimmick in *Pulp Fiction*, Tarantino, like Larry Bishop/Gomez in *Kill Bill Vol. 2*, playfully tortures his own characters, Jules and Vincent, stripping them of their *Reservoir Dogs*-like suits and dressing them up in his clothes, acting under the tutelage of the actor, Keitel, whom the director describes as a surrogate father.[31] As Warren, the owner of the Texas Chili Parlor in *Death Proof*, Tarantino embodies the male patriarch guilty of subjecting young women to his "leering,"[32] forcing them to drink shots of a drink he praises because of its color in a film where he handled the cinematography himself.[33] In *Django Unchained*, the slave-turned-bounty hunter is given a chance to slay his maker, Tarantino as Robert, the LeQuint Dickey Mining Co. employee, thus acting out his role as avenger on a metafictional level. Tarantino's voice has become sufficiently recognizable for him to recite a narrative voice-over in *The Hateful Eight*, underscoring the novelistic practices typical of his films by playing on the reader/viewer's tendency to confuse author and narrator. The fact that Tarantino's characters often die—notably in the films of Robert Rodriguez, *Desperado* (1995), *From Dusk Till Dawn* (1996), and *Planet Terror* (2007)—is clearly a snub to those who see the director as guilty of promoting violence and/or fetishizing their characters.

Another reflexive device, this one initiated in *Kill Bill*, is the casting of the same actor for two parts. In *Kill Bill*, Chia-Hui Liu's playing Johnny Mo and Pai Mei, and Michael Parks's playing Sheriff Earl McGraw and Esteban Vilhaio, reinforce the film's two-part structure. This device is used, albeit less conspicuously, in later films, with James Remar portraying Ace Speck and Butch Pooch in *Django Unchained*, and Tarantino acting as the movie's first scalped Nazi (fig. 63) [26:19] and an American soldier (the one who shouts: "We must destroy that tower!") in Goebbel's film [130:59] in *Inglourious Basterds*. Actors playing several parts has long been a common practice in theater, with Brecht turning it into an anti-illusionist device.[34] The device contributes to the theatricality of Tarantino's films and reflexively lays bare the artifice, of course, but it also participates in the political subtext and/or metafictional discourse. Tarantino's twin role as Nazi and American victim in the diegesis and the film-within-the-film connects the violence of his

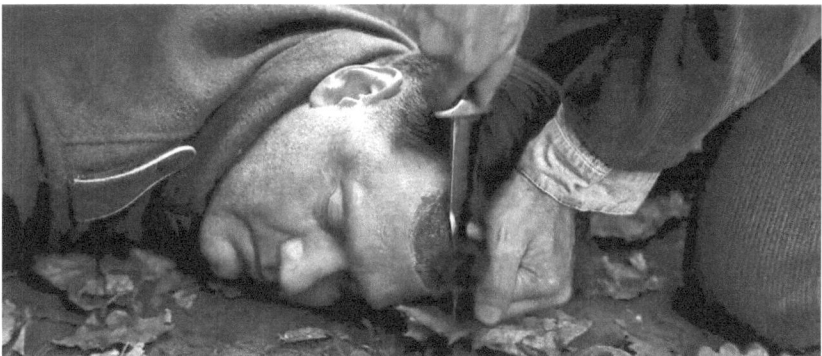

Fig. 63: *Inglourious Basterds*: The Basterds' first scalp, a Nazi soldier played by Tarantino.

film and the fictitious Nazi propaganda movie. Parks's parts as a father (to Edgar) who upholds the law and a surrogate father (to Bill) who exploits women structurally and thematically reinforce, as we have seen, the patriarchal framework of *Kill Bill*. Liu, on the other hand, becomes a bridge between Hong Kong and Japanese martial arts cinema; as a subordinate to O-Ren, the first character recognizes the power of this figure of hybridity who, as a Chinese-Japanese American woman wielding a samurai sword, embodies all that his second character, Pai Mei, despises. The Hong Kong martial arts star is thus made to incarnate the history of conflict and exchange between two nations and two film industries. In all three cases, the twin casting serves to undermine a clear-cut dichotomy. Making Remar play two very similar roles serves, conversely, to consolidate the figure of the white oppressor, and thus implies an indictment of the white South in its entirety.

Like many directors past and present, Tarantino has, after eight feature films, constituted a veritable stock company by working repeatedly with several actors. Samuel L. Jackson has played in six feature films (all except for *Reservoir Dogs* and *Death Proof*), Michael Madsen and Tim Roth[35] in three feature films (*Reservoir Dogs*, *The Hateful Eight*, *Pulp Fiction* for Roth, and *Kill Bill* for Madsen), and two for Uma Thurman (*Pulp Fiction*, *Kill Bill*), Christoph Waltz (*Inglourious Basterds* and *Django Unchained*), Bruce Dern and Walton Goggins (*Django Unchained*, *The Hateful Eight*), Michael Parks[36] and his son James (*Kill Bill*, *Death Proof*), and Eli Roth and Omar Doom (*Death Proof* and *Inglourious Basterds*). (Apparently, Leonardo DiCaprio, Brad Pitt, and Samuel L. Jackson are attached to star in Tarantino's ninth film.) If the presence of a character in several films can reinforce the fantasy model that underlies metafiction, especially when the films in question seem to exist in distinct realities (Sheriff McGraw and his son Edgar in *Kill Bill* and *Death Proof*), casting the same actors reminds the audience of the character's fictionality by drawing attention to the fact that s/he is just a part. It is also an invitation to compare the roles and connect the films. The story of a female assassin out for revenge, *Kill Bill*, as many online fans have surmised,[37] sounds like a sequel to the pilot for the series *Fox Force Five* Mia Wallace starred in [38:49–39:46]. The connection between the two movies is simultaneously established and annulled by the presence of Thurman, who cannot be both Beatrix the blonde and Mia the brunette, thus rendering uncertain the ontological borders between the two films—that is, unless Thurman were actually playing Mia playing Beatrix. But casting Thurman in the role of Beatrix does not just enable the playful titillation of ontological boundaries between story worlds, but it also sheds light on what links and distinguishes both roles: as the Bride, Thurman gets to crush the figure of the patriarch her previous character remained subjected to. This is also the case of Waltz's and Goggins's roles in Tarantino's films. As Schultz, Waltz's verbal eloquence is put to the service of humanist and romantic values rather than the racist and cynical ones that drive Landa. Mannix's siding with Major Warren is all the more unexpected as Goggins's character initially appears to be a comic continuation of the sadistic Billy Crash from *Django Unchained*, especially since Dern's General Sandy Smithers, who represents a father figure for Mannix, plainly recalls his previous role as Old Man Carrucan. In this respect, casting mainly Tarantino regulars in *The Hateful Eight* invites the viewer to see the movie not just as a reimagining of *Reservoir Dogs* and *Django Unchained* but of his entire œuvre.

If the return of familiar faces tends to reinforce the organic quality of the director's work, casting actors against the types they previously portrayed effectively thwarts audience expectations. It also constructs a more complex political and metafictional discourse on typecasting. Nowhere is this more patent than in the Jackson-Tarantino collaboration. The roles played by Jackson do more than just play off each other: Ordell Robbie, who is suave like Jules but comes to a bad end, or Major Warren Marquis, who resembles Django more than Stephen the butler. Each part corresponds to the type of black character the Hollywood industry—and, at a broader level, American culture—has restricted African American male actors to: the black gangster (*Pulp Fiction, Jackie Brown*), the piano player (*Kill Bill Vol. 2*), the Uncle Tom (*Django Unchained*), the Civil War soldier (*The Hateful Eight*). Yet in the lead roles, at least, Jackson is systematically given the opportunity to deconstruct these types. As we have seen in chapter 2, Jules is notable because he survives, Ordell because of his self-loathing tendencies, Stephen because the reassuring figure is reframed as demonic, Warren because the black bounty hunter ends up converting the Southern renegade. Jackson's voice-over in

Inglourious Basterds is particularly significant because the only time Jackson is allowed to portray a character who is not a staple African American male type is when he remains unseen. In the other films, Jackson's characters are types whose arcs end up going against type. As a whole, then, the Jackson-Tarantino collaboration reiterates the metafictional discourse proposed in *Jackie Brown*: that it is difficult for an actor to shed his/her skin, that freeing oneself from the (racial, gendered, etc.) types the industry pins on one's back is a perpetual struggle.

Casting, in the films of Quentin Tarantino, is thus a privileged means of establishing intertexual connections with past works, including the director's own; it is also a way of linking fiction and reality via the performer. As such, it largely contributes to Tarantino's films' political subtexts and metafictional discourses that are, as we have seen, intertwined. Tarantino's interest in film history encompasses the history of stars, actors, and less visible members of the crew such as stunt people. His films deliberately resort to typecasting in order to engage with the stars' images and the very notion of typecasting. The early films in particular—from *Reservoir Dogs* to *Death Proof*—are often as much about the stars and the types of roles they have played (including in Tarantino films) as about the characters. If using an actor to play several parts is an anti-illusionistic practice more typical of theater, the repeated casting of the same actor in several films draws attention to the actor behind the role, making the latest Tarantino movie a new reflection on Samuel Jackson's star image and on the types of roles African American actors have been given.

Juxtaposing Naturalistic and Theatrical Performances

Arguing that image supersedes talent in Tarantino's casting choices would be inaccurate and unfair. Tarantino is clearly a director who loves acting and actors, one who is very much aware of how essential good performances are to the effectiveness of a film. But his films also propose reflections on performance in film and beyond. The theatrical treatment of space functions as a frame, creating a stage on which a variety of acting schools can be examined: *Reservoir Dogs* contrasts Keitel's Method acting[38] with Roth's more spontaneous acting,[39] *The Hateful Eight* Russell's on-camera acting[40] to Jackson's more "theatrical" acting. Such scenes follow the Hollywood tradition of contrasting naturalistic and theatrical acting foregrounded by Viviani.[41] Where Tarantino departs from tradition, however, is that the theatrical performances are not relegated to the background or restricted to the roles of villains but regularly occupy center stage. This is most obviously the case in *The Hateful Eight*, when Jackson takes over Russell as lead actor a little over halfway through the film [105:37].

It is also evident in Brett's apartment scene in *Pulp Fiction*, where Jackson's and Travolta's acting styles are set against a less obviously theatrical space (fig. 60.1–60.2). As Vincent, Travolta displays the various clichés of Method acting:[42] mumbled, short lines—"Ain't hungry" [16:12], "Royale with cheese" [16:34], "Yeah, we happy" [18:13]; busying himself with his hands—pressed against his belly until he starts rolling a cigarette in the kitchen area and lights up [16:15]; and behaving almost pathologically bashful—he looks down throughout most of the scene. By contrast, Jackson uses "eloquent gestures" that verge on pantomime:[43] he holds his hand out to signify that Brett's friend lying on the bed shouldn't budge [14:36], congratulates him with an A-okay sign with his right hand [14:44], and makes the quasi-universal gesture of touching his mouth to signify his mental processes, momentarily resembling Rodin's famous statue *The Thinker* [15:00]. Jackson speaks in an emphatic tone, whether friendly—"Hamburgers! The cornerstone of any nutritious breakfast" [15:23]—or aggressive—"I don't remember asking you a goddamn thing" [17:27]—with the corresponding facial expressions highlighted in close-up. The contrast in acting styles is enhanced by the staging; the theatrical actor stands in center stage and is free to walk around, while the naturalistic actor is framed in a medium shot beside the turquoise kitchen counter. Travolta then becomes a stand-in of the spectator, his gestures as he smokes his cigarette calling attention to his presence offscreen to the left in the full shot of Jules domineering the room [18:20]; Travolta even jitters his right leg nervously, expressing both his character's anticipation of the moment when he will get to perform, and the viewer's anticipation as the tension builds up (fig. 60.2) [19:16]. Finally, the monologue becomes Vincent's cue to step in, Travolta crushing the cigarette and taking out his gun in order to ready himself to execute Brett [20:07]. In a scene which reflexively announces the paramount importance of acting, the performance styles largely contribute to the intertwined political subtext and metafictional discourse underlying the story of Jules and Vincent: the history of Hollywood racial and aesthetic conventions are toppled over, as the theatrical black supporting actor/character stands in the limelight, and the naturalistic white star/character is relegated to the role of sidekick. Granted, the characters are just playing parts, but the denouement of *Pulp Fiction*, as we have seen, confirms that Jules is the movie's true hero. And so the Jackson-Tarantino collaboration brought out the Richard III in the African American actor, making him a worthy successor of Laurence Olivier and Co.

With *Inglourious Basterds*, Tarantino found another actor capable of enhancing the theatricality of his dialogue in the person of Christoph Waltz, a well-known TV actor in Germany, whom Tarantino cast because of his talent and because he possesses a "linguistic genius" to match Landa's.[44] If several locations are made stagey in the film, the theatricality of the majority of the scenes featuring Waltz emanates not so much from the handling of space as from his performance, especially in static scenes where the characters are sitting around tables. This is obvious in Chapter One, but maybe even more so in the scene where Aldo and the Little Man get captured because of the face-off between Waltz's Landa and Pitt's Raine [124:01–130:29]. The six-minute-long scene resorts to mainly frontal medium shots of the characters edited in shot/reverse shot to contrast the two actors' styles: Landa/Waltz's eloquence versus Aldo/Pitt's silence and shorter lines; the former's abundant gestures and changes in tone versus the latter's limited body movements (his wrists, after all, are bound, so his body language is limited to shaking his head, grinning, or frowning). The scene appears to uphold the Hollywood convention of the foreign villain played by a theater actor opposed to the American hero played by a naturalistic actor—in this case, one who went out of his way to mimic a fairly authentic, though admittedly thick, rural Tennessee accent.[45] And yet the two do not stand on equal terms. Raine and especially the Little Man function as an audience even more so than Vincent in *Pulp Fiction* because they are literally imprisoned in that position. On a metafictional level, the star is forced to sit back and admire the talented foreign TV actor taking over the film just as his character is taking over the plot by offering to make a deal to end the war tonight. The scene, however, contributes to undercut the Hollywood dichotomy. First, the villain confesses that the sadistic Jew Hunter was nothing more than a role, very much like Jules's hitman character, and implies that he could just as easily play the part of a resident of Nantucket. Second, close attention to Pitt's own performance reveals that it, too, verges on pantomime—for instance, when he looks away and frowns to express embarrassment at the Little Man's nickname [125:05], or leans back to listen to Landa's proposition [128:36]. In fact, throughout the movie, Pitt, with his furrowed eyebrows and pursed lips, offers a caricature of a Brando or De Niro mug, two of the most famous American Method actors. The scene thus suggests that the the difference between Pitt's and Waltz's acting style is but one of degree, like the difference between their sadistic characters, and demonstrates that pantomime continues to inform Method acting, thus rejoining arguments made by Naremore and Viviani in their studies of Hollywood acting.[46]

Django Unchained furthers the reflection on performance by synthesizing the metafictional discourses of *Pulp Fiction* and *Inglourious Basterds*. Although the title and opening credits indicate that Waltz is not the star of the show, the Austrian-German actor is, again, allowed to occupy center stage from the moment he makes his entrance in the first scene [4:27]. In Daughtrey, Texas, it is the whole town that witnesses his performance. Waltz's costume—a white shirt and black vest—draws attention to his arms and hands, which serve to frame his head. Like Jackson, Waltz's performance verges on pantomime, resorting to universal expressions and gestures such as motioning to his audience with both hands [22:20], waving his left hand in order to indicate an approximate date [22:46], pointing at the warrant in his right hand [22:59], raising his eyebrows, and nodding when asking a question [22:48]. Like Jackson, Waltz speaks in a clipped fashion and an exaggerated tone. More so even than Travolta's Vincent, Foxx alternates between naturalistic expressions of anxiety—shuffling on his feet [22:27]—and acting as a stand-in for the audience by glancing repeatedly at Schultz and voicing his admiration at his performance in a one-liner: "I'll be damned" [22:35]. The contrast between the two acting styles is even more salient than in the previous films because both actors occupy the same frontal two-shot. At this stage, Hollywood conventions are partially preserved: the roles are racially segregated; theatricality is associated with the European, naturalism with the American, but Schultz is no villain and occupies center stage. However, the repetition of a similar scene at Big Daddy's plantation points to a significant evolution (fig. 61), as we have seen in chapter 2. Waltz's performance remains theatrical (his hands, elocution, and tone), but he lacks the absolute confidence displayed in the earlier scene. Conversely, Foxx's acting is slightly more theatrical: he marks his position at the beginning of the scene [38:28], doesn't fidget, and his Blue Boy costume draws attention away from Schultz in spite of the latter's speech, leading the viewer to look back and forth between the two men. Instead of pointing at a prop (the warrant), Schultz points twice at Django, who has participated in the execution [38:35, 39:10]. Django even acts as a prompter, providing information ("They were going by the name Schaeffer") for Schultz's monologue [38:54].

The arc of Django's empowerment is thus made manifest by Foxx's increasingly theatrical performance. Significantly, Foxx's final performance pits him against the other master of theatrical acting in Tarantino's films, Jackson, who Tarantino initially imagined in the role of Django.[47] Foxx's Django struts about, like Jackson's Jules Winnfield, on a mezzanine with the other characters looking up at him. His gestures verge on pantomime when

Fig. 64: *Django Unchained*: Django facing down Stephen, or Jaime Foxx ensuring the legacy of Samuel Jackson and Christoph Waltz as monologist extraordinaire.

he looks down at his clothes [158:15] or puts his left hand on his hip [157:38], and his gleaming burgundy suit highlights his shoulders and arms, and his white shirt, his hands (fig. 64). Again, the characters themselves are fully aware that they are acting roles. Stephen's casting off his own costume, notably his cane [158:23], is thus a recognition of Django's talent as an actor. On a metafictional level, then, *Django Unchained* is the story of how an African American actor comes to master a performance style that had historically been reserved for white European foreigners. The face-off between the two actors inscribes Django in the heritage of Jules, and Foxx in that of Jackson, so that Jackson as Stephen's acknowledgment of Foxx as Django's talent indicates that the older actor's succession is assured.

More time would be necessary to analyze thoroughly the subtleties of the wide variety of performances staged in each film. What I hope to have demonstrated is that the foregrounding of performance in Tarantino's films is more than just a means of reflexively laying bare the artifice: it produces a discourse on performance in Hollywood film. The scenes analyzed above are grounded in the aesthetic opposition between theatrical and naturalistic acting, often mirrored in one character watching another perform, only to deconstruct it by insisting on common features. If the acting in Tarantino's films would tend to confirm the contemporary trend of blending acting styles Viviani highlights, the centrality given to theatrical performances (of Jackson, Waltz, and others) inverts the Hollywood tradition of relegating them to the background. The play on performance also participates in the discourse on the politics of Hollywood conventions, whether by deconstructing the archetype of the European villain or by endowing African American male characters with a command of verbal language historically denied to them.

The Thematization of Acting and Its Ethics

It will not have escaped the reader that the performances in the scenes analyzed above are justified by character motivation, and thus that acting is overtly thematized. Recurrent in all the films, the theme of acting is predominantly treated obliquely through questions of duplicity and professionalism. If the diegeses of *Death Proof* and *Inglourious Basterds* feature actual performers (Lee the model, stuntpeople Mike, Kim, and Zoë, and German star Bridget von Hammersmark), almost all of Tarantino's main characters self-consciously play roles at one time or another. Many of them have something to hide: the dogs behind their aliases; Freddy Newandyke the undercover cop and Officer Marvin Nash who knows his true identity; Butch's betrayal of Marsellus Wallace in *Pulp Fiction*; the eponymous heroine's plot in *Jackie Brown*; Elle, who disguises herself as a nurse in *Kill Bill Vol. 1* [20:03–25:10] but then dupes Budd and lies to Bill about his brother's death in *Vol. 2* [66:09–73:48]; Mike's dark motives in *Death Proof*; Shosanna's intentions, and Hicox and Bridget von Hammersmark's team's identity in La Louisiane in *Inglourious Basterds*; the two bounty hunters' at work in *Django Unchained*; and the members of the Jody Domergue gang (Bob, Joe Gauge, and Oswaldo Mobray) in *The Hateful Eight*, most patently Daisy who, as Chapter Four indicates, "[ha]s got a secret." The roles the characters play are often linked to their jobs (as assassins, cops, spies, terrorists, thieves). As Ortoli has argued, the Hawksian theme of professionalism runs throughout Tarantino's films,[48] with characters voicing their resolve to maintain their professional selves—Mr. White and Mr. Pink's repetition of the word "professional" (five times) in *Reservoir Dogs*, Vincent Vega's "test of loyalty" monologue in *Pulp Fiction* [51:42–53:39], Stuntman Mike whose "identity *is* his social function."[49] Loyalty is not just loyalty to another individual, a boss (Cabot, Wallace, Bill), a fellow colleague (Freddy Newandyke, John Ruth), a lover (Bill, Broomhilda von Shaft), or one's family (Shosanna); it is, above all, loyalty to a code (the gangster, samurai,[50] or bounty hunter code), a contract (marriage), or a deeply rooted principle (love, humanism). There is an ethics to the act.

In *Reservoir Dogs*, this is dramatized in the disagreement between Mr. Pink and Mr. White. While Buscemi's character repeatedly insists on the importance of maintaining one's professionalism—"What was tellin' him your name when you weren't supposed to?" [30:54]—Mr. White invokes humanist values to explain why he violated Cabot's rules in the first place: "I mean, the man was dying in my arms. What the fuck was I supposed to do? Tell him I'm sorry! I can't give out that fuckin' information!" [31:27]. The two men's anger is then directed at Mr. Blonde who, by opening fire on the customers in the jewelry shop, transgressed both professional code (Mr. Pink: "Fuck, man, you panic on the inside. In your head, you know. And you give yourself a couple of seconds—you get a hold of the situation, you *deal* with it. What you don't do is start shootin' up the place and start killing people") and humanist values (Mr. White: "I mean, Jesus Christ, how old do you think that black girl was? Twenty? Maybe twenty-one?") [22:59–23:30]. After Mr. Pink has managed to prevent Mr. Blonde and Mr. White from indulging in a "playground" fight, Mr. Blonde concludes: "Wow. That was really exciting. I bet you're a big Lee Marvin fan, aren't you? Me, too. I love that guy" [36:16]. By debunking the authenticity of the emotions that seemed to be governing their behavior up to this point, his comment not only reduces their tough masculinity to an act and their dispute to play, but it implies that, if they cannot come together around a professional code or humanistic values, they can at least agree on their appreciation of an actor's persona. In other words, order is restored (at least momentarily) by reasserting the value of acting as performance and emptying it of the pretense of authentic emotion.

The thematization of acting in the first third of *Reservoir Dogs* ironically foreshadows "The Commode Story" chapter, which depicts Freddy Newandyke's composition of Mr. Orange in a series of scenes.[51] The transformation starts with Freddy's mentor Holdaway explaining that it can only be achieved through "naturalistic" acting of the Marlon Brando sort [66:50], and is finally complete when Freddy, like a Method actor, slips a ring on his finger (a symbol of the contract he has signed to play his part as thief) to get into character and, addressing his reflection, compares his role to that of another undercover cop, the title character in the TV show *Baretta* (ABC, 1975–78) [75:42–76:20].[52] If the flesh-and-blood actor (Freddy) and his character (Mr. Orange) in the mirror are ontologically separate, they threaten to fully merge, a possibility Holdaway senses in the diner when he points out that Freddy's view of the informant who got him in is skewed: "Long Beach Mike is not your fuckin' amigo, man. Long Beach Mike is a fuckin' *scumbag*. He's selling out his amigos" [66:17]. Mr. Orange's takeover of Freddy Newandyke climaxes when he reacts exactly according to Mr. Pink's professional code—"You know I don't wanna kill anybody. If I'm gettin' out of that door and you're standin' in my way, one way or the other you're getting out of my way" [22:14]—by killing the woman who shot him [86:30], and failing to keep act and self fully separate. The crime Freddy commits entails that, if there is an ethics to the act, sticking to character may be aesthetic, but it is not necessarily ethical.

Sticking to character at all costs does not always pay. Mr. Pink presumably gets arrested outside the warehouse [94:04], while Vincent Vega, who remains loyal to Marsellus to the end, dies on a toilet because he is locked into his role [91:47]. In *Death Proof*, Mike's pathological espousal of his professional role, which recalls Mr. Blonde's, leads to his demise. The revenge narrative that drives *Kill Bill* leads Beatrix to stick to her role as the Bride under all circumstances, whether confronted by avatars of the women she was (O-Ren in Chapter Five, Elle in Chapter Nine) or the woman she could have been (Vernita in Chapter One), until her discovery of B. B., and thus of another possible role, that of mother, leads her to momentarily crack in the last chapter. Her uncompromising stance casts a dark shadow over the happy ending, since the cycle of revenge and violence might be pursued by the next generation, represented by Vernita's daughter Nikki and by B. B., who has already evinced a capacity for violence [88:34–95:13]. As Luke Cuddy and Michael Bruce have noted, assessing the degree to which Beatrix has reached a form of enlightenment depends on whether she will extend compassion to Nikki in the future.[53]

The cost of breaking character is equally high in Tarantino's films. It ends in death for Freddy, Archie Hicox in *Inglourious Basterds*, Doctor Schultz in *Django Unchained*, and John Ruth in *The Hateful Eight*. Hicox, perhaps due to his focus on the verbal dimension of acting—the Nazis' interest in his accent [78:58]—is outed by Major Hellstrom because he pays less attention to his body language, forgetting to make the continental gesture when ordering four glasses of whiskey [88:57]. Schultz and Ruth, though both are hardened bounty hunters, like Mr. White, give in to their emotions: Ruth, enchanted by Daisy's song, momentarily lets his guard down [101:02–101:20], while Schultz's revulsion at the embodiment of the horrors of slavery that is Calvin Candie leads him to commit suicide in exchange for the pleasure of executing the slave owner [130:55].

Ultimately, it is lack of distance with the act that is the killer, more so even than lack of control over it. As Ortoli brilliantly concludes about the protagonists of *Pulp Fiction*, "following or refusing the programmatic aspect of the stories [and, more precisely, I would argue, of the acts] does not generate morality; what it does is assert the necessity of free will by adapting these stories."[54] Ortoli's remark illuminates the outcome of most of Tarantino's films. Indeed, much of the ethical dilemmas are dramatized according to the roles a character opts for. In *Pulp Fiction*, master performer Jules's decision to change his ways leads him to contemplate modeling his life on another role, that of the hero of *Kung Fu*, after honoring his role as hitman to the end [136:15]. When Vincent mocks his decision, Jules firmly answers: "I'll just be Jules, Vincent, no more, no less" [136:30]. Jules's capacity to maintain a distance between self and act was announced from the start, since it is he, and not Vincent, who utters the line: "Come on, let's get into character" [13:37]. The end of *Jackie Brown* is more ambiguous in this respect, as it hangs on the question of whether the heroine's feelings for Max Cherry are authentic, a question the heroine, who has successfully juggled with various parts for her various audiences (Ordell, the police), feels the need to answer in the farewell scene: "I didn't use you, Max" [145:25]. Indeed, room for hesitation lies in the fact that the mastermind's morning talk with Max is framed by her discussions with Ordell and the cops and thus reinforces this doubt, especially since the repetition of the lateral medium shot of Jackie opening and closing her door can function as either a juxtaposition or a counterpoint [53:15–53:51].

That talent is not as essential as distance is dramatized in the outcomes of *Inglourious Basterds* and *The Hateful Eight*. Aldo Raine, for instance, has been portrayed as a lousy actor incapable of passing as an Italian officer for one second, especially when faced with the linguistic genius Hans Landa [113:07–115:03], yet his final "masterpiece" is achieved when he decides not to violate his role, but to adapt it to the morality he "abide[s]" by:

> RAINE: Yeah, they made that deal. But they don't give a fuck about him. They need you.
> LANDA: You'll be shot for this!
> RAINE: Naw, I don't think so. More like chewed out. I've been chewed out before. [147:35–147:45]

As for the finale of *The Hateful Eight*, it hinges on Mannix's decision to move forward and embrace his role as new sheriff—and thus side with the bounty hunters and adhere to their code—or take up his past role as Southern "renegade" [144:28–152:35], a temptation Daisy Domergue is very much aware of, as she witnessed Mannix's slipping into his previous role when Ruth rejected his proposal to drink and break bread with him in Chapter Two [27:53–34:30].

The thematization of acting thus draws attention to the commonality between dramatic roles and social roles (such as professions), and thus plays on the theatrical metaphor of the *theatrum mundi*, which evokes "[t]his problem of the relationship for man to his roles," analyzed at length by Elizabeth Burns.[55] Scenes where actors "*act persons who are acting*" are not only reflexive.[56] As Naremore argues,

> In these moments when deception or repression are indicated, the drama becomes a metaperformance, imposing contrary demands on the players: the need to maintain a unified narrative image, a coherent

persona, is matched by an equally strong need to exhibit dissonance or expressive incoherence within the characterization. Thus, we could say that realist acting amounts to an effort at sustaining opposing attitudes toward the self, on the one hand trying to create the illusion of unified, individualized personality, but on the other suggesting that character is subject to division or dissolution into a variety of social roles.[57]

The paradox Naremore underlines is particularly interesting in the case of Tarantino's films because of the degree to which the social roles depicted in the diegeses are modeled on genre roles, thereby marking their artificiality twofold. This artificiality is laid bare through a play on "deception" or "repression" (conscious or unconscious role-playing), as in Naremore's analysis, or, I would add, on the destruction of prior roles. Tarantino's films are not realistically representing the fragmented subject of structuralist, poststructuralist, and postmodernist theories, but are artificially representing it. I have argued elsewhere that, from a psychoanalytical perspective, it is through the multiplication of these social roles, what D. W. Winnicott calls "false selves"—in this case, professional roles that are actually genre roles— that *Reservoir Dogs* creates the illusion of a true self.[58] But given the degree to which the thematization of acting ultimately serves to develop ethical concerns, I would specify that this "true self" is more precisely an ethical subject asserting her/his values by adapting her/his roles.

A term used to describe a specific treatment of space and performance in film, "cinematic theatricality" is, in effect, a fundamental quality of Tarantino's films, though it may vary in degree, from the most theatrical (*Reservoir Dogs, The Hateful Eight*) to the least (*Jackie Brown, Death Proof*). The characters' and actors' performances are played out on various spaces (indoor or outdoor, vast or intimate) that are rendered stagey through staging and framing; the sense of theatricality can be enhanced by performances that verge on pantomime and that contrast with more naturalistic acting. But in the films of Quentin Tarantino, cinematic theatricality is more than just a reflexive strategy that serves to point to the work's nature as a fiction made in a specific medium by blending in conventions from another medium; it acts as a frame for the films' metafictional discourses on movie stars, actors, and acting. These discourses, often grounded in an exploration of the actors' careers and star images, focus on types of roles, individual actors, and groups of actors. As such, the films reflect on how the Hollywood industry marginalizes specific members—aging and/or forgotten stars ("Vincent

Vega & Marsellus Wallace's Wife," *Jackie Brown*, *Kill Bill*), minority actors (*Django Unchained*), foreign or TV actors (*Inglourious Basterds*), stuntpeople (*Death Proof*)—and offer stories of their empowerment and conquest of center stage. The films' metafictional discourses on typecasting and performance are thus intertwined with their political subtexts and participate in the debunking of stereotypes based on class, ethnicity, gender, nationality, and race. As such, they are integral to the broader reflection on film and cultural history. Finally, I would argue that the high degree of cinematic theatricality also works to establish play as an underlying model of the sort described by Hutcheon, for though the thematization of acting is overt, the implication that the characters are always acting functions in a more covert fashion. A characteristic that has often been attributed both to metafiction and postmodernist fiction, playfulness is often derided as proof of these fictions' lack of real-world concerns. Yet it is often in this multiplication of roles that originate the films' ethical concerns, the complexity of which the essays in *Quentin Tarantino and Philosophy*, edited by Richard Greene and K. Silem Mohammad, testify to. As Burns has demonstrated in her study of theatricality, the theatrical metaphor points to the artificiality of social roles. In the films of Tarantino, the self-consciousness of the actor-characters confirms the political and philosophical adhesion to the poststructuralist view of identity as a construct analyzed in chapters 2 and 3.

CHAPTER EIGHT

"HE'S JUST NOT USED TO SEEIN' A MAN RIPPED APART BY DOGS IS ALL"

Violence and Spectacle

It is the former slave who steps in to explain to a puzzled and suspicious Calvin Candie why Schultz, a man interested in the Mandingo business, might have such a weak stomach in the first place [84:28]. Django passes off his associate's reaction as purely aesthetic: it is the form of execution that is shocking, not necessarily the reason. D'Artagnan's death would be even more revolting than that of Luigi, whose butchering had already elicited a queasy reaction Schultz had tried to mask [66:21], because he was not slain by another man but defiled by animals. However, this act is a form one could become habituated to, and Django's implication is that, as a white man interested in getting in the Mandingo business to have "a good bit of fun" [64:05], his employer should get over it in time. Yet the form of violence also carries ethical implications, as the use of "man" (instead of slave) indicates, for it is the enactment of Candie and his men's view that the slaves are just animals, and thus that such acts do not constitute abject degradations of the human. The risk of habituation is not just aesthetic, but ethical and political; it is because Candie and his men have been raised to see slaves as animals that they consider this form of punishment to be appropriate. Clearly, the act is just as culturally determined as the sentence.[1]

For the viewer who has followed the two bounty hunters' adventures, Django's answer raises another question concerning the aesthetics and ethics of violence. Schultz is not only accustomed to watching men die; he is responsible for the deaths of many. In fact, Django's intervention harks back to the moment when the apprentice bounty hunter hesitated to kill Smitty

Bacall before his son's very eyes, and Schultz argued that the father's guilt fully justified the act against Django's conscience [52:33–55:14], espousing a harder line even than the vengeful Bride who, in *Kill Bill Vol. 1*, accepts not to "murder [Vernita] in front of [her] child," not out of "mercy, compassion and forgiveness," but "rationality" [10:26]. The role reversal effected between the two scenes—Schultz acts as mentor in the West, while Django is better equipped to deal with the laws of the South[2]—underscores significant differences: the Mandingo fighter's death is not legally and morally justified, Smitty Bacall's is; the criminal is granted a more "honorable" and less painful mode of execution than the slave; D'Artagnan's plight elicits pleasure from his executioners, Smitty Bacall's doesn't, Django's face in frontal close-up expressing not righteousness, but solemnity as he watches the son discover his father's death [55:11], a situation typical of an Italian Western—most famously, the McBain family massacre in *Once Upon a Time in the West*—that is likely to have occurred on slave plantations as well. The difference in tone is emphasized by the narration which depicts Bacall's death amidst the silence in a very long shot, while D'Artagnan's death scene insists on the grotesque mauling through the use of closer shots, slow motion, and amplified noises, nonetheless displacing the aesthetics of violence onto the perpetrators and their weapons (the dogs).

Django's explanation implies that there are various acts, forms, and justifications of violence, that there are different ways of depicting and watching violence, and that the aesthetic, ethical, and political implications are intermeshed. More suprisingly, perhaps, given Tarantino's own comments in his early interviews, Django is also acknowledging the possibility of habituation in a specific sociocultural context—the antebellum South, but also the gladiator fights of antiquity (one of Candie's fighter's name is Samson, and Schultz proposes to name his the Black Hercules [101:06–102:35])—one that could lead to desensitization and dehumanization, so that an act of violence can be sadistically cheered on. By thematizing the question of watching a violent act, *Django Unchained* overtly comments on the relationship between violence and spectacle, and more precisely on the treatment of violence as spectacle in the fiction film. It demonstrates that not all scenes of violence are the same and that they should not all be received in the same manner. They are representations of events, no doubt, but each one is inscribed in a specific context that is complex and layered; this accounts for their ambivalence and for the fact that they elicit different reactions. This is further complicated by the fact that each individual's response is, of course, grounded in personal experience and sensibility. In so doing, the film is making a case against a form of censorship that would fail to take into account the manifold intricacies of representations of violence. It is not a simple issue with clear-cut answers, which explains why it continues to fuel fiery discussions to this day, notably with each release of a Tarantino film.

The reception of Tarantino's films has by and large been framed in discussions of violence.[3] Writing for the *Village Voice*, film critic Ella Taylor criticized the violence of his movies, associating it with a pejorative: "juvenility."[4] Hendrik Hertzberg in the *New Yorker* spoke against the "utter moral depravity" of *Django Unchained*, a film in which "there isn't much difference between" "the cruelty of the slavedriving villains and the avenging heroes."[5] Numerous academics have tackled the violence in Tarantino's films or used his films to deal with questions of violence in cinema: Henry A. Giroux (1995) on *Pulp Fiction*, Paul Gormley on *Reservoir Dogs* and *Pulp Fiction* (2005), Aaron Anderson (2005), Lisa Coulthard (2007), Maud Lavin (2010) on *Kill Bill*, Michael D. Richardson (2012) and Alexander D. Ornella (2012) on *Inglourious Basterds*, and William Brown (2015) on *Django Unchained*, not to mention the many discussions of violence in books and articles devoted to other topics (race, gender, catharsis, music). Aesthetic evaluations often consider whether or not the violence is gratuitous, realistic, cartoony, graphic, sadistic, masochistic, and/or fetishistic with very little attention to formal features such as lighting, camerawork, and editing, as if the aesthetics stemmed primarily from the nature of the act and not its filmic representation. Ethical and political considerations usually revolve around the question of whether or not the violence is justified by the situation and the overall context. For some, this comes down to asking whether the characters themselves are justified in committing such deeds; the characters' morals are thus projected onto the film in the assumption that the work is unquestionably aligned with the protagonist, and with the fear that the audience will automatically adhere to the protagonist's mindset.

Tarantino did very little to deflect some of the charges leveled at his work in his early interviews. Instead, he retorted cockily: "I love violence in movies,"[6] stated that violence was "fun"[7] (in *Reservoir Dogs*) or "funny"[8] (in films in general), and that, in the end, it was "a totally aesthetic subject."[9] A decade later, however, Tarantino admitted that he had deliberately resorted to a metonymical approach to violence for the Dreyfus family massacre in Chapter One of *Inglourious Basterds* because of the sensitive material;[10] he also felt the need to justify the "ugly violence and language" in *Django Unchained* as part of the context.[11] Again, it is mainly Tarantino the man's discourse on violence that has changed, not his practices as a director. While some took it for granted that *Reservoir Dogs* vainly indulges and privileges onscreen violence,[12] both Dan Jardine and Kate E. Temoney remind us that the infamous ear-cutting scene had already been left to the audience's imagination.[13] What follows is thus an analysis of both the treatment of the spectacle of violence and of the discourse on the relationship between violence and spectacle in film. I argue that the representations of violence are, in effect, complex and problematic, but that they are acknowledged as such both in the films' treatment of violence and in the fairly overt metafictional discourses.

Aesthetics, Ethics, and Politics

Excepting *Kill Bill*, the scenes of violence are neither numerous nor lengthy. With the never-ending Crazy 88 finale, the murders and fights of *Kill Bill Vol. 1* easily comprise 46.5 percent (over 47 minutes) of the film, and in spite of the briefer fight scenes,[14] *Vol. 2* is almost as violent as the first installment, the massacre, buried-alive, tutelage, murder, fight, and interrogation scenes totaling over 34 percent (42 minutes) of the film. *Death Proof* has three murder scenes and a car chase scene, comprising about 27 percent (approximately 30 minutes) of its runtime. *Django Unchained* is permeated with desecration (Big Ben's skull), torture, murder, shoot-outs, ambushes, so that such scenes comprise 23.5 percent (38 minutes) of the film's runtime, not including the marks of violence such as scars[15] and the system itself, the violence of which each slave, by her/his very presence, testifies to. The chase, fight, torture scenes, and shootings only make up 19 percent (approximately 18 minutes) of *Reservoir Dogs*, if you don't count Mr. Orange's bleeding from a gunshot throughout. Excluding the OD scene, *Pulp Fiction*'s killings and rape scene amount to 13.7 percent (almost 18 minutes) of the movie, 22.3 percent if you include the eleven-minute-long anti-climactic holdup in the diner. In *Inglourious Basterds*, almost all the scenes of violence (excepting Stiglitz's three murders and the brief flashback of the Basterds' ambush) come in twos—interrogations (Aldo questions Bridget, and Shosanna and Marcel beat up a man), scalpings (at the beginning of Chapter Two and at the end of the movie), executions (Rachtman, Bridget), shoot-outs (at the Louisiane and when Shosanna and Frederick kill each other), massacres (at Perrier's and in the movie theater)—for a total of 9.5 percent (a little over 14 minutes) of the film's runtime, confirming Susan Rubin Suleiman's remark that the film revises the combat movie genre by amping up the dialogue.[16] *The Hateful Eight*'s beatings, rape and ensuing gunfight, shoot-outs, massacre, and hanging make for a mere 6.9 percent (under 11 minutes) of its runtime, while the killings of Beaumont, Melanie, Louis, and Ordell, and the attempted murder of Jackie barely account for 6 percent (a little over nine minutes) of *Jackie Brown*.

The quantity of violence may seem to be a matter of genre (martial arts, horror, the gangster movie) and context (slavery), but not essentially; *Jackie Brown*, *Inglourious Basterds*, and *The Hateful Eight* prove that the treatment can vary, even in a WWII film or a Western horror movie. In hindsight, what is striking is that Tarantino's early films were considered highly violent when they are significantly less so compared to later movies like *Kill Bill*, *Death Proof*, and *Django Unchained*. In fact, the average Hollywood blockbuster contains at least as much violence as Tarantino's films. Two mainstream action movies roughly contemporary to *Pulp Fiction* and *Django Unchained*, *Die Hard 3* (John McTiernan, 1995) and *Iron Man 2* (Jon Favreau, 2010), comprise, respectively, 13.3 percent (about 16 minutes minutes) and 20.7 percent (over 24 minutes) of violent scenes (dangerous car chases, fights, killings, explosions), and the Marvel superhero movie was only rated PG-13.

What justifies the foregrounding of violence as a characteristic feature of Tarantino's films is the fact that the scenes of violence do occupy key positions, in opening scenes (*Pulp Fiction*, *Kill Bill Vol. 2*, *Inglourious Basterds*, *Django Unchained*, and especially *Kill Bill Vol. 1*), climaxes of a given scene ("The Gold Watch," Chapters Five, Six and Nine in *Kill Bill*, the end of the Austin part of *Death Proof*, Chapter Three in *The Hateful Eight*) or of the film (basically, all of them). The narratives build up to these explosive situations—and, in the case of the end of *Pulp Fiction*, to the lack thereof—quite dramatically, an effect that can be intensified by recourse to theatricality (Jules's behavior at Brett's apartment, Candie's theorizing around Ben's skull, and generally speaking the Mexican standoff motif which participates in the staginess). If these moments are emphasized for dramatic effect, the violence exists as an insidious potential throughout. After all, as thieves, hitmen, boxers, drug traffickers, assassins, serial killers, soldiers, slaves, and bounty hunters, the protagonists inhabit brutal worlds, and the premises involve violent situations: robbery, murder, persecution, guerilla warfare, terrorism, and, most frequently, revenge. The fact that violence is central both diegetically and dramatically is clearly enough to assert that it is core to the films and thus justified. The violent scenes are often foregrounded by the narration as well, either thanks to specific techniques like the quick zoom or, more generally, by introducing a stylistic break from a fairly classical form of narration to what Bordwell calls "intensified continuity," as we have seen in chapter 5. In this respect, Tarantino is, as Marsha Kinder has argued, indebted to Peckinpah (and, I would add again, Leone), the films sharing "a narrative orchestration of violence in which action sequences function like performative 'numbers' interrupting the linear drive of the plot with their sensational audiovisual

Fig. 65: *Inglourious Basterds*: The narration cuts to a high-angle establishing shot that tracks out from the execution of the dignified Sergeant Rachtman in the arena-like setting.

spectacle yet simultaneously serving as dramatic climaxes that advance the story toward closure."[17]

Another argument concerns how graphic the violence is at times. Generally speaking, Tarantino alternates between restrained and excessive depictions of violence, and between a bleak or comic-booky treatment. In the first case, the gore is not emphasized, and the narration distances itself from the violence through shot size, camera movement, or cuts. In the second case, the visuals and sound accentuate the violence in loud, bright-red outbursts, sometimes adorned with slow motion. Scenes that resort predominantly to the first approach include the torture of Officer Marvin Nash and the numerous deaths in *Reservoir Dogs*, the rape of Marsellus Wallace and the death of Marvin in *Pulp Fiction*, the massacre of the Dreyfus family and the execution of Sergeant Rachtman in *Inglourious Basterds* (fig. 65), the deaths of the Mandingo fighters in *Django Unchained*, and the rape of Smithers's son in *The Hateful Eight*. In these scenes, the violence either occurs offscreen or the narration cuts or moves away from it. Aesthetically speaking, these are scenes where the violence is distanced, not fetishized. Some scenes do indulge in excess; the lengthiest include the Bride's fight with the Crazy 88 in *Kill Bill Vol. 1* and Django's shoot-out with Candie's men in *Django Unchained*, where the impact of Django's bullets are depicted as explosions of blood, often in slow motion and accompanied with low distorted sounds, contrasting with the more realistic treatment in the scenes where slaves are mistreated or killed (fig. 66–67).[18] In alternating between the two aesthetics, the films of Tarantino tap into the traditional opposition between aesthetics of suggestion and "monstration,"[19] but the two can also be combined. Indeed, in some scenes, the act itself is depicted with restraint, the consequences

Fig. 66: *Django Unchained*: Big Fred looks sadly down at his victim, while Candie and the like exult.

Fig. 67: *Django Unchained*: Django shields himself with his adversaries' bodies, of which copious amounts of blood burst out.

with copious amounts of passive gore; this is the case of the torture scene in *Reservoir Dogs*—we see the severed ear, not the cutting [56:33–57:13]—and the killing of Marvin in *Pulp Fiction*—his death occurs offscreen, but Vincent and Jules are splattered in his blood [116:07–117:08]. The violence in these scenes impresses us as graphic because its depiction rests on a cause-effect scheme that makes sense in terms of cognition.

The aesthetics of violence in Tarantino's films is by no means homogeneous, and the violence is rarely "fetishized" and much less "eroticized," contrary to what some critics have claimed.[20] Moreover, these aesthetics largely depend, as we have noticed in chapters 2 and 3, on the politics underlying each act: the restrained approach often concerns scenes that are morally and/or politically problematic, the excessive approach scenes that are less so. The few scenes where the violence is eroticized are mostly justified politically. If the lengthy finale of *Kill Bill Vol. 1* presents itself predominantly as sensual spectacle, the eroticization of black bodies in *Django Unchained* fully participates in the film's attack on racist desires, as we have seen in chapter 3. In some cases, the restrained approach is justified aesthetically because it confers solemnity on a given situation. This is the case of the Mexican standoff in *Reservoir Dogs*, which is shown in a seven-second-long long shot (fig. 15) [92:09], the execution of Sergeant Rachtman in *Inglourious Basterds*, which cuts rapidly to a high-angle establishing shot that tracks out (fig. 65) [34:44], and all the deaths in *Jackie Brown*,[21] a movie that takes care to flesh out each protagonist.

The aesthetics are, in effect, very much grounded in an ethics, and not just in narrative and genre concerns, as Kinder contended about *Pulp Fiction*.[22] Generally speaking, the restrained approach recognizes the victim as an imagined human being; the excessive treats bodies as mere cinematic material. This is obvious in *Kill Bill* where the Crazy 88 are treated as interchangeable bodies that spout blood—they all wear the same masks and suit that conspicuously reference their sources (*Reservoir Dogs* and *The Green Hornet*)—while Vernita, O-Ren, and Bill, though singled out in close-ups and medium close-ups, are allowed more dignity in dying; a mere trickle of blood appears at the corner of Vernita's and Bill's mouths [*Vol. 1* 13:48, *Vol. 2* 118:45], while O-Ren retains her elegant poise, even with her brains exposed (fig. 68) [*Vol. 1* 97:13]. In *The Hateful Eight*, on the other hand, the increasingly graphic depictions of the deaths of Smithers in frontal medium shot [94:40], of O. B. and especially Ruth spouting red blood in medium close-ups [103:45–105:32], the slow motion shoot-out with Mobray and Mannix [118:37–119:26], the execution of Bob in medium shot [117:00], Jody in frontal close-up [143:18], Grough Douglass (formerly Joe Gauge) in slow motion [150:09], and Daisy covered in blood in frontal close-up [158:18], all[23] consolidate the protagonists' belonging to the "hateful" group referred to in the title, the restrained aesthetics being reserved exclusively for the innocent victims murdered in Chapter Five, whose deaths are either represented metonymically (the candy for Gemma, Charly's boots) or at a distance (brief medium shots for Minnie, Ed, Judy, and Sweet Dave) [129:50–133:26]. Irreverence is also what, in *Inglourious Basterds*, justifies the graphic treatment of Hitler's death [145:26–145:28] and Landa's mutilation; unlike Private Butz in Chapter Two [37:30–37:55], the Machiavellian villain is denied an ellipsis [148:54–149:30].

And yet a few scenes go against the golden rule of dignified restraint/ irreverent excess the films generally follow, yet another example of art cinema's tendency to violate the very norms it sets up. *Inglourious Basterds*, for instance, adopts the excessive approach to depict the deaths of Shosanna and Frederick, not so much in terms of the level of gore but in the use of slow motion: it serves to both insist on the characters' pain and delay their

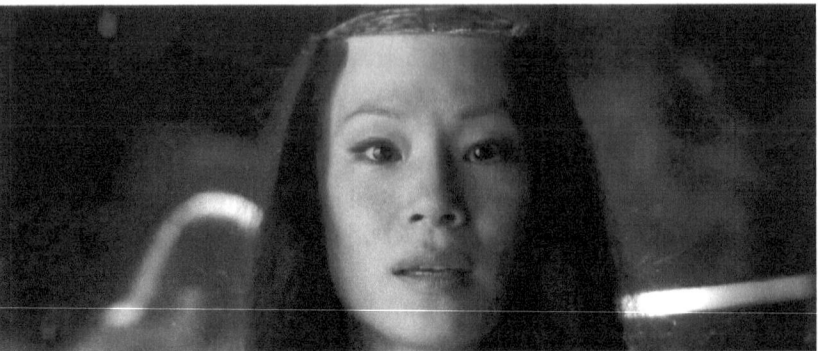

Fig. 68: *Kill Bill Vol. 1*: O-Ren, dignified even with the top of her brains exposed.

deaths, a cheesy farewell to the heroine and the impossible romance plot that contrasts with the rapid rhythm of the following scene featuring Donowitz and Ulmer timing their attack [141:05–141:48].[24] Conversely, in *Django Unchained*, Calvin Candie's inhumanity is visualized by the absence of blood when Schultz shoots him through the heart, the bullet-riddled white flower functioning as yet another metonymy of the sullying of Hollywood representations of the South (fig. 69) [131:02], much like the blood-sprayed cotton noted by Robert von Dassanowsky,[25] Heather Ashley Hayes, and Gilbert B. Rodman.[26] If Tarantino generally abides by the classic distinction between restraint and excess, then, each scene of violence has its specific aesthetics, ethics, and politics, and begs to be considered as such.

That the violence plays a core role in the narrative structure should be enough to dispel initial impressions that it is utterly gratuitous, at least aesthetically speaking. Discussions of the cathartic potential of violence follow traditional theories based on Aristotle's use of the word in the *Poetics*, whereby negative emotions can be purged notably through the build-up and shock of violence through art.[27] On one level, this is exactly what the use of violence as a structure seems to be designed for, as many Tarantino scholars have noted. Randall E. Auxier contends that, in *Pulp Fiction*, the transformation of flat genre archetypes into increasingly human characters is a condition for catharsis to be effective.[28] Ortoli describes both Bill's[29] and Mr. Orange's deaths as cathartic, the second because the expression of pain reminds us of our mortal bodies.[30] Hayes and Rodman's nuanced discussion of *Django Unchained* as a black film hints at the cathartic potential of the destruction of the villain's plantation when they suggest that "Django doesn't blow up Candieland because *he* needs to do so: he blows it up because *we* need him to do so."[31] Alexander D. Ornella and Dara Waldron have put forth

Fig. 69: *Django Unchained*: The inhuman Candie shot through a white flower in the heart by Dr. Schultz hardly bleeds.

some convincing arguments to qualify the degree of catharsis afforded by the finales of *Inglourious Basterds* and *Django Unchained*. For Ornella, "by denying our gaze to enjoy Hitler's death," previously set up as "the epitome of evil," "Tarantino denies us the moment of catharsis";[32] undermining a clear-cut dichotomy between good guys and villains should also prevent us from fully enjoying Raine's desecration of Landa. Waldron similarly observes that the potential catharsis is limited by the fact that, "[i]n making his adversary, the slave Stephen, the object of his revenge, Django is morally compromised as hero to the group he seemingly represents."[33]

Ethically ambivalent finales with morally compromised heroes are, in effect, a recurrent feature of Tarantino's films: from Mr. White who ends up killing those he previously esteemed as friends (Joe Cabot and Mr. Orange) in *Reservoir Dogs*, to Jules's changing his ways (but Vincent failing to do so) in *Pulp Fiction*, to Jackie Brown's victory tainted by her bittersweet parting with Max, to Beatrix's equally bittersweet victory over Bill, and to the hanging of Daisy Domergue, whose villainy is amply justified by the beatings and abuse she endures. Even in *Death Proof*, Abernathy, Kim, and Zoë's victory over Stuntman Mike is qualified by the fact that they sacrificed their friend Lee. Catharsis, in the films of Tarantino, is always limited and nuanced. I would not go so far as to argue that the films entirely deny the emotional purge Brecht sought to avoid in favor of critical consciousness.[34] Rather, the emotional purge of classical theory is tempered by an almost Brechtian critical catharsis. These qualified catharses could be seen as a means to have things both ways: the spectacle of violence and its critique, blockbuster entertainment and art-cinema commentary.

This is exactly the delicate balance Tarantino is aiming for. The nuanced catharses in Tarantino's films imply that underlying the Manichean

Hollywood and genre film conventions, and the uncomplicated spectacle of violence, lie complex ethical and political issues that cannot be entirely resolved. This explains why, as K. Silem Mohammad notes, the "films frequently start from and/or end up at a position of aporia."[35] As Hayes and Rodman conclude, Django may have destroyed Candieland, but Stephen's monologue reminds us that the destruction of the institution of slavery remains only a symbolic victory.[36] The "bloody satisfaction" of Tarantino's revenge narratives is systematically limited by the cycle of violence it entails (*Kill Bill*), by a potentially violent event taking place offscreen (*Death Proof*), by an abject villain's successfully authoring himself as hero of the history books to come (*Inglourious Basterds*), and by the sacrifice of the female element that comes at the cost of interracial male bonding (*The Hateful Eight*). The Mexican standoff epitomizes the complex ramifications of violence which can never be limited to a simple one-on-one face-off in Tarantino's movies; indeed, Richard Greene has convingly shown that such scenes in *Reservoir Dogs*, *True Romance*, and *Pulp Fiction* explore the complexity of reaching rational solutions, notably through cooperation; the same could be said of Chapter Four of *Inglourious Basterds*. The end of *Pulp Fiction* remains to this day, perhaps, the most Brechtian, because the end of violence is brought about by a negotiation that stresses doubt: Jules remains uncertain of how his interpretations of Ezekiel 25:17 relate to the situation (nor does he seem to realize the irony that his speech comes from a movie in which the hero fought against drug lords), though he is certain he wants the violence to stop nonetheless [146:44–148:33]; yet we leave the movie with the knowledge that violence will remain an integral part of Vincent's life.

The Thematization of Violence as Spectacle

The relationship between violence and spectacle is thematized in all of Tarantino's films, but varies in the degree of overtness. The infamous torture scene in *Reservoir Dogs*, for instance, reflects primarily on the performance and consumption of violence, and their sadomasochistic terms [54:10–60:27]. The sadistic Mr. Blonde turns the interrogation of Officer Nash into a show where the criminal dances for the policeman before straddling him. This nightmare lap dance—the dancer really is in control and really is deriving pleasure from the performance—reflects our own position as viewers,[37] "stuck in the middle with" the characters and made to endure the scene. By intervening and potentially blowing his cover, Mr. Orange represents another facet of the spectator who has given up the passive position to intervene as a moral agent and put an end to the horror (fig. 44). The scene thus conflates a series of responses to the spectacle of violence, organized according to a progression from sadomasochistic pleasure (as a consumer of a violent genre film, this is what you've paid to see) to empathy and moral outrage (for the victim, but also at yourself for being "stuck" in this uncomfortable situation in the first place).

Pulp Fiction similarly reflects on the relationship between violence, spectacle, and pleasure in the scene where Esmarelda Villalobos questions Butch about his feelings during and after the fight, which she has heard about on the radio [71:22–73:42]. The metafictional discourse, here, is verbal and a bit more overt. The Latina cab driver prompts the boxer to express his emotions. Butch's conclusion that he "do[es]n't feel in the least bit bad about it" is, however, contradicted by his initial reaction to his opponent's death ("Sorry about that, Floyd"); it is further disproven by the obvious relief he derives from punching Marsellus ("You feel that sting, big boy, huh? That's pride fuckin' with you, see!") [96:18], suggesting he may have had similar vindictive thoughts in mind when killing Floyd. Esmarelda is clearly a double of the ghoulish spectator (her last name means "town of wolves" in Spanish), disappointed that a fight ending in the death of an opponent was ellipticized [73:10], and the stereotypically sensual Latina thus stands as a parodic reminder of the erotic potential of violence. The portrayal of such a spectator is initially a promise of things to come: subsequent scenes will not disappoint viewer expectations, with Butch eliminating Vincent [91:47] and beating Marsellus with the very fists that killed the gangster's fighter. But it is also particularly ironic, given that both the rape of Marsellus and the death of Marvin mainly occur offscreen, and that the film's climax ends in peace. Like the torture scene from *Reservoir Dogs*, then, the film knowingly panders to sadomasochistic pleasures, foregrounding the viewer's role as an accomplice, but only up to a certain point, that is only insofar as it is dramatically justified.

The thematization of violence as spectacle is even more overt in Tarantino's third feature film, especially since its position in the opening scene lends it a programmatic value. While commenting on the video "Chicks with Gun," Ordell the arms trafficker explains to his friend Louis that his clients "want a .45" not because it's a reliable weapon, but because John Woo's 1989 "Killer had a .45" [5:13–5:45]. The arms trafficker's comments are "no small irony considering Tarantino's unabashedly violent body of work,"[38] and, in so doing, seem to provide fodder for Tarantino's detractors via the reference to the Hong Kong action film[39] and, more generally, for the defenders of the view that violence in fiction influences violence in reality. Yet Ordell's point is not that the violence actually derives from cinema—the social circumstances of his Los Angeles customers have little to do with those of Woo's characters. It has exclusively to do with style: anyone can appropriate the stylish style of a John Woo movie, but this by no means accounts for the violence governing one's life. In so doing, Ordell's comments reflexively draw attention to the displacement of stylistic concerns over social causes: those who point the finger at the influence of cinema are examining the surface, not the root of the evil. More precisely, they fail to see what underlies the concern with style: class, social mobility, white privilege—a point that the film dramatizes with its emphasis on costumes and through Ordell's complex relation to race.

Interestingly enough, the overt discourse on violence in the spectacular *Kill Bill* is focused exclusively on the ethics of violence, as if to counter the film's excesses. These concerns are addressed in *Vol. 1* by Hattori Hanzo's philosophy of revenge [15:26–15:57, 57:13–58:25, 102:07–102:25] and in *Vol. 2* by Bill's essentialist spiel on "natural born killers" [104:16–107:41]. Both draw attention to the generic status of the characters, equated with movie samurais, comic book superheroes, and even the protagonists of a film based on an idea by Tarantino. Both have a structural function: Hanzo's voice occurs at three significant moments in *Vol. 1* (at the end of Chapters One and Four, and in the epilogue), Bill's in both prologues and in the last chapter. In so doing, the disembodied male voices can be seen as the narration foregrounding patriarchal discourses' attempts to contain the taboo topic that is female violence. Both discourses are deconstructed by the narrative, though to various degrees. In fact, Bill's spiel has already been disproven before he makes it. For not only does Beatrix choose to take on the role of "Mother," but "Chapter Three: The Story of O-Ren," combined with the intertexual references to the rape-revenge genre, suggests that the killer's tendencies originate in trauma, not biology. The film also plays at confirming and invalidating Hanzo's statements. The first voice-over ("For those regarded as warriors...") only seems to confirm the Bride's lack of "compassion" in killing Vernita in front of her daughter. The second concerning the quality of Hanzo's sword is proven by Chapter Five, yet debunked by *Vol. 2* where the Bride is never in a position to actually "cut" any of her adversaries. The third statement by Hanzo ("Revenge is never a straight line...") has already been corroborated by both the plot and the structure of *Kill Bill Vol. 1*, but the idea that "it's easy to lose your way, to get lost, to forget where you came in" qualifies Hanzo's previous advice to "[s]uppress all human emotions and compassion," which is contradicted by Beatrix's tears as she watches Bill die in the end. In short, the film thematizes that the spectacle of violence cannot be fully dissociated from ethical and personal considerations, whose implications are made far more complex, notably through the feminine elements, than the heroic patriarchal discourses[40] that inform genre films. However, Hanzo's discourse is not assuredly deconstructed because its weakness may also stem quite simply from having been taken out of context. Indeed, his voice may actually be the Bride's inner voice, reflecting on the lessons she has learned.

In *Death Proof*, the relationship between violence and spectacle, also overtly thematized through a protagonist's words, takes a new turn by exploring the production of audiovisual fictions. Significantly, it is to his first potential victim that Stuntman Mike expresses his nostalgia for the "all-or-nothing days," "real cars smaking into real cars, real dumb people drivin'" [43:27]. As a proponent of analog over digital, the serial killer is very much speaking for Tarantino. In an article where she convincingly demonstrates that Rodriguez and Tarantino's *Grindhouse* laments the passing of theatrical exhibition in the digital age, Caetlin Benson-Alliott notes that *Death Proof* "wants to discover what [the human body] can do."[41] In a clever turnaround, Mike makes the filmmaking process over into fiction: the stuntcar meant to create an illusion becomes an actual weapon. His *modus operandi* thus symbolizes the return of the "real" violence erased in the production of the fiction inflicted on potential viewers who, like Pam, naïvely believe all special effects are harmless CGI and ignore the indispensable work of stuntpeople [43:20]. Kim and Zoë are able to retaliate because they are accustomed to channeling violence professionally. The film's metafictional discourse on violence as spectacle thus intertwines both aesthetic (analog versus CGI) and class (invisible performers versus visible ones) considerations.

Inglourious Basterds pursues the reflections on spectatorial responses to violence from *Reservoir Dogs* and *Pulp Fiction*. The boundary between violence as an act of war and violence as entertainment is blurred when the site where the Basterds have just ambushed a group of Nazis becomes the theatrical space for Donowitz's performance as the Bear Jew [31:57–35:20]. If the Basterds and the actual spectators have in common that they are watching the same act, the latter is not presented to the diegetic and the real audience in the same fashion. In spite of Raine's comment that "quite frankly watching Donnie beat Nazis to death is the closest we get to goin' to the movies," what the Basterds watch is a sick parody of a baseball game, one that might recall Al Capone's "headball" in *The Untouchables* (Brian De Palma, 1987). We, however, are watching a film. The mannerist style—close-ups, slow motion, Morricone's music from *The Big Gundown*—not only confers the solemnity of a ritual to the scene, but draws attention to its cinematic quality. This style is broken first by the violent act (in a series of five shots, medium and long), then by the very long shot that tracks out when Donowitz starts beating the man to death, a disruption that draws attention to the Basterds' less ambivalent response, as they enthusiastically applaud their fellow soldier. The act is the same, but the spectacle is different, and it is the different aesthetics that endow, or deny, the dying man with dignity. That is not to say that the Basterds' staging is without purpose: on the contrary, it is meant to impress the enemy with the depths of their inhumanness.

The scene has its mirror opposite in Chapter Five, when the Nazis watch a propaganda movie based on real events [136:08–136:40]. Like the Bear Jew's show, the spectacle of violence has a specific design: *Stolz der Nation* is propaganda meant to boost confidence in the Nazis, as Hitler explains [101:14]. The violence, which is simulated but based on real events, prompts varying reactions: enthusiasm in Hitler and apparently the rest of the audience, sadness in Zoller, who underwent both the real ordeal and its fictitious re-creation. *Inglourious Basterds*'s rejection of the Manichean representation of Nazis common to most Hollywood WWII movie thus enables the film to introduce a new parameter in its reflection on spectatorship. If "only a thoughtless viewer will not see him or herself reflected in shots of Hitler cackling as he watches Americans being slaughtered in *Nation's Pride*," as Ben Walters (2009-10) has stated, Zoller's reaction "suggests that what one will do and what one will watch need not coincide." Much like us (the real viewers) during the baseball execution scene, Zoller is not seeing the same thing, and his reaction seems to indicate that, unlike the Basterds, he derived no pleasure from killing his enemies. The film thus recognizes the possibility that the traumatic experience of actual violence can inform one's response to simulated violence.

Like *Django Unchained*, *The Hateful Eight* insists on the ethics underlying the spectacle of violence, but this time, the thematization narrows the discourse down to the question of justice. Appropriately enough, it is introduced by Oswaldo Mobray, who is passing as the local hangman. The man who "will perform the execution" of Daisy Domergue distinguishes between frontier justice and justice, concluding that "the man who pulls the lever that breaks your neck—will be a dispassionate man. And that dispassion—is the very essence of justice. For justice delivered without dispassion—is always in danger of not being justice" [47:14–48:51]. The execution may arouse strong, perhaps unsavory emotions in its audience, but the performer remains distanced from his role. Mobray's definition then serves as a frame to the subsequent scenes where justice is dealt by protagonists who are anything but "dispassionate."

The first occurs when Warren tells General Smithers of how he raped and killed his son. The possibly unreliable flashback is broken by a frontal close-up of Warren, who pauses in his account to address his prime spectator: "You're startin' to see pictures, ain't ya? Your boy—black dude's dingus in his

Fig. 70.1: *The Hateful Eight*: Warren raping Smithers's son in a pristine white setting.

Fig. 70.2: *The Hateful Eight*: Warren looking at Smithers and the camera: "Ya startin' to see pictures, ain't ya?"

Fig. 70.3: *The Hateful Eight*: General Smithers looks back in horror.

mouth. Him shakin', him cryin'. Me laughin' ... and *him* not understandin'. But you understand, don't you, Sandy?" (fig. 70.1–70.3) [93:06]. By allowing Warren to look right at the camera, momentarily breaking the fourth wall, the narration brings to the fore both the similarities and differences between the diegetic spectator's position and the viewer's: if the narration has already furnished the illustrations of Warren's account, both are struggling to assess the veracity of the words and images. Yet regardless of their truth, the "pictures" have the desired effect: they trigger strong emotions in the audience, sorrow and anger for Smithers, and maybe a combination of shock (at the content) and amusement (at the form) for other viewers. In any case, Warren is not pressing emotional buttons for their own sake: he is recounting a story, in which he killed a man out of self-defense but toyed with him first, that is, in effect, an inverted *mise en abyme* of the present situation. Underlying the spectacle of violence is thus a complex situation steeped in ethical, historical, and political implications: though acting as if he were on the witness stand disclosing his own sadism, Warren is, in fact, judging the Confederate general guilty of desecrating black soldiers before executing him. The scene proves how frail the boundaries between each position are. The revelation that Mobray is not a hangman calls into question the very possibility of dispassionate justice, especially since English Pete (formerly Mobray) is actually prepared to sacrifice himself to save Daisy Domergue [149:53]. It paves the way for the travesty of justice in the final scene, where Mannix sentences Daisy to hang, and the two men delight in watching her die, laughing with lust-filled eyes [158:18–159:38]—Warren again reveals his own sadism, shouting: "Hang on, Daisy. I wanna watch." An execution, the film seems to suggest, remains hateful entertainment (like Tarantino's eighth film), even when delivered by a soon-to-be representative of the law.

Clearly, the violence in Tarantino's films is not just material for entertainment; it is also the subject of a complex and ongoing metadiscourse that is distributed over the totality of his œuvre. The spectacles of violence in Tarantino's films can be moments that gleefully indulge in the choreography of bodies in space, but they also serve to dramatize the films' ethical and political concerns; even when emphasis is put on the former (as in *Kill Bill*), the flying bodies are also reflecting on the circulations in film history and their aesthetic and political implications.[42] What Greg M. Colón Semenza argues of *Inglourious Basterds*, that it "build[s] in multiple levels of reflexive meditation on movie violence and historical appropriation,"[43] is true of all of Tarantino's feature films. Although the degree of overtness may vary, the thematization of violence as spectacle includes considerations on differing responses to violence, the relationship between style and substance, the many ethical and political implications underlying various acts of violence, and even the violence that goes into making a movie. The common denominator, as the quote from *Django Unchained* suggests, seems to be that violence must be examined as a complex: there are various forms of violence, various and sometimes conflicting ethical reasons behind each instance, so that each violent scene must be analyzed in context. The fact that each film adds a nuance or proposes a novel angle indicates that it is anything but a closed discussion; it has evolved, as have Tarantino's comments in interviews, though not necessarily in parallel. As cinematic metafictions, the films testify, rather, to the intricacies of discourses on violence and the incapacity to provide an all encompassing discourse that would provide total resolution. One could advance that the thematization is nothing more than a clever means of having your cake and eating it, too, the metafictional discourse coughed up to excuse the guilty pleasures, and it is possible that this comes into play on some level. But the fact that the treatment of violence varies based on each situation suffices to qualify, if not counter, that argument. My hunch is that Tarantino's interest in violence is sincere, and that, like the reflexivity at work in many horror movies,[44] the metadiscourse is an attempt to work through obsessions that are at once personal and cultural. Viewers and audiences are absolutely right in identifying violence as a central—if not the most central—characteristic of Tarantino's films, not because it is graphic or gratuitous, but because violence stands at the nexus of aesthetics, ethics, and politics. It provides the dramatic climax (or anti-climax) where character arcs converge, and gender, historical, moral, Oedipal, racial questions are not so much resolved—they are only so on a narrative level—but revealed in all their complexity, providing at best a very ambivalent form of catharsis, a notion that remains operative today because it points to how indelibly intertwined the aesthetics and ethics of violence are.

CONCLUSION

The feature films of Quentin Tarantino are clearly inscribed in a long tradition of anti-illusionist fiction. They deploy an impressive arsenal of reflexive devices—chapter headings, conspicuous camerawork and editing, intertexuality, theatricality—some of which draw attention away from the diegesis to the medium of film by invoking another medium (comics, drama, the novel). These practices, however, do more than just flaunt the films' artificiality. Rather, they are integral to the production of metafictional discourses. These cinematic metafictions rely on many of the overt and covert strategies identified by Hutcheon in literary metafiction. On the formal level, the specifically cinematic reflexive devices, including the iconization of genre characters, draw attention to the films' building blocks. On a diegetic level, storytelling, role-playing, and making movies are thematized through dialogue, narrative, and *mises en abyme*, while the films themselves are primarily organized according to underlying fantasy and game models, notably through the play on identifying various references that many fans take part in online.

Much of the criticism of Tarantino's films, as we have seen, is due to the fact that they are metafictions. I would venture that the generalized attack on metafiction, instead of on certain works in particular, is underpinned by an unreasoned and overarching fear of fiction, an "antimimetic attitude" that has traversed Western thought since Plato:[1] the fear of a fiction that radically and unashamedly celebrates its own powers. If metafiction is about itself, Tarantino's feature films prove that it need not be solipsistic or vacuous; that depends entirely on the work under scrutiny. It will not have escaped the reader that my defense of these films started from a view that has often been put forth by the director's critics: that they are solely concerned with film history. But the films do more than just allude to film history; they engage with it on various levels—that is, with other films, but also with the history of production, exhibition, and reception, and even with film historiography. In a movie where film is used as a weapon, Landa's question "What will the history books read?" inevitably raises the question "What will the film history books read?" Engaging with film history, at least in the case of Tarantino's films, means engaging with cultural history (comics, drama, literature, music, television), whether high or low. It rests on the belief that culture is an integral part of history, that history informs culture, but also that culture can explore and interrogate history; in other words, it presupposes a dialogical relationship between culture and history where the two are placed on par. The scope of these metafictions is thus far-ranging temporally; it is equally so geographically, since cultural history is not restricted to the United States.

The metafictional discourses produced by a scene, a film, or the œuvre as a whole are varied. An issue like cinematic violence is so complex that each film offers a different take. Interest in the circulations between various industries can be expressed through plot and style (*Kill Bill*, *Inglourious Basterds*). Emphasis on performers and performance can highlight the tension between a star's image and mortal body (*Pulp Fiction*, *Jackie Brown*). In-depth analyses of the genre conventions the films reprise reveal an acute awareness that such conventions are racialized, gendered, connected to issues of class, and so forth. The deconstruction of gendered and racialized genre conventions is grounded in a reflection on the history of representations. Discussions about plot, characters, and character relationships are not enough to conclude on the politics of representation in a work of fiction with no regard of the medium; in film, such analyses require attention to acting, costume, lighting, camerawork, editing, music, and sound.

If the metafictional discourses propose different and even differing angles, the poetics and politics of Tarantino's cinematic metafictions intersect because the politics of representation are intertwined with the aesthetics of re-creation. We have seen that the political subtexts are partly produced through repetitions that invite comparisons, notably Tarantino's signature devices or the use of musical leitmotifs based on preexisting material. But with Tarantino, the prefix "re-" is self-consciously redoubled: the films often—and maybe even increasingly—re-represent and re-recycle.

This is patent in the frequent use of cover songs. It is especially obvious in the titles of the last three films. *Inglourious Basterds* borrows its title from a 1978 Italian exploitation film largely inspired by a Hollywood film, *The Dirty Dozen* (1967), the spelling mistakes and the absence of the article "the" asserting that the 2009 film itself is the bastard of a bastard.[2] If the second word in the title spells difference, *Django Unchained* wears its Italian Western heritage on its sleeves by citing the 1966 movie that was already an unavowed remake of *Yojimbo* (Akira Kurosawa, 1961), the same movie the first Italian Western, *A Fistful of Dollars* (Sergio Leone, 1964), was based on.[3] The title *The Hateful Eight* self-consciously points to its status as Tarantino's eighth feature film and inverts the terms of the famous Hollywood film *The Magnificent Seven* (Preston Sturges, 1960), a remake of an equally famous Japanese film, *Seven Samurai* (Akira Kurosawa, 1954). This was also the case of *Jackie Brown*, a title that alludes to Grier and Hill's 1974 follow-up to *Coffy*. All four titles draw attention to the numerous recyclings in time and circulations in space.

Again, the scope is much broader than most early viewers had realized, no doubt because an artistic project becomes more apparent and/or conscious in time, both to the filmmakers (and I include Tarantino regulars Jackson, Menke, Richardson, Roth, and the rest) and to the audience. Blending high culture (Shakespeare, Beethoven, Wagner, *Citizen Kane*, *8 ½*) and low culture (comics, exploitation films) references are now regarded as a myth of postmodernist practice.[4] In the films of Quentin Tarantino, mixing, or rather remixing, is, in effect, both an aesthetic and a political statement. It taps into networks of signification, as we have seen. But it also implies that all cultural productions can be valued for specific moments: any film, no matter how lowly, can have a moment of beauty.

Tarantino's love affair with the Italian Western is a prime example of this; many of these films are partially redeemed, in the eyes of some critics, by the scores composed by Morricone. I would argue that the fact that the Italian Western has provided the underlying structure of almost half of his films (*Kill Bill*, *Inglourious Basterds*, *Django Unchained*) should not be entirely put down to a question of taste, seeing that *The Good, the Bad and the Ugly* is the only Italian Western Tarantino includes in his list of favorite films. Rather, the Italian Western serves as a template for the very reason that it is so obviously *not* a model, but a derivative and an appropriation by another culture; it is a distorted reflection of the Hollywood Western, one informed by Japanese cinema, previous European Westerns (notably German), and Italian neorealism, one that aims to attack capitalism and totalitarianism by subverting the myth of the frontier, one that addresses specific Italian anxieties of the period. The Italian Western provides an ideal template for Tarantino because it is an ambivalent re-representation: one that glorifies figures while undermining their ethics, one that magnifies genre conventions to ritualistic proportions, one that exploits excessive violence while criticizing it. The Italian Western exemplifies that forms and meanings change in time and space, that recycled material is not drained of meaning but rather invested with new meanings through recontextualization. The sheer number of references from British,

French, German, Hong Kong, Italian, and Japanese cinema in the films of Quentin Tarantino complexifies their status as Hollywood or even American productions. It points to a global history of cinema that circulates beyond the dominant industry. The circulation is, in the first place, economic, but it ultimately escapes the industries' control, the products becoming material for aesthetic and political reworking. These films thus testify to the shizophrenic energies unleashed by capitalism, recalling, in this respect, Gilles Deleuze and Félix Guattari's theses that "monetary fluxes are perfectly schizophrenic realities."[5]

The films of Quentin Tarantino are not just characteristic of contemporary debates concerning historical and transnational circulations, the questioning of originality in art, or the notion that identities are performative and performed, copies of copies;[6] they actively engage with these issues. They also exemplify the convergence between contemporary fiction and poststructuralist ideas that foreground practices of recycling and resignification. They prove that metafiction need not be solipsistic and that postmodernism need not be vacuous because they consider that signs (actors, images, language, music, representations) are not empty but are, on the contrary, loaded with meaning. In short, Tarantino doesn't just recycle, as was first thought: he recycles to resignify. Therein lies the political potential of his films, and perhaps of metafiction and postmodern practices in general. And by positing an active spectator, like literary metafictions according to Hutcheon, they invite viewers to participate in the production of meaning, and thus reshape the material; this book is, no doubt, one such endeavor, as are various discussions in classrooms, at coffee machines, or online. Politically speaking, requiring participation is both an asset and a limitation: it is limiting because viewers who don't perceive the references or refuse the invitation will miss out on something, but it is empowering because it demands of the viewer that s/he does at least part of the work.

There is nothing original about this view or this approach either. Not only is it characteristic of metafiction, but it is characteristic of the way many contemporary filmmakers conceive filmmaking, including some who are rarely associated with Tarantino in discussions of contemporary American cinema. Jim Jarmusch, another filmmaker who reworks classic genres—the Western in *Dead Man* (1995), the vampire movie in *Only Lovers Left Alive* (2013)—has stated: "Nothing is original. Steal from anywhere that resonates with inspiration or fuels your imagination."[7] The particularity of Tarantino's feature films lies partly in the degree to which they are layered (overtly, covertly, linguistically, musically, structurally, and, of course, visually), a layeredness that, in my experience, rivals the work of an obsessive perfectionist like Vladimir

Nabokov. The individuality lies more precisely in the references chosen—the vast majority of them originate from the 1970s, Tarantino's formative years.

Tarantino is very much the descendant of the various film new waves, particularly the French New Wave and the New Hollywood. Like those filmmakers, he is intensely aware of film history;[8] like them, he aims to regenerate cinema and, literally, to save film. His poetics, as we have seen, mix the efficacy of classical cinema, the spectacle of blockbuster and exploitation movies, and the self-conscious sophistication of art cinema. In Tarantino's case, it is not so much a compromise as an ideal of an absolute cinema that would fuse the high and the low, blockbuster, exploitation and art, Woo and Godard, novel, film, TV shows, and comics, Shakespeare and Leonard. In short, the ideal includes eveything the screenwriter-director loves, and even things he says he hates (*The Birth of a Nation*, John Ford). The juggling act between overt and covert metafiction is consistent with the delicate balance the feature films strive for. In answer to the astute Gavin Smith, who had perceived the combination of realism and artifice in *Reservoir Dogs* and *Pulp Fiction*, Tarantino asserted that the reflexive devices "don't necessarily break the reality."[9] It is because Tarantino does not want to go all-out anti-illusionist and sacrifice entertainment that his films resemble the early and not the later Godard. In the end, it is not at all surprising that Tarantino's favorite film is *The Good, the Bad and the Ugly*, for he is very much following in the path of Leone. Like Leone, Tarantino wants to have things both ways: to celebrate the beauty of the icon while undercutting it. As if its redemption lied squarely in its poetic and political power to die and be born anew, a spectral image intimately connected to the past and temporarily projected on a column of smoke for the mere duration of a show.

NOTES

Introduction

1. Tarantino has often been quoted saying, "When people ask me if I went to film school, I tell them, 'No, I went to films.'"
2. Tarantino is an avid reader (Peary 86).
3. Bauer 237; Peary 37.
4. Peary 168.
5. Peary 27, 142, 150, 159. Janet Staiger told me that Tarantino had even sent an assistant to take notes at a conference where Clover and Linda Williams were speaking.
6. See <http://wiki.tarantino.info/index.php/Tarantino's_favorite_films>. Accessed on May 7, 2017.
7. Peary 6.
8. Peary 101.
9. Peary 190.
10. Morgan 24, 26.
11. Von Dassanowsky, "Dr. 'King' Schultz" 26, 31–32.
12. Peary 171.
13. Peary 192.
14. Peary 6, 20.
15. Peary 73.
16. Neupert 207.
17. <https://en.wikiquote.org/wiki/Quentin_Tarantino>. Accessed on May 7, 2017.
18. Genette, *Introduction à l'architexte* 87–88, my translation.
19. See <https://www.youtube.com/watch?v=AyeKbqp-Cz8>. Accessed on May 5, 2017.
20. Conard, "*Reservoir Dogs*" 107–9.
21. Jullier 109.
22. As such, this book is absolutely in agreement with Speck when he explains that, "if we treat the many references in *Django Unchained* not as a simple nod to fan expectations but as real intertexts, a political dimension is opened" (5). I argue that this is the case in all of Tarantino's films.

23. Bertelsen 9. She is, here, citing Linda Hutcheon.
24. Hutcheon, *Narcissistic* 18.
25. Waugh 2.
26. McHale, *Constructing Postmodernism* 202.
27. Hutcheon, A *Poetics of Postmodernism* 40.
28. Hutcheon, *Narcissistic* 7–8.
29. Stam xx.
30. Metz 10.
31. Stam xiv.
32. Stam 6–7, 20–21, 46–48, 102.
33. Stam 44, 255–61.
34. In the 2010s, bloggers regularly discuss whether films, shows, or video games haven't become "too meta." See, for example, Lady Salka's 12/3/2014 post on ladygeekgirl.wordpress.com or EwokD20's 11/2015 post on hub.cybercast.net.
35. Cerisuello 92–93, my translation.
36. Von Dassanowsky, *Quentin Tarantino's* Inglourious Basterds vii–ix.
37. Chinita 7.
38. Chinita 7–8.
39. McRoy 32.
40. Sinnerbrink 154.
41. <https://ruthlessculture.com/2016/02/11/review-rosencrantz-guildenstern-are-dead-1990>. Accessed on May 5, 2017.
42. Stam 159.
43. Stam 98–105, 219, 19.
44. Humphries, *Fritz Lang* 119, 121-22.
45. Stam 231.
46. Roche, *Making and Remaking* 147–52.
47. Hutcheon, *Narcissistic* 23.
48. Hutcheon, *Narcissistic* 48–56
49. Hutcheon, *Narcissistic* 71–86.
50. Hutcheon, *Narcissistic* 29.
51. Hutcheon, *Narcissistic* 30.
52. Hutcheon, *Narcissistic* 27.
53. Willis, "'Fire!'" 187.
54. In a discussion on movieforums.com, one blogger complained that Tarantino "gets credit for a level of originality he simply doesn't possess" because "younger," "undereducated" fans can't see the references <https://www.movieforums.com/community/showthread.php?t=16956>. Accessed on May 7, 2017.
55. Hutcheon, *Narcissistic* 8–16.
56. Hutcheon, *Narcissistic* 47.
57. Hutcheon, *Narcissistic* 152.
58. Sobchack 41.
59. Eco 71.
60. Nama 3.

Notes

Chapter One: "What Shall the History Books Read?": History and Film History

1. Thomas Leitch deals with the fidelity to true stories and history in chapter 11 of *Film Adaptation and Its Discontents*.
2. Stokes and Menegaldo 2008; Stokes 2014.
3. Grayzel 786.
4. Coates 2010.
5. Chermak and Bailey 639–40. The connection to the Western is reinforced by the fact that the James Gang belonged to Quantrill's marauders (Slotkin 133).
6. See Paul D. Escott's *"What Shall We Do with the Negro?" Lincoln, White Racism, and Civil War*.
7. Slotkin 638.
8. See Tricia Martineau Wagner's *Black Cowboys of the Old West*.
9. Holmes 75.
10. Hicox even looks like Field Marshal Bernard Law Montgomery.
11. German speakers have told me that the German dialogue in *Inglourious Basterds* is spot on.
12. Hayes and Rodman 196.
13. Von Dassanowsky, "Dr. 'King' Schultz" 31.
14. The major prison camps were in Virginia.
15. Nama 110; Kaster 77.
16. Meyer 19; Kligerman 137; Willis, "'Fire!'" 181.
17. Von Dassanowsky, *Quentin Tarantino's* Inglourious Basterds xii.
18. Von Dassanowsky, "Dr. 'King' Schultz" 18. Temoney also uses the term (125).
19. Stokes 53.
20. Stokes 51.
21. Hutcheon, *Narcissistic* 32.
22. Hutcheon, *Narcissistic* 76.
23. Hutcheon, *Narcissistic* 81.
24. Richardson 103.
25. For a discussion of "artistic license" in contemporary Hollywood films, see Toplin 1996.
26. Kligerman 139–40.
27. Meyer 18.
28. Kligerman 147–48; Ornella 237.
29. Von Dassanowsky, "Dr. 'King' Schultz" 18–20.
30. Von Dassanowsky, "Dr. 'King' Schultz" 31.
31. Niemeyer 47–48.
32. Richard Slotkin explains that, in the captivity narrative, values are tested by the passive victim (15).
33. Desilet 33.
34. Nama 110.
35. Nama 116.
36. Temoney 130.
37. See Von Klemperer 9.

38. <http://ingloriousbasterds.wikia.com/wiki/Hugo_Stiglitz>. Accessed on May 4, 2017.

39. Kligerman 151.

40. Kligerman suggests that the reference likens the movie theater to a courtroom (141).

41. Kligerman 148.

42. Nama 101.

43. Haber 135.

44. Tarantino says of this scene: "And I even love the fact that it's a Gestapo major who is calling America on its racist past" (Peary 172).

45. Nama 102.

46. Signficantly, the other fictional character is a Native American invented by the German writer Karl May.

47. Nama 101–2.

48. Slotkin argues that even in the "pro-Indian" *Broken Arrow* (Delmer Daves, 1950), Cochise is "an Indian we can trust, because he is literally and figuratively 'White'—that is he acts up to 'White' standard of nobility and honor, and he is played by a white actor" (375).

49. <http://wiki.tarantino.info/index.php/Major_Marquis_Warren>. Accessed on May 4, 2017.

50. <http://ingloriousbasterds.wikia.com/wiki/Ed_Fenech>. Accessed on May 4, 2017.

51. Semenza 74–75.

52. Willis, "'Fire!'" 169.

53. Imke Meyer says Chaplin's and Tarantino's Hitlers are both cartoony (29).

54. Django and Schultz's arrival in Daughtrey, Texas, replays that of Boss Nigger and Amos in the Western town, with the difference that Schultz feigns dismay at the shocked reception.

55. Peary 187; O'Brien 32; Nama 113; Speck, *Quentin Tarantino's* Django Unchained 7; Hayes and Rodman 197; Ortoli, "Quentin Tarantino : du cinéma d'exploitation."

56. Nama 111.

57. Bogle 4–7.

58. Desilet 33.

59. Geoffrey O'Brien even wonders whether the scene isn't a nod to *O Brother, Where Art Thou?* (Joel and Ethan Coen, 2000) (32).

60. Kligerman 145.

61. Meyer 18.

62. Kligerman 147, 153.

63. Hayes and Rodman 189, 197.

64. Semenza 77.

65. Tuhkunen 10, 83, 98–99.

66. Nama 111.

67. Willis, "'Fire!'" 186–87.

68. Kligerman 145. Ortoli (2015), who, like me, disagrees with this view, similarly remarks that Tarantino's referring to the film world—for instance, by citing *Sabotage* rather than a documentary—"can give the impression of maintaining a fake coherence which would not take into account the cultural environments of the images he invokes" (my translation).

69. Semenza 78.

70. Willis, "'Fire!'" 185.

71. The literature on World War II propaganda films is abundant.
72. Kligerman 155.
73. The Tennessee scenes were shot in Austin and California.
74. Anderson, "Stuntman Mike" 15.
75. Chumo II 23, 26.
76. Ritter 288.
77. Ritter 294.

Chapter Two: "Black Man, White Hell": Identity Politics Vol. 1: Race and Ethnicity

1. "Director Quentin Tarantino discusses *The Hateful Eight*," DGA Q&A in Los Angeles, December 5, 2015. <https://www.dga.org/Events/2016/jan2016/HatefulEight_QnA_1215.aspx>. Accessed on May 9, 2017.
2. Beltzer, "Dogs in Hell."
3. Allan, "When Is a Slur Not a Slur?"
4. Nama 10. Heather Ashley Hayes and Gilbert B. Rodman go so far as to define *Django Unchained* as a "black film," one of the most important contemporary ones at that, because of its actors, topic, influences, and its endeavor to "dismantl[e] systemic and institutional racism" (184).
5. Nama 6–7.
6. Nama 3.
7. I am referring to Gloria Anzaldúa's (1987) metaphor of the self as a crossroads. It parallels Kimberlé Williams Crenshaw's (1989) legal discussion of "intersectionality" and has been reprised by Judith Butler in *Bodies that Matter* (116–17), notably in her study of *Paris Is Burning* (Jennie Livingston, 1990) (121–40).
8. Perry 205.
9. hooks 59.
10. Perry 208 (on *Django Unchained*).
11. Cervulle 35–49 (on *Death Proof*). Weaver and Kathol 245, 265 (on *Django Unchained*).
12. Butler, *Bodies* 2.
13. Nama 23.
14. Jules's saying "Le Big Mac" also echoes *The Mack* (Roche, "French Fries" 296).
15. Ortoli, *Musée* 36–96.
16. Ortoli, *Musée* 218.
17. Nama 50–51.
18. Dargis 118.
19. Nama 51.
20. Crémieux, "Exploitation Cinema and the Lesbian Imagination."
21. Samuel L. Jackson said he wanted his character to look like the 1972 Super Fly and that Tarantino was initially reluctant. <http://www.thedailybeast.com/galleries/2013/11/28/ranking-samuel-l-jacksons-craziest-onscreen-hairdos-from-pulp-fiction-to-oldboy-photos.html>. Accessed on May 9, 2017.
22. Bogle 251–52.
23. Peary 163.

24. Nama 72.
25. Roche, "Choreographing Genre"; Nama 72.
26. Roche, "Quentin Tarantino's *Death Proof*" 86; Szaniawski 173–74.
27. Von Dassanowsky, *Quentin Tarantino's* Inglourious Basterds 19.
28. Nama says she becomes "a symbolic Native American warrior" (99).
29. Srinivasan 11.
30. Kligerman 155; Speck, "Is Tarantino Serious?" 195.
31. Nama 106–20.
32. Though Kate E. Temoney wonders whether the characterization of Stephen as a demonic Uncle Tom was intentional (137), interviews confirm that it was very much so (Peary 190).
33. Nama 104–5.
34. By the end of their winter stay in the mountains, Django has come to be recognized as a bounty hunter by a figure of authority, Sheriff Gus, who salutes him [57:09–58:01], as Tarantino points out (Peary 195).
35. Nama 109–10.
36. Peary 7.
37. Nama 19.
38. Nama 23.
39. Nama 17.
40. Freddy about Cabot: "He's a cool guy. He's funny; he's a funny guy" [71:10].
41. Nama 18.
42. Nama 17.
43. Nama 20.
44. Nama 18.
45. Nama 21.
46. Nama 20.
47. Nama 47.
48. Nama 48.
49. Nama 46.
50. Nama 51.
51. Nama 52.
52. Nama 51.
53. Nama 57.
54. Nama 58.
55. Ordell says to Jackie: "You scared of me? You got any reason to be nervous around me?" [51:28].
56. Nama 59.
57. Nama 61.
58. Nama 48.
59. Nama 58.
60. Ordell says: "Come on, man, you know how they do. Black man show up with $10,000 cash, first thing they wanna know is where I got it" [12:37]; "Plus [Beaumont's] from Kentucky, and I think they kind of prejudiced against brothers from down south out here" [13:10]; "A

forty-four-year-old black woman caught with less than two ounces, they calling that shit 'intent.' The same thing happen to a movie star, they call it 'possession'" [36:26].

61. Nama 56.

62. Dargus says: "Now you'll probably end up only serving a year and some change, but—if I was a forty-four-year-old *black* woman, desperately clinging on to this one *shitty* little job that I was fortunate enough to get, I don't think that I'd think that I had a year to throw away" [32:15].

63. Tierney 610.

64. Nama 81–82.

65. Bill is also shown tenderly caressing Sofie Fatale in *Vol. 1* [95:20].

66. Shanna: "Okay, mean girl in a high school movie, you through throwin' a tantrum?" [3:51]; Pam: "That pituitary case? Might have kicked my ass like a couple of times. Sorry, I'm built like a girl, not a *black* man" [30:34].

67. Nama 89.

68. Zoë says to Kim: "I'm sorry I called you black bitch" [94:38].

69. Nama 90.

70. I am, of course, reprising Vladimir Propp's (1928) typology of the function of characters in folk tales.

71. Nama compares the movie to *Beloved* (Toni Morrison's 1989 novel, adapted in 1998 by Jonathan Demme), as "a stirring assertion of the commitment and courage of black folk to love one another, despite the most callous of environments and under the most oppressive institutions" (116). James Edward Ford III similarly argues that the couple's "radical care for each other becomes synonymous with a critique of the state of emergency they inhabit" (208).

72. Nama 118–19.

73. As David G. Holmes points out, Broomhilda, Django, and Stephen represent "counter-arguments" to Candie's discourse (74).

74. Nama 111.

75. Leonard 273.

76. Nama 118.

77. This is, of course, reinforced by the fact that Minnie is said to despise Mexicans [115:18].

78. Nama 12.

79. In *Inglourious Basterds*, the high command of both factions—the Nazis at the restaurant [48:28], Winston Churchill and General Fenech in London [64:24]—are associated with luxury, while the size and sophistication of Landa's pipe contrasts with the French dairy farmer's more modest one [16:59]. Even Shosanna's plot is made possible because she owns a small movie theater.

80. The handling of filmic space reflects the fluidity of Marcel and Shosanna's relationship. Though Marcel is first introduced in high angle, as if to suggest a subordinate position to his employer Shosanna [46:48], he is later seen on the balcony even as Shosanna announces her plan [61:21].

81. Jacob Mey says that "[p]ragmatics studies the use of language in human communication as determined by the conditions of society" (6).

82. Abrams 2.

83. Mr. Pink to Mr. Blonde and Mr. White: "What are we in a playground here? Huh? Jesus, am I the only professional? Fuckin' guys, you're actin' like a bunch of niggers, huh? Have you worked with niggers, huh? Just like you. Always sayin' they're gonna kill each other."

84. Nama 20.

85. Eddie says to Joe Cabot about Mr. Blonde: "Ain't that a sad sight, Daddy. A man walks into prison a white man, he walks out talkin' like a fuckin' nigger. You know what? I think it's all that black semen's been *pumped* up your ass so far now it's backed into your fuckin' brain and it's comin' out your mouth."

86. Nama 21.

87. Nama 22.

88. Nama 22.

89. Cabot tells the dogs: "You get four guys all fightin' over who's gonna get to be Mr. Black. And they don't know each other so nobody wants to back down" [81:48].

90. Nama 47.

91. Nama 48.

92. Nama 47.

93. Nama 44–46.

94. Willis, "Style" 292.

95. Marsellus asks Butch, "You my nigga?" [23:05], then says to Vincent: "Vincent Vega's in the house? My nigga. Get your ass over here" [25:52].

96. Nama 43.

97. Allan 193.

98. Allan 194.

99. Allan 192.

100. Allan 195.

101. Marsellus to Jules: "Go back in there, chill them niggas out, and wait for the cavalry, which should be coming directly" [121:09].

102. Nama 46.

103. Allan 196.

104. Nama 41–42.

105. Army Archerd, "Lee has Choice Words for Tarantino," *Variety* (December 16, 1997). <http://variety.com/1997/voices/columns/lee-has-choice-words-for-tarantino-111779698>. Accessed on May 9, 2017.

106. The only racially inflected word used by a white character (Dargus) is "black woman" (see above).

107. Peary 104.

108. That Ordell also calls Mr. Walker a "cat" [5:52] and uses the n-word again at the end would tend to confirm this [131:13].

109. The stereotype is debunked, as the only customers who are actually mentioned are Korean.

110. Peary 103.

111. My use of the term is derived from Judith Butler, for whom the possibility to resignify depends on the gap between context and effects (*Excitable Speech* 14). Her view is grounded

in a pragmatic view of language, Butler citing J. L. Austin, one of the fathers of pragmatic linguistics (*Excitable Speech* 24).

112. In the DVD extra "Le Casting selon Tarantino."

113. Kim talking about men in the car: "Bitch, you might be actin' like you twelve years old, but he's just actin' like a man. You need to break that nigga off a piece. [. . .] Before you can *claim* a nigga, you gotta *claim* a nigga" [70:49]. Kim in the diner: "Motherfucker try to rape me, I don't wanna give him a skin rash. I wanna shut that nigga down. [. . .] Look, if I ever become a famous actress, I won't carry a gun. I'll hire me a dude dirt nigga and *he'll* carry the gun" [75:37]. Kim to Abernathy: "Set crush, nigga, please. You were his set wife" [68:32].

114. Like the use of the word "guy" (see chapter 3), the use of the n-word participates in foregrounding the fluidity of identity as a discursive construct.

115. Peary 189.

116. I have in mind, of course, Sigmund Freud's famous thesis that jokes and wordplay are indicative of unconscious desires.

117. Ford III 212.

118. Ruth to Daisy about Warren: "You ruin that letter of his, that nigger gonna stomp your ass to death" [20:08]; and to Warren about Mannix: "One thing I know for sure, this nigger-hatin' son of a gun ain't partnered up with you" [27:13].

119. He says to Bill about Hattori Hanzo: "Them Japs sure know how to hold a grudge, don't they?" [15:03]

120. According to Paul Fussell, the term became derogatory during and after World War II (117).

121. Today Germans use the words "Schwarzen" or "Afro-Deutsche," while German blacks have appropriated the English word "Nigger."

122. Allan 197.

123. Peary 103.

124. Nama 130.

125. Even the Rock, relegated to the offscreen in *Death Proof*, is eroticized, this time through discourse, with Lee praising "his big hands" and "mushy lips" [57:18].

126. Nama 110.

127. Nama 118; Leonard 273. For James Edward Ford III, the black ensemble cast's attention to looks and glances communicates a sense of the collective experience of slavery that goes beyond the black legendry the film develops: "Glances alone do not tear down plantations, but they reveal an alternative sociality taking shape through a committed effort to develop new ways of seeing beyond the state of emergency's prescriptions" (215).

128. Nama 108.

129. Nama 109.

130. Nama 110.

131. This is indexed on the costumes: Django changes from blue to khaki and brown, while the white-clad Big Daddy is replaced by the brownish-burgundy-red-clad Candie.

132. Candie says to Django: "Now bright boy, I will admit you're pretty clever. But if I took this hammer here, and I bashed in your skull with it, you would have the same three dimples—in the same place—as Old Ben."

133. Peary 191; Perry 200. See chapter 8.

134. Warren to General Smithers: "You want to know what your boy did? I pulled my big, black, pecker, out of my pants, and I made him crawl through the snow on all fours over to it. Then I grabbed me a handful of that black hair—and I stuck my big, black johnson—right down his goddamn throat. And it was full of blood, so it was warm. Oh, you bet your sweet ass it was—*warm*. And Chester Charles Smithers—*sucked* on that warm, black, dingus—for *long* as he could!"

135. Conard, "*Kill Bill*" 165. Both Elle and O-Ren appear in music video scenes that include similar fetishizing close-ups of their feet [*Vol. 1* 20:10, 67:36]. Nama goes so far as to describe O-Ren as "sexually subservient" (74).

136. Jungle Julia is even associated with Native Americans via the post of *Soldier Blue* [2:45].

137. Nama 87.

138. Nama 87.

139. Nama 88.

140. Lavin 118.

141. Nama 80–81.

142. Nama counters Armond White's critique of Vernita's death as mere "pop violence"; for him, Vernita is humanized through the gaze of her daughter and the close-up of her face, making it a "solemn and morbid" moment (77–78).

143. Washton Long, Baigell, and Heyd 8. Sara Lipton explores at length the history of grotesque representations of Jews in *Dark Mirror*.

144. Kligerman 155.

145. Speck, *Quentin Tarantino's Django Unchained* 9.

146. In *Totality and Infinity*, Emmanuel Levinas argues that the encounter with an other's face is a social and ethical experience that forces the subject to accept the other's reality.

Chapter Three: "That's the Excuse You Guys Use Whenever You Want to Exclude Me from Something": Identity Politics Vol. 2: Gender (and Sexuality)

1. Bernard 7; Peary 90.

2. Roche, *Making and Remaking* 104, 117.

3. Peary 142. It is possible that Tarantino picked up the central tenets of feminist film theory from Clover's book (Mulvey and Williams are summed up on page 8), but unlikely given his interest in film criticism and history.

4. Mulvey 14–26.

5. Clover 43.

6. Mulvey 29–38.

7. Daring, Rogue, Shannon, and Volcano 14.

8. See Place 47–68.

9. Peake 60.

10. Barbara Creed uses Carrie in her discussion of the figure of the "Witch" in *The Monstrous-Feminine* (73–83).

11. I like to think that the anonymous female character is a prostitute enjoying the social disruption produced by the black man in whom she sees her own oppression partly mirrored.

12. Conard, "Kill Bill" 165.

13. Anderson, "Mindful Violence"; Ortoli, *Musée* 355.
14. McGee 240.
15. Mabuse in Lang's 1933 *The Testament of Dr. Mabuse* is Michel Chion's prime example of the "acousmatic being [*acousmêtre*]" or bodiless voice (*La Voix* 45).
16. *Death Proof* further qualifies the idea that "male" film genres are for male audiences by having Marcy sport a T-shirt with the title of Sam Peckinpah's 1972 *Junior Bonner* written in Spanish (*L'ultimo Buscadero*) [9:37].
17. Clover 7.
18. Creed 124.
19. Clover 35.
20. Clover 18.
21. I use "hangout" rather than "teen flick" because the emphasis is on the protagonists hanging out with "[their] girls" [13:54].
22. In the DVD extra "Reservoir Girls."
23. No doubt Tarantino also had in mind another one of his favorite films, Richard Linklater's Austin-based *Dazed and Confused* (1993).
24. Clover 32.
25. Clover 151.
26. See page 15 of Quentin Tarantino's *Death Proof: A Screenplay* (New York: Weinstein Books, 2007).
27. Clover 49. Erich Kuersten (2008) says the former belong to a "college-like world," the latter to the "working world."
28. Brintnall 73.
29. This opposition is reinforced by the casting of two generations of actors, Lawrence Tierney and Harvey Keitel, which taps into their star images: Tierney the monolythic 1940s tough guy, Keitel the hysterical 1970s male.
30. Ortoli, *Musée* 166, my translation.
31. Bertelsen 22.
32. Ortoli compares the introduction of Marsellus to that of Don Corleone in *The Godfather* (Francis Ford Coppola, 1972) (*Musée* 163).
33. Both Todd F. Davis and Paul H. Schmidt describe Butch's turn away from violence and Jules's conversion as redemptions (Schmidt 45–46), Jules's associated with his "re-reading the text of his life" (Davis 65). Ortoli concludes that "it is because Butch has the courage to transgress the relative rules of safety in order to obey the rules of an absolute, whereas the killer [Vincent] will remain to the end a zealous instrument of the established power, that the first survives and the second dies" (*Musée* 167, my translation).
34. Ortoli explains that Butch must undergo an experience—escaping a putrid closed place—similar to that of his forefathers in Vietnam and Europe (*Musée* 85).
35. Kinder 84.
36. This impression is reinforced by the subsequent extreme close-ups of his finger pressing the remote and Ordell's muting the volume [4:41, 4:54].
37. Seen in this light, the backshot of Ordell, which comes later in the movie when he threatens Max over the telephone, reflects the character's own desperate attempt to reassert his power [131:48].

38. The extreme close-up of his mouth speaking in Beaumont's intercom [15:39] links him to Jackie speaking in his own intercom in close-up [91:34], as well as to Mia Wallace speaking into the microphone in extreme close-up [31:07].

39. Conard, "*Kill Bill*" 173.

40. See Freud's famous article "A Child Is Being Beaten" (1919).

41. Humphries, *American Horror* 159–60.

42. Hutchings 98.

43. I arrive at the opposite conclusion of Maxime Cervulle (2009), who considers that the second group's lack of solidarity implies that the film itself endorses post-feminism instead of calling it into question.

44. Landa's compliment to LaPadite confirms the association between milk and family: "Monsieur, à votre famille et à vos vaches, je dis bravo."

45. A betrayal that was foreshadowed in his failing to capture Shosanna in Chapter One.

46. Tarantino explains that Landa is outraged at Bridget's betrayal (Peary 181).

47. Raine says he might get "chewed out" for having executed Herman [147:42].

48. Candie is first presented as a voice, then in a very long backshot before he faces the camera. The shot then effects a quick zoom-in to an extreme close-up [63:37].

49. This is even the case of Doctor Schultz in *Django Unchained*, the gentle patriarch who, as a German bounty hunter, brings together the Euro-Western and the mythical story of Siegfried.

50. In *Django Unchained*, the female characters (Sheba, Lara Lee Candie-Fitzwilly, Cora, Broomhilda von Shaft, and the countless black slaves) are all confined to the domestic sphere and subjected to the white patriarchs (Big Daddy, Calvin Candie), the black characters more forcefully so.

51. Although the final images of Broomhilda promise a more egalitarian relationship between the two lovers, since she pulls out a rifle [155:14], and has been portrayed as a strong woman who repeatedly attempts to escape Candieland [88:03].

52. Butch, the gentle lover who gives Fabienne "oral pleasure," is in this respect an exception [76:30].

53. Ortoli, *Musée* 238.

54. Vincent to Mia: "Come on, girl, we're getting out of here."

55. Ray Nicolet exclusively uses the word "woman," while Louis follows his friend's example by calling Melanie a "bitch."

56. Ordell to Louis: "Go in there, grab that bitch by the hair, drag her fuckin' ass outta there!" [97:24].

57. Talking to Louis, Ordell later mourns his "little blonde-haired surfer girl" [136:47].

58. Ordell to Louis: "You know, she ain't pretty as she used to, and she bitch a whole lot more than she used to."

59. He uses "girl" again when he tries to behave casually at their final meeting [142:56].

60. Ruth says to the patrons at Minnie's: "When that sun comes out, I'm takin' this woman into Red Rock to hang." Significantly, Oswaldo Mobray, the phony executioner, always refers to Daisy as a "woman" [38:55, 41:28].

61. Bill tells Elle: "You all beat the hell out of that woman, but you didn't kill her" [*Vol. 1* 22:35]. Budd tells Bill: "That woman—deserves her revenge . . ." [*Vol. 1* 98:17; *Vol. 2* 16:49].

62. Bill to Beatrix: "But every once in a while, you can be a real cunt" [*Vol. 2* 114:48].

63. Conard, "*Kill Bill*" 165.

64. The Bride to her friends: "I'm not feeling very well, and this bitch is starting to piss me off."

65. This, of course, is the case in British English, where the word "cunt" is also used to refer to men.

66. In the screenplay, Mike even calls Julia "my fair lady" and kisses her hand (Tarantino 58).

67. In the second part of the film, Jasper's greeting them with "What you horny gals want?" and then "Right up here, ladies" [79:24] foreshadows Mike's attitude in the car chase scene.

68. The female characters in *Death Proof* use the word "woman" once, "lady" twice, and "girl" fifteen times (ten times in the first half of movie, probably because of the age difference).

69. Both definitions from urbandictionary.com.

70. In the DVD extra "The Guys of *Death Proof*," Roth kids that "[t]he girls just castrate us and neuter us at every turn, and we're essentially their bitches."

71. The Nazi characters (Goebbels, Landa, and Zoller) always use the French "Mademoiselle" and its German equivalent "Fräulein"—the equivalents of "Miss"—when addressing Shosanna and Bridget von Hammersmark. Not only do these words serve to emphasize the female characters' subordinate position, like the word "girl" in *Jackie Brown*, but the characters' verbal politeness conceals their potential for violence. This is established as soon as the opening scene when Landa compliments Perrier LaPadite for his daughters' beauty before having the Dreyfus family slaughtered, and is reiterated first when Major Hellstrom picks up Shosanna and demands she "get her *ass* in the car" (in German) [47:27], and later when Landa asks Bridget if he can "have a word with [her] in private" (in German) before strangling her [117:50]. The character of Esteban Vihaio in *Kill Bill Vol. 2* also conceals his mistreatment of women under a suave demeanor, the word "young lady" being, for him, synonymous with prostitute [80:21]. Such refined language serves to enhance, by contrast, the acts of violence. It suggests that masculinity is very often constructed through subjection of the female and the feminine, regardless of social, national, and racial background, and in practice if not in discourse.

72. Black characters like Ordell in *Jackie Brown*, Vernita in *Kill Bill Vol. 1*, and Kim in *Death Proof* use the b-word more often than the other protagonists.

73. Von Dassanowsky, "Dr. 'King' Schultz" 29.

74. By comparison, Stephen and Candie always position her as subservient, Stephen using the b-word and "your woman" when negotiating with Django [135:00], and Calvin describing her as "this lovely lady" when selling her [121:42].

75. Ortoli, *Musée* 277.

76. Mason 153.

77. Their costumes contrast with Holdaway's clothes.

78. Nama has demonstrated that "blackness signifies cool" in Tarantino's films (130), and consequently that "white cool" is modeled on "black cool."

79. See Susan Jeffords's *Hard Bodies*.

80. And Vincent will die in his suit [87:57]. For Ortoli, the reference to *The Killers* (1946) is even more evident in *Pulp Fiction* because of Jules and Vincent's conversing as they head toward their job (*Musée* 296).

81. Something similar occurs in *Inglourious Basterds*, with Raine, Donowitz, and Ulmer trading their men-on-a-mission outfits for classy suits they don as uneasily as they play their parts as Italians [111:08].

82. Ortoli, *Musée* 217, my translation.

83. Mia's transformation from a desirable to an abject body is announced by Jody's talking about piercings and genitals in close-up, the house in which Mia will be revived.

84. Nama 116.

85. "Masha and the bitches" correspond to Creed's figure of the *vagina dentata* that castrates through incorporation (105–21).

86. Miklitsch 291.

87. This is an instance where race and gender intersect: the stereotypical female and black performers (Mulvey 19; Bogle 118–21).

88. By contrast, her feet, which are all Jackie can see under the changing room panel, have little effect on the heroine when they trade bags [105:43].

89. The young black woman (Sheronda) is almost entirely desexualized in spite of the fact that Ordell hints that he has turned her into his sex slave.

90. The same can be said of Django in relation to his empowerment as a subject who endured the bodily and psychic trauma of slavery. He goes from being unclothed [1:00], to wearing a slaver's coat [10:11], a valet's outfit—one slave asks him: "You mean you wanna dress like that?" [32:08]—to a bounty hunter's getup [50:40], until he is forced to undergo the same transformation, this time on his own, from naked slave [137:30] to clothed slave [142:55] to avenger wearing Calvin Candie's clothes [156:37].

91. Landa compares Von Hammermask to an action movie heroine when he asks if her broken ankle is "[a] byproduct of kicking ass in the German cinema" [111:25].

92. Willis, "'Fire!'" 178.

93. Dima, "Tarantino's *Inglourious Basterds*"; Suleiman 83.

94. Nama 77–78.

95. Conard, "*Kill Bill*" 167.

96. Clover 35.

97. Conard, "*Kill Bill*" 169.

98. Conard, "*Kill Bill*" 170.

99. Conard, "*Kill Bill*" 172.

100. Conard, "*Kill Bill*" 174. See also Novoa 94.

101. Schlipphacke 124.

102. Like Mulvey's stars, Julia's hair contributes to her fetishization, Mike marveling: "Look at that hair" [29:52].

103. Humphries, *American Horror* 142–44.

104. In this scene, Tarantino, who describes himself as a foot fetishist (Bernard 217), is also making fun of himself.

105. Omar can also be seen lurking in the background when, after returning with her friends, Julia receives a text message from Christian Simonson [18:15].

106. Creed describes "the image of woman's cut and bleeding body" as a "symbolic form of castration" (125).

107. Linda Williams argues that the female character, like the monster, is "constituted as an exhibitionist-object by the desiring look of the male. There is not that much difference between an object of desire and an object of horror as far as the male look is concerned" (20–21).

108. Abernathy's transformation is typical of "revenge or self-defense stories" that are "in some measure *about* that transformation" (Clover 123).

109. Kaja Silverman interpreted the concept from a psychoanalytic perspective whereby "suture"—for instance, through the shot/reverse-shot technique—aims at masking "symbolic castration" and is thus "coded as male" (10–13).

110. Nigel M. Smith, "Jennifer Jason Leigh: 'Until Tarantino, I had forgotten who I was as an actress,'" *The Guardian* (January 8, 2016). <https://www.theguardian.com/film/2016/jan/08/jennifer-jason-leigh-interview-the-hateful-eight-quentin-tarantino>. Accessed on May 13, 2017.

111. This is also the case of Carrie (Williams, *Hearths* 240).

112. Roche, "Le Noir chez David Cronenberg" 45.

113. Peary 61.

114. The death of the two female protagonists in *Inglourious Basterds* is framed in an awareness of contemporary debates on rape culture. By strangling Bridget, Landa, the gentleman, perverts the Cinderella narrative [119:10–120:54] and confirms he is a monster like Mike, the foot fetishist from Tarantino's previous film. Zoller's bursting in after Shosanna has said "no" conjures up rape situations whereby "no" is understood as "yes" [138:55]. In an earlier scene, a female German soldier swears to protect a French civilian named Mathilde from the male soldiers [75:44].

115. Roche, *Making and Remaking* 101–18.

116. Ortoli, *Musée* 139, my translation.

117. Ortoli, *Musée* 114, my translation.

118. Conard, "*Kill Bill*" 167.

Chapter Four: "Revenge Is Never a Straight Line": A Neoformalist Approach Vol. 1: Narrative Structures and Paradigms

1. See the full review <http://www.telegraph.co.uk/culture/film/filmreviews/11311308/Reservoir-Dogs-review-raw-and-exciting.html#disqus_thread>. Bruce Williamson (*Playboy*) also commented on the structure; see <http://www.movie-film-review.com/devfilm.asp?rtype=1&id=9189>. Accessed on January 7, 2016.

2. Levy 144, 244.

3. Thompson and Bordwell 673.

4. Bordwell, *Narration* 49–50.

5. Tarantino has from the start asserted the novelistic structures of his films (Peary 23, 38, 75, 178). See also Ortoli 101. Bordwell on his blog concludes that Tarantino's films and the earlier examples of Hollywood films of the 1940s that were structured according to "blocks" and "chapters" are indebted both to the mystery and the "mild modernist" novel.

6. Tarantino: "I have said many times that there are two different worlds that my movies take place in [...] One of them is the 'Quentin Universe' of *Pulp Fiction* and *Jackie Brown*—it's

heightened but more or less realistic. The other is the Movie World. When characters in the Quentin Universe go to the movies, the stuff they see takes place in the Movie World. They act as a window into that world. *Kill Bill* is the first film I've made that takes place in the Movie World. This is me imagining what would happen if that world really existed, and I could take a film crew in there and make a Quentin Tarantino movie about those characters" (Charyn 168–69).

   7. Ortoli, *Musée* 104.
   8. Telotte 49.
   9. Ortoli also finds the "key" to *Pulp Fiction*'s structure in the chapter titles (*Musée* 157).
   10. Bertelsen 22.
   11. Ortoli even argues that the ampersand in the first title suggests that the link between the two characters is problematic, and that the dance scene and the shot of Mia and Vincent together when they go back home are the only moments where their parallel trajectories momentarily converge (*Musée* 162–64).
   12. Ortoli, *Musée* 102, 132.
   13. Conard, "*Kill Bill*: Tarantino's Oedipal Play" 170.
   14. Jenkins 27.
   15. Thompson, *Storytelling in the New Hollywood* 27–35; Bordwell, *The Way* 27, 29, 38.
   16. As it stands, the first act corresponds to chapters 1–3, the second to chapters 4–16, the third to chapters 17–22, the fourth to chapters 23–26, and the prologue to chapter 27.
   17. Quart 48–50.
   18. Though I agree with Kevin Howley that *Pulp Fiction* follows the classical paradigm, forcing it on the whole film—with the second scene as the "setup," "Vincent Vega & Marsellus Wallace's Wife" as the "complicating action," "The Gold Watch" as the "development," and "The Bonnie Situation" as the "climax"—is untenable.
   19. Frayling 236. In his review, Geoffrey O'Brien noted the "picaresque" quality of *Django Unchained*'s narrative (31).
   20. Each act is marked by a contract between two of the three main characters. Act 1: presentation of Angel Eyes, Tuco, and Blondie. Act 2: Tuco's revenge makes way to a new contract with Blondie who has found out the name of the grave. Act 3: they are captured, tortured in a concentration camp, and Angel Eyes makes a deal with Blondie; Act 4: Tuco and Blondie join forces again and take part in a battle for a bridge; Act 5: the showdown.
   21. It is especially overt in the bridge battle scene where the commanding officer laments the absurdity of war.
   22. Gordon 288.
   23. Lisa Coulthard attributes this "series of acts of violence" to the "revenge structure" ("Killing Bill" 167), while Maud Lavin describes the Bride as "comic-booky" and "videogamish" (108).
   24. See Charles Shiro Inouye's "Promoting Virtue and Punishing Vice: Tarantino's *Kill Bill* and the Return of Bakumatsu Aesthetics."
   25. The Japanese film actually has a more classical four-act structure, with a prologue, a backstory (the murder and rape of her parents), three confrontations, and an epilogue.
   26. Conard points out that *Vol. 1* is a frenetic martial arts movie, *Vol. 2* a slow Western ("*Kill Bill*" 163).

27. <http://www.davidbordwell.net/blog/category/directors-tarantino>. Accessed on January 15, 2016.

28. Bordwell, *Narration* 205.

29. Ortoli, *Musée* 261.

30. Bordwell, *Narration* 206.

31. In the DVD extra "Les interviews du gang : Quentin Tarantino (Mr. Brown)" of *Reservoir Dogs*: "Taking genre characters and genre situations, all right, and giving them a real life spin, have them sound like real people [. . .] and talk about shit other than *the plot*, all right. You know, most of us don't talk about *the plot* in our lives, all right. We talk all around things, and we talk about bullshit, and we talk about things that interest us. Gangsters don't just talk about gangster plot-related stuff" [6:50].

32. See online reviews: http://www.eatmybrains.com/showreview.php?id=315 and http://blogs.indiewire.com/criticwire/quentin-tarantino-death-proof-not-his-worth-movie (accessed on January 4, 2016). Maximilian Le Cain and Allen H. Redmond already felt Bill's Superman riff in *Kill Bill Vol. 2* was useless.

33. Bordwell, *Narration* 206.

34. Botting and Wilson 91, 95–96; Bertelsen 23.

35. Laurent Jullier notes that such a turn of events would have been unimaginable in classical cinema (107).

36. Charyn 40.

37. In the collected volume *Django Unchained: A Continuation of Meta-cinema*, both Brown and Temoney have noted that the film is fairly linear (130, 162).

38. Dawson 70.

39. Turim 2.

40. Genette, *Figures III* 90–95.

41. The sequence featuring Beatrix in a classroom is not a flashback but a fantasy, mediated by Elle's words [*KB2* 71:14–71:20].

42. Garner 198.

43. The same can be said of the use of the split screen in the scene where Max realizes Jackie has taken his gun, significantly located at the turning point of the movie when Jackie takes over Ordell's control of the narrative [50:12–50:43].

44. Ortoli, *Musée* 127, my translation.

45. The flashback of Shosanna and Marcel's preparations that opens the following chapter is less problematic because, though it fulfills a narrative function by providing the viewer information, it may quite simply represent Shosanna's memories [107:19–108:44].

46. Ortoli, *Musée* 459–60, 470.

47. Bordwell chooses to see this chapter as the present and the rest of the film as a flashback. This implies considering Chapters Six, Seven, Eight, Nine, and the beginning of the last chapter as flashbacks as well.

48. Maximilian Le Cain (2004) notes that "Tarantino has the chance of bringing *Kill Bill*'s structure full circle by proposing an alternative to the shattered normality-image of Vernita's home."

49. Luke Cuddy and Michael Bruce suggest that *Kill Bill*'s nonlinear structure might foreground a Buddhist sense of interconnectedness (195).

50. To my knowledge, Eve Bertelsen is the only other scholar to describe *Pulp Fiction* as an anthology film (13).

51. Howley describes Marsellus as "a motivating force that lends unity to *Pulp Fiction*'s disjointed narrative." Ortoli also insists on the character's being the central figure of power (*Musée* 43), whose rules Vincent subjects himself to (163), Butch disobeys (167), and Jules respects while realizing, like Butch, that they are limited by something higher, be it chance or the divine (169).

52. Schmidt 46.

53. Brooker 147.

54. Auxier 130.

55. Auxier 134.

56. http://inglouriousbasterds.wikia.com/wiki/Fonts_used. Accessed on September 12, 2017.

57. Bordwell, *Narration* 219.

58. The fact that the closure provided by each story is not of the scale anticipated by each premise, as Bertelsen has noted (23), can also be seen as characteristic of the art-cinema treatment of classical narrative.

59. Thompson and Bordwell 478.

60. Thompson and Bordwell 690.

Chapter Five: "Everything's the Same Except for One Change": A Neoformalist Approach Vol. 2: Narration and Style

1. Roche, "French Fries" 297.
2. Tarantino has admitted to liking long takes (Peary 41).
3. Bordwell, *The Way* 120–21.
4. Bordwell, *The Way* 184.
5. The lower ASL is permitted by the abundant use of slow motion in this scene.
6. See my 2014 study of the fight scenes in *Kill Bill*.
7. Thompson and Bordwell 323; Bordwell, *The Way* 122.
8. Bordwell, *Narration* 9–12.
9. Bordwell, *Narration* 184.
10. I am not including the frontal close-up of Major Warren in *The Hateful Eight* because it is justified by the reverse shot of General Smithers, but it, too, momentarily breaks the wall (fig. 70.2) [93:06].
11. A similar descending tracking shot occurs reveals the presence of Jody hiding under the floor in *The Hateful Eight* [118:19–118:28].
12. Tarantino calls these "forced perspectives" (Peary 66).
13. The camera movement also plays a structural role, the track-out reversing the opening track-in, which constructed the church as a significant microcosm [13:51–14:45].
14. The pan right from Fabienne and Butch's messy hotel bed has a similar effect in *Pulp Fiction* [80:22].
15. Bordwell, *Narration* 232.
16. Ortoli, *Musée* 47.

17. Ortoli, *Musée* 41.

18. Ortoli, *Musée* 45, my translation.

19. Ortoli, *Musée* 483–84; Semenza 77.

20. Tarantino has said that the scene was divided into three parts, all shot in different styles (Peary 15, 66).

21. This is also true of the two-shot of Mia and Vincent when they arrive at Jack Rabbit Slim's [34:14].

22. Significantly, it is also used when Ray Nicolette accepts Jackie's terms in Mark Dargus's office [61:12].

23. The split screen showing six members of the Crazy 88 during the end credits reenacts the House of Leaves scene, with the bloody face of the female fighter on the right compromising the cool confidence of the male icons [*Vol. 2* 124:46].

24. Ortoli, *Musée* 53.

25. Similar shots occur in the first two chapters of *The Hateful Eight*, when Major Warren [7:41] and later Sheriff Mannix [23:04] are framed by the doors and windows of the stagecoach, appropriately in the scenes that most recall another John Ford film, *Stagecoach* (1939). And Warren, Mannix, Bob, and O. B. are similarly framed by the barn doors at the beginning of Chapter Three [44:09].

26. McGee 237.

27. McGee 238.

28. Schlipphacke 118.

29. Brown, "Counterfactuals" 256.

30. Roche, "Choreographing Genre."

31. Ornella 106.

32. Brown, "Value and Violence" 172.

33. I have in mind Ed Tan's discussion of the risk of losing viewer interest because of habituation (111).

34. I did hesitate to include the extreme high-angle tracking shots mentioned in the first subpart.

35. Bordwell, *Narration* 211.

36. Bordwell, *Narration* 213.

37. Pastoureau 141.

38. Bill's brown environment contrasts with the Bride's.

39. Von Dassanowsky, "Dr. 'King' Schultz" 24. Ozierski concludes that the costume "reflects not only Django's foray into self-expression through sartorial taste, but also the wealth of his master, who is his employer, not owner" (43).

40. In an interview with Deadline.com (2016), DP Robert Richardson explained that, with 70mm Kodachrome, "the blacks are remarkable in their density without forcing an inherent contrast into the digital intermediate." <http://deadline.com/2016/02/oscars-robert-richardson-the-hateful-eight-live-by-night-cinematography-interview-1201701206>. Accessed on May 4, 2017.

41. Tarantino admits to an appreciation for "[p]rimary colors" and a dislike for "flat colors" (Peary 58).

42. Cavell 95.

43. Following Henri Bergson, Gilles Deleuze posits that "the only subjectivity is time, non-chronological time grasped in its foundation" (80).

44. Tarantino describes the zoom as "analytical" (Peary 67).

45. Another editing device used in *Kill Bill* is intercutting. It emphasizes a character's relative command over the narration: in Chapter Two, Bill's power over life and death when he tells Elle to abort the mission [23:00–24:41], and in Chapters Five and Eight, the Bride coming for her unsuspecting foes [64:35–66:18]. Again, it points to the Bride's replacing Bill as prime orchestrator.

46. This is confirmed by the three instances in *Vol. 2*: to depict the Bride walking across the desert to Budd's [64:25–65:10], to link the end of the Esteban Vihaio scene and return to the Bride on her way to kill Bill [87:24], and to introduce the hotel room flashback [113:55].

47. Bill's attempt to do so should, no doubt, remind the viewer that he destroyed the Bride's attempt at creating a family, as the family portraits of the Bride, Tommy, and their friends in Chapter Six suggest [2:55–4:58].

48. Roche, *Making and Remaking* 200.

49. Neupert 161.

50. Kligerman 154.

51. Nama 108–9.

52. Tarantino describes these scenes as the film's *Heart of Darkness* moment (Peary 190).

53. Yip 156.

54. Peckinpah himself got the idea from *Seven Samurai* and *Bonnie and Clyde* (Arthur Penn, 1967) (Prince 27).

55. This is also the case at the beginning of the rape scene in *Pulp Fiction* [102:08].

56. See Tasha Robinson's article "Does *The Hateful Eight*'s 70mm Roadshow Really Impact the Future of Film?" *The Verge* (December 8, 2015). <https://www.theverge.com/2015/12/8/9867742/the-hateful-eight-70mm-ultra-panavision-quentin-tarantino>. Accessed on May 5, 2017.

Chapter Six: "Lookin' Back on the Track, Gonna Do It My Way": The Use of Preexisting Music

1. According to Michel Chion, the soundtrack of *Apocalypse Now* (Coppola, 1979) was the first to include sound bites from the film (*Musique* 250).

2. Peary 158.

3. Garner 191.

4. Garner 198.

5. Garner 198–99.

6. Garner 189.

7. Garner 201.

8. Chion, *Audio-vision* 73.

9. Bernard 228.

10. Frayling 235.

11. This was the case during the shooting of the plantation scenes in *Django Unchained*. http://www.vanityfair.com/online/oscars/2012/07/jamie-foxx-django-unchained-quentin-tarantino. Accessed on April 27, 2017.

12. Frayling 235; Chion, *Musique* 355.
13. Peary 168.
14. Roche, "Irony in *The Sweet Hereafter*" 240.
15. The song is thus more than just "a musical emanation of the world" (Garner 193); it is also an ironic commentary on the men who are depicted as "losers" (Garner 195–96), as well as on the situation.
16. Garner 200.
17. Ortoli, *Musée* 167, 189.
18. Roche, "Quentin Tarantino's *Death Proof* (2007)" 338–40.
19. Thompson, *Music in the Social* 324, 977, 1114.
20. Chion, *Audio-vision* 12.
21. Chion, *Audio-vision* 35–36.
22. Mera describes "Un amico" as generating "tenderness" and suggesting "regret," thus making for a very "ambiguous" scene (452).
23. The late Sally Menke, Tarantino's editor from *Reservoir Dogs* to *Inglourious Basterds*, described the place of music in production and post-production in a 2009 interview: "Music is one of his obsessions, so I've cut a lot of great scenes to music. He's very specific and will play music on set all day to get everyone in the mood. I think he goes to sleep with his iPod on when we're filming, because the music becomes the rhythm of his directing. Oddly, I don't cut to music. I just make the scene work emotionally and dramatically, and then Quentin will come in and lay the track over it and we'll tweak it to the beats." <http://www.theguardian.com/film/2009/dec/06/sally-menke-quentin-tarantino-editing>. Accessed on April 26, 2017.
24. Miklitsch 292.
25. Ortoli, *Musée* 139.
26. Garner 194.
27. Ortoli, *Musée* 277.
28. Chion, *Musique* 66, my translation.
29. Coulthard, "Inglourious Music" 60.
30. Coulthard, "Inglourious Music" 67.
31. Ortoli, *Musée* 361.
32. Garner explains that "Misirlou" is actually a Greek standard (197).
33. Garner 190. See also Mera 439–40.
34. "Bath Attack" (Charles Bernstein) from *The Entity* (1982) [53:56–54:20].
35. Miklitsch 294.
36. Ortoli, *Musée* 287.
37. Roche, "Quentin Tarantino's *Death Proof*" 348.
38. Tony Williams argues that Boorman's sequel is a radically progressive film that attacks patriarchy (123–28).
39. Ortoli, *Musée* 449.
40. The reintroduction of slavery and extensive persecution of Native Americans and Latinos followed the emancipation of Texas from Mexico.
41. Fisher 88.
42. Ortoli, *Musée* 328.
43. The score thus taps into Nazism's appropriation of Beethoven (Mera 450).

314   Notes

44. "Strawberry Letter #23," prominently featured in *Jackie Brown*, also occurs in *Pulp Fiction* when Jules and Vincent walk by a door in Brett's apartment building [11:22–11:33]. However, the song is so faint in *Pulp Fiction* that it is doubtful any viewer would make the connection between two murder scenes featuring characters played by Jackson.

45. Von Dassanowsky, "Dr. 'King' Schultz" 31–32.

46. Kassabian 3.

47. Eco 71.

48. See https://sunglassesandcinema.quora.com/Kill-Bill-Vol-1. Accessed on April 26, 2017.

49. See http://www.mtv.com/news/1699409/django-unchained-music. Accessed on May 2, 2017.

50. Carr, "'To Be Actually Honest'" 55.

51. Mera argues convincingly that Tarantino's use of music in *Inglourious Basterds* is typical of music mashup culture, a practice that values not just playfulness but also the "search for resonant associations between tracks" (440).

52. See <http://www.wired.com/2015/12/ennio-morricone-hateful-eight-soundtrack>. Accessed on April 26, 2017.

53. Only Bob's rendition of "Silent Night" [85:37–89:45] and Daisy's of "Jim Jones at Botany Bay" [98:32–102:10] are performances.

Chapter Seven: "Come On, Let's Get into Character": Acting and Theatricality

1. Tarantino says he wanted to bring out the Richard III in Samuel Jackson (Peary 56) and describes Hans Landa's actions as "pure theatre" (Peary 181).

2. Peary 10, 23 64.

3. Morgan 21, 27.

4. Kligerman 139; Matuska 216.

5. Morgan 26.

6. Peary 104–5.

7. Loiselle and Maron 5.

8. Naremore describes frontality as "a presentational form" (241).

9. Bissonnette 140.

10. Naremore 239, 241, 243.

11. Naremore 43.

12. Corrigan 64.

13. André Loiselle and Jeremy Maron's definition—"cinematic theatricality refers to film representations that call attention to their own artifice" (5)—sounds like a definition of reflexivity.

14. I noticed while on a tour of the Evergreen plantation that the house does not have a dirt track leading to its gate, so the circle of dirt at the foot of the house was designed specifically for the movie.

15. Peary 51, 133; Morgan 22, 26.

16. Nigel M. Smith, "Jennifer Jason Leigh: 'Until Tarantino, I had forgotten who I was as an actress.'" theguardian.com, January 8, 2016. Accessed on March 22, 2017.

17. Dyer 60.

18. Dyer 63.

19. While promoting *The Piano* (1993), not only did Campion state that she didn't think of Keitel "as macho at all," but Holly Hunter said of him that "he brings a vulnerability to almost every character that he does." In Karen Schoemer, "Harvey Keitel Tries a Little Tenderness," *New York Times*, November 7, 1993. <http://www.nytimes.com/1993/11/07/movies/harvey-keitel-tries-a-little-tenderness.html?pagewanted=all>. Accessed on April 7, 2017.

20. Chumo II notes that Travolta approaches the dance floor with "caution" (19), and that Willis killing Travolta is the younger star killing the older star (21).

21. Peary 50.

22. Ortoli, *Musée* 236.

23. Peary 29.

24. Ortoli, *Musée* 217, 247, 252, 271.

25. Tierney 612; Roche, "Choreographing Genre."

26. Ortoli, *Musée* 285.

27. Chumo II 18.

28. Tarantino described Travolta as "the best-forgotten secret" in the industry (Peary 51).

29. The notable exception, a drama entitled *On the Edge* (Rob Nilsson, 1986), was a box-office flop.

30. Peary 86.

31. Peary 87. Chumo II sees Keitel as playing the part of the "producer" in this scene (24).

32. Peary 156.

33. Roche, "Quentin Tarantino's *Death Proof*" 352.

34. Goldsmith 168.

35. Roth is also the lead actor of the anthology film *Four Rooms*.

36. Parks also appears in *From Dusk Till Dawn*.

37. See fan theories, https://www.reddit.com/r/FanTheories/comments/15mbsy/pulp_fictions_fox_force_five_is_a_reference_to>. Accessed on March 27, 2017.

38. Keitel studied under Stella Adler and Lee Strasberg.

39. Roth received no formal training, refuses to do auditions, and is skeptical about training and techniques. See Dina Gachman, "Tim Roth to Share Life Lessons in Acting Today." <http://www.tim-roth.com/index.php?id=bruinfeb96>. Accessed on September 19, 2017. See also Jay Dixit, "Pulp Nonfiction: Tim Roth on Lying, Acting, and Not Being a 'Pretty Boy.'" <https://www.psychologytoday.com/blog/brainstorm/200912/pulp-nonfiction>. Accessed on December 3, 2009.

40. In the 1960s, Kurt Russell started acting in TV shows while still a teenager.

41. Viviani 31.

42. Naremore says that "short interjections" and keeping "busy" are typical of naturalistic acting (45).

43. Naremore studies such "codified gestures" indebted to the work of François Delsarte (52–67). Viviani brilliantly analyzes the transformation of the "eloquent gesture," one that aims at replacing speech in order to express a conscious or unconscious mental state (49), into a quasi-baroque ornament in contemporary acting (65).

44. Peary 162.

45. <http://english.stackexchange.com/questions/105682/in-which-accent-does-lieutenant-aldo-raine-brad-pitt-speak>. Accessed on April 7, 2017.

46. Naremore concludes that "despite the fact that film acting has usually been explained in roughly Stanislavksian terms, the players in classic Hollywood frequently relied upon an untutored application of principles Delsarte and Aubert tried to systematize" (63); "actors continue to practice the rhetoric of conventionalized expression; most of them simply explain their craft in a different way, exchanging new gestures for old" (64). Viviani's book insightfully demonstrates that, if the Method has become the norm of acting in film, many contemporary actors (Jack Nicholson and Al Pacino, to name two) seek to integrate Delsartian influences in their performances (141).

47. Peary 189.

48. Ortoli, *Musée* 32, 139. Jeremy Carr (2016) notes the Hawksian theme in *The Hateful Eight* where one's identity is "based on professional repute."

49. McRoy 228.

50. Bence Nanay and Ian Schnee show how, unlike Jules, Vincent never frees himself from "the hyper-cool and might-makes-right gangster values of the underworld" (184), while, for Rachel Robison, the DiVAS have a "warped view of Virtue Ethics" (84).

51. Roche, "Tarantino's Round Flat Characters" 411–31.

52. *Django Unchained* depicts a similar transformation, this time through a mostly linear narrative, with Schultz acting as Django's Holdaway by explaining that the bounty hunter profession requires "putting on an act" [26:53] and concocting their plan to get into Candieland [60:03–62:19], although the flashback proves that, as a slave, Django had already developed a talent for improvisation, a trait encapsulated in John Brittle's sadistic comment: "I like the way you beg, boy" [34:12].

53. Cuddy and Bruce 201.

54. Ortoli, *Musée* 80, my translation.

55. Burns 8.

56. Naremore 72.

57. Naremore 72.

58. Roche, "Tarantino's Round Flat Characters" 411–31.

Chapter Eight: "He's Just Not Used to Seein' a Man Ripped Apart by Dogs Is All": Violence and Spectacle

1. Weber 56–57.

2. In the collected volume on *Django Unchained* edited by Oliver C. Speck, both Robert von Dassanowsky and Dana Weber underline how "overwhelmed" Schultz is by the barbarity he witnesses (29, 56).

3. Mendehlson 38.

4. Peary 156.

5. Hendrik Hertzberg, "Djangled Nerves," *New Yorker* (March 7, 2013). <http://www.newyorker.com/news/hendrik-hertzberg/djangled-nerves>. Accessed on April 10, 2017.

6. Peary 25.

7. Peary 20.

8. Peary 43.
9. Peary 43. See also Peary 153.
10. Peary 179.
11. Peary 189.
12. Jullier 137–38.
13. Jardine 2004; Temoney 133.
14. Roche, "Choreographing Genre."
15. Nama 107.
16. Suleiman 77.
17. Kinder 68.
18. Samuel P. Perry also notices the contrast between fantastic and realistic violence in *Django Unchained*, and rightly concludes that "[b]lack people experience real harm and white people experience unrealistic harm" and "suffer little" (200), but comes to a different conclusion (for some reason, he sees this as proof of the film's "white supremacist agenda") than does Nama, who concludes that the film is "deadly serious" when it comes to representing the horrors of slavery (110).
19. Opposing suggestion to monstration is a recurrent concern in horror studies. See Roche, *Making and Remaking* 157, 188.
20. Perry 213; Anderson, Stephenson, and Anderson 228.
21. Beaumont gets shot in the trunk of Ordell's car at night in a very long shot [22:30], Melanie by Louis offscreen [112:17], Louis by Ordell in a backshot in which all we see is the blood splattering on the windshield [125:10], and Ordell in Max's dark office [143:04]; the latter is the only character whose dead face is filmed in a close-up [144:20].
22. Kinder 81.
23. The sympathetic O. B. is actually the exception, but his inclusion foreshadows the entry of the ninth "hateful" one, Jody.
24. It also allows more time for the scene to metafictionally comment on the Bazinian paradox of images astutely noted by Suleiman—"the image captured by the camera remains alive and eternally identical to itself, even after the death of the actual persons who appear in it" (84)—and for us to acknowledge this discourse.
25. Von Dassanowsky, "Dr. 'King' Schultz" 27.
26. Hayes and Rodman 197.
27. Golden 51–52.
28. Auxier 136.
29. Ortoli, *Musée* 251.
30. Ortoli, *Musée* 438.
31. Hayes and Rodman 190.
32. Ornella 234–35.
33. Waldron 154–55.
34. The distinction between "critical catharsis" and "emotional purgation" was made by Roland Barthes in "Brecht and Discourse." See also Carney, *Brecht and Critical Theory* 93.
35. Mohammad 112.
36. Hayes and Rodman 190–91.

37. Dan Jardine (2004) has similarly analyzed the scene as forcing the viewer to experience the policeman's terror.

38. Johnson 31.

39. Tarantino expressed his admiration for John Woo on numerous occasions at the time (Peary 32, 43).

40. Including the frontier hero mythology Samuel P. Perry (2014) claims underpins Tarantino's films from *Kill Bill* on in an unproblematic fashion.

41. Benson-Alliott 23.

42. Roche, "Choreographing Genre."

43. Semenza 66.

44. Clover 168, 232.

Conclusion

1. Schaeffer 34.

2. Ortoli, *Musée* 454–55.

3. Waldron 142–43.

4. McHale, *Cambridge Companion* 37.

5. Deleuze and Guattari 293, my translation.

6. I am reticent to invoke Jean Baudrillard because of his pessimistic view that the repetition of "simulacra" is steeped in loss (Poster 6–7); I would like to insist on the potential of resignification instead.

7. <http://www.moviemaker.com/archives/series/things_learned/jim-jarmusch-5-golden-rules-of-moviemaking>. Accessed on May 8, 2017.

8. Thompson and Bordwell 478.

9. Peary 61, 75.

FILMOGRAPHY AND BIBLIOGRAPHY

The Feature Films of Quentin Tarantino

Reservoir Dogs. With Harvey Keitel (Mr. White / Larry Dimmick), Tim Roth (Mr. Orange / Freddy Newandyke), Michael Madsen (Mr. Blonde / Vic Vega), Chris Penn (Nice Guy Eddie Cabot), Steve Buscemi (Mr. Pink), Lawrence Tierney (Joe Cabot), Edward Bunker (Mr. Blue), Quentin Tarantino (Mr. Brown), Randy Brooks (Holdaway). Production Design: David Wasco. Cinematography: Andrzej Sekula. Editing: Sally Menke. Live Entertainment / Dog Eat Dog Productions Inc., 1992. DVD. Metropolitan Video, 2004.

Pulp Fiction. Based on stories by Quentin Tarantino and Roger Avary. With Samuel L. Jackson (Jules Winnfield), Ving Rhames (Marsellus Wallace), Uma Thurman (Mia Wallace), John Travolta (Vincent Vega), Bruce Willis (Butch Coolidge), Rosanna Arquette (Jody), Peter Greene (Zed), Angela Jones (Esmarelda Villalobos), Harvey Keitel (Wolf), Phil LaMarr (Marvin), Maria de Medeiros (Fabienne), Amanda Plummer (Honey Bunny), Tim Roth (Pumpkin), Eric Stoltz (Lance), Quentin Tarantino (Jimmie Dimmick), Christopher Walken (Captain Koons), Frank Whaley (Brett), Duane Whitaker (Maynard). Production Design: David Wasco. Cinematography: Andrzej Sekula. Editing: Sally Menke. Miramax / A Band Apart / Jersey Films, 1994. DVD. Wild Side Vidéo, 2005.

Jackie Brown. Based on Elmore Leonard's novel *Rum Punch*. With Pam Grier (Jackie Brown), Samuel L. Jackson (Ordell Robbie), Robert Forster (Max Cherry), Bridget Fonda (Melanie Ralston), Michael Keaton (Ray Nicolette), Robert De Niro (Louis Gara), Michael Bowen (Mark Dargus), Chris Tucker (Beaumont Livingston). Production Design: David Wasco. Cinematography: Guillermo Navarro. Editing: Sally Menke. Miramax / A Band Apart / Lawrence Bender Productions / Mighty Mighty Afrodite Productions, 1997. DVD. TF1 Vidéo, 2004.

Kill Bill Vol. 1. With Uma Thurman (the Bride / Beatrix Kiddo), Lucy Liu (O-Ren Ishii), Vivica A. Fox (Vernita Green), Michael Bowen (Buck), Shin'ichi Chiba (Hattori Hanzo), Julie Dreyfus (Sofie Fatale), Daryl Hannah (Elle Driver), Chiaki Kuriyama (Gogo), Chia-Hui Liu (Johnny Mo), Michael Parks (Earl McGraw). Production Design: Yohei Taneda and David Wasco.

Cinematography: Robert Richardson. Editing: Sally Menke. Miramax / A Band Apart / Super Cool ManChu, 2003. DVD. TF1 Vidéo, 2004.

Kill Bill Vol. 2. With Uma Thurman (the Bride / Beatrix Kiddo), David Carradine (Bill), Daryl Hannah (Elle Driver), Helen Kim (Karen), Michael Madsen (Budd), Chia-Hui Liu (Pai Mei), Michael Parks (Esteban Vihaio). Production Design: David Wasco. Cinematography: Robert Richardson. Editing: Sally Menke. Miramax / A Band Apart / Super Cool ManChu, 2004. DVD. TF1 Vidéo, 2004.

Death Proof. With Kurt Russell (Stuntman Mike), Vanessa Ferlito (Arlene), Sydney Tamiia Poitier (Jungle Julia), Rose McGowan (Pam), Jordan Ladd (Shanna), Quentin Tarantino (Warren), Marcy Harriell (Marcy), Eli Roth (Dov), Omar Doom (Nate), Monica Staggs (Lanna Frank), Zoë Bell (Zoë Bell), Rosario Dawson (Abernathy), Tracie Thoms (Kim), Mary Elizabeth Winstead (Lee). Production Design: Steve Joyner. Cinematography: Quentin Tarantino. Editing: Sally Menke. Dimension Films / Troublemaker Studios / Rodriguez International Pictures / The Weinstein Company, 2007. DVD. TF1 Vidéo, 2011.

Inglourious Basterds. With Brad Pitt (Lt. Aldo Raine), Mélanie Laurent (Shosanna), Christoph Waltz (Col. Hans Landa), Michael Fassbender (Lt. Archie Hicox), Diane Kruger (Bridget von Hammersmark), Daniel Brühl (Frederick Zoller), August Diehl (Major Hellstrom), Omar Doom (Pfc. Omar Ulmer), Sylvester Groth (Joseph Goebbels), Jacky Ido (Marcel), Denis Ménochet (Perrier LaPadite), B. J. Novak (Pfc. Smithson Utivich), Eli Roth (Sgt. Donny Donowitz), Til Schweiger (Sgt. Hugo Stiglitz). Production Design: David Wasco. Cinematography: Robert Richardson. Editing: Sally Menke. Universal Pictures / The Weinstein Company / A Band Apart / Studio Babelsberg / Visiona Romantica, 2009. DVD. Universal 2010.

Django Unchained. With Jamie Foxx (Django), Christoph Waltz (Dr. King Schultz), Leonardo DiCaprio (Calvin Candie), Kerry Washington (Broomhilda von Shaft), Samuel L. Jackson (Stephen), Walton Goggins (Billy Crash), Don Johnson (Big Daddy), Dennis Christopher (Leonide Moguy). Production Design: J. Michael Riva. Cinematography: Robert Richardson. Editing: Fred Raskin. The Weinstein Company / Columbia Pictures, 2012. DVD. Sony Pictures, 2013.

The Hateful Eight. With Samuel L. Jackson (Major Marquis Warren), Jennifer Jason Leigh (Daisy Domergue), Kurt Russell (John Ruth), Walton Goggins (Sheriff Chris Mannix), Demián Bichir (Bob), Bruce Dern (General Sandy Smithers), Tim Roth (Oswaldo Mobray / English Pete), Michael Madsen (Joe Gage / Grouch Douglass), James Parks (O. B.), Dana Gourrier (Minnie Mink). Production Design: Yohei Taneda. Cinematography: Robert Richardson. Editing: Fred Raskin. Music by Ennio Morricone. Double Feature Films / FilmColony, 2015. DVD. M6 Vidéo, 2016.

Books and Articles on Tarantino

Allan, Keith. "When Is a Slur Not a Slur? The Use of Nigger in *Pulp Fiction*." *Language Sciences* 52 (2015): 187–99.
Anderson, Aaron. "Mindful Violence: The Visibility of Power and Inner Life in *Kill Bill*." *Jump Cut* 47 (Winter 2005). <https://www.ejumpcut.org/archive/jc47.2005/KillBill>. Accessed on May 3, 2017.
Anderson, Aaron. "Stuntman Mike, Simulation, and Sadism in *Death Proof*." *Quentin Tarantino and Philosophy*. Eds. Richard Greene and K. Silem Mohammad. Chicago and La Salle, IL: Open Court, 2007. 12–20.
Anderson, Reynold, D. L. Stephenson, and Chante Anderson. "'Crowdsourcing' 'The Bad-Ass Slave': A Critique of Quentin Tarantino's *Django Unchained*." *Quentin Tarantino's Django Unchained: The Continuation of Metacinema*. Ed. Oliver C. Speck. New York and London: Bloomsbury, 2014. 227–42.
Auxier, Randall E. "Vinnie's Very Bad Day: Twisting the Tale of Time in *Pulp Fiction*." *Quentin Tarantino and Philosophy*. Eds. Richard Greene and K. Silem Mohammad. Chicago and La Salle, IL: Open Court, 2007. 123–40.
Bauer, Erik. "The Mouth and the Method: Eric Bauer Talks with Quentin Tarantino about *Jackie Brown*." *Film/Literature/Heritage: A Sight and Sound Reader*. Ed. Ginette Vincendeau. London: BFI, 2001. 231–41.
Beltzer, Thomas. "Dogs in Hell: *No Exit* Revisited." *Senses of Cinema* 6 (2000). <http://sensesof cinema.com/2000/feature-articles/dogs>. Accessed on December 23, 2017.
Benson-Alliott, Caetlin. "*Grindhouse*: An Experiment in the Death of Cinema." *Film Quarterly* 61.1 (Fall 2008): 20–24.
Bernard, Jami. *Quentin Tarantino: The Man and his Movies*. New York: HarperPerennial, 1995.
Bertelsen, Eve. "'Serious Gourmet Shit': Quentin Tarantino's *Pulp Fiction*." *Journal of Literary Studies* 15.1–2 (1999): 8–32.
Bordwell, David. "Directors: Tarantino." davidbordwell.net <http://www.davidbordwell.net/blog/category/directors-tarantino>. Accessed on April 26, 2017.
Botting, Fred, and Scott Wilson. "By Accident: The Tarantinian Ethics." *Theory, Culture & Society* 15.2 (1998): 89–113.
Bradley, Regina N. "I Like the Way You Rhyme, Boy: Hip Hop Sensibility and Racial Trauma in *Django Unchained*." *Sounding Out!* (January 18, 2013). <https://soundstudiesblog.com/2013/01/28/i-like-the-way-you-rhyme-boy-hip-hop-sensibility-and-racial-trauma-in-django-unchained/>. Accessed on April 26, 2017.
Breen, Marcus. "Woof, Woof: The real bite in *Reservoir Dogs*." *Australian Humanities Review* 4 (December 1996). <http://australianhumanitiesreview.org/1996/12/01/woof-woof-the-real-bite-in-reservoir-dogs>. Accessed on September 15, 2017.
Brintnall, Kent L. "Tarantino's Incarnational Theology: *Reservoir Dogs*, Crucifixions and Spectacular Violence." *Cross Currents* 54.1 (Spring 2004): 66–75.
Brooker, Peter, and Will Brooker. "Pulpmodernism: Tarantino's Affirmative Action." *Pulping Fictions: Consuming Culture across the Literature/Media Divide*. Eds. Deborah Cartmell, I. Q. Hunter, Heidi Kaye, and Imelda Whelehan. London and Chicago, IL: Pluto Press, 1996. 135–51.

Brown, William. "Counterfactuals, Quantum Physics, and Cruel Monsters in Quentin Tarantino's *Inglourious Basterds*." *Quentin Tarantino's* Inglourious Basterds: *A Manipulation of Metacinema*. Ed. Robert von Dassanowsky. New York and London: Continuum, 2012.

Brown, William. "Value and Violence in *Django Unchained*." *Quentin Tarantino's* Django Unchained: *The Continuation of Metacinema*. Ed. Oliver C. Speck. New York and London: Bloomsbury, 2014. 161–76.

Carr, Jeremy. "Familiar Refrains and Minor Variations: Quentin Tarantino's *Hateful Eight*." *Senses of Cinema* 78 (March 2016). <http://sensesofcinema.com/2016/feature-articles/the-hateful-eight>. Accessed on April 17, 2017.

Carr, Joi. "'To Be Actually Honest': An Interview with Reginald Hudlin, Writer, Producer, Director, and Executive." *Black Camera* 7.2 (Spring 2016): 45–61.

Cervulle, Maxime. "Quentin Tarantino et le (post)féminisme : Politiques du genre dans *Boulevard de la mort*." *Nouvelles questions féministes* 28 (2009): 35–49.

Charyn, Jerome. *Raised by Wolves: The Turbulent Art and Times of Quentin Tatantino*. New York: Thunder's Mouth Press, 2006.

Chumo II, Peter N. "'The Next Best Thing to a Time Machine': Quentin Tarantino's *Pulp Fiction*." *Post Script* 15.3 (Summer 1996): 16–28.

Coates, Kristen. "Hyperreality in *Inglourious Basterds*: Tarantino's Interwoven Cinematic World in 1940s France." *Film Stage* (June 26, 2010). Accessed on September 11, 2017.

Conard, Mark T. "*Kill Bill*: Tarantino's Oedipal Play." *Quentin Tarantino and Philosophy*. Eds. Richard Greene and K. Silem Mohammad. Chicago and La Salle, IL: Open Court, 2007. 163–75.

Conard, Mark T. "*Reservoir Dogs*: Redemption in a Postmodern World." *The Philosophy of Neo-Noir*. Ed. Mark T. Conard. Lexington: University Press of Kentucky, 2007. 101–16.

Coulthard, Lisa. "Inglourious Music: Revenge, Reflexivity, and Morricone as Muse in *Inglourious Basterds*." *Quentin Tarantino's* Inglourious Basterds: *A Manipulation of Metacinema*. Ed. Robert von Dassanowsky. New York and London: Continuum, 2012. 57–70.

Coulthard, Lisa. "Killing Bill: Rethinking Feminism and Film Violence." *Interrogating Post-Feminism*. Eds. Yvonne Tasker and Diane Negra. Durham, NC: Duke University Press, 2007. 153–75.

Cuddy, Luke, and Michael Bruce. "Could Beatrix Kiddo Reach Enlightenment? Traces of Buddhist Philosophy in *Kill Bill*." *Quentin Tarantino and Philosophy*. Eds. Richard Greene and K. Silem Mohammad. Chicago and La Salle, IL: Open Court, 2007. 189–201.

Dargis, Manohla. "Pulp Instincts." *Action/Spectacle Cinema*. Ed. José Arroyo. London: BFI, 2000. 117–21.

Davis, Todd F. "Shepherding the Weak: The Ethics of Redemption in Quentin Tarantino's *Pulp Fiction*." *Literature Film Quarterly* 26.1 (1998): 60–66.

Dawson, Jeff. *Quentin Tarantino: The Cinema of Cool*. New York: Applause Books, 1995.

Desilet, Gregory. "*Django Unchained*: How *Not* to do Screen Violence." *Screens of Blood: A Critical Appoach to Film and Television Violence*. Jefferson, NC: McFarland, 2014. 24–38.

Dima, Vlad. "Tarantino's *Inglourious Basterds*: Film Kills." *Bright Lights Film Journal* 66 (November 2009). <http://brightlightsfilm.com/tarantinos-inglourious-basterds-film-kills/#.WRXdz4Xw_nI>. Accessed on May 12, 2017.

Ford, James Edward, III. "Blackness and Legend." *Black Camera* 7.1 (Fall 2015): 199–217.

Garner, Ken. "'Would You Like to Hear Some Music?' Music in-and-Out-of-Control in the Films of Quentin Tarantino." *Film Music: Critical Approaches*. Ed. K. J. Donnelly. Edinburgh, UK, and New York: Edinburgh University Press / Continuum, 2001. 188–205.

Giroux, Henry A. "Racism and the Aesthetic of Hyper-Real Violence: *Pulp Fiction* and Other Visual Tragedies." *Social Identities: Journal for the Study of Race, Nation and Culture* 1.2 (Aug 1995): 333–55.

Gormley, Paul. "Chapter Four: Miming Blackness: *Reservoir Dogs* and 'American Africanism'" and "Chapter Five: Trashing Whiteness: *Pulp Fiction*, *Se7en*, *Strange Days* and Articulating Affect." *The New-Brutality Film: Race and Affect in Contemporary Hollywood Cinema*. Bristol UK, and Portland, OR: Intellect, 2005. 137–81.

Greene, Richard. "Quentin Tarantino and the Ex-Convict's Dilemma." *Quentin Tarantino and Philosophy*. Eds. Richard Greene and K. Silem Mohammad. Chicago and La Salle, IL: Open Court, 2007. 149–59.

Greene, Richard, and K. Silem Mohammad, eds. *Quentin Tarantino and Philosophy*. Chicago and La Salle, Illinois: Open Court, 2007.

Hayes, Heather Ashley, and Gilbert B. Rodman. "Thirteen Ways of Looking at a Black Film: What Does It Mean to Be a Black Film in Twenty-First Century America?" *Quentin Tarantino's* Django Unchained: *The Continuation of Metacinema*. Ed. Oliver C. Speck. New York and London: Bloomsbury, 2014. 179–204.

Hertzberg, Hendrik. "Djangled Nerves." *New Yorker*, March 7, 2013. <http://www.newyorker.com/news/hendrik-hertzberg/djangled-nerves>. Accessed on April 10, 2017.

Holmes, David G. "Breaking the Chains of Science: The Rhetoric of Empirical Racism in *Django Unchained*." *Black Camera* 7.2 (Spring 2016): 73–78.

hooks, bell. "Cool Cynicism: Pulp Fiction." *Reel to Real: Race, Class and Sex at the Movies*. New York and London: Routledge, 1996. 59–64.

Howley, Kevin. "Breaking, Making, and Killing Time in *Pulp Fiction*." *Scope: An Online Journal of Film and TV Studies* (May 2004). <https://www.nottingham.ac.uk/scope/documents/2004/may-2004/howley.pdf>. Accessed on April 26, 2017.

Inouye, Charles Shirô. "Promoting Virtue and Punishing Vice: Tarantino's *Kill Bill* and the Return of Bakumatsu Aesthetics." *Post Script* 28.2 (Spring 2009): 92–100.

Jardine, Dan. "The Killing Fields (on *Reservoir Dogs*)." *Film Journal* 1.10 (October 2004). <http://archive.is/Gc32>. Accessed on May 3, 2017.

Johnson, Mary. "*Jackie Brown*: The Art of Talking Trash." *Creative Screenwriting* 5.1 (1998): 29–32.

Jordan, Jessica Hope. "Women Refusing the Gaze: Theorizing Thryth's 'Unqueenly Custom' in *Beowulf* and the Bride's Revenge in Quentin Tarantino's *Kill Bill, Volume I*." *Heroic Age: A Journal of Early Medieval Northwestern Europe* 9 (October 2006). <http://www.heroicage.org/issues/9/forum2.html>. Accessed on May 14, 2017.

Kaster, Gregory L. "*Django* and *Lincoln*: The Suffering Slave and the Law of Slavery." *Quentin Tarantino's* Django Unchained: *The Continuation of Metacinema*. Ed. Oliver C. Speck. New York and London: Bloomsbury, 2014. 75–90

Kligerman, Eric. "Reels of Justice: *Inglourious Basterds*, *The Sorrow and the Pity*, and Jewish Revenge Fantasies." *Quentin Tarantino's* Inglourious Basterds: *A Manipulation of Metacinema*. Ed. Robert von Dassanowsky. New York and London: Continuum, 2012. 135–62.

Kuersten, Erich. "The Foxy, the Dead, and the Foxier: Re-Visiting *Death Proof.*" *Bright Lights Film Journal* (January 2008). <http://brightlightsfilm.com/the-foxy-the-dead-and-the-foxier-revisiting-death-proof/#.WRYSN4Xw_nI>. Accessed on May 12, 2017.

Lavin, Maud. "Violence: *Kill Bill* and *Murder Girls.*" *Push Comes to Shove: New Images of Aggressive Women*. Cambridge, MA: MIT Press, 2010. 106–55.

Le Caine, Maximilian. "Tarantino and the Vengeful Ghosts of Cinema." *Senses of Cinema* 32 (July 2004). <http://sensesofcinema.com/2004/beyond-the-grave-of-genre/tarantino>. Accessed on April 17, 2017.

Leonard, David J. "Django Blues: Whiteness and Hollywood's Continued Failures." *Quentin Tarantino's* Django Unchained*: The Continuation of Metacinema*. Ed. Oliver C. Speck. New York and London: Bloomsbury, 2014. 269–86.

Matuska, Agnes. "Tarantino's *Kill Bill* and the Renaissance Tradition of Revenge Plays." *Shakespeare and his Collaborators over the Centuries*. Eds. Pavel Drábek, Klára Kolinská, and Matthew Nicholls. Newcastle-upon-Tyne, UK: Cambridge Scholars, 2008. 211–20.

McGee, Patrick. "Conclusion: *Kill Bill*, or Why Shane Always Comes Back." *From* Shane *to* Kill Bill*: Rethinking the Western*. Hoboken, NJ: Wiley-Blackwell, 2006. 235–44.

McRoy, Kay. "'The Kids of Today Should Defend Themselves Against the '70s: Simulating Auras and Marketing Nostalgia in Robert Rodriguez and Quentin Tarantino's *Grindhouse*." *American Horror Film: The Genre at the Turn of the New Millenium*. Ed. Steffen Hantke. Jackson: University Press of Mississippi, 2010. 221–34.

Mendehlson, Daniel. "It's Only a Movie." *New York Review of Books* 50.20 (December 18, 2003): 38, 40–41.

Mera, Miguel. "Inglo(u)rious Basterdization: Tarantino and the War Movie Mashup." *The Oxford Handbook of Sound and Image in Digital Media*. Eds. Carol Vernalis, Amy Herzog, and John Richardson. New York: Oxford University Press, 2013. 437–61.

Meyer, Imke. "Exploding Cinema, Exploding Hollywood: *Inglourious Basterds* and the Limits of Cinema." *Quentin Tarantino's* Inglourious Basterds*: A Manipulation of Metacinema*. Ed. Robert von Dassanowsky. New York and London: Continuum, 2012. 15–36.

Miklitsch, Robert. "Audiophilia: Audiovisual Pleasure and Narrative Cinema in *Jackie Brown*." *Screen* 45.4 (Winter 2004): 287–304.

Mohammad, K. Silem, "'I Didn't Know You Liked the Delfonics': Knowledge and Pragmatism in *Jackie Brown*." *Quentin Tarantino and Philosophy*. Eds. Richard Greene and K. Silem Mohammad. Chicago and La Salle, IL: Open Court, 2007. 111–22.

Morgan, Kim. "The Interview: Quentin Tarantino." *Sight & Sound* 26.2 (February 2016): 18–27.

Nama, Adilifu. *Race on the QT: Blackness and the Films of Quentin Tarantino*. Austin: University of Texas Press, 2015.

Nanay, Bence and Ian Schnee. "Travolta's Elvis Man and the Nieztschean Superman." *Quentin Tarantino and Philosophy*. Eds. Richard Greene and K. Silem Mohammad. Chicago and La Salle, IL: Open Court, 2007. 177–88.

Novoa, Adriana. "Rough Awakenings: Unconscious Women and Rape in *Kill Bill* and *Talk to Her*." *Rape in Art Cinema*. Ed. Dominique Russell. New York: Continuum, 2010. 83–96.

O'Brien, Geoffrey. "Heart of Dixie." *Film Comment* (January–February 2013): 30–33.

Ornella, Alexander D. "Disruptive Violence as Means to Create a Space for Reflection: Thoughts on Tarantino's Attempts at Audience Irritation." *Quentin Tarantino's* Inglourious

Basterds: *A Manipulation of Metacinema*. Ed. Robert von Dassanowsky. New York and London: Continuum, 2012. 215–46.

Ortoli, Philippe. *Le Musée imaginaire de Quentin Tarantino*. Paris: Cerf-Corlet, 2012.

Ortoli, Philippe. "Quentin Tarantino : du cinéma d'exploitation au cinéma." *Transatlantica* 14.2 (2015). <https://transatlantica.revues.org/7909>. Accessed on April 26, 2017.

Ozierski, Margaret. "Franco-faux-ne: Django's Jive." *Quentin Tarantino's* Django Unchained: *The Continuation of Metacinema*. Ed. Oliver C. Speck. New York and London: Bloomsbury, 2014. 39–50.

Peake, Glenn. "Icons, Iconoclasts, and Ideology: The Strange Case of Quentin Tarantino." *University of Dayton Review* 24.1 (Fall 1996): 55–61.

Peary, Gerald, ed. *Quentin Tarantino: Interviews*. Jackson: University Press of Mississippi, 2013.

Perry, Samuel P. "Chained to It: The Recurrence of the Frontier Hero in the Films of Quentin Tarantino." *Quentin Tarantino's* Django Unchained: *The Continuation of Metacinema*. Ed. Oliver C. Speck. New York and London: Bloomsbury, 2014. 205–225.

Reilly, Ian. "'Revenge Is Never a Straight Line': Transgressing Heroic Boundaries: Medea and the (Fe)Male Body in *Kill Bill*." *Studies in Popular Culture* 30.1 (Fall 2007): 27–50.

Richardson, Michael D. "Vengeful Violence: *Inglourious Basterds*, Allohistory, and the Inversion of Victims and Perpetrators." *Quentin Tarantino's* Inglourious Basterds: *A Manipulation of Metacinema*. Ed. Robert von Dassanowsky. New York and London: Continuum, 2012. 93–112.

Ritter, Kelly. "Postmodern Dialogics in *Pulp Fiction*: Jules, Ezekiel, and Double-Voiced Discourse." *The Terministic Screen: Rhetorical Perspectives on Film*. Ed. David Blakesley. Carbondale, IL: Southern Illinois University Press, 2007. 286–302.

Robison, Rachel. "'I'm a Bad Person': Beatrix Kiddo's Rampage and Virtue." *Quentin Tarantino and Philosophy*. Eds. Richard Greene and K. Silem Mohammad. Chicago and La Salle, IL: Open Court, 2007. 75–84.

Roche, David. "Choreographing Genre in *Kill Bill Vol. 1 & 2* (Quentin Tarantino, 2003 & 2004)." *Miranda* 10 (2014). <https://miranda.revues.org/6285?lang=fr>. Accessed on May 4, 2017.

Roche, David. "French Fries, French Foxes and Crazy Frenchmen in Quentin Tarantino's *Pulp Fiction* (1994) and Roger Avary's *Killing Zoe* (1994): Reading Hollywood 'Frenchness' / French Readings." *Bulletin du CICLAHO* 5 (2010): 291–311.

Roche, David. "Quentin Tarantino's *Death Proof* (2007): Subverting Gender through Genre or Vice Versa?" *Generic Attractions: New Essays on Film Genre*. Eds. María del Mar Azcona and Celestino Deleyto. Paris: Michel Houdiard, 2010. 337–53.

Roche, David. "Tarantino's Round Flat Characters: A (Mainly) Verbal Study of *Reservoir Dogs* (1992)." *Bulletin du CICLAHO* 6 (2012): 411–31.

Schlipphacke, Heidi. "*Inglourious Basterds* and the Gender of Revenge." *Quentin Tarantino's* Inglourious Basterds: *A Manipulation of Metacinema*. Ed. Robert von Dassanowsky. New York and London: Continuum, 2012. 113–34.

Schmidt, Paul H. "Charming Pigs and Mimetic Desire in Quentin Tarantino's *Pulp Fiction*." *University of Dayton Review* 24.1 (Fall 1996): 43–53.

Semenza, Greg M. Colón. "The Ethics of Appropriation: *Samson Agonistes*, *Inglourious Basterds*, and the Biblical Samson Tale." *Adaptation* 7.1 (2004): 62–81.

Speck, Oliver C. "Is Tarantino Serious? The Twofold Image of the *Auteur* and the State of Exception." *Quentin Tarantino's* Inglourious Basterds: *A Manipulation of Metacinema*. Ed. Robert von Dassanowsky. New York and London: Continuum, 2012. 193–214.

Speck, Oliver C, ed. *Quentin Tarantino's* Django Unchained: *The Continuation of Metacinema*. New York and London: Bloomsbury, 2014.

Srinivasan, Srikanth. "The Grand Illusion." *Quentin Tarantino's* Inglourious Basterds: *A Manipulation of Metacinema*. Ed. Robert von Dassanowsky. New York and London: Continuum, 2012. 1–13.

Suleiman, Susan Rubin. "The Stakes in Holocaust Representation: On Tarantino's *Inglourious Basterds*." *Romanic Review* 105.1–2 (2014): 69–86.

Szaniawski, Jeremi. "Laisse tomber les filles: (Post)Feminism in Quentin Tarantino's Death Proof." *Situating the Feminist Gaze and Spectatorship in Postwar Cinema*. Ed. Marcelline Block. Newcastle-upon-Tyne, UK: Cambridge Scholars, 2008: 168–91.

Taubin, Amy. "The Men's Room." *Action/Spectacle Cinema*. Ed. José Arroyo. London: BFI, 2000. 122–26.

Telotte, J. P. "Fatal Capers: Strategy and Enigma in Film Noir." *Journal of Popular Film and Television* 23.4 (Winter 1996): 163–70.

Temoney, Kate E. "The 'D' is Silent, but Human Rights Are Not: *Django Unchained* as Human Rights Discourse." *Quentin Tarantino's* Django Unchained: *The Continuation of Metacinema*. Ed. Oliver C. Speck. New York and London: Bloomsbury, 2014. 123–40.

Tierney, Sean M. "Themes of Whiteness in *Bulletproof Monk*, *Kill Bill*, and *The Last Samurai*." *Journal of Communication* 56 (2006): 607–624.

Von Dassanowsky, Robert, ed. "Dr. 'King' Schultz as Ideologue and Emblem: The German Enlightenment and the Legacy of the 1848 Revolutions in *Django Unchained*." *Quentin Tarantino's* Django Unchained: *The Continuation of Metacinema*. Ed. Oliver C. Speck. New York and London: Bloomsbury, 2014. 17–38.

Von Dassanowsky, Robert, ed. *Quentin Tarantino's* Inglourious Basterds: *A Manipulation of Metacinema*. New York and London: Continuum, 2012.

Waldron, Dara. "Hark, Hark, the (dis)Enchanted Kantian, or Tarantino's 'Evil' and its Anti-Cathartic Resonance." *Quentin Tarantino's* Django Unchained: *The Continuation of Metacinema*. Ed. Oliver C. Speck. New York and London: Bloomsbury, 2014. 141–60.

Walters, Ben. "Debating *Inglourious Basterds*." *Film Quarterly* 63.2 (Winter 2009–10). <https://filmquarterly.org/2009/12/01/talking-point-debating-inglorious-bastards>. Accessed on May 3, 2017.

Weaver, Ryan J., and Nichole K. Kathol. "Guess Who's Coming to Get Her: Stereotypes, Mythification, and White Redemption." *Quentin Tarantino's* Django Unchained: *The Continuation of Metacinema*. Ed. Oliver C. Speck. New York and London: Bloomsbury, 2014. 243–68.

Weber, Dana. "Of Handshakes and Dragons: Django's German Cousins." *Quentin Tarantino's* Django Unchained: *The Continuation of Metacinema*. Ed. Oliver C. Speck. New York and London: Bloomsbury, 2014. 51–74.

Willis, Sharon. "'Fire!' in a Crowded Theater: Liquidating History in *Inglourious Basterds*." *Quentin Tarantino's* Inglourious Basterds: *A Manipulation of Metacinema*. Ed. Robert von Dassanowsky. New York and London: Continuum, 2012. 163–92.

Willis, Sharon. "'Style,' Posture, and Idiom: Tarantino's Figures of Masculinity." *Reinventing Film Studies*. Eds. Christine Gledhill and Linda Williams. London and New York: Arnold, 2000. 279–95.

Film Criticism and Theory

Abrams, Nathan. *The New Jew in Film: Exploring Jewishness and Judaism in Contemporary Cinema*. New Brunswick, NJ: Rutgers University Press, 2012.

Bissonnette, Sylvie. "Committed Theatricality." *Stages of Reality: Theatricality in Cinema*. Eds. André Loiselle and Jeremy Maron. Toronto, Buffalo and London: University of Toronto Press, 2012. 135–59.

Bogle, Donald. *Toons, Coons, Mulattoes, Mammies & Bucks: An Interpretive History of Blacks in American Films*. Fourth edition. New York and London: Continuum, 2001 [1973].

Bordwell, David. *Narration in the Fiction Film*. Madison: University of Wisconsin Press, 1985.

Bordwell, David. *Poetics of Cinema*. New York and London: Routledge, 2007.

Bordwell, David. *The Way Hollywood Tells It: Story and Style in Modern Movies*. Berkeley, Los Angeles, and London: University of California Press, 2006.

Cavell, Stanley. *The World Viewed: Reflections on the Ontology of Film*. New York: Viking Press, 1971.

Cerisuelo, Marc. *Hollywood à l'écran : les métafilms américains*. Paris: Presses de la Sorbonne Nouvelle, 2000.

Chinita, Fátima. "The Tricks of the Trade (Un)exposed." *Networking Knowledge* 7.4 (2014). <ojs.meccsa.org.uk/index.php/netknow/article/view/353/183>. Accessed on May 5, 2017.

Chion, Michel. *L'Audio-vision : son et image au cinéma*. Paris: Armand Colin, 2013 [1990].

Chion, Michel. *La Musique au cinéma*. Paris: Fayard, 1995.

Chion, Michel. *La Voix au cinéma*. Paris: Éditions de l'Étoile / *Cahiers du cinéma*, 1982.

Clover, Carol. *Men, Women, and Chainsaws: Gender in the Modern Horror Film*. Second edition with a new preface by the author. Princeton and Oxford, UK: Princeton University Press, 2015 [1992].

Corrigan, Timothy. *Film and Literature: An Introduction and Reader*. Upper Saddle River, NJ: Prentice Hall, 1999.

Creed, Barbara. *The Monstrous-Feminine: Film, Feminism, Psychoanalysis*, London and New York: Routledge, 1993.

Crémieux, Anne. "Exploitation Cinema and the Lesbian Imagination." *Transatlantica* 14.2 (2015). <https://transatlantica.revues.org/7869?lang=en>. Accessed on September 24, 2017.

Dyer, Richard. *Stars*. London: BFI, 1998 [1979].

Fisher, Austin. *Radical Frontiers in the Spaghetti Western: Politics, Violence and Popular Italian Cinema*. London: I. B. Tauris, 2011.

Frayling, Christopher. *Sergio Leone: Something To Do with Death*. London and New York: Faber and Faber, 2000.

Gordon, Andrew M. *Empire of Dreams: The Science Fiction and Fantasy Films of Steven Spielberg*. London, Boulder, New York, Toronto, and Plymouth, UK: Rowman & Littlefield, 2008.

Haber, Karen. *Kong Unbound: The Cultural Impact, Pop Mythos, and Scientific Plausibility of a Cinematic Legend*. New York: Gallery Books, 2005.

Humphries, Reynold. *The American Horror Film: An Introduction*. Edinburgh: Edinburgh University Press, 2002.

Humphries, Reynold. *Fritz Lang: Genre and Representation in his American Films*. Baltimore, MD, and London: Johns Hopkins University Press, 1989.

Hutchings, Peter. "Tearing Your Soul Apart: Horror's New Monsters." *Modern Gothic: A Reader*. Eds. Allan Lloyd Smith and Victor Sage. Manchester: Manchester University Press, 1996. 89–103.

Jeffords, Susan. *Hard Bodies: Hollywood Masculinity in the Reagan Era*. New Brunswick, NJ: Rutgers University Press, 1994.

Jenkins, Henry. *Convergence Culture: Where Old and New Media Collide*. Updated and with a New Afterword. New York and London: New York University Press, 2006 [2008].

Jullier, Laurent. *L'Écran post-moderne : un cinéma de l'allusion et du feu d'artifice*. Paris: L'Harmattan, 1997.

Kassabian, Anahid. *Hearing Film: Tracking Identifications in Contemporary Hollywood Film Music*. New York and London: Routledge, 2001.

Kinder, Marsha. "Violence American Style: The Narrative Orchestration of Violent Attractions." *Violence and American Cinema*. Ed. David J. Slocum. New York: Routledge, 2001. 63–100.

Leitch, Thomas. *Film Adaptation and Its Discontents: From* Gone with the Wind *to* The Passion of Christ. Baltimore, MD: Johns Hopkins University Press, 2007.

Levy, Emanuel. *Cinema of Outsiders: The Rise of American Independent Film*. New York: New York University Press, 1999.

Loiselle, André, and Jeremy Maron. *Stages of Reality: Theatricality in Cinema*. Toronto, Buffalo, and London: University of Toronto Press, 2012.

Mason, Fran. *American Gangster Cinema: From* Little Caesar *to* Pulp Fiction. Basingstoke, UK, and New York: Palgrave Macmillan, 2002.

McRoy, Jay. *Nightmare Japan: Contemporary Japanese Horror Cinema*. Amsterdam: Rodopi, 2007.

Metz, Christian. *Impersonal Enunciation, or the Place of Film*. Trans. Cormac Deane. Afterword. Dana Polan. New York: Columbia University Press, 2016 [1991].

Mulvey, Laura. *Visual and Other Pleasures*. Bloomington and Indianapolis: Indiana University Press, 1989.

Naremore, James. *Acting in the Cinema*. Berkeley, Los Angeles, and London: University of California Press, 1988.

Neupert, Richard. *A History of the French New Wave Cinema*. Second edition. Madison: University of Wisconsin Press, 2007 [2002].

Quart, Alissa. "Networked." *Film Comment* 41.4 (July–August 2005): 48–51.

Place, Janey. "Women in Film Noir." *Women in Film Noir*. Ed. E. Ann Kaplan. London: BFI, 1998. 47–68.

Prince, Stephen. "Introduction: Sam Peckinpah, Savage Poet of American Cinema." *Sam Peckinpah's* The Wild Bunch. Ed. Stephen Prince. Cambridge: Cambridge University Press, 1999. 1–6.

Roche, David. "Irony in *The Sweet Hereafter* by Russell Banks (1991) and Atom Egoyan (1997)." *Adaptation* 8.2 (2015): 237–53.

Roche, David. "Le Noir chez David Cronenberg ou la persistence des obsessions." *CinémAction* 151 (2014): 39–47.

Roche, David. *Making and Remaking Horror in the 1970s and 2000s: Why Don't They Do It Like They Used To?* Jackson: University Press of Mississippi, 2014.

Silverman, Kaja. *The Acoustic Mirror: The Female Voice in Psychoanalysis and Cinema*. Bloomington: Indiana University Press, 1988.

Sinnerbrink, Robert. *New Philosophies of Film: Thinking Images*. London and New York: Continuum, 2011.

Slotkin, Richard. *Gunfighter Nation: The Myth of the Frontier in Twentieth-Century America*. Norman: University of Oklahoma Press, 1998 [1992].

Sobchack, Thomas. "Genre Film: A Classical Experience" (1975). *Film Genre Reader III*. Ed. Barry Keith Grant. Austin, TX: University of Texas Press, 2003. 102–13.

Stam, Robert. *Reflexivity in Film and Literature: From* Don Quixote *to Jean-Luc Godard*. New York: Columbia University Press, 1985 [1982].

Stokes, Melvyn. *American History through Hollywood Film: From the Revolution to the 1960s*. London, New Delhi, New York, and Sydney: Bloomsbury, 2014.

Stokes, Melvyn, and Gilles Menegaldo, eds. *Film and History / Cinéma et histoire*. Paris: Michel Houdiard, 2008.

Tan, Ed S. *Emotion and the Structure of Narrative Film: Film as an Emotion Machine*. Second edition. New York and London: Routledge, 2011 [1996].

Thompson, Kristin. *Storytelling in the New Hollywood: Understanding Classical Narrative Technique*. Cambridge, MA, and London: Harvard University Press, 1999.

Thompson, Kristin, and David Bordwell. *Film History: An Introduction*. Third edition. New York: McGraw Hill International, 2010 [1994].

Toplin, Robert Brent. *History by Hollywood: The Use and Abuse of the American Past*. Urbana and Chicago: University of Illinois Press, 1996.

Tuhkunen, Taïna. *Demain sera un autre jour : Le Sud et ses héroïnes à l'écran*. Pertuis: Rouge Profond, 2013.

Turim, Maureen. *Flashbacks in Film: Memory and History*. London and New York: Routledge, 2013.

Viviani, Christian. *Le Magique et le vrai : L'acteur de cinéma, sujet et objet*. Aix-en-Provence: Rouge Profond, 2015.

Williams, Linda. "When the Woman Looks." *The Dread of Difference: Gender and the Horror Film*. Ed. Barry Keith Grant. Austin, TX: University of Texas Press, 1996 [1984]. 15–34.

Williams, Tony. *Hearths of Darkness: The Family in the American Horror Film*. Updated edition. Jackson, MS: University Press of Mississippi, 2014 [1996].

Yip, Man-Fung. *Martial Arts Cinema and Hong Kong Modernity: Aesthetics, Representation, Circulation*. Hong Kong: Hong Kong University Press, 2017.

General Criticism and Theory

Anzaldúa, Gloria. *Borderlands / La Frontera: The New Mestiza*. San Francisco, CA: Aunt Lute Books, 1987.

Barthes, Roland. "Brecht and Discourse: A Contribution to the Study of Discursivity." Trans. Richard Howard. *The Rustle of Language*. New York: Hill and Wang, 1986 [1984]. 212–22.

Burns, Elizabeth. *Theatricality: A Study of Convention in the Theatre and in Social Life*. London: Longman, 1972.

Butler, Judith. *Bodies That Matter: On the Discursive Limits of "Sex."* New York and London: Routledge, 1993.

Butler, Judith. *Excitable Speech: A Politics of the Performative*. New York and London: Routledge, 1997.

Carney, Sean. *Brecht and Critical Theory: Dialectics and Contemporary Aesthetics*. London and New York: Routledge, 2005.

Chermak, Steven M., and Frankie Y. Bailey, eds. *Crimes and Trials of the Century: Notorious Crimes, Criminals, and Criminal Trials in American History*. Santa Barbara, CA: ABC-CLIO, 2016.

Daring, C. B., J. Rogue, Deric Shannon, and Abbey Volcano, eds. *Queering Anarchism: Addressing and Undressing Power and Desire*. Oakland, CA: AK Press, 2012.

Deleuze, Gilles. *Cinema 2: The Time-Image*. Trans. Hugh Tomlinson and Robert Galeta. London and New York: Continuum, 1989 [1985].

Deleuze, Gilles, and Félix Guattari. *L'Anti-Œdipe : Capitalisme et schizophrénie*. Paris: Minuit, 1972–1973.

Eco, Umberto. *L'Œuvre ouverte*. Paris: Seuil, 1965 [1962].

Escott, Paul D. *"What Shall We Do with the Negro?" Lincoln, White Racism, and Civil War*. Charlottesville: University of Virginia Press, 2009.

Fussell, Paul. *Wartime: Understanding and Behavior in the Second World War*. New York and Oxford: Oxford University Press, 1989.

Freud, Sigmund. "A Child Is Being Beaten" (1919). *Standard Edition of the Complete Psychological Works of Sigmund Freud*. Ed. James Strachey. London: Hogarth, 1953–74. 17: 177–204.

Freud, Sigmund. *Jokes and their Relation to the Unconscious*. New York: Norton, 1989 [1905].

Genette, Gérard. *Figures III*. Paris: Seuil, 1972.

Genette, Gérard. *Introduction à l'architexte*. Paris: Seuil, 1979.

Genette, Gérard. *Palimpsestes : la littérature au second degré*. Paris: Seuil, 1982.

Golden, Leon. "Catharsis." *Transactions and Proceedings of the American Philological Association* 93 (1962): 51–62.

Goldsmith, Barclay. "Brecht and Chicano Theatre." *Brecht Sourcebook*. Eds. Carol Martin and Henry Bial. London and New York: Routledge, 2000. 163–72.

Grayzel, Solomon. *A History of the Jews: From the Babylonian Exile to the Present*. Philadelphia: Jewish Publication Society, 1968.

Hutcheon, Linda. "Historiographic Metafiction: Parody and the Intertextuality of History." *Intertextuality and Contemporary American Fiction*. Eds. Patrick O'Donnell and Robert Con Davis. Baltimore, MD: Johns Hopkins University Press, 1989. 3–32.

Hutcheon, Linda. *Narcissistic Narrative: The Metafictional Paradox*. Waterloo, ON: Wilfrid Laurier University Press, 1980.

Hutcheon, Linda. *A Poetics of Postmodernism: History, Theory, Fiction*. New York: Routledge, 1988.

Levinas, Emmanuel. *Totality and Infinity: An Essay on Exteriority*. Trans. Alphonso Lingis. The Hague and Boston: M. Nijhoff Publishers, 1979 [1971].
Lipton, Sara. *Dark Mirror: The Medieval Origins of Anti-Semitic Iconography*. New York: Metropolitan Books / Henry Holt and Company, 2014.
McHale, Brian. *The Cambridge Introduction to Postmodernism*. New York: Cambridge University Press, 2015.
McHale, Brian. *Constructing Postmodernism*. London and New York: Routledge, 1992.
Mey, Jacob L. *Pragmatics: An Introduction*. Malden, MA, and Oxford, UK: Blackwell Publishing, 2001 [1993].
Niemeyer, Mark. "'A Partial Reassurance of Fratricide': Redefining National Unity in *Adventures of Huckleberry Finn*." *Mark Twain Journal* 54.2 (Fall 2016): 35–59.
Pastoureau, Michel. *Bleu*. Paris: Seuil, 2000.
Poster, Mark. "Introduction." *Jean Baudrillard: Selected Writings*. Stanford, CA: Stanford University Press, 2002 [1988]. 1–12.
Propp, Vladimir. *Morphology of the Folktale*. Austin: University of Texas Press, 1968 [1928].
Ricardou, Jean. "La population des miroirs." *Poétique* 22 (1975): 196–226.
Schaeffer, Jean-Marie. *Pourquoi la fiction?* Paris: Seuil, 1999.
Thompson, William Ford, ed. *Music in the Social & Behavioral Sciences: An Encyclopedia*. Los Angeles, London, New Delhi, Singapore, and Washington DC: Sage, 2014.
Von Klemperer, Klemens. *German Resistance Against Hitler: The Search for Allies Abroad, 1938–1945*. Oxford: Oxford University Press, 1992.
Wagner, Tricia Martineau. *Black Cowboys of the Old West: True, Sensational, and Little-known Stories from History*. Lanham, MD: Rowan & Littlefield, 2010.
Washton Long, Rose-Carol, Matthew Baigell, and Milly Heyd, eds. *Jewish Dimensions in Modern Visual Culture: Antisemitism, Assimilation, Affirmation*. Waltham, MA: Brandeis University Press, 2010.
Waugh, Patricia. *Metafiction: The Theory and Practice of Self-Conscious Fiction*. London and New York: Routledge, 1984.
Williams Crenshaw, Kimberlé. "Demarginalizing the Intersection of Race and Sex: A Black Feminist Critique of Antidiscrimination Doctrine, Feminist Theory and Antiracist Politics." *University of Chicago Legal Forum* 140 (1989): 139–67.

INDEX

8 ½ (Federico Fellini, 1963), 6, 9, 290
12 Years a Slave (Steve McQueen, 2013), 22
400 Blows, The (François Truffaut, 1959), 9

"About Her" (Malcolm Mclaren, 2004), 164, 196, 227, 230
Abrams, Nathan, 52, 299n
acousmatic being, 80, 303n
"Across 110th Street" (Bobby Wormack, 1972), 164, 226, 228, 232
Adler, Stella, 315n
Adventures of Huckleberry Finn (Mark Twain, 1884), 19
"Ain't No Grave (Can Hold My Body Down)" (Johnny Cash, 2003), 234
Alamo, The (John Wayne, 1960), 238
Allan, Keith, 32, 55, 63, 297n, 300–301n
allohistory, allohistorical, 18
allusion, 6, 10
Altman, Robert: *Kansas City* (1996), 254; *Nashville* (1975), 127; *Short Cuts* (1993), 127, 253–54
analepsis, internal heterodiegetic or homodiegetic, completive and repeating, 149–50
Anderson, Aaron, 31, 79, 272, 297n, 303n
Anderson, Chante, 276, 317n
Anderson, Reynold, 276, 317n
anempathetic music, 230
Anzaldúa, Gloria, 33, 297n

"Apple Blossom" (The White Stripes, 2000), 123, 164, 227
architextuality, 6
Argento, Dario: *The Bird with the Crystal Plumage* (1970), 237; *The Cat O'Nine Tails* (1971), 237
Aristotle, 278
Arrowhead (Charles Marquis Warren, 1953), 25
art-cinema narration, 147, 170, 192
Aubert, Charles, 316n
Austin, J. L., 301n
Auxier, Randall E., 157, 278, 310n, 317n
Ayers, Roy: "Aragon" (1973), 225, 236; "Brawling Broads" (1973), 236; "Escape" (1973), 236; "Exotic Dance" (1973), 236; "Vittrone's Theme" (1973), 236

"Baby It's You" (Smith, 1969), 229, 232, 234
"Baby Love" (The Supremes, 1964), 232
Bacalov, Luis, 235; "Django" (1966), 64, 184, 190, 226, 231–32, 235; "The Grand Duel" (1972), 230
Baigell, Matthew, 71, 302n
Bailey, Frankie Y., 17, 295n
"Bang Bang" (Nancy Sinatra, 1966), 224
Bardot, Brigitte, 118–19
Baretta (ABC, 1975–78), 265
Barth, John, 7
Barthelme, Donald, 7

Index

Barthes, Roland, 279, 317n
Battle of Algiers, The (Gillo Pontecorvo, 1966), 238
Battle Royale (Kinji Fukasaku, 2000), 37, 233
"Battle Without Honor or Humanity" (Tomoyasu Hotei, 2001), 164, 232–33
Battleship Potemkine (Sergei M. Eisenstein, 1925), 215
Baudrillard, Jean, 318n
Bauer, Erik, 3, 293n
Bazin, André, 317n
Bell, Zoë, 255
Beloved (Toni Morrison, 1987; Jonathan Demme, 1998), 299n
Beltzer, Thomas, 32, 297n
Bend of the River (Anthony Mann, 1952), 23
Benson-Alliott, Caetlin, 283, 318n
Bergson, Henri, 312n
Bernard, Jami, 3, 302n, 306n, 312n
Bernstein, Charles: "Bath Attack" (1982), 313n; "White Lightning" (1973), 232, 239
Bertelsen, Eve, 6, 84, 142, 147, 294n, 303n, 308–10n
Big Gundown, The (Sergio Sollima, 1966), 238
Billson, Anne, 127, 307n
Birth of a Nation, The (D. W. Griffith, 1915), 25–27, 50, 292
Bishop, Larry, 255–56
Bissonnette, Sylvie, 244–45, 247, 250–51, 314n
Black Sunday (John Frankenheimer, 1977), 80
Blade Runner (Ridley Scott, 1982), 253
Blazing Saddles (Mel Brooks, 1974), 25
Blow-Up (Michelangelo Antonioni, 1966), 9
Bogle, Donald, 25, 37, 110–11, 296–97n, 306n
Bonnie and Clyde (Arthur Penn, 1967), 77, 202, 312n
Boorman, John: *Deliverance* (1972), 6, 35; *Exorcist II: The Heretic* (1977), 235, 242, 237, 313n
Bordwell, David, 13, 127, 128, 141, 144, 146–47, 158, 159, 161, 163–65, 172, 192, 292, 307–11n, 318n
Borges, Jorge Luis, 7
Born to Kill (Robert Wise, 1947), 253

Boss Nigger (Jack Arnold, 1975), 25, 296n
Botting, Fred, 147, 309n
Bradley, Regina N., 225, 241
Brando, Marlon, 261, 265
Brecht, Bertold, 8, 256, 317n; Brechtian, 244, 279–80
Breen, Marcus, 230
Brintnall, Kent L., 84, 303n
Broken Arrow (Delmer Daves, 1950), 296n
Brooker, Peter, 157, 310n
Brooker, Will, 157, 310n
Brown, James, 241–42
Brown, William, 149, 187, 190, 272, 309n, 311n
Bruce, Michael, 266, 309n, 316n
Buck and the Preacher (Sidney Poitier and Joseph Sargent, 1972), 25
Bulletproof Heart (Marke Malone, 1994), 127
"Bullwinkle Part II" (The Centurians, 1964), 106, 164, 201–2, 226, 230
Burch, Noël, 7
Burns, Elizabeth, 267, 269, 316n
Butler, Judith, 34, 57, 297n, 300–301n

Cain, James M., 3
Calvino, Italo, 7
Campion, Jane, *The Piano* (1993), 252, 315n
Carpenter, John: *Big Trouble in Little China* (1986), 253; *Escape from New York* (1981), 253; *Halloween* (1978), 81–82; *The Thing* (1982), 32, 40, 220, 235–36, 242, 253
Carney, Sean, 279, 317n
Carr, Jeremy, 149, 316n
Carr, Joi, 314n
Carradine, David, 37, 40, 70, 252–54
"Cat People (Putting out the Fire)" (David Bowie, 1982), 114, 164, 226
catharsis, 278–79, 317n
Cavell, Stanley, 198, 311n
Cerisuello, Marc, 8–9, 294n
Cervantes, Miguel de, 8
Cervulle, Maxime, 34, 76, 304n
Chandler, Raymond, 3
Charlie's Angels (ABC, 1976–81), 37, 79
Charyn, Jerome, 308–9n

Chermak, Steven M., 17, 295n
China Doll (David Mamet, 2015), 244
Chinita, Fátima, 8–9, 294n
Chion, Michel, 80, 225–26, 230, 233, 239, 303n, 312–13n
Christie, Agatha, 40
Chumo, Peter N., II, 31, 254, 297n, 315n
cinematic theatricality, 244–45, 314n
"Cissy Strut" (The Meters, 1969), 226–28, 232–33
citation, 6, 10
City on Fire (Ringo Lam, 1987), 6, 27, 146
"Claire's First Appearance" (Jacques Loussier, 1968), 232
classical narration, 165
Clover, Carol, 76, 80–82, 116, 287, 293n, 302–3n, 306–7n, 318n
Coates, Kristen, 17, 295n
Coen, Ethan and Joel: *The Hudsucker Proxy*, 254; *O Brother, Where Art Thou?* (2000), 296n
"Comanche" (The Revels, 1961), 230–31
comics, comic-booky, 6, 15, 146, 224, 275, 288–90, 292, 308n
Commando (Mark L. Lester, 1985), 114
Conard, Mark T., 6, 68, 79, 89, 99, 114, 116–18, 126, 143, 146, 293n, 302n, 304–7n, 308n
Confederate (HBO, in development), 15
constructivism, 33–34
Coover, Robert, 7
Coppola, Francis Ford, 33; *Apocalypse Now* (1979), 312n; *The Godfather* (1972), 303n
Corbucci, Sergio, 6; *Django* (1966), 64, 182, 190, 289–90, 235; *The Great Silence* (1968), 23; *The Hellbenders* (1967), 238
Coulthard, Lisa, 76, 146, 224–25, 234, 272, 308n, 313n
Craven, Wes: *The Last House on the Left* (1972), 235–37; *Scream* (1996), 10
Creed, Barbara, 80, 108, 121, 302–3n, 306n
Crémieux, Anne, 35, 297n
Cronenberg, David, 123–24; *eXistenZ* (1999), 254
Crouch, Stanley, 32

CSI (CBS, 2000–2015), 3
Cuddy, Luke, 266, 309n, 316n

Dargis, Manohla, 35, 297n
Darieux, Danielle, 113–14
Daring, C. B., 77, 302n
Davis, Todd F., 86, 303n
Dawn of the Dead (Zack Snyder, 2004), 9–10
Dawson, Jeff, 3, 5, 149, 309n
Dawson, Rosario, 37, 47, 69
Dazed and Confused (Richard Linklater, 1993), 303n
De Niro, Robert, 245, 261
De Palma, Brian, 3, 192; *Blow Out* (1981), 250–51; *Carrie* (1976), 78, 123, 252, 302n, 307n; *Sisters* (1972), 185; *The Untouchables* (1987), 283
deacousmatization, 87
Deer Hunter, The (Michael Cimino, 1978), 253
Deleuze, Gilles, 203, 291, 312n, 318n
Delsarte, François, 315–16n
Dern, Bruce, 257–58
Desilet, Gregory, 22, 295–96n
DiCaprio, Leonardo, 253–54, 257
"Didn't I (Blow Your Mind This Time)" (The Delfonics, 1969), 227–28
Die Hard (John McTiernan, 1988; Renny Harlin, 1990; McTiernan, 1995), 252, 273
Dillinger (Max Nosseck, 1945), 253
Dima, Vlad, 114, 306n
Dirty Dozen, The (Robert Aldrich, 1967), 16, 24–25, 289
Dirty Mary Crazy Larry (John Houch, 1974), 80, 147
Doctorow, E. L., *Ragtime* (1975), 7
Domergue, Jean-Baptiste, 93
"Don't Let Me Be Misunderstood" (Santa Esmeralda, 1977), 234
Doom, Omar, 72, 257
"Down in Mexico" (The Coasters, 1956), 37, 164, 232
Dreyfus, Alfred, 23
Du Bois, W. E. B., 49
Duel in the Sun (King Vidor, 1946), 76

Dumas, Alexandre, 16–17, 22; *The Three Musketeers* (1844), 19
Dyer, Richard, 252, 314–15n

Eastern Condors (Sammo Hung Kam-Bo, 1987), 238
Eco, Umberto, 11–12, 240, 294n, 314n
eloquent gesture, 315n
empathetic music, 230
Entity, The (Sidney J. Furie, 1982), 79, 313n
epic structure, 145
E.R. (NBC, 1994–2009), 3
Escott, Paul D., 17, 295n

fabula, 128
Faster, Pussycat! Kill! Kill! (Russ Meyer, 1965), 81, 122
Ferlito, Vanessa, 37
Ferrara, Abel: *Bad Lieutenant* (1992), 253; *The King of New York* (1990), 253
Fielding, Henry, 8
film genres: action movie, 4, 6, 50, 75, 79, 99, 107, 114, 122–23, 147, 162, 164–65, 218, 252, 274–75, 306n; blaxploitation, 6, 25, 33–37, 39, 50, 72, 79, 105, 110, 113, 172–75, 190, 192, 222, 236, 252, 290, 297n; boxing movie, 35, 105, 202; buddy movie, 39–40, 77; car movie, 34, 38, 80–82, 229; film noir, 34–35, 77, 79, 82, 103, 114, 146, 167, 193–94, 198, 202, 222; gangster movie, 34–35, 77, 79, 84, 94, 105, 107, 264, 274, 309n, 316n; Gothic, 18, 37, 40, 65, 78, 171, 217, 220, 222, 242; hangout movie, 81–82, 101, 303n; heist movie, 34, 77–78, 84, 127, 152, 171; horror, 9, 12, 32, 34, 39–40, 65, 78, 87, 117, 121, 125, 143, 152, 164, 171, 212, 220, 222, 234–35, 237, 274, 287, 307n, 317n; martial arts movie, 6, 35, 46, 79, 87–88, 115, 141, 143, 146, 149, 190, 211, 225, 241, 253–54, 257, 274, 308n; mystery, 78, 148, 152, 176, 307n; plantation film, 39–40, 78, 197; 253; rape-revenge, 79–80, 82–83, 118, 189, 223, 237, 282; samurai, 61, 70, 128, 187, 211, 223, 235, 264; slasher, 10, 38, 76, 80–82, 89–90, 120–22, 145, 147, 152, 229, 237; teen flick, 37, 191, 254, 303n; war movie, 15–16, 26, 34–35, 38–39, 196, 198, 222, 274, 284; Western, 6, 15, 17–18, 23, 25–26, 32, 34–35, 39, 64, 78–79, 88, 143, 145–46, 149, 152, 171, 187, 190, 197–98, 211, 217–18, 220, 222–23, 225, 234–35, 238, 242–43, 271, 274, 289–91, 295–96n, 304n, 308n, 318n
Final Girl, 75, 81–82
Fisher, Austin, 238, 313n
Fleischer, Richard: *Mandingo* (1975), 25, 58–59; *Tough Enough* (1983), 255
"Flower of Carnage" (Meiko Kaji, 2003), 234–35
Ford, John, 292; *The Searchers* (1956), 185–87, 192, 213; *Stagecoach* (1939), 311
Ford, James Edward, III, 58–59, 299n, 301n
Fort Massacre (Joseph M. Newman, 1958), 143
Forster, Robert, 255
four-act structure, 144
Four Rooms (Allison Anders, Alexandre Rockwell, Robert Rodriguez, Quentin Tarantino, 1995), 3, 315n
Fowles, John, 7
Foxx, Jamie, 253–54, 262–63
Frayling, Christopher, 145, 226, 308n, 312–13n
Frederickson, Don, 7
French New Wave, 8, 35, 122, 212, 222, 292
Freud, Sigmund, Freudian, 58, 89, 301n, 304n
Friday the 13th (1980–2009), 81, 147
Fujiawara, Chris, 160
Fussell, Paul, 301n

Gainsborough, Thomas, 197
García Márquez, Gabriel, 7
Garner, Ken, 151, 225–26, 228, 233–34, 309n, 312–13n
Genette, Gérard, 6, 127, 149–51, 155, 293n, 309n
German Expressionism, 29, 71, 73, 214–15, 222
Get Shorty (Barry Sonnenfeld, 1995), 255
"Girl, You'll Be a Woman Soon" (Urge Overkill, 1992), 96, 227–28, 234
Giroux, Henry A., 272

Glory (Edward Zwick, 1989), 18
Godard, Jean-Luc, 5, 7, 124–25, 211, 222, 292; *Band of Outsiders* (1964), 147; *Breathless* (1960), 147; *Contempt* (1963), 9; *Tout va bien* (with Jean-Pierre Gorin, 1972), 9
Goggins, Walton, 257–58
Golden, Leon, 278, 317n
Goldsmith, Barclay, 256, 315n
Gone in 60 Seconds (H. B. Halicki, 1974), 80–81
Gordon, Andrew, 146, 308n
Gormley, Paul, 272
Graduate, The (Mike Nichols, 1967), 110, 183, 192
Grand Budapest Hotel, The (Wes Anderson, 2014), 141
Grayzel, Solomon, 17, 295n
Grease (Randal Kleiser, 1978), 106, 226, 252
Great Dictator, The (Charles Chaplin, 1940), 25, 296n
Green Berets, The (Ray Kellogg, John Wayne, and Mervyn LeRoy, 1968), 23–24
Green Hornet, The (ABC, 1966–67), 116, 233, 254
"Green Leaves of Summer, The" (Nick Perito, 1960), 234
Greene, Richard, 269, 280
Grier, Pam, 35, 40, 110, 187, 226, 252, 255
Guattari, Félix, 291, 318n
Gun Crazy (Joseph H. Lewis, 1950), 77

Haber, Karen, 23, 296n
Halloween (Rob Zombie, 2007), 9
Hamilton, Anthony, 241; "Freedom" (2012), 241
Hammett, Dashiell, 3
Hang 'Em High (Ted Post, 1968), 23
Hannah, Daryl, 253
Hannah and Her Sisters (Woody Allen, 1986), 176–77, 192
Hawks, Howard, Hawksian, 21, 252, 264, 316n; *His Girl Friday* (1940), 4; *Rio Bravo* (1959), 4, 81; *Scarface* (1932), 166; *Sergeant York* (1941), 215

Hayes, Heather Ashley, 17, 25–26, 33, 278, 280, 295–97n, 317–18n
Heart of Darkness (Joseph Conrad, 1899), 5, 312n
Hertzberg, Hendrik, 272, 316n
Heyd, Milly, 71, 302n
Hill, Jack: *The Big Doll House* (1971), 226, 236; *Coffy* (1973), 79, 110, 113, 236, 252; *Foxy Brown* (1974), 36, 110, 113, 252, 290; *Switchblade Sisters* (1975), 80
Hitchcock, Alfred, 3; *Aventure Malgache* (1944), 29; *Bon Voyage* (1944), 29; *Rear Window* (1954), 9, 245; *Sabotage* (1936), 28–29, 185, 296n
Hogan's Heroes (CBS, 1965–71), 25
"Hold Tight" (Dave Dee, Dozy, Beaky, Mick, and Tich, 1966), 230–31
Holmes, David G., 17, 295n, 299n
hooks, bell, 34, 297n
Howley, Kevin, 157, 308n, 310n
Hudlin, Reginald, 241
Hughes, John, 196
Humphries, Reynold, 9, 89, 120, 294n, 304n, 306n
Hunter, Holly, 315n
Hutcheon, Linda, 7–11, 18, 30, 269, 288, 291, 294–95n
Hutchings, Peter, 90, 304n
hypotext, 6

"I Got a Name" (Jim Croce, 1973), 219
"I Gotcha" (Joe Tex, 1972), 104
Ido, Jacky, 72
Indiana Jones films (1981–2008), 146, 165
independent cinema, indie cinema (US), 149, 159, 222
Inglorious Bastards, The (Enzo G. Castellari, 1978), 16, 24–25, 143, 289
Inouye, Charles Shiro, 146, 308n
intensified continuity, 163
intersectionality, 33–34
intertextuality, 6
Iron Man 2 (Jon Favreau, 2010), 273
"Ironside" (Quincy Jones, 1967), 228

Italian Western, 4, 6, 23, 37, 64, 190, 220, 234–35, 238, 243, 271, 289–90, 292

Jackson, Samuel L., 28–29, 224, 244, 257–60, 262–63, 297n, 314n
Jardine, Dan, 272–73, 317–18n
Jarmusch, Jim: *Dead Man* (1995), 292; *Only Lovers Left Alive* (2013), 292
Jarry, Alfred, 8
Jay-Z, 69
Jeffords, Susan, 105, 305n
Jenkins, Henry, 144, 308n
JFK (Oliver Stone, 1991), 18
"Jim Jones at Botany Bay" (traditional, early nineteenth century), 123, 227, 314n
Johnson, Dwayne "The Rock," 47
Johnson, Mary, 281, 318n
Jordan, Jessica Hope, 76
Jullier, Laurent, 6, 272, 293n, 309n, 317n
Jungle Book, The (Rudyard Kipling, 1894), 60

Kalifornia (Dominic Sena, 1993), 253
Karate Kiba (Ryuichi Takamori and Simon Nuchtern, 1976), 6, 31, 280
Kassabian, Anahid, 240, 314n
Kaster, Gregory L., 18, 295n
Kathol, Nichole K., 34, 297n
Kawin, Brice, 7
Keitel, Harvey, 252, 254, 256, 259, 303n, 315n
Keys, Alicia, 69
Killers, The (Robert Siodmak, 1946), 35, 103, 233, 305n
Kinder, Marsha, 86, 274–75, 277, 303n, 317n
King Kong (Merian C. Cooper and Ernest B. Schoedsack, 1933), 23–24, 62
Kligerman, Eric, 18–19, 23, 26, 28–29, 39, 72, 215, 244, 295–98n, 302n, 312n, 314n
Kubrick, Stanley, 8; *The Killing* (1956), 78, 147; *Lolita* (1962), 9
Kuersten, Erich, 82, 303n
Kung Fu (ABC, 1972–75), 35, 88, 187, 252–54, 266
Kuriyama, Chiaki, 37

Kurosawa, Akira: *Seven Samurai* (1954), 290, 312n; *Yojimbo* (1961), 290

Lady Snowblood (Toshiya Fujita, 1973), 37, 79, 146, 159, 174–75, 235
Lang, Fritz, 29; *House by the River* (1950), 9; *The Testament of Dr. Mabuse* (1933), 80, 303n; *The Woman in the Window* (1944), 9
"Last Race, The" (Jack Nitzsche, 1965), 237
Laurent, Mélanie, 72
Lavin, Maud, 70, 76, 146, 272, 302n, 308n
Law Abiding Citizen (F. Gary Gray, 2009), 253
Lawrence of Arabia (David Lean, 1962), 219
Le Cain, Maximilian, 309n
Lee, Bruce, 37, 254n; *Game of Death* (1978), 37, 79, 254
Lee, Spike, 56, 300n
Legend, John, 241; "Who Did That to You?" (2012), 241
Legend of Nigger Charley, The (Martin Goldman, 1972), 25
Leigh, Jennifer Jason, 227, 252–53
Leitch, Thomas, 15, 295n
Leonard, Elmore, 3, 292; *Rum Punch* (1992), 35, 78, 147, 308n
Leonard, David J., 50, 299n, 301n
Leone, Sergio, 124–25, 147, 159, 220, 274; *A Fistful of Dollars* (1964), 290; *The Good, the Bad and the Ugly* (1966), 4, 145, 159, 226, 290, 292, 308n; *Once Upon a Time in the West* (1968), 37, 39, 79, 91, 143, 238, 271
"Let's Stay Together" (Al Green, 1972), 231
Levinas, Emmanuel, 74, 302n
Levy, Emmanuel, 127, 307n
Lévy, Pierre, 144
Lincoln (Steven Spielberg, 2012), 18–19
Lipton, Sara, 71, 302n
"Little Green Bag" (George Baker, 1970), 164, 224, 227–28, 232–33, 240
Liu, Chia-Hui, 256–57
Loiselle, André, 244, 314n

338　Index

"Long Time Woman" (Pam Grier, 1971), 226, 236
Losers, The (Jack Starrett, 1970), 6

Mack, The (Michael Campus, 1973), 172–75, 192, 222, 297n
Madonna, 77; "Like a Virgin" (1984), 94, 148
Madsen, Michael, 4, 257
Magnificent Seven, The (Preston Sturges, 1960), 290
Magnolia (P. T. Anderson, 1999), 127
Man from Okinawa, The (Akinori Matsuo, 1978), 144
Man in the High Castle (Philip K. Dick, 1962; Amazon, 2015–), 15
Mann, Michael: *Collateral* (2004), 253; *Miami Vice* (2006), 253
Maron, Jeremy, 244, 314n
Marvin, Lee, 265
Mason, Fran, 103, 305n
Massacre (Alan Crosland, 1934), 143
Matuska, Agnes, 244, 314n
May, Karl, *Winnetou* trilogy (1875–80), 24, 296n
McCalmont, Jonathan, 9
McGee, Patrick, 79, 186, 303n, 311n
McHale, Brian, 7, 290, 294n, 318n
McRoy, Jay, 9, 264, 294n, 316n
Memento (Christopher Nolan, 2000), 127
Mendehlson, Daniel, 272, 316n
Menegaldo, Gilles, 15, 295n
Menke, Sally, 4, 313n
Mera, Miguel, 224–25, 242, 313–14n
Mercenaries / Dark of the Sun, The (Jack Cardiff, 1968), 238
metafiction, 7–12; cinematic metafiction, 9
metafilm, 8
Metz, Christian, 7, 294n
Mey, Jacob, 299n
Meyer, Imke, 18–19, 25–26, 38–39, 295–96n
Miklitsch, Robert, 110, 224, 232, 236, 306n, 313n
"Misirlou" (Dick Dale and the Del Tones, 1963), 224, 234

Mississippi Burning (Alan Parker, 1988), 18
Mohammad, K. Silem, 269, 280, 317n
monstrous-feminine, 108
Morgan, Kim, 293n, 314n
Morricone, Ennio, 225–26, 235, 242, 290; "Un amico" (1973), 231, 313n; "Ancora qui" (2012), 241; "Bestiality" (1982), 228–29; "Despair" (1982), 235; "Dopo la congiura" (1967), 238; "Eternity" (1982), 235; "A Fistful of Dollars" (1964), 241; "I quattro passaggeri" (2015), 242; "L'inferno bianco" (2015), 242; "Un monumento" (1967), 232, 238; "La musica prima del massacro" (2015), 242; "Narratore letterario" (2015), 242–43; "Neve" (2015), 242; "Norme con ironie" (1970), 230; "Paranoia prima" (1971), 230, 237; "La resa" (1966), 283; "Unexpected Violence" (1970), 237; "The Verdict (Für Elise)" (1966), 234, 238
Morton, George, 17
Mulvey, Laura, 76, 103, 110–11, 120–21, 302n, 306n
Murphy, Audie, 17
music video aesthetics, 70, 106, 113, 116–17, 163–65, 172, 233–34, 302n
"My Touch of Madness" (Jermaine Jackson, 1976), 233

Nabokov, Vladimir, 7, 291–92
Nama, Adilifu, 12–13, 18, 22–26, 32–35, 37, 39–44, 46–55, 64–66, 68–70, 91, 105, 108, 115, 174, 217, 273, 294–302n, 305–6n, 312n, 317n
Nanay, Bence, 316n
Naremore, James, 245, 250–51, 260–61, 267–68, 314n, 316n
Neupert, Richard, 5–6, 212, 293n, 312n
New Hollywood, 33, 149, 159, 184, 221, 292
New York Undercover (Fox, 1994–99), 56
Nicholson, Jack, 316n
Niemeyer, Mark, 19, 295n
"Night the Lights Went Out in Georgia, The" (Reba McEntire, 1991), 77
Nikita (Luc Besson, 1990), 6, 35, 37, 202

No Exit (Jean-Paul Sartre, 1944), 32
"Nobody But Me" (The Human Beinz, 1967), 227, 231
Novoa, Adriana, 306n
"Now You're All Alone" (David Hess, 1972), 231, 235–36

O'Brien, Geoffrey, 25–26, 145, 296n, 308n
Ocean's Eleven (Steven Soderbergh, 2001), 253
Olivier, Laurence, 260
On the Edge (Rob Nilsson, 1986), 315n
O'Neil, Eugene, 5
Ornella, Alexander D., 19, 190, 272, 278–79, 295n, 311n, 317n
Ortoli, Philippe, 12, 25, 35, 79, 84–86, 94, 103, 106, 126, 141–43, 147, 154–55, 157, 160, 172, 175, 185, 224, 228, 232–34, 237–38, 253–54, 264, 266, 278, 289, 296–97n, 303–11n, 313n, 315–18n
Ozierski, Margaret, 197, 311n

Pabst, G. W., *White Hell of Pitz Palu* (1929), 71
Pacino, Al, 244, 316n
Package, The (Andrew Davis, 1989), 255
Palmer, Tim, 245, 314n
Paris Is Burning (Jennie Livingstone, 1990), 297n
Parks, Michael, 256–57, 315n
Passion of Joan of Arc, The (Carl Theodor Dreyer, 1928), 39
Pastoureau, Michel, 194, 311n
Pawnbroker, The (Sidney Lumet, 1964), 35
Peake, Glenn, 77, 302n
Peary, Gerald, 3–5, 293n, 296–98n, 300–302n, 304n, 307n, 310–12n, 313–16n, 318n
Peckinpah, Sam, 218, 222, 274, 312n; *Junior Bonner* (1972), 303n
Penn, Chris, 83
Perry, Samuel P., 33, 67, 275–76, 297n, 301n, 317–18n
Pitt, Brad, 23, 253–54, 257, 261
Place, Janey, 77, 302n

plagiarism, 6
Plato, 288
Plot Against America, The (Philip Roth, 2004), 15
Poster, Mark, 318n
Power Rangers (1993–99), 79
pragmatics, 52, 62–63, 102, 299n
Prince, Stephen, 312n
prolepsis, 155
Propp, Vladimir, 48, 299n
Puccini, Giacomo, 5
Pynchon, Thomas, 7

Quart, Alissa, 144, 308n
queering, 77

Redmond, Allen H., 309n
reflexivity, 7–10
Reilly, Ian, 76
Remains of the Day, The (Kazuo Ishiguro, 1989; James Ivory, 1993), 25–27, 50
Remar, James, 256–57
resignification, 57, 300–301n
Richardson, Michael D., 18, 272, 295n
Richardson, Robert, 4, 311n
Ritter, Kelly, 31, 297n
Robinson, Tasha, 312n
Roche, David, 9–10, 37–38, 75–76, 123–25, 160–61, 187, 211, 227–29, 237, 254, 256, 265, 268, 273, 286, 294n, 297–98n, 302n, 307n, 310n, 312–13n, 315–17n
Rodman, Gilbert B., 17, 25–26, 33, 278, 280, 295–97n, 317–18n
Rodriguez, Robert, 225–26; "Calling the Hateful Bitch" (2004), 241; *Desperado* (1995), 256; *From Dusk Till Dawn* (1996), 3, 256, 315n; *Planet Terror* (2007), 256, 283
Rogue, J., 77, 302n
Ross, Rick, 241–42; "100 Black Coffins" (2012), 241
Roth, Eli, 102, 254–55, 257, 305n; *Hostel* (2005) and *Hostel II* (2007), 25, 256
Roth, Tim, 257, 259, 315n
Roxanne (Fred Schepisi, 1987), 253

Russell, Kurt, 40–41, 236, 253–54, 259, 315n
RZA, 225–26; "Bannister Fight" (2003), 231, 241; "Black Mamba (instrumental)" (2003), 241; "Crane" (2003), 241; "Yakuza Oren 1" (2003), 241

Salome, Where She Danced (Charles Lamont, 1945), 141
Samurai Fiction (Hiroyuki Nakano, 1998), 6
Saturday Night Fever (John Badham, 1977), 35, 105, 226, 252
Schaeffer, Jean-Marie, 288, 318n
Schlipphacke, Heidi, 76, 118, 187, 306n, 311n
Schmidt, Paul H., 86, 157, 303n, 310n
Schnee, Ian, 316n
Schultz, Carl, 19
Schweiger, Til, 23
Scorsese, Martin, 33; *Mean Streets* (1973), 245, 252; *Shutter Island* (2010), 253; *Taxi Driver* (1976), 4
Semenza, Greg M. Colón, 25–26, 28–29, 175, 286, 296n, 318n
Seven-Year Itch, The (Billy Wilder, 1955), 200
Shadow Warriors (KTV, 1980–), 128
Shaft (Gordon Parks, 1971), 25
Shakespeare, William, 8, 290, 292; *Richard III* (1633), 260, 314n
Shakur, Tupac, 241–42
Shannon, Deric, 77, 302n
Shaw Brothers, 37, 187, 192, 222; *Clan of the White Lotus* (Lieh Lo, 1980), 143; *Executioners from Shaolin* (Chia-Liang Liu, 1977), 143; *The Shaolin Avengers* (Cheh Chang, 1976), 143
"Silent Night" (traditional), 314n
Silverman, Kaja, 76, 122, 203, 307n
Sinnerbrink, Robert, 9, 294n
Slotkin, Richard, 17, 24, 295–96n
Slumber Party Massacre, The (Amy Holden Jones, 1982), 143
Smith, Gavin, 5, 125, 292
Sobchack, Thomas, 294n
Soldier Blue (Ralph Nelson, 1970), 119, 302n

Soul of Nigger Charley, The (Larry G. Spangler, 1973), 25
Sound and the Fury, The (William Faulkner, 1929), 62
Space Sheriff (Toei, 1982–83), 79
Speck, Oliver C., 6–7, 12, 19, 39, 72, 271, 293n, 298n, 302n, 316n
Splash (Ron Howard, 1984), 253
Srinivasan, Srikanth, 39, 298n
"Staggolee" (Pacific Gas and Electric, 1970), 90, 231, 233
Staiger, Janet, 293n
Stam, Robert, 7–9, 294n
Stanislavski, Constantin, 316n
star image, 252
Star Trek (1966–), 5
Stephenson, D. L., 276, 317n
Stokes, Melvyn, 15, 18, 295n
Strasberg, Lee, 315n
"Strawberry Letter 23" (Brothers Johnson, 1977), 231, 314n
"Stuck in the Middle with You" (Stealers Wheel, 1972), 227–28, 230–32, 236
Sukiyaki Western Django (Takashi Miike, 2007), 25
Suleiman, Susan Rubin, 114, 273, 306n, 317n
Super Fly (Gordon Parks Jr., 1972), 79, 297n
syuzhet, 128
Szaniawski, Jeremi, 37–38, 76, 298n

Tan, Ed, 311n
Targets (Peter Bogdanovich, 1968), 215
Tasker, Yvonne, 105
Taubin, Amy, 76
Taylor, Ella, 272
Telotte, J. P., 142, 308n
Temoney, Kate E., 22, 39, 149, 272–73, 295n, 298n, 309n, 317n
Texas Chain Saw Massacre, The (Tobe Hooper, 1974), 143, 211
Thinker, The (Auguste Rodin, 1904), 260
Thompson, Kristin, 13, 127, 144, 161, 159, 164, 292, 307n, 308n, 310n, 318n

Thompson, William Ford, 229, 313n
Thriller: They Call Her One Eye (Bo Arne Vibenius, 1973), 37, 79–80
Thurman, Uma, 4, 70, 257–58
Tierney, Lawrence, 40, 83, 253, 303n
Tierney, Sean M., 46, 254, 299n, 315n
To Hell and Back (Jesse Hibbs, 1955), 17
Tom Jones (Tony Richardson, 1963), 9
Toolbox Murders, The (Dennis Donnelly, 1978), 121
Toplin, Robert Brent, 19, 295n
Travolta, John, 40, 171, 226, 228, 244, 252, 254–55, 260, 262, 315n
True Romance (Tony Scott, 1993), 56, 253
Tuhkunen, Taïna, 26, 297n
Turim, Maureen, 149, 309n
"Twisted Nerve" (Bernard Herrmann, 1968), 227, 232, 239

"Unchained (The Payback/Untouchable)" (Claudio Cueni, 2012), 59, 164, 234
Usual Suspects, The (Bryan Singer, 1995), 127

van Beethoven, Ludwig, 19, 290, 313n; "Für Elise" (1867), 17, 239
Vanishing Point (Richard C. Safarian, 1971), 80–81, 101, 147, 175
Verdi, Giuseppe, "Dies Irae (Requiem)" (1874), 25
Village of the Giants (Bert I. Gordon, 1965), 237
Vindicator, The (Jean-Claude Lord, 1986), 255
Virginian, The (NBC, 1962–71), 25
Viviani, Christian, 250, 259–61, 263, 315–16n
Volcano, Abbey, 77, 302n
von Dassanowsky, Robert, 7–8, 12, 15, 17–19, 38–39, 102, 197, 239, 271, 278, 293n, 295n, 298n, 305n, 311n, 314n, 316–17n
von Klemperer, Klemens, 22

Wagner, Richard, 290; "Ride of the Valkyries" (1851), 26

Wagner, Tricia Martineau, 17, 295n
Wait Until Dark (Frederick Knott, 1966), 244
Waldron, Dara, 278–79, 389–90, 318n
Walken, Christopher, 253
Walsh, Martin, 7
Walters, Ben, 284
Waltz, Christoph, 257–58, 261–63
Washton Long, Rose-Carol, 71, 302n
Watchmen (Dave Gibbons and Alan Moore, 1986–87; Zack Snyder, 2009), 15
Waugh, Patricia, 7, 294n
Wayne, John, 23
Weaver, Ryan J., 34, 297n
Weber, Dana, 270–71, 316n
Welles, Orson: *Citizen Kane* (1941), 79, 191, 290; *F Is for Fake* (1973), 9
White, Armond, 302n
White Lightning (Joseph Sargent, 1973), 239
Wicked Dreams of Paul Schultz, The (George Marshall, 1968), 143
Williams, Linda, 121, 293n, 302n, 307n
Williams, Tony, 237, 307n, 313n
Williams Crenshaw, Kimberlé, 33, 297n
Williamson, Fred, 25
Willis, Bruce, 252–54, 315n
Willis, Sharon, 10, 18, 25, 28–29, 54–55, 76, 113–14, 294–96n, 300n, 306n
Wilson, Scott, 147, 309n
Winnicott, D. W., 268
Wizard of Oz, The (Victor Fleming, et al., 1939), 29, 39, 80, 190
Woo, John, 147, 292, 318n; *Broken Arrow* (1996), 255; *The Killer* (1989), 281–82
"Woo Hoo" (The 5.6.7.8's, 2003), 232

Yip, Man-Fung, 218, 312n
"You Never Can Tell" (Chuck Berry, 1964), 228, 232

Zola, Émile, 23

www.ingramcontent.com/pod-product-compliance
Lightning Source LLC
Chambersburg PA
CBHW030333240426
43661CB00052B/1618